The Greenwood Encyclopedia of Asian American Literature

The Greenwood Encyclopedia of Asian American Literature

———— VOLUME ONE: A–G ————

Edited by Guiyou Huang

Greenwood Press
Westport, Connecticut • London

Library of Congress Cataloging-in-Publication Data

The Greenwood encyclopedia of Asian American literature / edited by Guiyou Huang.
   p. cm.
  Includes bibliographical references (p.   ) and index.
   ISBN 978–0–313–34157–1 (set : alk. paper) — ISBN 978–0–313–34158–8 (v. 1 : alk. paper)
— ISBN 978–0–313–34159–5 (v. 2 : alk. paper) — ISBN 978–0–313–34160–1 (v. 3 : alk. paper)
  1. American literature—Asian American authors—Encyclopedias. 2. American literature—Asian
American authors—Bio-bibliography—Dictionaries. 3. Asian American authors—Biography—
Dictionaries. 4. Asian Americans—Intellectual life—Encyclopedias. 5. Asian Americans in
literature—Encyclopedias. I. Huang, Guiyou, 1961-
  PS153.A84G74 2009
  810.9'895—dc22   2008027502

British Library Cataloguing in Publication Data is available.

Library of Congress Catalog Card Number: 2008027502
ISBN: 978–0–313–34157–1 (set)
     978–0–313–34158–8 (vol. 1)
     978–0–313–34159–5 (vol. 2)
     978–0–313–34160–1 (vol. 3)

First published in 2009

Greenwood Press, 88 Post Road West, Westport, CT 06881
An imprint of Greenwood Publishing Group, Inc.
www.greenwood.com

Printed in the United States of America

The paper used in this book complies with the
Permanent Paper Standard issued by the National
Information Standards Organization (Z39.48-1984).

10 9 8 7 6 5 4 3 2 1

Contents

✦

List of Entries

✦

Guide to Related Topics

✦

Hua, Chuang
Hwang, David Henry
Jen, Gish
Jin, Ha
Kingston, Maxine Hong
Kwa, Lydia
Lai, Larissa
Lau, Carolyn Lei-Lanilau
Lau, Evelyn
Lee, C. Y.
Lee, Gus
Lee, Li-Young
Lee, Sky
Lee, Yan Phou
Leong, Russell
Lim, Shirley Geok-Lin
Lin, Yutang
Liu, Aimee E.
Liu, Eric
Loh, Sandra Tsing
Lord, Bette Bao
Louie, David Wong
Lowe, Pardee
Lum, Darrell H.Y.
Lum, Wing Tek
Mah, Adeline Yen
McCunn, Ruthanne Lum
Min, Anchee
Ng, Fae Myenne
Ng, Mei
Nieh, Hualing
Nunez, Sigrid
Song, Cathy
Tan, Amy
Thien, Madeleine
Tsiang, H. T.
Tsui, Kitty
Wah, Fred
Wang, Ping
Wong, Elizabeth
Wong, Jade Snow
Wong, Shawn Hsu

Woo, Merle
Yang, Rae
Yau, John
Yee, Paul
Yep, Laurence Michael
Yung, Wing

Filipino American Literature
Barroga, Jeannie
Barry, Lynda
Brainard, Cecilia Manguerra
Bulosan, Carlos
Carbò, Nick
Filipino American Anthology
Filipino American Autobiography
Filipino American Literature
Filipino American Novel
Filipino American Poetry
Filipino American Short Story
Gonzalez, N.V.M.
Hagedorn, Jessica
Rosca, Ninotchka
Santos, Bienvenido Nuqui
Tabios, Eileen
Ty-Casper, Linda
Villa, Jose Garcia

Genres
Asian American Children's Literature
Graphic Novel
Hawaiian Literature
Indian American Film
Korean American Adoptee Literature

Identity and Stereotyping
Asian American
Asian American Stereotypes
Asian Pacific Islanders
Biraciality
Charlie Chan
Fu Manchu

Gay Male Literature
Hawaiian Pidgin
Hybridity
Issei, Nisei, Sansei
Korean American Adoptee Literature
Lesbian Literature
Model Minority
Pan-Asian Ethnicities
Queer Identity and Politics
Suzie Wong
Yellow Peril

Ideologies, Legislation, and Policies

Asian American Political Activism
Asian American Studies
Asian Canadian Studies
Chinese Exclusion Act (1882)
Colonialism and Postcolonialism
Feminism and Asian America
Model Minority
Multiculturalism and Asian America
National Origins Act of 1924
Nationalism and Asian America
Orientalism and Asian America
Queer Identity and Politics
Racism and Asian America
Sexism and Asian America

Indian American Literature

Alexander, Meena
Ali, Agha Shahid
Ali, Samina
Desai, Kiran
Divakaruni, Chitra Banerjee
Ganesan, Indira
Gawande, Atul
Gill, Myrna Lakshmi
Indian American Anthology
Indian American Autobiography
Indian American Film
Indian American Literature

Indian American Short Story
Iyer, Pico
Kumar, Amitava
Lahiri, Jhumpa
Lakshmi, Vijay
Malladi, Amulya
Mara, Rachna
Mehta, Gita
Mehta, Ved Parkash
Mistry, Rohinton
Mohanraj, Mary Anne
Mootoo, Shani
Mukherjee, Bharati
Nair, Meera
Parameswaran, Uma
Rama Rau, Santha
Rao, Raja
Seth, Vikram
Suri, Manil
Tharoor, Shashi
Vazirani, Reetika
Verghese, Abraham
Viswanathan, Kaavya

Japanese American Literature

Ai
Aoki, Brenda Wong
Gotanda, Philip Kan
Goto, Hiromi
Hahn, Kimiko
Hongo, Garrett Kaoru
Houston, Jeanne Wakatsuki
Houston, Velina Hasu
Iko, Momoko
Inada, Lawson Fusao
Inouye, Daniel K.
Japanese American Autobiography
Japanese American Internment
Japanese American Literature
Japanese American Poetry
Japanese American Short Story

Kadohata, Cynthia
Kaneko, Lonny
Kogawa, Joy
Kono, Juliet Sanae
Mirikitani, Janice
Mori, Kyoko
Mori, Toshio
Mura, David
Murayama, Milton
Nishikawa, Lane
Okada, John
Okita, Dwight
Roripaugh, Lee Ann
Saiki, Patsy Sumie
Sakamoto, Edward
Sakamoto, Kerri
Shiomi, Rick A.
Sone, Monica
Suyemoto, Toyo
Takei, George
Uchida, Yoshiko
Watada, Terry
Watanabe, Sylvia A.
Yamamoto, Hisaye
Yamanaka, Lois-Ann
Yamashita, Karen Tei
Yamauchi, Wakako

Korean American Literature
Cha, Theresa Hak Kyung
Chee, Alexander
Choi, Susan
Kang, Younghill
Keller, Nora Okja
Kim, Myung Mi
Kim, Richard
Kim, Ronyoung
Kim, Suki
Kim, Susan
Korean American Adoptee Literature
Korean American Autobiography

Korean American Literature
Korean American Novel
Lee, Chang-Rae
Lee, Don
Lee, Marie G.
Lee, Mary Paik
Pak, Gary
Song, Cathy
Trenka, Jane Jeong

Movements and Organizations
Association for Asian American
    Studies
Bamboo Ridge Press
Civil Rights Movement and Asian
    America
RAWI
Third World Students' Strikes

Places and People
Angel Island
Asian American
Asian Diasporas
Asian Pacific Islanders
Chinatowns
Gold Mountain
Pearl Harbor
Transcontinental Railroad

Social Issues
Assimilation/Americanization
Chin, Vincent
Filial Piety
Hawaiian Pidgin
Japanese American Internment

South Asian American Writers
Ahmed, Sharbari (Bangladeshi)
Naqvi, Tahira (Pakistani)
Ondaatje, Michael (Sri Lankan)
Selvadurai, Shyam (Sri Lankan)

Shamsie, Kamila (Pakistani)
Sidhwa, Bapsi (Pakistani)
Suleri, Sara (Pakistani)

Vietnamese American Literature
Bao, Quang
Cao, Lan
Hayslip, Le Ly
Lam, Andrew
Law-Yone, Wendy

lê thi diem thúy
Truong, Monique
Vietnamese American Literature
Vietnamese American Novel
Vietnamese American Short Story

Wars, The Military
Korean War (1950–1953)
Vietnam War (1959–1975)
World War II (1939–1945)

Preface

✦

The writing of Asian Americans dates back to the last years of the nineteenth century, and, following World War II in the middle of the twentieth century, experienced a notable rise that began to shape an identity of its own. Catalyzed by the civil rights movements of the 1960s and inspired by women's liberation movements in the 1970s, Asian American literature has since produced works that have caught the attention of mainstream literary critics who started to take serious note of this distinct voice in the expanding canon of American literary writing now called Asian American. In the last three decades, this emerging branch of American literature has thrived in virtually every major genre—the novel, short fiction, autobiography, poetry, anthology, and drama—a strong testimony, which is evident in the hundreds of monographs, reference works, and critical anthologies, and thousands of articles published in different venues in the United States and Canada, as well as secondary works produced in foreign languages in many Asian (China, Japan, and Korea, to mention just three) and European countries (Great Britain, Germany, and Spain, to also cite three).

While market research indicates a real demand for a comprehensive reference tool that reflects the history, complexity, multiplicity, and richness of Asian American literature, there does not exist a reference work of encyclopedic scope to facilitate the study and teaching of this field, except for some single-genre and single-volume reference books, such as the five bio-bibliographical critical sourcebooks published by Greenwood since 2000: *Asian American Novelists*, *Asian American Autobiographers*, *Asian American Poets*, *Asian American Playwrights*, and *Asian American Short Story Writers*. However, these reference works include only entries on writers of different genres. Unlike the above-mentioned sourcebooks, *The Greenwood Encyclopedia of Asian*

American Literature contains entries on writers as well as entries on special topics, events, and terms, and, as a result, its coverage surpasses that of any single existing reference work on Asian American literature. This encyclopedia is thus designed to fill a reference gap to support and advance the study and teaching of Asian American literature at all levels.

The encyclopedia covers Asian American literature from the late 1890s to 2007, written by North American (U.S. and Canadian) writers of Asian descents, and comprises entries on authors, works, themes, genres, events, and special topics, presented in political, social, historical, cultural, and international contexts. It includes 272 alphabetically arranged entries, each of which discusses its topic in considerable depth and concludes with a list of further information resources. The encyclopedia closes with a selected General Bibliography of print and electronic resources that consist of literary anthologies, critical studies, and periodicals. Each of the entries falls into one or more of sixteen broad categories listed in the "Guide to Related Topics" in the front of the encyclopedia. This Guide is provided out of the belief that librarians, reviewers, and students will find it helpful in locating topics and in understanding the scope of the encyclopedia as well as the relatedness of the topics.

The encyclopedia is arranged alphabetically by the last names of the writers covered, or, in the case of other topics, by the first non-article word of the entry title. In the great majority of entries, for ease of reference, **boldface** cross-references highlight topics that appear in other entries. Additional cross-references are provided by "See also" lines that follow the text of some entries.

Although writers constitute the majority of the entry topics in the three volumes, a considerable number of entries are (what the editor deems to be) influential Asian American literary works such as Kingston's *The Woman Warrior*, Bulosan's *America Is in the Heart*, and the anthology *Aiiieeeee!*, to name only three. Another major entry type comprises general topics on different genres or subgenres broadly grouped by ethnicity, such as "Chinese American Drama," "Asian American Children's Literature," or "Indian American Films."

Other than writers, works, and genres, the encyclopedia consists of a range of entries on historically important events, such as the building of the Transcontinental Railroad, the Civil Rights movements, Japanese American Internment, the murder of Vincent Chin, and Japan's 1941 attack on Pearl Harbor. These events all had significant impact at different times throughout twentieth-century U.S. history on the life and literature of Asian Americans, and they are thus included to provide historical, social, cultural, and even legal backgrounds against which to read and understand the writers and their works. Just as important is the inclusion of many terms and concepts, such as *the model minority; issei, nisei,* and *sansei; the yellow peril; Asian Diasporas;* or *sexism and Asian America,* which are explored in one form or another in writings by Asian American writers.

The Greenwood Encyclopedia of Asian American Literature is designed to be accessible to high school and college students and general readers, although English teachers and college professors of literature and ethnic studies can use it for reference and teaching purposes because the encyclopedia provides a wealth of information about writers' personal and educational experiences, along with reviews and critical analyses of their major works, and, in the case of topical entries, definitions of important terms and discussions of politically significant events or legislation. The user of this reference work will notice the following important features:

1. Although the focus is on literature, the encyclopedia is clearly interdisciplinary, including topics in different disciplines written by experts in history, cultural studies, geography, anthropology, sociology, political science, race relations, linguistics, and arts.
2. The entries have depth and breadth (and, in many cases, length) and are thus suitable for both the general reader and the specialist because each entry offers discussions based upon research and provides material for further reading.
3. A great many contributors are well-established scholars in their fields, and because of the broad diversity of their ethnic, geographical, linguistic, and national backgrounds, they offer a wide spectrum of perspectives on their respective topics. In this regard, the scope of the book is truly international; its 104 contributors hail from many different countries (see the "About the Editor and Contributors" section for biographical details).

This encyclopedia may be used in several ways. For example, the encyclopedia presents relevant, reliable biographical information on major Asian American writers, which typically includes educational achievements and cultural upbringing. A reader will also be able to find critical reviews or analyses of works of a chosen writer discussed in that entry. And if a reader is interested in reading more about a particular writer or in doing further research, he or she will have the benefit of bibliographical information at the end of each entry. Of course, for various reasons, not every American writer of Asian descent is included here, but the rich material offered in this encyclopedia will guide the reader to other writers and topics. For high school teachers and college instructors of American literature, and more specifically of Asian American literature, this reference work will be a convenient as well as comprehensive source of research information for the study of a continuously growing field of literature and the social and political milieu in which its writers work.

Guiyou Huang
April 2008, Miramar, Florida

Acknowledgments

✦

This 3-volume encyclopedia is the culmination of the enthusiastic work of over a hundred scholars from many parts of the world, most notably the United States, Canada, some Asian countries, and a few European countries. Obviously, this book owes its publication to all its fine contributors. It also benefited enormously from an advisory board that consists of Prof. Shirley Geok-lin Lim of the University of California at Santa Barbara; Prof. Emmanuel S. Nelson of SUNY-Cortland; Prof. Viet Thanh Nguyen of the University of Southern California; Prof. Gayle K. Sato of Meiji University, Japan; and Prof. Eleanor Ty of Wilfrid Laurier University, Canada. Most of these advisory members also contributed entries, and all of them provided advice on various aspects of the book, especially in the initial preparatory stage of the project; they also helped identify qualified contributors to write entries. In addition, I would also like to thank Prof. Elaine H. Kim of the University of California, Berkeley for her help in recommending contributors.

Dr. George Butler, supervising editor at Greenwood Press, has always been generous with his time and provided professional guidance throughout the two years during which the manuscript was prepared. Dr. John Wagner, senior development editor at Greenwood Press, answered my questions concerning various matters and handled the contracts issued to authors all over North America, Asia, and Europe. To George and John I am very grateful.

I also want to thank Greenwood Press for granting me permission to use two articles previously published in *The Greenwood Encyclopedia of Multiethnic American Literature* (2005), edited by Professor Emmanuel S. Nelson, and in *Asian American Short Story Writers*, edited by Professor Guiyou Huang (2003), respectively.

Ms. Lisa Connery, Project Manager, and her team at Publication Services, Inc., provided excellent copyediting for the book. Ms. Erica Alfonso, my administrative assistant, helped with the general bibliography. To them I am indebted.

Most importantly, my wife, Dr. Yufeng Qian, and my son, George Ian, have always been very understanding and supportive of my time commitment to scholarly work. To them I dedicate these volumes.

A

✦

✦ ABU-JABER, DIANA (1959–)

Arab American novelist, short story writer, essayist, columnist, reviewer, food critic, and associate professor of English, Diana Abu-Jaber came into prominence as a storyteller of the cultural duality of home and exile in an immigrant's life with the publication of her widely acclaimed first novel *Arabian Jazz* (1993). Daughter of a Jordanian father and an American mother, Abu-Jaber grew up in a little town outside Syracuse, New York, having moved intermittently between Jordan and the United States since she was seven. She earned her bachelor's degree from the State University of New York, Oswego, in 1980; her master's degree from the University of Windsor in 1982, where she studied with Joyce Carol Oates; and her PhD in English and creative writing in 1986 from the State University of New York, Binghamton, where she worked with John Gardner. She taught creative writing and film studies at the University of Nebraska, the University of Michigan, the University of California at Los Angeles, and the University of Miami. In 1990 she was a visiting professor of English at Iowa State University. From 1990 to 1995, she worked as assistant professor of English at the University of Oregon. Since 1996 she has been an associate professor and writer-in-residence at Portland State University, Oregon, where she teaches literature and creative writing.

Arabian Jazz reflects Abu-Jaber's unwavering faith in the dignity of human beings and their capacity to survive; she writes about pain and passion, trials and traumas, impediments and optimism, and fears and hopes with extraordinary sensitivity that appeals simultaneously to her readers' minds and hearts. With an inevitable sense of two worlds (Jordan and the United States) in her delineation of an immigrant's new situation, she has added new insight into the Arab American issues of race, ethnicity, gender, culture, and identity through the real and imagined constructs of home and exile. *Arabian Jazz* narrates the cultural displacement of the Jordanian family of Matussem Ramoud, a widower living with his two daughters, Jemorah and Melvina, in Euclid, New York, and his relatives and friends who frequently meet to share feelings of loneliness and longing in the United States, their new country of exile. Matussem's sister, Fatima, is obsessed with the idea of marrying off her nieces (Jemorah and Melvina) within her own community of immigrants, a scenario through which Abu-Jaber links sexuality and reputation with the identity of an Arab American. Fatima's self-imposed duty, in the absence of Matussem's deceased wife — to find Arab boys for her nieces and to preserve the family's name and honor — puts her in conflict with Melvina, who is a dedicated nurse at the local hospital. Both Melvina and Jemorah feel racial discrimination like the children of their invisible neighbors, the Ellises, Otts, and Beevles, and their sense of exile is also linked with their father's behavior, who, like Shaharazad, tells them many stories in a language that reveals his distinctive ethnic self with irreconcilable dualities. Jemorah and Melvina grow up in their father's house, which resounds with the thunder of drumming and jazz music and heated conversations in Arabic among friends and relatives. For some time pursued by her classmate Gilbert Sesame, Jemorah is ambivalent about living a life of uncertainty amid the opportunities of freedom and work in her adopted country; this ambivalence is expressed through her love affair with Ricky Ellis, whom she visualizes as a mythical Pan, a beautiful monster, and through Melvina's love affair with her patient-lover Larry Fasco. However, their assimilation into the culture of the new country is resisted by the pull of divergent threads of their own culture. Memories of the past haunt Matussem and his sister Fatima; the former recalls his growing up as the only male child surrounded by sisters, and the latter is tormented by memories of the burial of female children. Like their father and aunt, Jemorah and Melvina live between home and homelessness with memories of their dead mother.

With her impressive storytelling Abu-Jaber weaves a complex plot in which characters like Matussem and Fatima and Jemorah and Melvina, who are caught between two different cultures, feel out of place in their new hybrid space. By bringing Jemorah close to Ricky Ellis and Nassir, Abu-Jaber suggests a kind of rebirth of the immigrant personality out of a duality that is not only cultural but also personal, driven by an individual's desire to move fully into one's own life. Her representations of race, ethnicity, gender, and diaspora are interspersed with ethnic humor, irony, and satire.

The ethnic humor of *Arabian Jazz* is transformed into a discourse of cuisine and coincidence in Abu-Jaber's second novel, *Crescent* (2003), which tells the agonizing tale of an immigrant's life. The plot centers around Sirine, the beautiful and talented

Iraqi American chef, who works at the restaurant of Um-Nadia and whose life moves along the pulls of Aziz's rhythmic poetry, Nathan's moving photographs, Hanif's attractive voice, and memories of her dead parents. Sirine, the daughter of an Iraqi father and an American mother, learned about food from her parents. In the opinion of Um-Nadia, Sirine dreams and wakes to the thoughts of cooking, and soon she would be Hanif's Cleopatra and the American Queen of Sheba. Um-Nadia's comments, based on her observations of the customers who throng her restaurant, mostly Arabs, reveal the loneliness caused by displaced identities. Like Fatima in *Arabian Jazz,* Hanif Al Eyad, the Iraqi professor and Sirine's uncle in *Crescent,* is a victim of his troubled past, a past that is haunted by distressing memories of political persecution by oppressive regimes, instead of by cultural constraints of furtive burials of female children as in the case of Fatima. Sirine's uncle tries to forget his pain of homelessness and loneliness by telling ongoing fables, which he calls moralless tales of Aunt Camille and her son, Abdelrahman Salahadin. By appropriating the elements of *Arabian Nights* to the narrative structure of *Crescent,* Abu-Jaber not only adds flavor of the indigenous oral tradition and dimensions of magical realism to the story, but she also seems to resist the monolithic discursive practices of the West. The use of a discourse of cuisine is a potent cultural signifier of the emotional bond that immigrants maintain with their families, communities, and home countries. Even for a person like Sirine, who has never been to her father's home in Iraq, she nonetheless searches for her roots by making a blend of Middle Eastern and Western cuisine for an Arabic Thanksgiving dinner at Um-Nadia's restaurant. *Crescent* is also the tragic but enduring love story of Sirine and Hanif, which ends in ambivalence, underscoring the uncertainties and emotional confusion of an outsider in a new country.

For Abu-Jaber, writing is wonderfully therapeutic. Her memoir, *The Language of Baklava* (2005), traces her family's journey through the metaphors of food, blending in each dish the ingredients of memory, faith, and love, which are so distant and yet so close. Remapping the adjustments of a growing child-narrator between Jordan and the United States through this unique experiment of combining autobiography with the cultural and emotional nuances of food, Abu-Jaber investigates her own heritage against the backdrop of her new encounters with conflicting cultures. Packed with people, foreign and familiar, filled with the aroma of a variety of recipes with inspiring descriptions, and overflowing with bright, flickering lights of primordial memories, *The Language of Baklava* is as much a celebration of an immigrant's home (which is always on the move) as it is an attempt at understanding a biracial upbringing in a multiethnic society.

Origin (2007), Abu-Jaber's latest novel, unfolds the mystery of sudden infant deaths, which creates an atmosphere of anguish and panic. Lena Dawson, the protagonist, is a fingerprint expert at a crime laboratory in the city of Syracuse, New York, who has been trained through a yearlong correspondence course of the FBI Fingerprint Classification School. The infant deaths bring her to examine her own childhood as an orphan. These incidents make her think through her continued existence, which could have easily been cut short.

Abu-Jaber has also written short stories and nonfiction that unmistakably deal with issues of identity and migration in a multicultural and multiracial society. Some of Abu-Jaber's short fiction, such as "Desert" (1991), "Billets-Doux" (1991), "In Flight" (1993), "Hindee" (1994), "My Elizabeth" (1995), "Irene" (1996), "Marriage" (1997), "Arrival" (1999), "Tale of Love and Drowning" (2001), "For the Time Being" (2002), and "Madagascar" (2003), have been published in reputed magazines and anthologized (see Chandra Prasad, ed. *Mixed: An Anthology of Short Fiction on the Multiracial Experience*. New York: Norton, 2006). She has regularly written and spoken on issues of race, ethnicity, identity, multiculturalism, and the culinary arts. She acknowledges William Faulkner, Toni Morrison, John Cheever, John Updike, Louise Erdrich, Jamaica Kincaid, and, more importantly, Anton Chekhov, and Maxine Hong Kingston as her inspiration and the power that opened for her the ways to understand and appreciate the hard realities of the world through the magic of the written word, even in the most adverse and challenging circumstances. **See also** Asian Diasporas; Assimilation/Americanization; Multiculturalism and Asian America.

Further Reading

Cherif, Salwa Essayah. "Arab American Literature: Gendered Memory in Abinader and Abu-Jaber." *MELUS* 28.4 (Winter 2003): 207–228.

Field, Robin E. "Diana Abu-Jaber: A Prophet in Her Own Town." An Interview with Diana Abu-Jaber. *MELUS* 31.4 (Winter 2006): 208–225.

Majaj, Lisa Suhair. "Arab American Literature and the Politics of Memory." In *Memory and Cultural Politics: New Approaches to American Ethnic Literature,* eds. Amritjit Singh, Joseph Skerret, Jr., and Robert E. Hogan. Boston: Northeastern University Press, 1996. 266–290.

———. "Arab-American and the Meaning of Race." *Arab Perspective* 15.35 (1998): 320–331.

———. "New Directions: Arab American Writing at Century's End." In *Post-Gibran: Anthology of New Arab American Writing,* eds. Munir Akash and Khaled Mattawa. Syracuse, NY: Syracuse University Press, 1999. 66–77.

Salaita, Steven. "Sand Niggers, Small Shops, and Uncle Sam: Cultural Negotiation in the Fiction of Joseph Geha and Diana Abu-Jaber." *Criticism* 43.4 (Fall 2001): 423–444.

Shakir, Evelyn. "Arab-American Literature." In *New Immigrant Literatures in the United States: A Sourcebook to Our Multicultural Literary Heritage,* ed. Alpana Sharma Knippling. Westport, CT: Greenwood Press, 1996. 3–18.

Shalal-Esa, Andrea. "Diana Abu-Jaber: The Only Response to Silencing is to Keep Speaking." An Interview with Diana Abu-Jaber. *Al-Jadid* 8.39 (Spring 2002): 4–6.

ANIL K. PRASAD

✦ AFGHAN AMERICAN LITERATURE

Afghan American literature is contemporary literature by Americans of Afghan descent. Afghans came as refugees to the United States after the 1979 Soviet invasion of Afghanistan. This was the first incident of mass migration for Afghans. Since the United States officially supported the mujahideen, the nationalist movement countering the Soviet forces, 1986 marked the largest migration of Afghan refugees to the United States. Currently there are approximately 75,000 Afghan Americans. The number continues to grow.

The terminology of *Afghan* is complex and should be clarified before discussing the term *Afghan American*. *Afghan* is a name that Ahmad Shah Durrani had chosen for Afghanistan after he brought together what is modern-day Afghanistan in 1747. The ancient names of Afghanistan are Ariana, Bakhtar, and Khorasan. Afghanistan was built mostly through the efforts of Pashtuns, or Afghans, an ethnolinguistic group occupying the southern and northeastern parts of the land. The name *Afghan* means "people who cause suffering," and it came to be the name of the land of Afghans; the *-istan* means "land." In Afghanistan, up until the 1970s, the common reference to Afghan meant Pashtun. Other groups were known as Farsiwan, meaning Persian-speakers, Tajiks (northeast region), Uzbeks (northern region), Turkmen (northern region), Kazak (northern region), or Hazara (central region). The term *Afghan* as an inclusive term for all ethnic groups was an effort begun by the "modernizing" King Amanullah (1909–1921), who went as far as printing the four different languages on the four corners of his money. Later this was continued by King Mohammad Zahir, who tried to unify the country under the banner of Afghan. Before the era of television or a national railway system that could unite the ethnically diverse people living in the extreme high and low terrains of Afghanistan, which easily allowed for isolation, the term *Afghan* to mean all Afghans did not quite permeate into the cultural society until after the 1979 Soviet invasion and later in the exile community. It was as in exilic consciousness that the term *Afghan* was used in reference to all ethnic groups, their shared culture, and their shared trauma as survivors of war.

The term *Afghan American* is a post–9/11 creation. As an American ethnic community, Afghans did not come to speak of themselves as Afghan Americans until post–9/11 required this particular community to voice their opinions and offer their assistance and expertise in the situation in Afghanistan. In this historical light, it is clear that Afghan American cultural production is a rather new concept and one that is struggling to define and create a niche for itself within the discourse of multicultural America, as well as within the context of Afghanistan. Afghan American writers discuss current politics in their fiction and prose and address the internal community issues of ethnic and linguistic unity. The Afghan Americans of note to list are Khaled Hosseini, Mir Tamim Ansary, and Farooka Gauhari. After some time, the attention shifted to the war in Iraq, and so Afghan Americans, like Afghanistan, have been brushed aside. These authors have mostly written memoirs about their return to post-Taliban Afghanistan: *Come Back to Afghanistan: A California Teenager's Story* (2006) by Said Hyder Akbar, with Susan Burton; *Torn Between Two Cultures: An Afghan American Woman Speaks Out* (2004) by Maryam Qudrat Aseel; *A Bed of Red Flowers: In Search of My Afghanistan* by Nilofar Pazira (Afghan Canadian); and *My War at Home* (2006) by Masuda Sultan.

The first Afghan American woman writer is Farooka Gauhari, a biologist at the University of Nebraska. Her memoir, *Searching for Saleem: An Afghan Woman's Odyssey* (1986), did not feature her American life. The memoir documented her escape from Afghanistan after the Soviet invasion. Saleem is her husband, a general under King Mohammad Zahir (reigned 1933–1973) and later President Mohammad Daoud (1973–1978), who disappears the first night of the April Coup (Saur Revolution) in 1978. Currently, she is working on a book documenting the history of Pashtuns in Afghanistan. Afghan-centered literary works from this period were mainly a preoccupation with the mujahideen, the nationalist counter-Soviet guerrilla groups. This is the only work that is written by an Afghan woman.

Mir Tamim Ansary is the son of an Afghan father and an American mother who was raised in Lashkargah, Afghanistan, and returned to the United States as a teenager. His rise to fame on the topic of Afghanistan began with an e-mail that stated his outrage about the War on Terrorism in Afghanistan with an in-depth explanation of the contemporary issue in Afghanistan. This e-mail reached as far as the *Oprah Winfrey Show* and was read on air. Afterward, the children's book author and journalist wrote his memoir *West of Kabul, East of New York* (2002). Currently, Ansary has completed a historical novel set in Afghanistan, *The Malang of Kabul*, set in the nineteenth-century Anglo-Afghan Wars. He is based in California.

No other Afghan writer has achieved the fame and acclaim of the California-based doctor Khaled Hosseini. Born in Kabul, Afghanistan, to a diplomat and high school teacher, Hosseini was an internist from 1994–2006. Hosseini's first novel, *The Kite Runner* (2002), was on the bestseller list of the *New York Times* for two years. This novel has made such an impact on readers that it has been translated into plays and also released as a Hollywood film. His latest novel, *A Thousand Splendid Suns*, was released in June 2007. Whereas his first novel focused on stories of brotherhood and men, his latest book enters the world of Afghan women. Vividly written with an abashed prose style, both novels have put Afghanistan back on the cultural map of the world. Hosseini, like many of the writers whose books have reached a mainstream market, is an avid humanitarian and has worked with the United Nations to help the war-traumatized people in Afghanistan.

Afghan American literature is surprisingly unlike the majority of Asian American literature, even Iranian American literature (Iran and Afghanistan share a language, Persian), which is spearheaded by bestselling female authors; its literary renaissance has featured mainly male authors. However, there is a growing movement of women authors who left Afghanistan as children whose narrative styles are fragmented and intermingled with Afghan folktales. Fitting within the rubric of American multicultural literature, these narratives are about growing up in America. These women writers are Wajma Ahmady, Sahar Muradi, Khaleda Maqsudi, and Zohra Saed. Many are also filmmakers and video artists such as Lida Abdul and Sedika Mojadidi. This generation of writers has developed a new kind of narrative structure, poetic nonfiction at the cusp of memoir, fiction, and folktales. Their works can be found in recent anthologies about Muslim American or Asian American women writers.

Afghan American literature is at its nascent phase. With the catapult of master storyteller Khaled Hosseini, the publishing world has taken notice of this new face in the larger American tapestry. The maturation of the second generation of Afghan Americans and the new relationship between Afghanistan and the United States promise a new literary genre within American literature.

Further Reading

Afzal-Khan, Fawzia, ed. *Shattering Stereotypes: Muslim Women Speak Out*. Northampton, MA: Olive Branch Press, 2005.

Handal, Nathalie, Ravi Shankar, and Tina Chang, eds. *Contemporary Voices from the East: A Norton Anthology of Poetry*. New York: Norton, 2007.

Husain, Sarah, ed. *Voices of Resistance: Muslim Women on War, Faith and Sexuality*. Emeryville, CA: Seal Press, 2006.

Nazemi, Latif. "A Look at Persian Literature in Afghanistan." (Online 2007) *Art & Thought* section in www.qantara.de.

ZOHRA SAED

✦ AHMED, SHARBARI (1971–)

Bangladeshi American playwright, writer, and actress, Sharbari Ahmed gained immediate attention for her first play *Raisins Not Virgins* (2001) about the identity conflicts of a young Muslim woman from Bangladesh in New York City. Ahmed's play, which she produced and also starred in, and her short stories and screenplays reflect her international cultural framework. Born in Dhaka, Bangladesh, and brought up in Connecticut and Ethiopia, Ahmed studied Chinese in Beijing, China, before graduating from Marymount College, Tarrytown, New York, in 1994. She attended New York University and was awarded an MA in creative writing and English literature in 1997.

Ahmed has also taught English, fiction, and poetry at Manhattanville College, Purchase, and at New York University.

Raisins Not Virgins premiered at the Producers Club II in New York City in 2003. Set a year before September 11, 2001, the play deals with how to live as a Muslim in North America. According to Ahmed, the play's title does not refer to the article "Challenging the Quran," published by *Newsweek* in July 2003, which discusses issues of authenticity in translations of the Quran, but refers to earlier reports about a controversial study by an anonymous professor of Semitic languages, who uses the pseudonym of Christoph Luxenberg. Luxenberg's analysis of Syriac and Arabic words in the Quran also includes the phrase "not virgins but grapes" (qtd. in Kroes), which Ahmed refers to in the title of her play.

Not unlike José Rivera's Puerto Rican American heroine Marisol Perez in his play *Marisol* (1992), who embarks on a spiritual odyssey through an apocalyptic New York City at the brink of a new millennium, 29-year-old Sahar Salam, the female protagonist of Ahmed's comedy, tries to negotiate her cosmopolitan urban identity with her religious identity as a Bangladeshi Muslim. Both women characters encounter a menagerie of impressive characters who challenge their former beliefs. Although Sahar's religious identity is clearly important, it is but one element of her journey toward self-discovery. In a manner reminiscent of the female *bildungsroman,* Ahmed is as interested in showing the spiritual maturation of her protagonist as she is in tracing Sahar's sociopolitical and emotional education. Initially bound by the religious and cultural traditions of her parents' generation, Sahar has to learn to differentiate between her self-perception and the perceptions of others.

Ahmed has also written a screenplay based on *Raisins Not Virgins* and, in collaboration with Julie Rajan, the screenplay *The Sacrifice*. Her short stories and essays have been published in literary journals such as the *Gettysburg Review, Catamaran, Chowrangi,* and *Asian Pacific American Journal,* and include "Hanging It" (1998), "Sonali" (1998), "A Boy Chooses to Go to the Moon" (2000), "Pepsi" (2003), "Wanted" (2003), and "The Ocean of Mrs. Nagai" (2005). Ahmed's work often portrays the more personal, individual aspects of intercultural encounters, as is also evident in her short story "Pepsi." As in *Raisins Not Virgins,* Ahmed resorts to embedded history lessons and comedic devices to reveal the complexities of religions and cultural concepts and to identify potential gaps in communication and the dangers of misunderstanding.

"Pepsi," like *Raisins Not Virgins*, which is marked by its autobiographical impetus, chronicles a day in the life of Zara, the precocious 10-year-old daughter of a Bangladeshi diplomat in Ethiopia. Feeling neglected by her busy parents and not part of the group of haughty international "Third Culture Kids," Zara seeks a substitute family in their Ethiopian Jewish gardener Ato Rosa and the Ethiopian children literally playing beyond the walls of Zara's gated community. Like Lilia, the young first-person narrator in Jhumpa **Lahiri's** short story "When Mr. Pirzada Came to Dine" from her collection the *Interpreter of Maladies* (1999), it is through a personal encounter with these children and joining them in a game called Pepsi that Zara not only gains personal confidence but also learns that racial prejudices know no geographical boundaries and that poverty leads to strong social divisions. In a similar vein, the Bangladeshi American Ella in "Wanted," who was adopted by a couple from New Jersey, recognizes the intricate connection between personal lives and politics and that there is hardly any escape from it on a return trip to Dhaka right before her thirtieth birthday. Ahmed's work is marked by its transnational focus, which stretches not only from North America to South Asia but also repeatedly includes references to Israel and Palestine. Her broad geographical, linguistic, and cultural framework provides the necessary context for her characters' increasing intercultural understanding.

Ahmed's nonfiction work includes "A Place in the Sun" (2003), "Chasing Clark Gable's Smile" (2004), "Transcending a Troubled Past" (2005), and an introduction to Jane Austen's *Sense and Sensibility* as part of the Barnes and Noble Digital Library (2002). She is currently working on a novel set at the time of the Bangladesh Liberation War of 1971, entitled *A Small War*.

Further Reading
Interview with Sharbari Z. Ahmed. http://www.adhunika.org/heroes/sharbari_ahmed.html.
Kroes, Richard. "Missionary, dilettante or visionary?" Rev. of Ch. Luxenberg, *Die Syro-Aramäische Lesart des Qur'an.* http://www.livius.org/opinion/Luxenberg.htm.
Srikanth, Rajini. *The World Next Door: South Asian American Literature and the Idea of America.* Philadelphia: Temple University Press, 2004.
Theil, Stefan. "Challenging the Quran." *Newsweek* (28 July 2003): 40.

CHRISTIANE SCHLOTE

✦ AI (1947–)

A poet of mixed Native American, African American, and Japanese heritage, Ai is known as a dangerous writer for her ferocious and forceful dramatic monologues with dark, edgy subjects centered on sex and violence. Born on October 21, 1947, in Albany, Texas, Ai had her multicultural heritage from her Japanese father and her Choctaw, Cheyenne, African American, Dutch, and Scots-Irish mother. Known as Florence Haynes in her childhood, Ai grew up with her mother and stepfather primarily in Tucson, Arizona, and also lived in San Francisco and Los Angeles. At the age of 14, when Ai was studying at Mount Vernon Junior High School in Los Angeles, an advertisement for a poetry-writing contest caught her attention. Though she had to move back to Tucson and failed to enter the contest, Ai discovered her talent for writing poetry, which became the way for her to express feelings she could not otherwise. In 1969, Ai received her BA in Japanese at the University of Arizona and then her MFA at the University of California at Irvine in 1971. In graduate school, Ai resumed use of her legal name, Florence Anthony, which sounded more poetic to her. However, after Ai learned about the affair between her mother and Michael Ogawa, her Japanese biological father, she adopted Ai, which means "love" in Japanese, as her pen name, and she legally changed her name to Florence Ai Ogawa in 1973. In the same year, Ai published her first book of poems, *Cruelty*. In the following thirty years, she published six more books of poems, including *Killing Floor* (1979), which won the Lamont Poetry Award from the American Academy of Poets; *Sin* (1986), a recipient of the American Book Award from the Before Columbus Foundation; *Fate* (1991); *Greed* (1993); *Vice* (1999), a winner of the National Book Award for Poetry; and *Dread* (2003). She wrote a novel, *Black Blood* (1997), which was sold but never published. Apart from the awards for her poetry publications, Ai also held the Radcliffe Institute Fellowship in 1975 and the Massachusetts Arts and Humanities Fellowship in 1976; in addition, she received recognition from the Guggenheim Foundation in 1975 and the National Endowment for the Arts in both 1978 and 1985. Furthermore, she received the Ingram Merrill Award in 1983 and the St. Botolph Foundation Grant in 1986. After graduating from the University of California at Irvine, Ai worked as a visiting poet at Wayne State University (1977–78) and at George Mason University (1986–87), as writer-in-residence at Arizona State University (1988–89), and as a visiting associate professor at the University of Colorado, Boulder (1996–97). From 2002 to 2003, Ai held the Mitte Chair in Creative Writing at Southwest Texas State University. Currently living in Stillwater, Oklahoma, she is an English professor at Oklahoma State University and vice president of Native American Faculty and Staff Association.

Ai, who started writing poetry at the age of 14, attributed her greatest inspiration to fiction, especially Latin American fiction, such as Miguel Angel Asturias's *Men of Maize* and Gabriel Garcia Marquez's *One Hundred Years of Solitude*, which inspired her to write "Cuba, 1962," a poem that marked the beginning of her new interest in exploring other dimensions of the characters in her poetry. Inspired also by the candid feelings expressed by Spanish and Latin American poets like Miguel Hernandez, Pablo Neruda, along with American poets Galway Kinnell and Phil Levine, Ai never fears or feels embarrassed in revealing her feelings in poetry. She chose to write poetry in the dramatic monologue form, for she took to heart the opinion of her first poetry teacher, Richard Shelton, that the first-person voice was always the strongest when writing. Ai's poems are almost all dramatic monologues of different characters, be they well-known or anonymous, eminent or despised, dead or alive, men or women, telling their stories in crude language with stark and disturbing topics, including brutal sex, violence, child abuse, murder, necrophilia, and torture.

According to critic Claudia Ingram, the speakers of Ai's poems are obviously trapped in their "cultural definition" and "their unbearable identities seem always at the point of being shattered and remade, or simply shattered" (572). Although they are not able to "transcend" it, "they speak in such a way as to profoundly unsettle the very positions from which they speak" (572). Thus, when reviewing her works, reviewers tend to believe it is the poet who is telling her own stories behind the masks of characters, and they classify her poems and characters according to color, race, sex, and creed. However, although Ai acknowledges the importance of race as a "medium of exchange" (Ai 1974, 58) in the United States and that her characters have shared her struggles as a multiracial woman, she refuses to be catalogued, and so do her poems and characters. Ai refers to herself as "simply a writer" (Kearney 1978, 4) who intends to transcend cultural boundaries in her poetry. She also regards herself as "the playwright, the director and the actor" (Elliot 2008) who uses dramatic monologues to depict individuals instead of herself. Because she is a wide reader, Ai finds in history, newspapers, and literary works interesting subjects and personas, of which she prefers scoundrels because "they are more rounded characters" (PBS). Then she steps into these personas, creates "an entire psychology" (Elliot 2008) for them, and lends them her voice so that they are able to speak.

In 1973, Ai published *Cruelty*, whose original title was "Wheel in a Ditch," which symbolized the chariot's wheels in Ezekiel's vision where the "spirit of man [was] trapped, stuck and not able to pull himself out." As the original title indicates, the individuals depicted in *Cruelty* are anonymous, mostly women, struggling in poverty or stuck in small towns. Critic Duane Ackerson describes these characters in *Contemporary Poets* as "people seeking transformation, a rough sort of salvation, through violent acts." Their dramatic monologues deal with harsh topics including violence, rape, suicide, abortion, fracture, hanging, child abuse, and insatiable sexual desires through ambiguous and horrifying images. Although retaining the subjects of sex and violence, Ai's second book, *Killing Floor*, witnesses a change in her poetry writing. As critic Rachel Hadas comments in the *Oxford Companion to Twentieth-Century Poetry*, Ai moves her preoccupation from personal violence to historic atrocity, and her imagination opens out into a public arena, the domestic turned political, which can be observed in poems such as "Pentecost" on the Mexican Revolution of 1910 and "Nothing But Color" for the Japanese writer Yukio Mishima. In subsequent volumes, such as *Sin, Fate, Greed,* and *Vice,* Ai replaces the anonymous speakers of her earlier works with real individuals and poems that tend to be longer, for she gives each character more freedom to speak. Monologues of cultural icons such as J. Edgar Hoover, Jimmy Hoffa, Elvis Presley, Lenny Bruce, and James Dean, who returned from death, reborn in Ai's verse, express "more about the American psyche than about the real figures and Ai intends it this way" (Ackerson 1996, 14). In *Dread,* her latest book dedicated to survivors of childhood trauma, besides writing on current events like the collapse of the World Trade Towers, Ai draws upon her personal life and family history, including the affair between her mother and Japanese father. Presently Ai continues to work on her first memoir and to contribute poems and articles to journals.

Further Reading

Ackerson, Duane. "Ai: Overview." In *Contemporary Poets,* 6th edition; ed. Thomas Riggs. New York: St. James Press, 1996. 13–14.

Ai. "On Being 1/2 Japanese, 1/8 Choctaw, 1/4 Black, and 1/16 Irish." *Ms.* 6 (1974): 58.

Ciuraru, Carmela, ed. *First Loves: Poets Introduce the Essential Poems that Captivated and Inspired Them.* New York: Scribner, 2000. 21, 28–32.

Elliot, Okla. "Interview with Ai." *The Pedestal Magazine* 25 June 2008. <http://www.thepedestalmagazine.com/Secure/content/cb.asp?cbid=345>.

Hadas, Rachel. "Ai." In *Oxford Companion to Twentieth-Century Poetry,* ed. Ian Hamilton. Oxford: Oxford University Press, 1994. 6–7.

Heuving, Jeanne. "Divesting Social Registers: Ai's Sensational Portraiture of the Renowned and the Infamous." *Critical Survey* 9.2 (1997): 108–120.

Ingram, Claudia. "The Flames of Language and of Love: Enactments of Intersubjectivity in Twentieth-Century Poetics." PhD Thesis. University of Oregon, 1993.

———. "Writers of Mixed Ancestry." In *The Oxford Companion to Women's Writing in the United States,* eds. Cathy N. Davidson and Linda Wagner-Martin. New York: Oxford University Press, 1995. 572.

———. "Writing the Crises: The Deployment of Abjection in Ai's Dramatic Monologues." *Literature Interpretation Theory* 8.2 (1997): 173–191.

Irwin, Therese Catherine. "Voices in the Mirror: Sacrifice and the Theater of the Body in Dramatic Monologues of Ai and Frank Bidart." PhD Diss. University of Southern California, 2002.

Kearney, Lawrence, and Michael Cuddihy. "An Interview with Ai." *Ironwood* 2 (1978). <http://www.english.uiuc.edu/maps/poets/a_f/ai/kearney.htm>.

Kilcup, Karen. "Dialogues of the Self: toward a theory of (re)reading Ai." *Journal of Gender Studies* 7.1 (1998): 5–20.

Moore, Lenard D. "Poetry Reviews." Rev. of *Vice: New and selected poems,* by Ai. *Black Issues Book Review* 2.2 (2000): 44–45.

"PBS Interview with Ai." PBS Online News Hour: The National Book Award for Poetry. 25 June 2008. http://www.pbs.org/newshour/bb/entertainment/july-dec99/ai_nba_11-18.html7.

JINGJIE LU

✦ *AIIIEEEEE!* (1974)

A groundbreaking anthology of Asian American literature, published by Howard University Press in 1974 and edited by Frank **Chin**, Jeffery Paul **Chan**, Lawson Fusao **Inada**, and Shawn Hsu **Wong**, *Aiiieeeee!'s* peculiar title originates from the often heard cry of capitulation sung out by stereotyped depictions of Asians in mainstream American films, usually followed by their on-screen demise. Like the anthology itself, the editors suggest that the title is a move toward reclamation.

BACKGROUND

More than a simple collection of literary excerpts, *Aiiieeeee!* was an audacious attempt to carve out space for Asian American literature at the popular and institutional levels. During their early development as burgeoning writers and scholars, Chin, Chan, Inada, and Wong noticed a dearth of readily available literary material written by Asian Americans, which to them seemed counterintuitive, considering the fact that Chinese, Japanese, and Filipino Americans were already well into their fifth, third, and second generations, respectively. Based in the Bay Area of Northern California, they sought each other out and began to actively search for Asian American texts by scouring local used bookstores. Through this method, they managed to discover some of the books included in the anthology, including Toshio **Mori's** *Yokohama, California* and John **Okada's** *No-No Boy*, both of which, until that point, had languished in obscurity. Armed with a copy of these "recovered" books, they would try to contact the authors to learn more about the Asian American literary heritage for which they had been searching. From there, their discussions led to the idea for *Aiiieeeee!*, which, after being rejected by several publishing houses, was put out by historically black Howard University's new publishing division. It became an instant hit, garnering reviews and attention from numerous literary journals and popular periodicals such as the *New York Times*, the *New Yorker*, and *Rolling Stone*. Asian American scholars credit *Aiiieeeee!* and its editors, sometimes begrudgingly, as one of, if not the single most important moment in Asian American literary history, which established the genre as a serious cultural and academic area of study. About a decade and a half later, *Aiiieeeee!* was revised and expanded upon as *The Big Aiiieeeee!* (1991), including a new introduction and a larger collection of works.

WHAT SET IT APART

The defining feature of *Aiiieeeee!*, other than the selection of rediscovered Asian American works, is the collectively written preface and introductions. The introduction, titled "Fifty Years of Our Whole Voice," sets out to define the canon and is divided into two parts, one introducing Chinese and Japanese American literature, which was written by the editors, and the other introducing Filipino American literature, written by Oscar Peñaranda, Serafin Syquia, and Sam Tagatac. The section on Filipino American literature largely laments the lack of literary legacies and the role political, cultural, and linguistic imperialism played in defining Filipino American works. The section written by the editors is more aggressive in its efforts to define Chinese and Japanese American literature. Polemical and pugilistic in tone, they rail against what they perceive as brainwashed, self-loathing Asian American writers pandering to mainstream white readerships. Although it ostensibly functions as a kind of overview of the ignored history of Asian American literature, it is apparent that, although it was imperative to the editors to define exactly what Asian American literature is, it was just as important to define what it is not. To this end, the introduction lends considerable space to attacking Asian American writers—Chinese American writers in particular—who, they posit, internalized white, racist stereotypes to such a successful degree that they ended up recycling the same stereotypes in their works, which was even more damaging to the larger Asian American community as they authenticated those images with their ethnicity. These authors, they contend, should be excluded from the canon because they are not truly **Asian American** but successfully indoctrinated puppets of the white, racist structure that raised them. Some of the early writers who incurred their collective wrath include Virginia Lee, Pardee **Lowe**, and Jade Snow **Wong**. Later, in the expanded *The Big Aiiieeeee!* Amy **Tan** and Maxine Hong **Kingston** would also be attacked for similar reasons. In contrast, they laud works they judge as representative of the "real" community, such as Louis **Chu's** *Eat a Bowl of Tea,* which discusses the stark reality of Chinese American bachelor society without any of the romanticizing of Jade Snow Wong. They also suggest a narrow definition of Asian American writers, including a prerequisite of having been American-born without any strong ties to East Asia rather than an immigrant. This is illustrated in their discussion of Japanese American literature, specifically John Okada's *No-No Boy,* where they outline a rejection of any notion of an Asian American dual identity, opting instead for a unified self.

CRITICISM

Although *Aiiieeeee!* was well respected for its instrumental role in establishing Asian American literature, critics immediately attacked the contentious introduction written by the editors. They bristled at the harsh tone and pointed out the exclusion of Korean American and South Asian American literature from the anthology. With the even more vitriolic introduction to *The Big Aiiieeeee!*—this time signed off by Frank Chin alone—critics accused him of being misogynistic, chauvinistic, and, again, narrow-minded in defining Asian American literature, most notably by scholars King-Kok Cheung and Susan Koshy, who have since sought to define Asian American literature within a more global, transnational scope. Furthermore, the new introduction, titled "Come All Ye Asian American Writers of the Real and the Fake," sparked a long-running feud between Chin and Maxine Hong Kingston, on whom he focused most of his criticism. Some of the controversy surrounding their provocative rhetoric, however, might be understood as a matter of methodology. In an interview, Shawn Wong, now a professor of ethnic studies at the University of Washington, revealed that the editors intentionally sought to provoke a strong reaction when they wrote the introduction. Unsatisfied with the ensuing response, they revised *Aiiieeeee!* with the goal of creating more controversy to galvanize other scholars into investing themselves in the direction of Asian American literature. Moreover, their vituperative tone can be explained by the radical 1960s tradition they were educated in, when ethnic tensions and angry calls for equality were at their most visible. Regardless of how the literary community reacted to *Aiiieeeee!*, it was successful in the sense that it sparked a conflagration of dialogue.

CONTENT

In addition to its famed introductions and preface, the anthology includes excerpts from novels, short stories, and poetry from Carlos **Bulosan**, Jeffery Paul Chan, Diana **Chang**, Frank Chin, Louis Chu, Momoko **Iko**, Wallace Lin, Toshio Mori, John Okada, Oscar Peñaranda, Sam Tagatag, Shawn Hsu Wong, Hisaye **Yamamoto**, and Wakako **Yamauchi**.

Further Reading

Cheung, King-Kok. "Re-viewing Asian American Literary Studies." In *An Interethnic Companion to Asian American Literature*. New York: Cambridge University Press, 1997. 1–36.

Daniels, Roger. Rev. of *Aiiieeeee! The Pacific Historical Review* 44.4 (1975): 571–572.

Koshy, Susan. "The Fiction of Asian American Literature." *The Yale Journal of Criticism* 9 (1996): 315–346.

Li, David Leiwei. "The State and Subject of Asian American Criticism." *American Literary History* 15.3 (2003): 603–624.

Partridge, Jeffrey F.L. "Aiiieeeee! and the Asian American Literary Movement: A Conversation with Shawn Wong." *MELUS* 29.3–4 (2004): 91–102.

DAVID ROH

✦ ALEXANDER, MEENA (1951–)

Meena Alexander is one of the most important contemporary poets of the South Asian diaspora. Although a distinguished memoirist, fiction writer, and academic, it is Alexander's achievement in poetry, a genre that does not dominate the literary market, that has earned her the most sustained critical acclaim.

Biography

Alexander was born in Allahabad, India, on February 17, 1951, the eldest of three daughters of Syrian Christian parents from the southern state of Kerala. After spending the first four years of her life in Allahabad and briefly in Pune, with periodic visits to the ancestral homes of her grandparents in Tiruvella and Kozencheri in Kerala, her father left to work as a meteorologist in Khartoum, Sudan, thus precipitating the first of Alexander's many border crossings. Already immersed in multiple languages in India: her mother tongue Malayalam; Hindi in Allahabad; classical Sanskrit; and English, the legacy of British colonial rule, she was also exposed to Arabic and French in Khartoum. After attending school in Khartoum, she entered the University of Khartoum at the age of 13 and graduated with bachelor's degrees in English and French at the early age of 18. She continued her education at Nottingham University in the United Kingdom, where she received a PhD in English in 1973. Her first poems were published in Arabic translation during her student years in Khartoum.

Returning to India after her doctoral research, Alexander held academic positions in Miranda House in Delhi and in the Central Institute of English and Foreign Languages in Hyderabad. It was in Hyderabad that she met and married David Lelyveld, the American historian of South Asia, and accompanied him to New York to begin her new life in the United States. She began her academic career in Fordham University, followed by Hunter College. Presently, she is Distinguished Professor in English and Women's Studies at Hunter College and the Graduate Center of the City University of New York. Her scholarly publications include *The Poetic Self: Towards a Phenomenology of Romanticism* (1979) and *Women in Romanticism: Mary Wollstonecraft, Dorothy Wordsworth and Mary Shelley* (1989). She lives in New York City with her husband and two children, Adam and Swati.

Meena Alexander's first poems, "The Bird's Bright Ring" and "Without Place," were published during her teaching years in India by the Calcutta Writers Workshop in the 1970s. In the United States, her first poems to be published were "House of a Thousand Doors" (1988) and "The Storm: A Poem in Five Parts" (1989). The 1990s saw a profusion of poetry, autobiography, and fiction from Alexander. Works such as *Fault Lines, Nampally Road, Manhattan Music,* and *The Shock of Arrival* signaled the arrival of a distinctive and original voice in South Asian American literature, a voice that distilled the experiences of multiple geographic locations and expressed a racialized, female identity. Alexander's poetic achievement has continued to grow in the new millennium. Her 2002 collection of poems won the PEN Open Book Award. This was followed by the 2004 collection *Raw Silk*. In 2003 Alexander published a revised version of *Fault Lines* with a coda titled *Book of Childhood*.

There are several unifying aspects in Alexander's oeuvre, even though she has worked in different genres. Her poetic and fictional works stem from events recollected in her autobiography. Different aspects of her memoir illuminate several poems she has written, and her poems resonate and deepen the experience of reading her memoir. Thus the works are not contained in distinct literary and generic boundaries but flow into each other, much like the rivers and the oceans that she has crossed and that often form the symbolic landscape of her poetry.

LANGUAGE AND ART

In Alexander's writing, the multiple migrations of her biography have resulted in a poetic vocabulary that is a hybrid palimpsest of various languages. Although she has chosen to write in English, she is acutely aware of the burden of English as a colonial language, and she infuses it with the rhythms of her mother tongue Malayalam, Hindi, and Marathi, as well as the spoken Arabic of her Khartoum adolescence to claim it as her own. She refused to learn the Arabic or Malayalam scripts as a child, unconsciously associating the formal script of a classical language with public authority. On the other hand, she is highly receptive to the musical cadences of these languages and consciously uses them in her poetry. A most remarkable example of this is the poem "Illiterate Heart" from the anthology of the same name. The intermeshing of English with Malayalam and French conveys the sense of fracture and dislocation, as well as artistic choice and agency.

The choice of poetic language is also enmeshed in Alexander's reflections on her colonial education. The entry into a colonial language is marked by an almost physical violence as painful as a separation from the ancestral home at Tiruvella by the oceanic passage to Sudan. It is in Khartoum that Alexander is tutored in proper English diction by the Scottish teacher Mrs. Mcdermott. Alexander's reminiscences of the painful process of saying these words in a manner intended to subdue her original Indian accent are recorded as bodily and epistemic violence in *Fault Lines*. Ironically, it is this same rigorous training in British elocution that marks her accent as "other" in North America. The immersion into the colonial episteme is precipitated by Alexander's choice of studying English and French poetry, culminating in a dissertation in Romanticism. It is during her time in England that she feels a profound sense of alienation from the literary figures she is studying, such as Wordsworth, and the realities of her own history. She returns to India to forge a connection with her own cultural history. This profound questioning of colonial pedagogy is also represented in the novel *Nampally Road*, where the heroine, Mira Kannadical, a young lecturer in Hyderabad, feels a sense of disconnect between the Romantic poets she is teaching at the university and the political actions of a repressive postcolonial state that interrupt the very notion of the university as a space of intellectual freedom. Mira grapples with what it means to be a writer at a time of social and political ferment. Through the debates between Mira and her lover, Ramu, Alexander seems to meditate on the complementary roles of poetry and activism in the postcolonial nation state. Although Ramu is at times disparaging of poetry, it is through the poetic imagination that Alexander conceptualizes the possibility of establishing solidarity with the subaltern. Through her imaginative empathy with Rameeza, a victim of rape by the police, Alexander is able to envision a path to recovery, rehabilitation, and social justice.

FEMINISM: TRAUMA AND RECOVERY

Alexander's preoccupation with the abject female body surfaces in various works. She represents the condition of being female as one encompassing the physical and psychic burden of shame. In *Fault Lines* she writes of being haunted by the image of the well in Kerala, into which unmarried pregnant women had jumped to commit suicide. Her female relatives tell her of the dishonor these women brought to their families and that the only liberation from their sexual transgression was through death. Alexander returns to this memory again in "Poem by the Wellside" in *The Shock of Arrival,* which depicts the poet persona looking into the water of the well and identifying with the women who committed suicide. The poem dramatizes the struggle of the poet persona against the oppressive sense of shame engendered in the female psyche by a patriarchal society. This scene of a protagonist looking into a well where a woman has committed suicide recurs in the life of Sandhya Rosenblum, the heroine of *Manhattan Music.*

Another recurring figure of the traumatized female body in Alexander's oeuvre is the stone-eating girl. Alexander mentions in *Fault Lines* her own act of swallowing a stone, followed by the encounter with the stone-eating girl. The stone-eating girl sits under a tree, covered in mud, and swallows pebbles in public view. This is interpreted as another act of shamelessness by Alexander's Aunt Chinna. However, Alexander feels an instinctive affinity with this symbol of female abjectness. The act of swallowing a stone seems to imply the internalizing of traumatic memory; speech will metaphorically mark the reversal of silence and the uncovering of buried memory.

One of the most significant changes in Alexander's revision of *Fault Lines* is to uncover in the 2003 memoir the long-buried childhood memory of sexual molestation at the hands of her beloved grandfather Ilya. It is only after feeling physically ill and seeking help through therapy in the late 1990s in New York that Alexander is able to gradually remember the psychic and physical trauma that her memory had unconsciously suppressed. This incident leaves her not only with a sense of betrayal against the grandfather she had loved and implicitly trusted but also with a sense of anger and sorrow at her mother's inability to protect her from this abuse or to discern what was going on. Although the revelation of this traumatic memory is shocking, many episodes in the 1993 version of her memoir seem to foreshadow this crisis. The moments of nervous breakdown in the 1993 edition seem to reflect a buried psychic trauma resurfacing in the form of bodily manifestations. In her novel *Manhattan*

Music, Sandhya Rosenblum falls into a state of nervous breakdown after her adulterous affair with Rashid. She virtually transforms into the girl in the well she had heard about when she attempts suicide by trying to hang herself by the neck. There seems to be a repetition of the trope of the female body being punished for transgressive sexuality. Aunt Chinna is another character who loses her mental equilibrium in the poem of the same name, collected in *The Shock of Arrival.*

Alexander's writings do not represent women as passive victims. Whether it is Rameeza in *Nampally Road* or Sandhya in *Manhattan Music,* they are always juxtaposed against characters like Little Mother, Mira Kannadical, Draupadi, and Sakhi, who strive to reverse conditions of female oppression through their intellectual, creative, literary, or activist projects. Although women have to bear the violence wreaked on them by traditional or diasporic patriarchies, Alexander always delineates a path toward rehabilitation, restoring hope in feminist agency and intervention. This is often envisioned through the formation of strategic alliances between women of differing socioeconomic and cultural groups. Female friendships and relations of nurturance abound in her works, examples of which include the one between Sandhya and Draupadi in *Manhattan Music* and the one between Rameeza and Little Mother, which begins to develop at the end of *Nampally Road.*

RACE, RELIGION, AND VIOLENCE

Although Alexander has declared that she is more of a poet than a fiction writer, her novel *Manhattan Music* is an important testament to **Asian American** life. In many ways, this novel is a work with the largest canvas sweep, because it encompasses the geographies of home and migration for a number of racially diverse characters. Whereas Sandhya Rosenblum shares Alexander's own South Indian background, Draupadi Dinkins is of racially mixed heritage. Some of her ancestors migrated from India to work in the Caribbean sugar plantations, intermarried with Japanese and other races, and eventually migrated to New Jersey. Alexander is obviously positing a complex notion of South Asian American identity. The mainstream perception of South Asian immigration is that of a **model minority** consisting of highly educated immigrants with professional degrees. This is only true of immigrants who arrived in the phase after 1970. This presentation in the media erases the memory of Indian immigrants who came in as agricultural laborers in California in the early years of the twentieth century and the even earlier migrations of Indians as indentured laborers in the plantations of the Caribbean. Moreover, Alexander is committed to exposing the continuing racism against immigrants even at the present time. In *Manhattan Music,* she recreates the stoning of Indian women by skinheads in suburban New Jersey. Alexander has been personally subjected to incidents of racialized stereotyping and verbal abuse, which she has narrated in *Fault Lines.* This prevailing atmosphere of racial profiling and suspicion is intensified in the aftermath of September 11, 2001. In her poem "Kabir Sings in a City of Burning Towers" in *Raw Silk*, Alexander reflects on her decision not to wear a sari while traveling to the Graduate Center, where she teaches, but to carry the sari folded into a ball and to change into it in the women's bathroom of her school. She imagines the mystical poet Saint Kabir speaking to her and chastising her for succumbing to the times and erasing marks of ethnicity from her body in public space.

Alexander has theorized and reflected deeply on the place of poetry in the public sphere, especially the function of poetry during a time of violence. She returns to the lyric form in the aftermath of 9/11 to bear witness to the horrors unfolding in the city she has made her home. "Aftermath," "Invisible City," and "Pitfire" form a triptych in *Raw Silk* and collectively mourn the tragedy of these events. Although many poems in *Raw Silk* concern themselves with 9/11 and its aftermath, this is by no means the first time that Alexander's poetry has grappled with events in the public sphere. In a poem titled "Color of Home," Alexander laments the brutal killing of Amadou Diallo by the New York police. In an earlier poem "For Safdar Hashmi Beaten to Death Just outside Delhi," Alexander voices her indignation at the repressive mechanisms of the Indian state that chose to silence one of the most progressive theater directors, who was committed to Marxist ideology in his street plays.

In *Raw Silk,* her most recently published volume of poems, Alexander returns to the question of India as a secular democracy, in the wake of large-scale violence against the Muslim minority. Alexander visited the refugee camps in Gujarat that housed the survivors of the Godhra incident, in which 2,000 Muslims lost their lives and innumerable Muslim women were raped and tortured, as the state's legal apparatus provided immunity to the perpetrators of these heinous acts. More disappointingly, the chief minister of Gujarat was re-elected by an overwhelming majority through an effective playing of the communal card. Alexander writes a series of lyrics, addressed to Gandhi, the father of the Indian nation and apostle of nonviolence, asking him to comment on what is happening in his home state. These poems are arguably the most politically charged of Alexander's poetry, because she is challenging the conscience of the Indian nation by reminding the country of its foundational principles of equality and religious tolerance. She exposes the enormous gulf between the ideals of nationalism and the travesty of a democracy that India has become. These poems were originally published in the leading Indian newspaper the *Hindu*. Although these poems are terrifying in their evocation of communal carnage in restrained and spare language, they interweave references to Sufi saints such as Wali Gujarati, thus invoking a history of tolerance, cultural pluralism, love, and spiritual healing. Alexander's poetry forms a bridge between the consciousness of the poetic self, the internal workings of memory, and the violent events in the public sphere. She considers poetry, in the contemporary context, to be an attempt to bear witness to traumatic events in the public sphere and to seek clarity and understanding at a time of confusion and unrest. **See also** Feminism and Asian America; Hybridity; Indian American Autobiography; Multiculturalism and Asian America; Racism and Asian America.

Further Reading

Alexander, Meena. *Fault Lines.* New York: Feminist Press, 1993. Rev. ed. Preface by Ngugi wa Thiong'o. New York: Feminist Press, 2003.

———, ed. *Indian Love Poems.* New York: Everyman's Library/Knopf, 2005.

———. *Illiterate Heart.* Evanston, IL: Triquarterly Books/Northwestern University Press, 2002.

———. *Manhattan Music: A Novel.* San Francisco: Mercury House, 1997.

———. *Nampally Road: A Novel.* San Francisco: Mercury House, 1991.

———. *Quickly Changing River: Poems.* Evanston, IL: Triquarterly Books/Northwestern University Press, 2008.

———. *The Poetic Self: Towards a Phenomenology of Romanticism.* New Delhi: Arnold-Heinemann, 1979; Atlantic Highlands, NJ: Humanities Press, 1981.

———. *Raw Silk.* Evanston, IL: Triquarterly Books/Northwestern University Press, 2004.

———. *River and Bridge: Poems.* New Delhi: Rupa, 1995; Toronto: Toronto South Asian Review Press, 1996.

———. *The Shock of Arrival: Reflections on Postcolonial Experience.* Boston: South End Press, 1996.

———. *Women in Romanticism: Mary Wollstonecraft, Dorothy Wordsworth and Mary Shelley.* London: Macmillan, 1989; Lanham, MD: Barnes and Noble, 1989.

Bahri, Deepika, and Mary Vasudeva. "Observing Ourselves Among Others: An Interview with Meena Alexander." In *Between the Lines: South Asians and Post-Coloniality,* eds. Deepika Bahri and Mary Vasudeva. Philadelphia, PA: Temple University Press, 1996. 35–53.

Ballerstadt-Dutt, Reshmi. "Forging States of Belonging: Migrant Memory, Nation, and Subjectivity in Meena Alexander's Memoir *Fault Lines.*" *South Asian Review* 27.2 (2006): 93–115.

Basu, Lopamudra. "The Poet in the Public Sphere: A Conversation with Meena Alexander." *Social Text* 20.3 (2002): 31–39.

Dave, Shilpa. "The Doors to Home and History: Post-Colonial Identities in Meena Alexander and Bharati Mukherjee." *Amerasia* 19.3 (1993): 103–114.

Gairola, Rahul Krishna. "Western Experiences: Education and 'Third World Women' in the Fiction of Tsitsi Dangarembga and Meena Alexander." *Jouvert A Journal of Postcolonial Studies* 4.2 (2000). http://social.chass.ncsu.edu/jouvert/v4i2/con42.htm.

Gunew, Sneja. "Mouthwork: Food and Language as the Corporeal Home for the Unhoused Diasporic Body in South Asian Women's Writing." *Journal of Commonwealth Literature* 40.2 (2005): 93–103.

Maxey, Ruth. "An Interview with Meena Alexander." *Kenyon Review* 28.1 (2006): 187–194.

Mukerji, Sumitra. "Towards the Creation of a Vital Aesthetics: A Survey of Contemporary Indian English Poetry and Criticism with Special Reference to Meena Alexander." *Journal of the School of Languages* 3 (1993): 1113–1123.

Perry, John Oliver. "Contemporary Indian Poetry in English." *World Literature Today* 68.2 (1994): 261–272.

Rai, Sudha. "Diasporic Location and Matrilineage: The Poetry of Sujata Bhatt, Meena Alexander and Chitra Banerjee Divakaruni." In *Indian Feminisms*, eds. Jasbir Jain and Avadesh Kumar. New Delhi, India: Creative, 2001. 176–189.

Ray, Sangeeta. "Ethical Encounters: Spivak, Alexander and Kincaid." *Cultural Studies* 17.1 (2003): 42–55.

Rustomji-Kerns, Roshni. "An Interview with Meena Alexander." *Weber Studies: An Interdisciplinary Humanities Journal* 15.1 (1998): 18–27.

Shankar, Lavina Dhingra. "Postcolonial Diasporics 'Writing in Search of a Homeland': Meena Alexander's *Manhattan Music, Fault Lines* and *The Shock of Arrival*." *Literature, Interpretation, Theory* 12.3 (2001): 285–313.

Tharu, Susie. "A Conversation with Meena Alexander." *Chandrabhaga: A Magazine of World Writing* 7 (1982): 69–74.

LOPAMUDRA BASU

✦ ALI, AGHA SHAHID (1949–2001)

Agha Shahid Ali was a Kashmiri American poet who was born in New Delhi on February 4, 1949, and died in Northampton, Massachusetts, on December 8, 2001. He grew up Muslim in Kashmir and was later educated at the University of Kashmir, Srinagar, and the University of Delhi. In 1984 he earned his doctorate in English from Pennsylvania State University and in 1985 received a master's degree in fine arts from the University of Arizona. Ali won fellowships from the Pennsylvania Council on the Arts, the Bread Loaf Writers' Conference, the Ingram-Merrill Foundation, the New York Foundation for the Arts, the Guggenheim Foundation, and was awarded a Pushcart Prize. He was a professor at the University of Delhi, Penn State, SUNY Binghamton, Princeton University, Hamilton College, Baruch College, the University of Utah, and Warren Wilson College.

Ali's volumes of poetry include *Call Me Ishmael Tonight: A Book of Ghazals* (2003), *Rooms Are Never Finished* (2001), *The Country Without a Post Office* (1997), *The Beloved Witness: Selected Poems* (1992), *A Nostalgist's Map of America* (1991), *A Walk Through the Yellow Pages* (1987), *The Half-Inch Himalayas* (1987), *In Memory of Begum Akhtar and Other Poems* (1979), and *Bone Sculpture* (1972). In addition, he wrote *T. S. Eliot as Editor* (1986), translated *The Rebel's Silhouette: Selected Poems* by Faiz Ahmed Faiz (1992), and edited the anthology *Ravishing Disunities: Real Ghazals in English* (2000).

Ali was born in Kashmir, a region known for its stunning mountainous landscapes and streams, and grew up in a sophisticated household often visited by musicians and writers and in which relatives and visitors recited poetry in Persian, Urdu, Hindi, and English. He attended the area's privileged Catholic school where he learned about Christianity and Hinduism. His parents often encouraged his free exploration of the two religions. Writing his first poems at 12, Ali felt it only natural to write them in English. Given this linguistically diverse upbringing, Ali's poetry never ceased to investigate the intersection of Kashmiri cultures as well as Kashmiri and Western cultures, an examination heightened by Kashmir's ongoing territorial disputes and bloody war. By claiming English for his poetry and Urdu as his mother tongue, Ali asserted an identity that encompassed two seemingly contradictory stances of embracing the colonial culture of English and the native culture of Kashmir.

Ali claimed he had always known he would venture to the United States, even sending his first poems out to journals abroad and not to those in his native region. Ali moved to the United States in 1976 and quickly pursued a doctorate at Pennsylvania State University with a dissertation that would appear as *T.S. Eliot as Editor* (UMI Research Press, 1986). He then received an MFA in creative writing from the University of Arizona, where he was able to find some time to write and to take in a new part of the United States. Ali's first professorial position was at Hamilton College in Upstate New York in 1987, moving on to the MFA in English program at the University of Massachusetts, Amherst, in 1993. He claimed that teaching never hindered his production of poetry, and he made time to write no matter what other duties filled his schedule. He also drew inspiration and direction from his good friend and reader James Merrill until Merrill's death in 1995. This friendship perhaps solidified Ali's dedication to form, beautiful surfaces, and formal aspects in his work.

Puzzled by the dedication to minimalism he found in American poetry, Ali filled his own poems with effulgence and lush imagery. Given the rich mix of cultural influence in the household in which he grew up and with no fixed stylistic or experimental agenda, he felt no allegiance to a particular tradition. Instead, he spent time asserting his maximalist poetic style against the constraints of the traditional Arabic form of the *ghazal*, always gesturing toward sources such as Milton, Shakespeare, Greek myth, Arabic legends, and so on. Ali felt a certain pleasure at confounding politically correct interpretations of what was considered South Asian or Kashmiri, delighting in mentions of his homeland in the work of American and European authors such as Emily Dickinson and Oscar Wilde. The political subjects of his poetry tended to represent not only the conflicts in Kashmir but also the political fights he observed in Arizona's Native American populations and the loss of their culture, sometimes blending or blurring the lines between them in his poems. Historical loss, even of other cultures, gave Ali a vehicle for his natural poetic gift of expressing grief. Extreme pitches of emotion, however, were not the ultimate aesthetic goal in Ali's poetry. He espoused "formal distancing devise(s)" (Benvenuto 2002, 267) to gain distance on the rich and forceful emotions that seemed inherent in his favorite subject matters. Ali himself appreciated the mix of cultures that informed his imagination and kept his attention to cultural boundaries fluid and generous, never harboring ill feeling toward one culture over another.

Making his home in western Massachusetts for over 10 years, Ali authored several volumes of poetry, often dealing with the flashpoints of violence and bloody conflict in Kashmir and his mother's death in Northampton, Massachusetts, in 1997. They include *The Half-Inch Himalayas* (Wesleyan University Press, 1987), *The Beloved Witness* (Viking, 1992), *A Nostalgist's Map of America* (Norton, 1991), *The Country without a Post Office* (Norton, 1997), and *Rooms Are Never Finished* (Norton, 2003). He edited a book of *ghazals*, *Call me Ishmael Tonight* (Norton, 2004). He also published a translation of poetry by Faiz Ahmed Faiz from Urdu entitled *A Rebel's Silhouette* (University of Massachusetts Press, 1995).

In the last years of his life, Ali suffered from brain cancer while teaching at New York University and—though he had decided to travel to Kashmir to die with his family and father at his side—he remained in western Massachusetts. He died on December 8, 2001, and was buried near Amherst, the final resting place of his beloved Emily Dickinson (Ghosh 2007, 36).

Further Reading

Benvenuto, Christine. "Interview with Agha Shahid Ali." *The Massachusetts Review* 43.2 (Summer 2002): 261—276.

Ghosh, Amitav. "'The Ghat of the Only World': Agha Shahid Ali in Brooklyn." Jan. 24, 2002. *The Nation.* Mar. 30, 2007. 31–36. http://www.thenation.com/doc/20020211/ghosh/3.

CYNTHIA ARRIEU-KING

✦ ALI, SAMINA (1970–)

Born in the city of Hyderabad in South India, Samina Ali immigrated to the United States with her parents when she was only six months old. In 1993, she graduated with a BA in English from the University of Minnesota and afterward acquired an MFA from the University of Oregon. Ali currently lives with her four-year-old son Ishmael in San Francisco. Pieces of her writings have appeared in diverse publications such as *Words Matter, Reading and Writing in the Second Wave of Multiculturalism, Our Feet Walk the Sky, Self* and *Child* magazines, the *New York Times,* and the *San Francisco Chronicle.* Barbara Deming Memorial Fund and the Rona Jaffe Foundation have provided her with funds to write. Ali also has given lectures about her novel and the role of Islam at the PEN/Faulkner Conference, the American Consulate in Italy, and at universities in the United States. Her interviews also illuminate her thoughts and beliefs. Ali has had a writer's mind all along, but it took years for her to pen a novel because of insecurities and fears. Ali got married when she was only 19 years old, and she returned to the United States after eight months. The writings about Muslim women by authors such as Marianna Ba, Nawal El Saadawi, and Sara **Suleri** have influenced her greatly. Her debut novel, *Madras on Rainy Days*, was published by Farrar, Straus and Giroux in January 2004. Although India is home to the second-largest Muslim population in the world, no immigrant Muslim from India has contributed substantially to Indian American literature. Ali's novel placed before Western and South Asian readers the problems, tribulations, and travails of Muslim women. With the publication of *Madras on Rainy Days*, Ali arrived on the scene of American immigrant literature with a bang. Although Ali might not yet be labeled as a great writer because she has only one novel to her credit, readers have been captivated by her portrayal of "possession" and "self-possession" of the main character in a lyrical language. The novel was the winner of the French award Prix Premier Roman Etranger in 2005. It was short-listed for the PEN/Hemingway Award in Fiction and the California Book Reviewers Award, and it was named one of the top-five best debut novels by *Poets & Writers*.

The protagonist in *Madras on Rainy Days* is Layla, who was brought up mainly in the United States with frequent sojourns to Hyderabad. While in school, she had a deep relationship with her boyfriend Nate that resulted in an abortion. The secret remained with her when she came to Hyderabad at the age of 19 after a year of college in Minneapolis for an arranged marriage with Sameer, a handsome engineer. Layla entered a world of chador-clad women, conservatism, suppression of inner feelings, and living by the norms of a rigid society. The city of Hyderabad had a special place in the Islamic culture of the South Asian subcontinent. A place of orthodoxy, it was the capital of the princely state of Hyderabad in pre-independent India. Now, it is the state capital of the province of Andhra Pradesh. It is no mere coincidence that the Bangladesh author Taslima Nasreen was threatened and heckled here in a literary function on August 9, 2007, by obscurantist forces of Islam. A city of rich Muslim culture blended with Hindu customs, it has also witnessed communal riots. The house of Ali once faced the wrath of a gang of Hindu communalists while she was living in that city. In a masterly way, Ali portrays the life of a newly married Muslim woman in Hyderabad and her yearning to become her own person. Behind the chador and burka, her inner spirit was being suppressed. Surrounded by the old city walls of Hyderabad was an unchanging world. Layla married into this world of tradition as an abiding and dutiful Muslim daughter. But her young and independent spirit was still there, deep inside. Strangely enough, she liked her new home and loving in-laws. However, the couple both had secrets of their own, which could devastate the lives of their spouses. On their honeymoon night, while the monsoon rain lashed the city of Madras (Chennai), the couple began to lay bare their true selves. When Layla discovered that Sameer was unable to consummate their marriage, she earnestly requested her family to allow her to leave the husband, to which she was entitled according to the laws of Islam. But Layla was forced to go on with her married life. She then began to delve into pages of the Quran and discovered the rights granted to a woman. She had rights over property, marriage, future, and, most importantly, over her body as granted by the Prophet Muhammad and Islamic jurisprudence. In the end, she began to assert herself and her rights. Layla was mistress of her own life henceforth. She could distinguish between Islam as a religion and as practiced by the self-proclaimed guardians of that religion.

Layla's stature among the readers rises when the arc of the novel comes to Sameer's understanding the angst of his wife. He did not object to her going back to the United States, thus enabling her freedom. Ali does not criticize Muslim males for criticism's sake. With empathy, she understands their condition, particularly that of gay Muslims. In the autobiographical novel, the character of Layla and the author are merged. Neither are aggressive, bra-burning femme fatales. They are, however, both devout Muslims, endeavoring to assert the rights of Muslim women as prescribed in the Quran. It was not for publicity's sake that Ali cofounded the American Muslim woman's organization *Daughters of Hajar*. It was born out of deep conviction. She has marched to the mosque in Morgantown, West Virginia, along with other women demanding equal rights. *Madras on Rainy Days* stands out as a saga of women's assertion against injustice, inequality, and male-controlled cultural norms. The world of immigrant literature is waiting for her second novel, which deals with the life of a Pakistani male.

Further Reading

Ali, Samina. *Madras on Rainy Days*. New York: Farrar, Straus and Giroux, 2004.

Champeon, Kenneth. *World of Muslim Women*. Web site: http://www.bookpage.com/0401bp/fiction/madras.html.

Rakoff, Joanna. *Madras on Rainy Days*. Web site: http://query.nytimes.com/gst/fullpage.html?res=9A02E5D71138F93BA35751C0A9629C8 B63.

Sawnet, Samina Ali. Web site: http://www.sawnet.org/books/authors.php?Ali+Samina.

University of Oregon. *Literary Reference: News Letter of the Creative Writing Program*, Spring 2006.

Vashisht, Kanupriya. *Samina Ali*. Web site: http://www.eastwestmagazine.com/content/view/34/52/.

PATIT PABAN MISHRA

✦ *AMERASIA JOURNAL*

The *Amerasia Journal* is a leading multidisciplinary scholarly journal in **Asian American studies** published three times a year (winter, spring, and fall) since March 1971 by the UCLA Asian American Studies Center, one of the oldest programs in Asian American studies in the United States, with the mission to promote understanding of the lived history and the living reality of Asian Americans and Pacific Islanders. *Amerasia* is the earlier of the two journals under the Center, the other one being *AAPI Nexus: Asian Americans and Pacific Islanders Policy, Practice, and Community,* which debuted in 2003.

Amerasia in the past three and a half decades has been committed to reflecting the profound social changes that have taken place among Asian Americans and Pacific Islanders, such as the unprecedented increase in their population, their ever-growing panethnicity, and their dynamic interactions with American society.

Since the historic premiere issue of *Amerasia,* the journal has published over 30,000 pages of scholarly and creative writings by both veteran and up-and-coming scholars and writers, providing a publishing venue for proven talents as well as the young talents who are determined to share their interpretation of the individual and collective experiences of new immigrants and descendents of the old immigrants from Asia. The journal has expanded its concerns under the categories of "Asian American studies and movement," "Asian Americans and U.S.-Asia relations," "Asians in the Americas," "authors/books/films reviewed," "bibliographies," "comparative ethnic and race relations," "culture, arts and media," "education," "ethnic and racial identity," "gender and women studies," "Hawaii and the Pacific," "immigrants, refugees and migration," "labor, business and economy," "legal, political and civil rights issues," "literature, literary criticism and commentaries /essays," "multicultural Asians," "poetry," "religion," "sexual politics and identities," "short stories, memoirs and novel experts," "testimonies to the Commission on Wartime Relocation," "war and peace issues," and "**World War II** and Japanese Americans."

Although scholarly oriented, *Amerasia* has never concealed its political concerns and preferences; many of its issues revolve around the status quo and the status quo ante, which cannot be missed by a glance at some of its titles: *Salute to 60s/70s: San Francisco Status Strike* (Vol. 15, No. 1, 1989), *Satyagraha: Political Culture of South Asian Americans* (Vol. 25, No. 3, 1999), and *Challenging Race and Racism; Retrospective Look at China's Cultural Revolution* (Vol. 27, No. 2, 2001).

The journal often draws attention to specific ethnic groups within the Asian American community, such as *Japanese American Nisei* (Vol. 13, No. 2, 1987) and *Chinese Americans: Rural & Urban Lives* (Vol. 14, No. 2, 1988). In *Vietnamese Americans: Diaspora and Dimensions* (Vol. 29, No. 1, 2003), a new generation of Vietnamese and American scholars and writers examine the experience of Vietnamese Americans and their sophisticated connections to Vietnam, employing approaches that include education, economics, ethnic studies, history, literature, political science, public health, religion, and society. Under the title of *What Does It Mean To Be Korean Today?* are two issues (Vol. 29, No. 3, 2003/2004 and Vol. 30, No. 1, 2004) dedicated to the commemoration of 100 years of Korean migration to the United States, addressing issues relevant to Korean migration history, youth, race relations, the Internet, and Koreatown.

Amerasia also publishes special issues in honor of highly respected individuals who have made great contributions to Asian American studies. The journal's first two issues were in honor of Rocky Chin and Yuji Ichioka, and this tradition is still alive in its recently published issues, such as *A Tribute to Miné Okubo* (Vol. 30, No. 2, 2004) and *Edward Said's Orientalism & Asian American Studies* (Vol. 31, No. 1, 2005). *Edward Said's Orientalism & Asian American Studies* is a special tribute to the influence of Edward Said's book, *Orientalism,* on Asian American studies, including papers on gender and **feminism**, identity politics, queer studies, translation in relation to the theme contributed by Moustafa Bayoumi, Ali Behdad, et al.

Asian American literature is also a theme regularly investigated and surveyed in this journal, for instance, *Asian American Literature* (Vol. 9, No. 2, 1983), *Korean Women, Literature* (Vol. 11, No. 2, 1985), and *Asian American Poetry* (Vol. 20, No. 3, 1994). Another feature of *Amerasia Journal* is its book review section, which comprises a sizable portion of every issue. The book reviews are commonly around 800–1,000 words in length, concise yet informative, reporting basic information about the books and making critical assessment of the books' scholarly value. Among many others, the following books are reviewed in the journal: *Dragon Ladies: Asian American Feminists Breathe Fire* by Sonia Shah; *A Resource Guide to Asian American Literature* edited by Sau-ling Cynthia Wong and Stephen H. Sumida; *Khmer American: Identity and Moral Education in a Diasporic Community* by Nancy J. Smith-Hefner; *A Single Square Picture: A Korean Adoptee's Search for Her Roots* by Kathy Robinson; and *Becoming American, Being Indian: An Immigrant Community in New York City* by Madhulika S. Khandelwal.

Amerasia has been indexed and abstracted in *America: History and Life; Bibliography of Asian Studies; Writing on American History; Arts and Humanities Citations Index; Sage Race Relations Abstracts;* and the *Western Quarterly. Amerasia*'s library and individual subscribers are worldwide, coming from the United States, Canada, Central America, Latin America, the United Kingdom, Italy, Poland, China, Japan, India, Korea, Australia, and the former Soviet Union. Some of the journal's contributors include Prosy Abarquez-Delacruz, Moustafa Bayoumi, Grace Lee Boggs, Sucheng Chan, Edward Chang, Gordon Chang, Jeff Chang, Frank **Chin**, Rey Chow, Catherine Ceniza Choy, Lowell Chun-Hoon, Roger Daniels, Enrique de la Cruz, Philip Vera Cruz, Arif Dirlik, Yen Le Espiritu, Chris Friday, Richard Fung, Emma Gee, N.V.M. **Gonzalez,**

Jessica **Hagedorn**, Arthur A. Hansen, Bill Hing, Lane Ryo Hirabayashi, Marlon Hom, Sharon Hom, Velina Hasu **Houston**, Evelyn Hu-Dehart, Amir Hussain, Yuji Ichioka, Jerry Kang, Ketu Katrak, Peter Kiang, Nazli Kibria, Elaine H. Kim, Maxine Hong **Kingston**, Harry Kitano, Amitava **Kumar**, Scott Kurashige, Him Mark Lai, Wally Look Lai, Vinay Lai, Bill Lann Lee, K.W. Lee, Lisa Lowe, Kingsley Lyu, Martin Manalansan, Sunaina Mara, Mari Matsuda, Valerie Matsumoto, Ruthanne Lum **McCunn**, Davianna Alegado McGregor, Pyong Gap Min, Alice Yang Murray, Franklin Ng, Angela Oh, Gary Okihiro, Glenn Omatsu, Michael Omi, Gary Pak, David Palumbo-Liu, Vijay Prashad, Robert Chao Romero, Steve Masami Ropp, Roshni Rustomji-Kerns, E. San Juan, Alexander Saxton, Paul Spickard, Rajini Srikanth, Dana Takagi, Eileen H. Tamura, Haunani-Kay Trask, Mililani B. Trask, Monique **Truong**, Karen Umemoto, Urvashi Vaid, Linda Vo, L. Ling-chi Wang, Shawn **Wong**, Hisaye **Yamamoto**, Eric K. Yamamoto, Michael Yamamoto, Karen Tei **Yamashita**, Wakako **Yamauchi**, Eui-Young Yu, Henry Yu, Judy Yung, and Helen Zia, among many others.

The current editor of *Amerasia* is Russell **Leong**, with Brandy Liên Worrall-Yu as associate editor. The editorial board members include Edward Taehan Chang, Arif Dirlik, Yen Le Espiritu, Chris Friday, Richard Fung, Emma Gee, Jessica Hagedorn, Lane Ryo Hirabayashi, Marlon Hom, Sharon K. Hom, Ketu H. Katrak, Him Mark Lai, Pyong Gap Min, Don T. Nakanishi, Robert A. Nakamura, Franklin Ng, Glenn K. Omatsu, Vijay Prashad, E. San Juan, Jr., Alaxander Saxton, Dana Takagi, Sau-ling C. Wong, Karen Tei Yamashita, Helen Zia, and Renee Tajima-Peña. *Amerasia's* ISSN is 00447471. Contact: UCLA Asian American Studies Center Press, 3230 Campbell Hall, Box 951546, Los Angeles, CA, 90095-1546; e-mail at aascpress@aasc.ucla.edu. Phone number: (310) 825-2968; fax number: (310) 206-9844.

Further Reading
Said, Edward W. *Orientalism*. New York: Vintage, 1979.
UCLA Asian American Studies Center Web site: www.aasc.ucla.edu.

LINGLING YAO

✦ *AMERICA IS IN THE HEART* (BULOSAN)

Published in 1946, *America Is in the Heart: A Personal History* is the best known work of Filipino American author Carlos **Bulosan**. Scholars have generally concluded that the work is a blend of autobiography, history, and novel. The book is based on events in Bulosan's life and the lives of other Filipino migrant laborers, filtered through the first-person point of view of a narrator who undergoes a number of name changes: born as Allos in the Philippines, he becomes Carlos upon coming to the

United States, and then Carl after his political transformation into a left-wing labor activist, journalist, and organizer (but following critical convention, the narrator will be referred to as Carlos here). Set during the Depression and ending on the eve of American involvement in **World War II**, the book is a record of the racist crimes of violence and labor exploitation committed by American society against Filipino migrant laborers. The book is also the story of how Carlos went from being a Filipino laborer to a writer and an American.

The book is divided into four parts. Part I documents Carlos's life in the Philippines, where he is the son of poor peasant farmers. Part II charts his immigration to the United States and the racist brutalities he endures as a migrant laborer at the hands of whites. Part III is a record of his self-education in both literature and politics and the rise of his political consciousness as he works as a radical journalist, organizing other poor laborers and people of color. Part IV shows Carlos as a published poet who finally reconciles with America, soon after **Pearl Harbor** and in the looming shadow of World War II. As a history, the book documents the intricate relationship between U.S. foreign policy abroad in the Philippines and its domestic policies at home concerning race, class, gender, and sexuality. Young Carlos leaves the Philippines because of the circumstances of his poverty in a land that is an American colony, and he chooses the United States because of that colonial tie. Although other Asians were forbidden from entering the United States after the passage of the **National Origins Act of 1924**, Filipinos continued entering because they were not technically foreigners or aliens but U.S. nationals, exempt from immigration restrictions. The seemingly liberal Tydings-McDuffie Act of 1934, which promised independence to the Philippines, was actually designed by the U.S. Congress to eliminate this loophole by turning Filipinos into aliens ineligible for immigration.

As Bulosan shows, American anti-Filipino sentiment was a complex mix of racism, class antagonism, and sexual anxiety. In the Philippines, these feelings were muted, given the relatively small presence of Americans. What Bulosan depicts in Part I is the seemingly benevolent attitude of American colonizers and the American colonial system that taught young Carlos such stories as the biography of Abraham Lincoln. Inspired by this and other stories, young Carlos aspires to immigrate to the United States. At the same time, Carlos's family is mired in poverty and its attendant problems: the fatal illness of a sister, the forced and unhappy marriages of his brothers, and the gradual loss of the family land, sold to pay for a brother's education. The exploitative, feudalistic class structure in the Philippines was both a legacy of Spanish colonial rule and American acquiescence to its perpetuation after the United States conquered the Philippines in the Philippine–American War (1899–1902). While the young Carlos does not recognize this history, the mature Carlos narrating the story interjects a sharp class analysis of these feudal relations perpetuated by Filipino elites against the Filipino peasantry. Young Carlos finally flees from the Philippines and, at the beginning of Part II, encounters his first taste of American racism on the journey there, when a young white woman calls Carlos and the other Filipino migrants "savages" and "monkeys."

These insults set the tone for Part II, where Carlos experiences a litany of abuse in the western United States: labor exploitation and poverty, physical violence and sexual humiliation, residential segregation and antimiscegenation statutes. As Bulosan puts it succinctly, "It was a crime to be a Filipino in California" (121). By the 1930s and Carlos's arrival in the United States, Filipinos had taken the place of earlier racial scapegoats, the Chinese and the Japanese. Those groups, too, were subject to the same intensity of white hatred that characterized the history of **racism and Asian America**, but immigration restrictions had virtually eliminated new Chinese and Japanese immigrants. In addition to the racial and economic discrimination shared with Chinese and Japanese immigrants, Filipinos were subject to a much greater degree of white sexual hysteria. Bulosan documents the sometimes sexual nature of the violence directed against Filipinos by white men, and the racist depictions of Filipino migrants that fueled that violence. Most of the Filipino migrants were men, and these racist depictions commented upon their desire for white women and the dangers Filipinos posed to these women, and, implicitly, to white men as sexual competition.

Although sex with white women was a clear taboo, sexual relations with women of color were not. Bulosan generally depicts these sexual relations with women of color as moments of degradation for Filipino men. White women, in contrast, generally represented the best of American possibility. In Part III, Carlos's life is saved by white women such as Marian, "the song of my dark hour," who prostitutes herself to give him money for his education. Other white women, such as Alice and Eileen Odell, give him books and mentor him. The combination of this informal education and the politicizing that Carlos undergoes through his experiences with racism and labor organizing transform Carlos into an intellectual and an aspiring writer. In his radicalization, Carlos becomes part of the wider movement to the left taken by the American intelligentsia during the 1930s. American writers and other artists were responding to the economic terror of the Great Depression, as well as to the totalitarian terror of fascism overseas. Carlos hears the urgent call to organize Filipino migrants and other poor laborers against the domestic forces of racism and labor exploitation directed against them and feels the need to tell their untold stories. Bulosan's story of Carlos's transformation into a radical writer-activist committed to both racial and class politics is one of the earliest accounts of **Asian American political activism**, and certainly one of the most influential. The editors of the 1974 Asian American literary anthology *Aiiieeeee!* excerpted *America Is in the Heart*, helping to establish its place in the new canon of Asian American literature.

By the end of Part III, Carlos has completed the first phase of his informal education, carried out while he is recovering from a bout of tuberculosis. He asks himself, "Would it be possible for an immigrant like myself to become a part of the American dream?" At the same time, he argues for the necessity of reclaiming Philippine folklore and national heroes like José Rizal. Through Part IV, Carlos matures as a writer, finding predecessors not only in Philippine culture but also in earlier Asian American writers such as Yone Noguchi and Younghill **Kang**. Carlos also finds his way into the contemporary literary scene by reading writers like Carey McWilliams, Louis Adamic, and John Fante, authors who in Bulosan's life would become his champions. Carlos also matures as a political organizer, becoming more involved with the Communist Party and developing an ever-more inclusive class and racial consciousness. The bombing of Pearl Harbor abruptly diverts his attention from the radical problems of domestic inequality to the global struggle against fascism, leading to the famous conclusion of the book in which Carlos sees the American earth "like a huge heart unfolding warmly to receive me" (326).

Perhaps not surprisingly, the American public positively received *America Is in the Heart* and Bulosan. Yet, within the book, there are clear signs of Bulosan's radical critique of the failures of American democracy and its promises of equality, given both to people of color within the nation and to colonial peoples ruled overseas by the United States. Rather than subtracting from the book's power, these tensions around the representation of the United States have only added to the book's fascination for successive generations of critics. One of the most written-about texts in Asian American literature, *America Is in the Heart* is probably the best known example of **Filipino American autobiography**, and arguably of **Filipino American literature**.

Further Reading

Bulosan, Carlos. *America Is in the Heart*. Seattle: University of Washington Press, 1973 (originally published 1946).

Espiritu, Augusto Fauni. *Five Faces of Exile: The Nation and Filipino American Intellectuals*. Stanford: Stanford University Press, 2005.

Kim, Elaine H. *Asian American Literature: An Introduction to the Writings and Their Social Context*. Philadelphia: Temple University Press, 1982.

Lee, Rachel. *The Americas of Asian American Literature*. Princeton, NJ: Princeton University Press, 1999.

San Juan, E., Jr. *On Becoming Filipino: Selected Writings of Carlos Bulosan*. Philadelphia: Temple University Press, 1995.

Wong, Sau-ling Cynthia. *Reading Asian American Literature*. Princeton, NJ: Princeton University Press, 1993.

VIET THANH NGUYEN

✦ ANGEL ISLAND

A hilly, grassy, and tree-covered island, Angel Island is the largest island in San Francisco Bay. As the top of Mt. Livermore reaches a height of 788 feet, Angel Island overlooks Marin County, San Francisco, the Golden Gate, and the entire Bay Area. The earliest-known visitors to the island were Miwok Indians, who used it as a fishing-and-hunting site for more than 6,000 years. After the war between Mexico and the United States, Angel Island became part of the United States in 1848. Starting from the Civil War and for almost 100 years, the island served to house a variety of military installations, a Public Health Service quarantine station, and an immigration station. Now the island is a state park.

The historical significance of Angel Island in Asian American history and literature lies in the fact that it was once the site of an immigration station that existed to detain Chinese immigrants. This immigration station was designed to be the main entry point into the United States for immigrants from Australia, New Zealand, Canada, Russia, and especially Asia. Often called the "Ellis Island of the West" or "the Guardian of the Western Gate," the immigration station was opened on January 21, 1910, and closed in November 1940. More than 1 million people were processed here, most of whom were allowed to enter the United States immediately or without much delay. However, for Chinese immigrants who were not welcome because of the **Chinese Exclusion Act** of 1882, it evokes unforgettable and bitter memories. Between 1910 and 1940, approximately 175,000 Chinese immigrants were detained and processed at Angel Island, and about one-tenth of that number were deported. The amount of time Chinese immigrants were detained here ranged from several days to two or three years. The immigrants had to suffer poor food, miserable living conditions, and, above all, tormenting interrogations. An interrogation usually lasted several hours a day and would continue for several days. The Chinese immigrants were asked detailed and often absurd questions. If they failed to give the right answers, they would be deported. When they could no longer endure the long confinement or the thought of deportation, some of them even committed suicide. The Chinese immigrants thus called Angel Island "Devil's Pass."

During the time Chinese immigrants were detained at Angel Island, many of them scribbled, brushed, or carved poems in Chinese on the barrack walls to express their disappointment, homesickness, loneliness, frustration, humiliation, agony, anger, and even hatred toward the white racists. For fear of being prosecuted, most writers of these poems chose not to sign their names. Thus, many poems remain anonymous. A few of the poems were copied by those who passed the interrogation and were able to enter the United States; consequently, they were published in Chinatown newspapers, journals, or books. Most of the poems, however, were locked up and forgotten when the immigration station closed in 1940. They remained unknown to the public until 1970.

In 1970 the poems inscribed on the barrack walls were discovered by a park ranger, Alexander Weiss, and, several years later, efforts were made to recover the long-forgotten anguished voices of the detainees. These poems were collected in several books. The earliest and most complete collection was made by Him Mark Lai, Genny Lim, and Judy Yung, three descendants of Angel Island inmates. They undertook a project of collecting more than 135 poems from the barrack walls, translating them into English, and publishing them in 1980 in a book titled *Island: Poetry and History of Chinese Immigrants*. Along with the poems, they also interviewed 39 people, most of whom had been detained at the station. The interviews serve as oral histories. The editors also presented more than 20 photographs that help to illustrate the history of the period. They dedicated the book to "the pioneers who passed through Angel Island" (Lai, Lim, and Yung 1980, book cover). These resurrected poems not only express the emotional responses of the detainees to racial prejudice but also shatter the stereotype that Chinese immigrants were poorly educated peasants and passive, silent, and uncomplaining "Orientals." Moreover, the recovered poems also lead to a resurrected history, as Charles Solomon commented, "This moving volume documents a neglected chapter of American history" (qtd. in "Him Mark Lai," *Contemporary Authors Online*).

Some of the poems appeared in other books. In an attempt to recover Asian American folk and oral traditions, Marlon K. Hom collected some of the poems under the title of "Immigration Blues" in his book *Songs of Gold Mountain: Cantonese Rhymes from San Francisco Chinatown*. In 1994, Paul Lauter selected 13 of the Angel Island poems in English translation for inclusion in *The Heath Anthology of American Literature*. The fact that some of the poems were anthologized indicates that they have entered the canon of American literature. Xiao-Huang Yin translated and discussed some of the poems in his essay "Plea and Protest: The Voices of Early Chinese Immigrants."

It should be noted that the immigration station at Angel Island is frequently mentioned in the writings of Chinese American writers such as Sui Sin Far (Edith Maude Eaton), Maxine Hong **Kingston**, Amy **Tan**, Shawn Hsu **Wong**, Frank **Chin**, and William Poy Lee, whose ancestors might have entered the United States by way of Angel Island and might have experienced the confinement and torturing interrogations. The literary representations indicate that Angel Island has become a memorial for Chinese Americans.

Further Reading

Daniels, Roger. "No Lamps Were Lit for Them: Angel Island and the Historiography of Asian American Immigration." *Journal of American Ethnic History* 17.1 (1997): 3–18.

D'Emilio, Frances. "The Secret Hell of Angel Island." *American West* 21 (May–June 1984): 44–51.

"Him Mark Lai." In *Contemporary Authors Online*. 2006. Thomson Gale. 3 April 2007. <http://galenet.galegroup.com/servlet/>.

Hom, Marlon K. "Immigration Blues." In *Songs of Gold Mountain: Cantonese Rhymes from San Francisco Chinatown*. Berkeley: University of California Press, 1987. 71–90.

Lai, Him Mark, Genny Lim, and Judy Yung, eds. *Island: Poetry and History of Chinese Immigrants on Angel Island 1910–1940*. San Francisco: Hoc Doi, 1980.

Lauter, Paul, et al., eds. *The Heath Anthology of American Literature*. Vol. 2. Lexington: D.C. Heath, 1994. 1755–1762.

Strom, Yale. *Quilted Landscape: Conversations with Young Immigrants*. New York: Simon and Schuster, 1996.

Takaki, Ronald. *Strangers from a Different Shore*. New York: Penguin Books, 1989.

Yin, Xiao-Huang. "Plea and Protest: The Voices of Early Chinese Immigrants." *Chinese American Literature Since the 1850s*. Urbana: University of Illinois Press, 2000. 11–52.

KUILAN LIU

✦ AOKI, BRENDA WONG (1953–)

Solo performer, storyteller, teacher, and recording artist using a performance aesthetic influenced by commedia dell'arte, Japanese Kyogen, and contemporary jazz, Brenda Wong Aoki's work explores issues of identity in contemporary multicultural America. Of Japanese, Chinese, Spanish, and Scots descent, Aoki's mixed heritage informs much of her work. Born in Salt Lake City, Utah, and raised in Long Beach, California, she received her bachelor's degree from the University of California at Santa Cruz in 1976. She began creating and performing solo pieces in 1988. Her many performance venues have included San Francisco's Yerba Buena Center for the Arts, the Kennedy Center in Washington DC, the San Diego Repertory Theatre, and Sapporo University in Sapporo, Japan. Her stories have been issued on CD, incorporated into video, and anthologized. Currently, Aoki is on the faculty of the Theater Arts Department at UC Santa Cruz, while she continues to tour and create new work.

Aoki's first solo performance, *Tales of the Pacific Rim* (1990), dramatized traditional Japanese ghost stories, casting her in the mode of the conventional storyteller. Many of her subsequent performances have adhered to this genre, including *Obake!* (1991) and *Mermaid Meat and Other Stories* (1997), a libretto commissioned by the Berkeley Symphony Orchestra. Simultaneously, however, in the early 1990s, Aoki joined a handful of performers who began to use the embodied autobiographical narrative as a political tool to expand the notion of identity. In 1992, she created *The Queen's Garden*, her first performance to receive national attention. As she documents in the performance, growing up in Southern California gave her early, practical experience with the tensions created at the intersections of race and class. Later, Aoki would become a community organizer, active in a burgeoning Asian American movement. This early activism is reflected in *The Queen's Garden*. The piece takes on such hot-button issues as gang violence, drug addiction, and teenage pregnancy with sensitivity and without oversimplification. It loosely follows Aoki's transformation from pudgy adolescent to weekday model minority/weekend street gang member to college-educated activist. Although "Brenda" is the central figure, the piece has a diverse cast of characters, each with their own story and all played by Aoki. Set mostly in an impoverished neighborhood enclosed by freeways and oil fields, *The Queen's Garden* evokes a world in which the comedy and the tragedy of life constantly collide. It deploys extremely specific details of dialect, landscape, and circumstance to make greater observations about the repercussions of poverty and racism. *The Queen's Garden* has been performed across the country. In addition, Aoki performs selections from the piece in the video *Do 2 Halves Really Make a Whole?* (1995). In 1999, Aoki recorded *The Queen's Garden* on CD with music by Mark Izu. The recording won an Indie Award for Best Spoken Word Album, presented by the Association for Independent Music.

Aoki continued the personal narrative of *The Queen's Garden* in *Random Acts of Kindness* (1994), about her life as a performing artist. A later work in 1998, *Uncle Gunjiro's Girlfriend,* departs from the explicit memoir but remains personal. The piece tells the story of the brother of Aoki's grandfather, a Japanese immigrant. In 1909, Gunjiro Aoki fell in love with Helen Emery, the daughter of the Archdeacon of San Francisco's Grace Cathedral. The relationship prompted outrage, resulting in the addition of the Japanese to the lists of racialized "Others" legally barred from marrying in California. Eventually, the couple was able to marry in Tacoma, Washington. Helen, however, like other Caucasian women before and after her, lost her citizenship. As a historical narrative, *Uncle Gunjiro's Girlfriend* reflects and comments on contemporary racial politics. It is a reminder, for example, that antimiscegenation laws were not revoked in the United States until 1967—and that the legacy of racial hatred and discrimination remains with us still.

Aoki's autobiography-as-activism underscores much of her work. But to call her work didactic, or even overtly political in a Brechtian sense, would be misleading. Aoki is primarily a storyteller, spinning complicated, funny, and often intensely beautiful tales intended to enrapture her audience. Her stories resemble morality tales without the clearly defined moral. Her 1997 fable "Mermaid Meat," for example, seems to follow the lines of a classic Japanese ghost story, replete with the iconic figures of Mermaid, Fisherman, and Fisherman's Daughter. At the tale's conclusion, however, the story turns strikingly contemporary in its exploration of the complicated relationships between women.

Although Aoki's stories have the language of literature, they are aesthetically completed by her distinctive performance style. Her performances are as much about the body and movement as they are about dramatic reading. A mixed medley of dance training in her childhood is in evidence, as is her experience with commedia dell'arte.

Moreover, her training in Kyogen and Noh, both genres of traditional Japanese theatre, informs her entire movement aesthetic. In the late 1970s and early 1980s, Aoki trained and performed at San Francisco's Theatre of Yugen with Yukio Dori. She also traveled to Japan to study with Noh master Nomura Shiro. Though her work diverges from the classical, her training emerges in her intense and precise gestural language, as well as her flexible, almost musical voice. Aoki presents a dramatic figure as she transforms her body, including a curtain of long black hair, into props and scenery.

Although Aoki is not a musician in the conventional sense, her performances can be recognized within the idiom of jazz. Her work depends upon rhythm, repetition, and the building of momentum. Although she does not improvise, the performances alternate between disciplined control and unexpected outburst. Moreover, she often collaborates with husband Mark Izu, using live jazz to underscore her work. Together, they founded First Voice as a way to promote the music and stories of people experiencing the intersection of cultures. They have created three audio recordings of Aoki's stories accompanied by Izu's score.

Aoki has twice been a National Endowment for the Arts Fellow. She has received four Dramalogue Awards for her work, as well as a Critics' Circle Award and an ASCAP special award for innovative libretto. In 2007, Aoki was awarded the Japan-United States Friendship Commission Creative Artist Exchange Fellowship, which involved a five-month residency in Japan. **See also** Multiculturalism and Asian America; Racism and Asian America.

Further Reading

Bonney, Jo. *Extreme Exposure: An Anthology of Solo Performance Texts from the Twentieth Century.* New York: Theatre Communications Group, 2000.

Cheng, Scarlet. "Speaking of the Unspoken." *Los Angeles Times* 30 April 2000: Calendar: 48, 82. First Voice Web site: www.firstvoice.org.

Perkins, Kathy A., and Roberta Uno, eds. *Contemporary Plays by Women of Color: An Anthology.* New York: Routledge, 1996.

JENNIFER CHAN

✦ ARAB AMERICAN LITERATURE

In contrast to what many might assume, Arab American literature is not a new genre in the United States, but rather one that is over a century old, dating back to at least 1911 with the publication of Ameen Rihani's *The Book of Khalid*. It also includes the establishment of *Al Rabitah al Qalamiyah* (The Pen League), a vibrant and active group of Arab American writers that included such eminent immigrant writers as

Rihani, Gibran Khalil Gibran, Elia Abu Madi, and Mikhail Naimy. After the 1930s, little was heard of Arab American writers, but this group's canon experienced a resurgence in the 1970s.

The First Generation: The Late 1800s–1930s

The earliest Arab American writers were mostly Lebanese and Syrian immigrants, known as *al-mahjar,* or "immigrants." Between the years of 1880 and 1924, almost 100,000 Arabs emigrated from greater Syria, headed for the Americas. Many who landed in the United States settled in large urban regions, such as Detroit, New York, and Philadelphia. The swelling numbers of Arab immigrants— many of whom did not identify themselves as Arabs but rather by their individual countries or regions, such as "Syrians"—were indicated by the increasing number of Arab-language publications to serve this community. *Kawkab Amerika,* founded in 1892, was the first of many Arab-language newspapers, for example, and in the early 1900s nine such newspapers were in existence. *Syrian World,* a literary journal, was also established at this time, and it gave voice to many prominent playwrights, poets, and critics of Arab origin.

In her overview essay on the history of Arab American literature, poet, memoirist, and playwright Elmaz Abinader refers to Ameen Rihani as "the father of Arab American literature" (2000). This is an apt title, popularly applied to Rihani, considering that he was the first to note the crossroads of Arab and American literary trends in his work. Born in Lebanon in 1876, Rihani was sent to the United States by his father, with a relative, at the young age of 12 to help with the family business of silk manufacturing. While living in New York and working with his father and uncle, Rihani read voraciously and was especially attracted to the literature of William Shakespeare and Victor Hugo. Later he also became a fan of Henry David Thoreau, Ralph Waldo Emerson, Leo Tolstoy, and Arab poets such as Abu-Ala. His readings greatly influenced his writing, both in English and Arabic. An admirer of the work of Walt Whitman, Rihani was the first to introduce free verse to Arab poetry, publishing work that modeled this new style as early as 1905. Today's modern Arabic poetry is most popularly written in free verse by such poets as Adonis and Mahmoud Darwish. In 1911, Rihani published *The Book of Khalid,* the first English-language novel by a writer of Arab origin; it focused on the immigrant experience, drawing from Rihani's personal life, with a philosophical edge—Khalid, the protagonist, is depicted as a new prophet whose vision transcends worlds and continents.

Gibran Khalil Gibran, coincidentally, provided the illustrations for the first edition of Rihani's *The Book of Khalid* but would later become perhaps more well-known than his prolific friend. Like Rihani, Gibran, who was born in 1883 in Lebanon and arrived in the United States at the age of 12, traversed two worlds and two languages quite easily; he befriended prominent American writers such as Sherwood Anderson and Eugene O'Neill, while also working actively within *Al-Rabitah al Qalamiyah*. As a result, his canon assumed a universal appeal. Most of his early work was written in Arabic, but, after the late 1910s, he wrote mostly in English. His opus, *The Prophet*, first published in 1923, has remained one of the best-selling American books of all time; it remains the best-selling book by its publisher, Alfred A. Knopf. During the 1960s, *The Prophet* experienced a resurgence of popularity as members of America's counterculture movements seized on its poetic language to express their rage and hopes.

THE 1960s – 1970s

The 1940s through the 1960s were relatively quiet years in Arab American literature, but two important writers made their mark in the ensuing decades: the 1960s and 1970s.

Born in 1925, Etel Adnan is a Lebanese American, born to a Muslim, Turkish father and a Greek, Christian mother. She writes in both English and French, and her most well-known work is *Sitt Marie Rose*, published by Post-Apollo Press in 1982. The novel, considered a classic and published in 10 languages, features a young Lebanese woman who deeply sympathizes with the plight of the Palestinian people during the turbulent 1980s; for her active work on behalf of the Palestinians, she is punished by her Lebanese compatriots. Her life, cut short by violence, represents the tragedy of the wars in the Middle East.

Poet Samuel Hazo was born in 1928 to Lebanese and Syrian immigrants. Currently McAnulty Distinguished Professor of English Emeritus at Duquesne University, Hazo founded the International Poetry Forum in 1966 at the University of Pittsburgh. Chosen as the first state poet of the Commonwealth of Pennsylvania in 1993 (a position he held for 10 years), he has authored over 20 books of poetry, fiction, and nonfiction, including *The Holy Surprise of Right Now, The Rest Is Prose, Stills, Feather, As They Sail,* and *Spying for God.* A translator of many works, he has also been a National Book Award finalist.

THE 1980s – PRESENT

Since the 1980s, a new and exciting crop of Arab American writers has emerged who are born in the United States and have made the search for an Arab American identity one of their major literary themes. There is also more concern among this new generation with political events in the Middle East, primarily the question of Palestine after the 1967 war and the occupation of the Gaza Strip and West Bank.

Much of the new literature was given voice in the form of anthologies, of new and established writers merging their efforts to express the Arab American experience. In 1982, Gregory Orfalea published a booklet, sponsored by the American-Arab

Anti-Discrimination Committee (ADC), entitled *Wrapping the Grape Leaves: A Sheaf of Contemporary Arab American Poets*. The small booklet would mark a resurgence in Arab American writing, such that, in 1988, Orfalea and Sharif Elmusa edited an expanded edition, a full-length anthology entitled *Grape Leaves: A Century of Arab-American Poetry*, which was published by the University of Utah Press. The collection helped to reinvigorate the discussion of Arab American literature, and it sparked the compilation and publication of other anthologies, most notably *Food for Our Grand-mothers: Writings by Arab-American and Arab-Canadian Feminists* (edited by Joanna Kadi) and *Post Gibran: Anthology of New Arab American Writing* (edited by Khaled Mattawa and Munir Akash). These anthologies—as well as the formation of such organizations as **RAWI (The Radius of Arab American Writers, Incorporated)** and the establishment of periodicals centered on Arab American and Arab writing, such as *Mizna* and *Al-Jadid*—offered encouragement for new writers by establishing that an audience for such work did exist.

Many Arab American writers in the last 30 years have left their mark on the American literary canon. Of these, Naomi Shihab Nye, a Palestinian American poet, essayist, and young adult author is perhaps best known. Born to a Palestinian father and an American mother in Missouri in 1952, Shihab Nye has authored several important collections of poetry, namely *The Words Under the Words* (1995), *What Have You Lost?* (1999), and *19 Varieties of Gazelle: Poems from the Middle East* (2002). Her young adult novel *Habibi,* published in 1997, was recognized by the American Library Association as the Best Book for Young Adults and broke new ground in young adult literature by taking on the Arab-Israeli conflict as its central theme; *Habibi* was also named an ALA Notable Book, a New York Public Library Book for the Teen Age, and a Texas Institute of Letters Best Book for Young Read-ers. She has also edited several important anthologies, such as *The Space Beneath Our Footsteps* (1998), bringing together the voices and visions of many Arab poets and artists.

Lawrence Joseph, born in 1948 in Detroit, Michigan, is a lawyer by profession as well as an acclaimed poet. His poetry collections include *Shouting at No One* (1983), *Curriculum Vitae* (1988), and *Before Our Eyes* (1993). In 1997, he published *Lawyerland,* a nonfiction book that examined the attitudes of lawyers; it was repub-lished by Farrar, Straus and Giroux, which also published his fourth poetry collec-tion, *Into It,* in 2005.

Diana **Abu-Jaber** broke onto the literary scene with her first novel, *Arabian Jazz,* published in 1993 by Harcourt. The novel features Jemorah, nicknamed Jem, the daughter of a deceased American mother and an Arab immigrant father still plunged in mourning. Torn between two cultures, Jem is at a crossroads, searching for her per-sonal identity and happiness, which can only result from the reconciliation of the various forces in her life. The novel's humor emanates from its satirical presentations of Jem's Arab relatives and the New York Arab community. The novel won the 1994 Oregon Book Award and was nominated for the PEN/Faulkner Award. Her second book, *Crescent,* traced the experiences of an Iraqi American woman, also searching for happiness and fulfillment, and won the 2004 PEN Center USA Award for Literary Fiction and the Before Columbus Foundation's American Book Award. Abu-Jaber's memoir *The Language of Baklava* recounts Abu-Jaber's personal experiences of growing up between Jordanian and American cultures.

Other memoirists have emerged onto the Arab American literary scene in recent years. Fay Afaf Kanafani's reputation as a writer is based on a single memoir, *Nadia, Captive of Hope,* which details her traumatic childhood and disastrous marriage in Palestine and Lebanon before her arrival in the United States. Elmaz Abinader, a skilled poet and playwright, is perhaps best known for her work *Children of the Roojme: A Family's Journey from Lebanon,* which was first published in 1991 by W.W. Norton to wide acclaim as an intimate account of an immigrant family's experiences crossing continents and searching for home. Edward Said, the renowned literary critic, published his own memoir, *Out of Place,* in 1999, shortly before his death, also to positive reviews. Most interestingly, Evelyn Shakir documents the personal life experiences of many Arab American women, both immigrants and first generation, in her monumental work *Bint Arab: Arab and Arab American Women in the United States,* published in 1997.

The last three decades have seen many short story collections and novels by Arab American writers, including some, such as Mona Simpson, who do not identify themselves or their work as Arab American in theme or nature. Those who do — that is, those who write about themes of Arab identity or concerns of the Middle Eastern community in the United States — include poets Nathalie Handal, D.H. Melhem, Khaled Mattawa, Suheir Hammad, and Dima Halal; short story writers Joseph Geha and Laila Lalami; and novelists Mohja Kahf, Samia Serageldin, and Rabbih Alammeddine.

Further Reading

Abinader, Elmaz. "Children of al-Mahjar: Arab American Writing Spans a Century." *U.S. Society & Values: Electronic Journal of the Department of State.* February 2000: Vol. 5, No. 1. Retrieved February 2007 from http://usinfo.state.gov/journals/itsv/0200/ijse/toc.htm.

Orfalea, Gregory. *The Arab Americans: A History.* Northampton, MA: Olive Branch Press, 2006.

Salaita, Steven. *Arab American Literary Fictions, Cultures, and Politics* (American Literature Readings in the Twenty-First Century). New York: Palgrave Macmillan, 2006.

SUSAN MUADDI DARRAJ

✦ ASIAN AMERICAN

The increasing globalization and transnational activities bring about more diversity in the Asian American population and community. Before **World War II**, Asian Americans consisted mainly of immigrants from China, Japan, and the Philippines, including a small number from Korea and India. Recently, the population of Asian Americans in the United States has increased to over 1.2 million, including immigrants from more than 20 Asian countries or regions.

Asian American is a term used today to refer to all Asian immigrants, inhabitants, or American-born citizens of Asian origins. The term came into being in the late 1960s in the wake of the Asian American movement. According to King-Kok Cheung (2000, 5), "The term grew out of the frustration felt by many American-born citizens of Asian extraction at being treated as perpetual foreigners in the United States, even if their roots in this country go back several generations." In 1968 a group of activists of the Asian American movement in Berkeley founded the Asian American Political Association. Unsatisfied with the prevailing term *Oriental,* which was used to designate the category of Americans with Asian origins, these activists coined *Asian American* as a counterblast. Unlike the prevailing word *Oriental,* which signified a caricatured image of submissiveness and periphery, *Asian American* cultivated a sense of ethnic unity that was tied to a neither American nor Asian cultural awareness. The term was later accepted by American official institutions and applied in the population census of 1980.

Ostensibly intelligible as the term is, its denotation and connotation are far from easy to define. Is *Asian* a geographical term or a racial/ethnic term? Is *American* a category measured by acquisition of citizenship, birthplace, or location of inhabitance? The official definition presented by the immigration laws and federal statistics of its population constitution is by no means a fixed one, thus intensifying the complexity of the term. The Immigration and Nationality Act Amendments passed in 1965 conveyed a transformation of *Asia* as a racial origin to *Asia* as a birthplace, which is but one example of the flexibility of official definition of *Asian.*

As a category term of a group of people, *Asian American* is even controversial to the people of that category. Frank **Chin,** in his preface to *Aiiieeeee! An Anthology of Asian American Writers,* used "the birth of the sensibility as the measure of being an Asian American" (1991, xiii). Here the sensibility refers to that "related to but distinct from Asia and white America" (Chin 1991, xiii) or a sense of one's ethnic identity as neither Asian nor American but in between. Chin's term seems too limited for its application. In terms of Chin's definition, no matter whether they have acquired American citizenship, those newcomers with Asian origins cannot be included in the category of Asian Americans because of their intimacy with Asian culture and their security in ethnic identity as Asian. However, given the significance of Chin's term in calling for expression of the Asian American experience as a target of racial discrimination, the definition could be regarded as a strategy rather than a reflection of reality. The official definition and the definition given by the group are strategic rather than realistic or objective.

Because of the discursive nature of definitions, any attempt to be objective in defining Asian Americans as an ethnic category will result in failure. Being objective means to reflect faithfully the ontological appearance of an object. If the object loses or never has ontological significance, the reflection of the object can by no means be objective. So the definition used here can be far from nondiscursive.

The first Asian immigrants in large numbers to the United States were Chinese who were recruited for the sugar industry in Hawaii in the 1830s and the building of the Central Pacific Railroad in the 1860s. The Japanese immigrants arrived in the 1880s, and other Asians, mainly from Korea, India, and the Philippines, entered the United States after the turn of the century. The early Japanese, Korean, and Filipino immigrants shared a common experience with those from China as migrant labors (Scupin 2003, 245). By the 1920s the immigration from Asia decreased drastically in reaction to a series of highly restrictive immigration laws enacted by the U.S. Congress. After World War II, these laws were liberalized, which opened "the door to a new wave of Asian immigration" (Aguirre and Tuner 1995, 152). In 1965 the Immigration and Nationality Act Amendments was passed that abolished the old national origins quota system and restricted immigration from non-European countries. Due to the implementation of the Act of 1965, the civil rights movement, and the Asian American's tradition of family sponsorship, Asian immigrants entered at a rapid rate. Unlike other post-1965 Asian newcomers, the Southeast Asians, including those from Vietnam, Cambodia, and Laos, mainly arrived as refugees because of the **Vietnam War**. The U.S. legislative attitude toward Asian immigrants has largely been determined by its domestic economy and labor demand. Early immigration laws ensured unlimited entry of Chinese immigrants due to the large demand for labor for the sugarcane industry and railway construction. The repeal of the **Chinese Exclusion Act** can be attributed largely to the economic prosperity in the 1940s. The nursing shortage in the 1970s and the shortage of technically trained personnel in the computer industry led to easier entry for Asian immigrants (Scupin 2003, 256).

In 2000 there were 10,477,300 Asian Americans making up 4.83 percent of the total population of the United States. Chinese Americans are the largest Asian ethnic group in the country. Its population has increased dramatically from less than 200,000 before 1945 to over 3 million today, occupying almost 1 percent of the whole population of the United States. Most Asian Americans inhabit the western United States. There is, however, a steady rise of Asian American inhabitants in the Northeast and the South, respectively accounting for 19.9 and 19.05 percent of the total Asian American population in 2000 (Chen 2003, 51–53). Over 90 percent of Asian Americans reside in urban districts. In terms of the current number of Asian American inhabitants, New York ranks first among all the cities in the United States, followed by Los Angeles, Chicago, Houston, and Philadelphia.

As the Asian immigrants before World War II were instrumental in the development of the commercial, industrial, and agricultural infrastructure of the West, those who arrived after the war, and in most cases were highly educated, have contributed greatly to America's economic development. As Martin N. Marger pointed out, these immigrants relieved the United States of a severe shortage in medical and engineering professionals (Chen 2003, 58). Because of their improved educational background, more Asian Americans are finding their way to executive, managerial, and administrative positions, and there is a great rise in their income. According to the U.S. Census Bureau (1998), in 1995 the median income of Asian and Pacific Islander families was close to that of non-Hispanic families. However, the seemingly high family income of the Asians can be explained partly by the fact that there are more wage earners in Asian American families than in white families. And "despite their representation in high-status professions, Asian Americans hold jobs in the low level of these professions" (Aguirre and Tuner 1995, 155). In other words, a glass ceiling, a restrictive line for their promotion, does exist.

Besides barriers to occupational mobility, Asian Americans suffer other forms of discrimination. Early Asian immigrants encountered nationalistic reactions, ranging from negative or even demonizing images fostered by the media to mob violence and denial of citizenship. They also experienced segregation in public places such as schools and restaurants well into the 1950s. The existence of "**Chinatowns**," "Koreatowns," and "Little Tokyos" indicates that segregation persists. Rather than a result of the Asians' preference to live with their own kind, as the popular belief perceives, it is a response to hostility in the host society (Aguirre and Tuner 1995, 177). In addition to discrimination inflicted by whites, Asian Americans suffer hostility from other minority groups, and even from its own group. The Los Angeles racial disturbance in 1992 caused an economic loss totaling 350–400 million dollars for Korean merchants. Misrepresenting the racial disturbance as a conflict between Korean storeowners as ruthless exploiters of African American customers, the media diverted the African Americans' protest against white society and changed it into violence against Korean merchants (Scupin 2003, 257).

Public prejudice against Asian Americans is caused largely by a negative image created by the media. The seemingly positive image "**model minority**" by no means gives a faithful presentation of Asian Americans. It fails to present the extreme poverty of those Asian Americans who have not "made it," especially those Southeast Asian refugees who came in the 1980s. Not only does the image of the model minority fail to present the diversity among Asian Americans in terms of economic achievement, education, and occupation, the term also covers up the discrimination inflicted on Asian Americans. Far from a new and constructive image for Asian Americans, the model minority is but another racial stereotype.

Further Reading
Aguirre, Adalberto, Jr., and Jonathan H. Turner. *American Ethnicity: The Dynamics and Consequences of Discrimination*. New York: McGraw-Hill, Inc., 1995.

Chen, Yiping. "An Analysis of the Characteristics of Asian Americans and Their Social, Economic and Political Influence." *Ethnics in the World* 2 (2003): 50–61. (In Chinese.)

Cheung, King-Kok, ed. *Words Matter: Conversations with Asian American Writers*. Honolulu: University of Hawaii Press, 2000.

Chin, Frank, Jeffery Paul Chan, Lawson Fusao Inada, and Shawn Hsu Wong, eds. *Aiiieeeee! An Anthology of Asian American Writers*. New York: Mentor, 1991.

Lee, Jennifer, and Min Zhou. *Asian American Youth: Culture, Identity, and Ethnicity*. New York: Routledge, 2004.

Scupin, Raymond, ed. *Race and Ethnicity: An Anthropological Focus on the United States and the World*. Upper Saddle River, NJ: Prentice Hall, 2003.

XUEPING ZHOU

✦ ASIAN AMERICAN CHILDREN'S LITERATURE

Asian American children's literature comprises multicultural children's picture books and longer works, both fiction and nonfiction, featuring Asian American themes and characters and books written by Asian American authors. In the past, books featuring Asian American themes and characters often depicted stereotypical characters and plots, but presently many Asian American children's stories depict the complex experiences of Asian Americans and work to dispel **Asian American stereotypes**.

In the twentieth century, as children's literature came of age, children's books featuring Asians and Asian Americans have, with a few exceptions, increased continuously. The **civil rights movement** initiated the provision of more multicultural children's literature. Unfortunately, many early books portrayed stereotypical Asian Americans, and, for decades, the only children's literature depicting Asian American themes, characters, and culture was written by authors who were outsiders to the culture. Many times, both the story and the pictures were stereotypical, even negative, and failed to portray the complex nature of Asian Americans and the Asian American experience honestly. Children's stories often portrayed Asian Americans as looking the same or at least being similar in appearance, and in the stories Asian Americans were overly polite or in roles of servitude. The other extreme was presenting Asian American characters whose only interest was martial arts. *Five Chinese Brothers,* written by Claire Bishop and illustrated by Kurt Wiese, was published in 1938 but remains in print and is sometimes referred to as a classic. The story depicts a Chinese folktale about five brothers who stand up for each other when one of them is sentenced to death. Although the story remains popular today, multicultural children's literature experts point to the problems within this text. In the illustrations, all the brothers look exactly alike, something that may reinforce stereotypes that people of different ethnic backgrounds all look alike. Although some adults may question the power of one story in reinforcing stereotypes in children's minds, research in children's literature and child development indicates that children's books are one way children learn about the world around them; therefore, young children who read or have *Five Chinese Brothers* read to them may begin to make assumptions about the appearance of Chinese people.

Presenting Asian Americans honestly in children's literature, even in more modern children's books, is no easy task. Many teachers use the 1984 book *In the Year of the Boar and Jackie Robinson* by Bette Bao **Lord** in their classrooms as a way to open discussions about Asian American experiences in the United States. The book is well written, but members of the Asian American community point out that the main character, Shirley Temple Wong, seems too concerned, almost obsessed, with assimilation into American culture, even to the point of completely disregarding her Chinese heritage. Although this is certainly one aspect of the Chinese American experience, some critics worry that the book oversimplifies the Chinese American experience by having the main character focus so much on assimilation. In their article "Beyond Chopsticks and Dragons: Selecting Asian-American Literature for Children," authors Valerie Ooka Pang, Carolyn Colvin, MyLuong Tran, and Robertta H. Barba contend that the book does not accurately portray the struggle recent immigrants to the United States might encounter as they try to find balance between two cultures. Again, these points might seem subtle to adults who choose Asian American literature for children, but they are nonetheless significant.

Although Asian American children's literature continues to struggle (as do other types of multicultural children's literature) to gain a wider variety of quality children's books that depict honest experiences of Asian Americans, progress has been significant in recent years, and a number of Asian American children's books in print today represent quality Asian American children's literature. As with any type of multicultural literature, there exists a great debate over whether outsiders can depict the complex experiences of a culture in Asian American children's literature, but many insiders write and publish quite prolifically, making a great range of quality Asian American children's books available to children, their parents, and teachers. Quality Asian American children's books present culturally pluralistic themes, provide positive portrayals of Asian American characters, are historically accurate, include authentic illustrations that avoid depicting characters of the same background in the exact same way, and provide strong and engaging plots and characterizations. Children's literature scholars and educators also point out that books about Asian Americans should be set in the United States, where the Asian American characters are clearly portrayed as Americans. Research indicates that many American students still see Asian Americans as foreigners, so children's books that emphasize the long history of Asian Americans in this country can be beneficial to all students.

Taro Yashima is one of the first Asian American children's authors to present believable images of Asian Americans. His book *Umbrella* was published in 1958 but remains a good example of Asian American children's literature. The story, intended for young children, is about Momo, a Japanese American girl who eagerly anticipates a rainy day that will allow her to use the new red umbrella and rain boots that she received for her birthday. The story builds anticipation for the rain, focusing on an experience that any child might experience, no matter their cultural background. This kind of culturally pluralistic plot that appeals to all children works to build connections between cultures when children are young.

Allan Say is considered one of the most important children's literature writers today, and his books provide accurate portrayals of modern Asian Americans while avoiding the popular stereotypes. In 1994, his picture book *Grandfather's Journey* won the Caldecott Medal, the most prestigious award for a children's picture book. In *Grandfather's Journey*, Say tells the story of his own grandfather, who emigrated from Japan to the United States and then went back to Japan. Say describes how his grandfather loved both countries and felt homesick for one when he was in the other. The illustrations in the book are of the highest quality and portray the Japanese American characters with Asian features but each with their own characteristics, unlike the characters in *Five Chinese Brothers* who all look exactly alike. In Say's 2004 book *Music for Alice*, Say tells the story of Alice, a Japanese American who grew up in California and loved to dance. She married a Japanese American businessman and moved to Seattle, but, when the Japanese attacked **Pearl Harbor**, which launched the United States' involvement in **World War** II, Alice and her husband Mark had to report to an internment camp in Portland, Oregon. In this story, **Japanese American internment** is portrayed with historical accuracy, and the internment does not break Alice's and Mark's spirit. Even when Mark's business is lost because of his internment, the couple tries to make the best of it and begins farming in eastern Oregon. At the end of the book, Alice returns to Portland, where she participates in ballroom dancing. Say's story provides an honest depiction of history while at the same time addressing a topic that reaches across cultures—the love of dancing.

Laurence **Yep** is the most prolific Chinese American children's book writer and is the recipient of the Laura Ingalls Wilder Award, an award that honors the body of work of an American author who has made a lasting contribution to children's literature. His novels *Dragonwings* and *Dragon's Gate* are both Honor Books for the Newberry Medal, an award honoring the most distinguished contribution to children's literature in the United States each year. His 1975 book *Dragonwings* is a fictional account of Fung Joe Guey, the first Chinese American aviator. The novel accurately describes prejudices and difficult living conditions for Chinese Americans in San Francisco in 1900. This novel and other novels by Yep emphasize the benefits of valuing one's culture while working to make a better life.

Other important Asian American children's writers include Janet Wong, Jeanne Lee, Yoshiko Uchida, Paul Yee, and Suzy Kline. Whereas children's books with Asian American themes were once only written by outsiders to the culture, today many Asian American children's writers publish books in a variety of genres that honestly depict the Asian American experience. **See also** Assimilation/Americanization.

Further Reading

Aoki, Elaine M. "Are You Chinese? Are You Japanese? Or Are You a Mixed-Up Kid? Using Asian American Children's Literature." *The Reading Teacher* 34 (1981): 382–385.

Ishizuka, Kathy. *Asian American Authors.* Berkely Heights, NJ: Enslow, 2000.

Jenkins, Esther C., and Mary C. Austin. *Literature for Children about Asians and Asian Americans.* New York: Greenwood Press, 1987.

Lu, Mei-Yu. "Multicultural Children's Literature in the Elementary Classroom." May 2007. www.ericdigests.org.

Pang, Valerie Ooka, et al. "Beyond Chopsticks and Dragons: Selecting Asian-American Literature for Children." *The Reading Teacher* 46 (1992): 216–224.

CRYSTAL McCAGE

✦ ASIAN AMERICAN POLITICAL ACTIVISM

Popular misperceptions of Asian Americans' political apathy have persisted, contradictory to the reality of their strong and longstanding tradition of political activism. The discrepancy between perception and reality comes partly from a tendency to focus narrowly on electoral participation. To appreciate Asian American political activism fully, we must go beyond electoral politics and adopt a broader perspective.

Historically, anti-Asian racism has been an overshadowing fact in the Asian American experience. In the pre-**World War II** years, it deprived Asian Americans of their political and socioeconomic rights, as is evidenced by state and federal legislation in a wide range of areas, such as taxation, property ownership, marriage, education, and employment. Because of the principle established in the 1790 Naturalization Act that only free white men could become naturalized citizens, a majority of Asian Americans did not have the right to vote. What is more, racism also constantly threatened their existence in this country. The exclusion of Asian immigration, which runs through all major early immigration legislation activities before World War II, beginning from the 1882 **Chinese Exclusion Act** to the immigration acts of 1917 and 1924, became a major policy of the U.S. government. While keeping aspiring Asian emigrants out, the anti-Asian forces also tried to eradicate Asian communities already in the country using legislative and political power as well as violence. This is most clearly seen in the internment of over 100,000 Japanese Americans, many of them citizens, on the West Coast. Throughout the second half of the nineteenth century and much of the twentieth century, therefore, Asian Americans devoted much of their political energy and resources to fighting racism.

Chinese Americans started such struggles shortly after the gold rush, which brought the Chinese forty-niners, the first major Asian immigrant group, to the New World. They publicly and defiantly denounced anti-Chinese rhetoric on numerous occasions. Early in the 1850s, soon after California Governor Bigler issued his oral attacks on the Chinese, for example, the Chinese responded by publishing a firm and lengthy rebuttal. Chinese Americans also unwaveringly defended their rights within the legal system. Although the numerically small and predominantly immigrant community was politically vulnerable, it won a few critical victories. One of them was the Supreme Court ruling in the 1898 *Wong Kim Ark v. United States* case, which concluded that "a child born in the United States, of parents of Chinese descent. . . . becomes at the time of his birth a citizen of the United States" (http://supreme.justia.com/us/169/649/case.html). The ruling upheld a fundamental constitutional principle established by the Fourteenth Amendment, which is cited several times in the ruling. Asian American immigrant activists also fought legal battles in an effort to gain the right to become naturalized citizens, as is exemplified by the *Takao Ozawa v. United States* and *United States v. Bhagat Singh Thind* cases. In the latter case, Asian Indians strategically appropriated the racial requirement for citizenship by arguing that they were indeed "white." But all such efforts to gain citizenship for Asian immigrants failed.

Many Asian immigrants worked in the United States as laborers. Therefore, Asian American political activism can also be found in their struggle against economic exploitation. For example, in what is known as the Great Strike, unionized Japanese plantation workers in Hawaii stood up, in enormous solidarity and strength, to the extremely powerful plantation owners backed by the government. In another strike against Hawaiian plantation owners in 1920, organized by Japanese and Filipino labor unions, workers came together across ethnic boundaries in a struggle for economic justice. Asian labor activism also grew strong among farm laborers and cannery workers in California and Seattle as well as in many other cases.

Overall, ethnic solidarity was not a constant occurrence in the experiences of Asian Americans, who were divided by political, cultural, linguistic, and religious differences. Such divisions further weakened their political strength. Sometimes, transnationalism became a useful tool in their struggle for social justice. The rise of Japan as a new world power, for example, helped to gain important concessions from the U.S. government that benefited Japanese Americans in what is known as the Gentlemen's Agreement of 1908. Under the agreement, the restriction of Japanese immigration was left to the Japanese government and, more importantly, allowed the children and wives of Japanese immigrants already in the United States to continue to come until the passage of the Japanese Exclusion Act of 1924. As a result, the Japanese American community was the first and, for a long time, the only Asian community to transition from a bachelor society to a family-based one. Japan's international status also helped Japanese Americans win another victory: because of the intervention of the Roosevelt Administration, the Board of Education of San Francisco allowed Japanese students to attend integrated public schools, whereas Chinese students in the city had to go to segregated schools.

Strongly believing that the status of the immigrants in the United States was closely tied to that of their mother country in the international geopolitical hierarchy, Chinese Americans dedicated enormous energy and resources to strengthening China. Chinese American transnationalism became an effective instrument for political mobilization, which also helped bring their struggle for civil rights to a trans-Pacific arena. For example, in 1905 their compatriots in China launched a national boycott of American goods in protest of American exclusion policy, forcing the U.S. government to adjust its treatment of Chinese Americans, who took part in that movement with great enthusiasm and pride. During the long war against Japanese aggression in China from 1937 to 1945, Chinese Americans donated millions of dollars to help China. The slogan "to save China, to save ourselves" clearly captured the mentality of Chinese Americans, who, by organizing popular fundraising events, such as the "Bowl of Rice," launched under the auspices of the United Council for Civilian Relief of China in the late 1930s, successfully grasped the wartime opportunity to combat racial bias, which became increasingly difficult to defend after Pearl Harbor, morally and militarily. In spite of all its apparent limitations, the repeal of all Chinese exclusion acts in 1943 represents a turning point in Asian American history, which not only marked the beginning of the collapse of Asian exclusion but also gave an Asian immigrant group the right to become naturalized citizens for the first time in American history. It was a vital victory of Chinese American political activism, won in a transnational theater.

Transnational connections do not benefit all Asian Americans, of which the Japanese American experience during World War II serves as a strong reminder. In the post–World War II anticommunist red-scare environment, the loyalty of Chinese Americans was also scrutinized.

The 1965 Immigration Reform Act, which abolished the racist quota system, opened the United States' door to new waves of Asian immigration. Post-1965 immigration has significantly increased the Asian American population (from less than a million, or 0.3 percent of the nation's total population in 1960 to more than 14 million, or 5 percent of the national population in 2005). It has also increased its diversity and made all Asian American groups, with the exception of Japanese Americans, predominantly immigrant communities. Such a preponderance of immigrants is one of the main reasons for a relatively low voter turnout rate among Asian American communities. In New York City at the end of the 1990s, for example, only 38 percent of eligible Asian voters in the **Chinatown** area were registered, which is much lower than the rates for African Americans (88 percent), Latinos (64 percent), and whites (85 percent) in lower Manhattan.

The influx of immigrants also helps to explain the continued importance of transnationalism in Asian life as a vehicle for political mobilization. The massive protest in 1999 over small business owner Truong Van Tran's decision to display the flag of the Communist Republic of Vietnam and the portrait of its founder, Ho Chi Minh, lasted almost two months and drew crowds of up to 15,000 protesters in the largest Vietnamese American community in Westminster, California, showing the lasting impact of anticommunism among Vietnamese Americans.

Economic exploitation remains a focal point of Asian American political activism. More frequently than the prewar years, however, such exploitation comes from Asian American business owners. For instance, the 1982 strike of Chinese women garment workers, which drew more than 20,000 in public rallies, was launched against ethnic Chinese sweatshop owners.

Asian Americans continue to spend much of their political activism and energy on fighting racial discrimination, which has become less visible than before. In higher education, for example, efforts to limit Asian American enrollment have been carried out under the guise of reducing the "overrepresentation of a **model minority**."

A significant event in the development of Asian American political activism is the protest over the brutal murder of Vincent **Chin** in 1982 in Detroit by two white workers in the automobile industry, which faced increasing competition from Japanese automakers. The white workers mistook Chin for Japanese. The murder and the light sentence that the county court gave the two white men (three years' probation and a $3,000 fine) triggered one of the largest pan-Asian American political protests. Since then, efforts have accelerated in developing pan-ethnic political consciousness, as is embodied by the formation of a growing number of political organizations, such as the political action committee known as 80-20, whose goal is to create an Asian American voting bloc. Such activities represent one of the most important new developments in Asian American political activism. **See also** Japanese American Internment; Racism and Asian America.

Further Reading

Chang, Gordon, ed. *Asian Americans and Politics: Perspectives, Experiences, Prospects.* Washington DC: Woodrow Wilson Center Press, 2001.

Fong, Timothy P. *The Contemporary Asian American Experience: Beyond the Model Minority.* Upper Saddle River, NJ: Prentice Hall, 1998.

Jung, Moon-Kie. *Reworking Race: The Making of Hawaii's Interracial Labor Movement.* New York: Columbia University Press, 2006.

Kim, Hyung-chan, ed. *Asian Americans and the Supreme Court: A Documentary History.* New York: Greenwood Press, 1992.

Le Espiritu, Yen. *Asian American Panethnicity: Bridging Institutions and Identities.* Philadelphia: Temple University Press, 1992.

Lien, Pei-te. *The Making of Asian America through Political Participation.* Philadelphia: Temple University Press, 2001.

Nakanishi, Don T., and James S. Lai. *Asian American Politics: Law, Participation, and Policy.* Lanham, MD: Rowman & Littlefield, 2003.

U.S. Supreme Court United States v. Wong Kim Ark, 169 U.S. 649 (1898). <http://supreme.justia.com/us/169/649/case.html>

Wei, William. *The Asian American Movement.* Philadelphia: Temple University Press, 1993.

YONG CHEN

✦ ASIAN AMERICAN STEREOTYPES

Asian American stereotypes refer to the inaccurate representations of Asian Americans, their communities, lifestyles, and the values commonly associated with these diverse ethnic communities in American literature and culture. Because their emergence can be traced back to early American literature and specifically to discourses on flows of immigration from different parts of Asia, primarily China and Japan, from the middle of the nineteenth century onward, it is vital to distinguish between different forms of and modifications to the typecasting over the centuries. Its ongoing revision and yet reinforcement constitute the major problems of their continuing pervasiveness in popular literature and culture. Despite growing divergence into more complex representations, including self-representations, of Asian Americans, they can most usefully be grouped into a triangulation of such modes of stereotyping. They are roughly framed by a chronological development: first, what may be termed the traditional types of the Asian in early American fiction and non-fiction writing, as well as early films, from **Fu Manchu** and **Charlie Chan** onward, and their literary legacies; second, the results of a revisionism that has ironically engendered its own sets of stereotypes; third, a self-reflexive play with stereotyping and the larger problematics underpinning its popular presence in contemporary cultural discourses. The latter development has moreover given rise to the similarly often self-ironic repackaging of both traditional and newly emerging stereotypes in Asian American fiction and film.

What have now come to be seen as the traditional stereotypes of the Asian American were created in nineteenth-century and early twentieth-century popular fiction by primarily white American writers, including Sax Rohmer, creator of Fu Manchu, and Earl Derr Biggers, author of the Charlie Chan novels, as well as Mark Twain, Jack London, Bret Harte, and Ambrose Bierce. Twain's "John Chinaman in New York" (1899), for example, marked out the easy typecasting of the Chinese immigrant as helpless, although in many early narratives, he was also emphatically loyal to the Anglo American heroes. The Chinese servant in particular functioned primarily as comic relief. Rohmer's Fu Manchu, however, embodied a more sinister stereotype: featuring in a series of novels, from *The Return of Dr. Fu Manchu* (1916), also familiar as *The Devil Doctor,* to the 1959 *Emperor Fu Manchu,* Rohmer's last completed novel, the eponymous arch villain is a foreign, incommensurately alien, master criminal, whose knowledge and ability to adapt to the challenges of a different culture single him out as a threat to humankind at large and Anglo American culture in particular.

Like Twain's fictionalization of victimized Asian immigrants in nineteenth-century America, Biggers's Charlie Chan novels were originally meant as a defensive, early revisionist reaction to the popularity of Fu Manchu and his various spin-offs. Although essentially ambiguous in its depiction of the role of the Chinese American, the series was thus conceived as a counterpoint to the hitherto prevailing fictionalizations of **Yellow Peril** discourse. Informed largely by post-Darwinian conceptualizations of race, such narratives of the threat posed by waves of immigrants and their intermarriages in a predominantly white Anglo American culture dominated representations of Asian Americans from the 1880s onward. The "Asian" in American fiction was primarily Chinese, primarily male, either a comically innocuous servant or sidekick on the one hand, or a dangerously clever, enigmatic, criminal mastermind on the other. Published from 1925 to 1932, the Charlie Chan novels, in contrast, posited an intellectual, able, ethnic Chinese detective. Popularized primarily by film adaptations from the 1920s onward, they have entered the popular imagination, in different ways reinforcing numerous stereotypes of the placid, Confucius-quoting Chinese American.

Such inadvertent reinforcements of traditional typecasting and the creation of even more invidious modes based on their opposites intriguingly form central points of criticism of Asian American literature. Seminal critical studies, such as Elaine Kim's 1982 *Asian American Literature: An Introduction to the Writings and Their Social Context,* have even traced a direct continuity, or specific linkages, between the representation of Asian Americans in early fiction by non-Asian American writers and early autobiographical writing by first- and even second-generation immigrants. The bulk of recent criticism, including Asian American academics Cynthia Sau-ling Wong and Shirley Geok-Lin **Lim**, has furthermore rested on the quickly stereotyped juxtaposition of the China-born mother and the American-born daughter in the internationally popular fiction of Asian American women writers. Such influential literary and controversially autobiographical works as Maxine Hong **Kingston's *The Woman Warrior*** (1976) and *China Men* (1980), as well as the fiction of Amy **Tan** and Fae Myenne **Ng**, have indisputably contributed much to the sheer variety of fictional representations of Asian Americans and their experiences in contemporary American society or, alternatively, the renegotiation of their protagonists' often hybrid heritage. Yet they have also engendered new stereotypes that an expanding market of the New Literatures in English has capitalized on. The popular media at large, however, primarily channelled the stereotyping. In a tellingly titled study, *In her Mother's House: The Politics of Asian American Mother-Daughter Writing,* Wendy Ho speaks pointedly of "a consumer market for Tan's mother-daughter text that the major publishing houses were happy to accommodate (the nature of the beast) and the mainstream, sometimes tributary, media were happily recommending to readers, unfortunately in rather stereotypical ways" (1999, 44).

This consumer market was consolidated by the film adaptation of Amy Tan's first novel, *The Joy Luck Club* (1989), in 1991. The dichotomous structure of this new typecasting of Asian American family life has generated a proliferation of Asian American narratives, primarily by women writers. They share an equation of generational conflicts with cultural clashes, setting an Asia (almost exclusively China) of the past against a multicultural yet often dysfunctional, micropolitical family structure in the present-day United States. Testifying to the ongoing process of revisionism that characterizes the creation, solidification, and then vigorous rejection of such mass-market new stereotypes, both Tan's and Kingston's own recent fiction has significantly moved away from this disconcertingly popular juxtaposition.

If one of the most central stereotypes of the Asian American is moreover a peculiarly misleading identification with the Chinese diaspora, to the exclusion of the descendants of immigrants from other parts of Asia, in particular South and North Asia, these contemporary Asian American women writers have thereby instigated a significant move in leaving the recasting of China and the overseas, or diasporic, Chinese behind. Their novels self-ironically satirize the expected structures that they nonetheless tend to reinforce, as readers are not always aware of the subtle ambiguities underpinning them. In eschewing the much criticized evocation of an exoticized China of the past, Tan's *Saving Fish from Drowning* (2005) hence marks a crucial departure. A multiethnic group of American tourists, accompanied by the disembodied—dead—Chinese American narrator, travels to Burma (Myanmar), in the process coming to terms with their own preconceptions and prejudices. In a similar move, Kingston's *The Fifth Book of Peace* (2003) deals primarily with Vietnam. The multiplicity of the Asian American experience and the ongoing "re-presentation" of Asia in fiction by Asian American writers has become the center of a self-conscious, often self-ironic exploration of the making of the stereotypes themselves.

But while fiction has become more variegated in its representations of Asian Americans and their different histories, Hollywood films have simultaneously begun to play out long-standing stereotypes with a different focus on self-irony. Thus, the growing popularity of Jackie Chan movies made in Hollywood has directed new attention to the presence of minority groups in the United States, today and in the past. *Shanghai Noon* (2000), *Shanghai Knights* (2003), and the casting of Chan as the hero's "French" butler in *Around the World in Eighty Days* (2004), based on Jules Verne's novel of 1873, have done much to put the Chinese immigrant back into the Wild West of the popular imagination. At the same time, however, their play with established stereotypes has ironically tended to reinforce as much as to satirize them. **See also** Asian Diasporas.

Further Reading

Button, Peter. "(Para-)humanity, Yellow Peril and the postcolonial (arche-)type." *Postcolonial Studies* 9.4 (2006): 421–447.

Hagedorn, Jessica, ed. *Charlie Chan Is Dead: An Anthology of Contemporary Asian American Fiction*. New York: Penguin, 1993.

Ho, Wendy. *In Her Mother's House: The Politics of Asian American Mother-Daughter Writing*. Walnut Creek, CA: AltaMira Press, 1999.

Kim, Elaine H. *Asian American Literature: An Introduction to the Writings and Their Social Context*. Philadelphia: Temple University Press, 1982.

Lim, Shirley Geok-lin, and Amy Ling, eds. *Reading the Literatures of Asian America*. Philadelphia: Temple University Press, 1992.

Wong, Sau-ling Cynthia. *Reading Asian American Literature: From Necessity to Extravagance*. Princeton, NJ: Princeton University Press, 1993.

Wu, William. *The Yellow Peril: Chinese Americans in American Fiction, 1850–1940*. Hamden, CT: Archon Books, 1982.

TAMARA S. WAGNER

✦ ASIAN AMERICAN STUDIES

Asian American studies emerged as an academic discipline because of the civil rights struggles of the 1960s and 1970s. The Asian American movement drew attention to conditions of social and economic disadvantage affecting the Asian community that had been invisible to mainstream American society by creating parallels with aspects of African American and Chicano experience. Together with calls for improvements in housing, health, and education provision and measures to tackle high unemployment, the Asian American movement also encouraged the efforts of student activists, who protested the invisibility of Asian American culture in the perspective of the mainstream and the absence of Asian American historical and cultural experience from college and university curricula. The acceptance of the term *Asian* to encompass groups including South Asian, Filipino, and East Asian communities posed an ongoing issue in Asian American cultural studies: how the concept of *Asia* is to be defined in the Asian American context. The religious, linguistic, ethnic, and geographical diversity of "Asia" has underpinned long-term debates within the field of Asian American studies, as the field continually renews itself in response to changing patterns of Asian immigration to the United States.

This issue was addressed by the writer and scholar Frank **Chin** in the introduction to the groundbreaking anthology that he coedited, *Aiiieeeee!: An Anthology of Asian American Writers* (1974). Chin proposed a sharp distinction between Asia and America, between those writers born in the United States of Asian descent and those writers who are Asian-born immigrants to the United States. Chin argued that only U.S.-born Asians could be appropriately termed *Asian Americans*. This claim was controversial because Chin excluded from the category of Asian American writers those writers who were first-generation American immigrants, and consequently Chin foregrounded the descendants of East Asian (Chinese and Japanese) migrants who had a history of settlement in the United States that went back several generations. So writers from more recent immigrant groups, such as South Asians and Vietnamese, were excluded from the category of **Asian American** writers. Indeed, how to determine whether a writer is "Asian American" is a fraught business. Possible criteria to make this determination include citizenship or residency in the United States; Asian ancestry, though this raises the tricky question of how a mixed-race writer would be included; texts that engage issues of Asian American ethnicity might legitimate a writer as "Asian American," though this potentially excludes writers who do not write about their ethnicity; and the degree of congruence between textual subject matter and the objectives of the Asian American movement (such as bringing to visibility the history and experience of this excluded ethnic group), though this would exclude writers who depict a quest for assimilation into the United States as an "American" rather than an "Asian American" subject.

Early anthologies of Asian American literature tended to privilege writers from one of three Asian groups: Chinese, Japanese, and Filipino. *Asian American Authors* (1972), edited by Kai-yu Hsu and Helen Palubinskas, featured works by two generations of American writers, with priority given to American-born Asian authors over Asian-born American writers. This selection was in keeping with Frank Chin's restrictive definition of Asian American writers, set out in the introduction to *Aiiieeeee!: An Anthology of Asian American Writers* (1974), coedited by Chin, Jeffery Paul **Chan**, Lawson Fusao **Inada**, and Shawn **Wong**. The editors of *Aiiieeeee!* promoted in their selection an approach to Asian American writers defined by Asian parentage and U.S. birth. The same group of editors published a companion anthology in 1991; *The Big Aiiieeeee!: An Anthology of Chinese American and Japanese American Literature* is, as the title indicates, even more restrictive in which Asian groups can be included in the category of Asian America, though Eurasian writers such as Diana **Chang** and Edith Maude **Eaton** (Sui Sin Far) are included. In the same year that the first *Aiiieeeee!* anthology appeared, David Hsin-fu Wand edited *Asian-American Heritage: An Anthology of Prose and Poetry* (1974), a collection that extended the field of Asian American literature to include Koreans and South Pacific Islanders. Two years after the publication of *The Big Aiiieeeee!* the Filipina American writer Jessica **Hagedorn** published *Charlie Chan Is Dead: An Anthology of Contemporary Asian American Fiction* (1993). Hagedorn's anthology is liberal in its remit and representation of the category of contemporary Asian America.

Other Asian American literature anthologies do not so much represent the changing demographics of Asian Americans but instead address issues of gender, sexuality, and race. For example, *The Forbidden Stitch: An Asian American Women's Anthology* (1989), edited by Shirley Geok-lin **Lim**, Mayumi Tsutakawa, and Margarita Donnelly, was the first anthology of Asian American women's writing and represented a landmark both in its emphasis upon gender and in the range of documents (poetry, stories, art, and reviews) that are included. As Shirley Lim remarks about the selection of writers, the diversity is so great that the unity of the anthology is continually in peril; however, this is the inherent risk of any project based upon the category "Asian American." A later anthology, conceived in this style, is Rajini Srikanth's *Bold Words: A Century of Asian American Writing* (2001), which includes writers of Chinese, Filipino, Japanese, Korean, South Asian, and Southeast Asian American heritage, with equal representation of male and female writers; however, the anthology uses a more conventional generic selection of literary texts that fall into the categories of memoir, fiction, poetry, and drama. Moving away from gender more narrowly perceived toward the issues of sexual difference and queer identities, David Eng and Alice Y. Hom edited the award-winning anthology *Q & A: Queer in Asian America* (1998), which brings together essays, personal testimonies, fiction, and art that address the intersection of

Asian American racial identity with queer sexuality at the turn of the twentieth century. A further example of the attempt to complicate received understandings of what constitutes Asian American literature and culture is represented by the anthology edited by Nora Okja **Keller** and Marie Hara: *Intersecting Circles: The Voices of Hapa Women in Poetry and Prose* (1999). This collection focuses on the work of women of part-Asian, mixed-race ancestry, which puts into question the racial and ethnic bases of Asian American identities.

Through the history of literary anthologies, which institutionalize and crystallize understandings of the category of Asian American cultural production, the complex contexts within which "Asian America" is constituted begin to become clear. The difficulty of this category, together with its necessity within a dominant immigrant culture that obscures the civil rights and cultural traditions of Asian minority communities, forms part of the effort to continually revise the basis of vibrant, relevant Asian American studies. **See also** Assimilation/Americanization.

Further Reading

Cheung, King-Kok, ed. *An Interethnic Companion to Asian American Literature.* Cambridge: Cambridge University Press, 1997.

Chin, Frank, Jeffery Paul Chan, Lawson Fusao Inada, and Shawn Hsu Wong, eds. *Aiiieeeee!: An Anthology of Asian American Writers.* Washington, DC: Howard University Press, 1974.

Eng, David. *Racial Castration: Managing Masculinity in Asian America.* Durham, NC: Duke University Press, 2001.

Kim, Elaine H. *Asian American Literature: An Introduction to the Writings and Their Social Context.* Philadelphia: Temple University Press, 1982.

Lee, Rachel. *The Americas of Asian American Literature: Gendered Fictions of Nation and Transnation.* Princeton, NJ: Princeton University Press, 1999.

Li, David Lei-Wei. *Imagining the Nation: Asian American Literature and Cultural Consent.* Stanford, CA: Stanford University Press, 1998.

Lim, Shirley Geok-lin, and Amy Ling, eds. *Reading the Literatures of Asian America.* Philadelphia: Temple University Press, 1992.

Ling, Jinqi. *Narrating Nationalisms: Ideology and Form in Asian American Literature.* New York: Oxford University Press, 1998.

DEBORAH L. MADSEN

✦ ASIAN CANADIAN STUDIES

The emergence of Asian Canadian studies is a late twentieth-century development, emerging largely from Canada's adoption of an official policy of multiculturalism in 1985. The early history of Asian immigrants in Canada was marked by legislative exclusion and racial hostility. From 1885, Chinese immigrants were required to pay a substantial (indeed, intentionally prohibitive) head tax that was not levied against any other class of immigrants, and as early as 1878 restrictions were placed on who could employ Asian workers in British Columbia. In 1907, in one of the most infamous acts of concerted anti-Asian violence, a mob destroyed Vancouver's **Chinatown** and much of the adjoining Japanese neighborhood or ghetto. Such events were followed in 1923 by a draconian immigration exclusion act that virtually stopped Asian immigration to Canada. With the outbreak of **World War II**, Canada forcibly evacuated Japanese North Americans from the Pacific Coast to detention camps in the Canadian interior, an act that preceded U.S. President Franklin D. Roosevelt's Executive Order 9066, which removed Japanese Americans from the West Coast and detained them in internment camps. Some 23,000 Japanese Canadians, 75 percent of whom were citizens, were interned; families were broken up as able-bodied men were sent to labor camps. After the war, attempts were made to send ("repatriate") inmates to Japan rather than return them to their Canadian homes, and camp inmates were not permitted to return to British Columbia until four years after the end of the war. Only in 1947 were Asian Canadians granted the right to vote.

It was with the introduction of a national policy of multiculturalism, with the Canadian Multiculturalism Act of 1985, that an appropriate context for the study of the cultural heritage of Asian migrants to Canada became possible. Glenn Deer, in his introduction to the special issue of the journal *Canadian Literature,* devoted to Asian Canadian writing, observes that the hyphenated term *Asian-Canadian* is a product of early 1980s multicultural thinking. In the same issue of the journal, Terry Watada begins his essay, "Go for Broke: The Spirit of the 70s," with the reminder: "In 1969, there was no such thing as Asian Canadian writing, at least not as a genre. In fact, there was no such thing as an Asian Canadian. Japanese Canadians were Japanese; Chinese Canadians were Chinese. The generic term was 'Oriental'" (1999, 80). The title of his article refers to the battle cry of the 442 Battalion, the all-nisei company that fought for the United States in World War II to stake a claim for American identity and allegiance. Watada reminds also that the movement for government redress of the civil rights violations suffered by Japanese Canadians had its origins at the same moment in the 1980s. This movement drew upon the recently published histories of the Japanese Canadian internment, a history that was not told until the 1970s. In September 1988, Canadian Prime Minister Brian Mulroney offered an official apology and the promise of compensation to all victims of the internment program. The story of Japanese Canadian internment and the successful struggle for redress was told by Roy Miki and Cassandra Kobayashi in the book *Justice in Our Time: The Japanese Canadian Redress Settlement* (1991).

Despite this history of anti-Asian hostility and exclusion, an Asian migrant culture flourished in Canada. In 1939 *The New Canadian,* a Japanese Canadian community newspaper, was established, to which one of the best known modern Canadian writers, Joy **Kogawa**, later contributed. Her novel about the Japanese Canadian internment experience, *Obasan* (1981), and then Chinese Canadian Sky **Lee's** novel *Disappearing Moon Café* (1990), marked the beginning of a significant English-language Asian literary presence in Canada. Alan Hotta and Ron Tanaka were influential agents behind various attempts to create and coordinate an Asian Canadian cultural community. Californian poet and academic Tanaka brought the consciousness-raising cultural politics of the Asian American movement to Canada; Hotta helped to establish the *Powell Street Review,* a Japanese Canadian cultural magazine. The Chinese Canadian Writers Workshop, formed by Tamio Wakayama and Takeo Yamashiro, published the first English-language Chinese Canadian newspaper, *Gum San Po.* Prominent writers such as Paul **Yee** and Sky Lee participated in the Chinese Canadian Writers Workshop, which was the precursor to the Asian Canadian Writers Workshop, which has involved such celebrated authors as Wayson **Choy**, Denise **Chong**, and Lien Chao. Chao's book, *Beyond Silence: Chinese Canadian Literature in English* (1997), is one of the first full-length studies of this growing area of literary creativity, and, in her account of the emergence of Chinese Canadian literature, Chao emphasizes the important context of the Asian Canadian community and community activism as a formative agent.

The first anthology of Asian Canadian writing, *Inalienable Rice: A Chinese & Japanese Canadian Anthology* (1979), edited by Garrick Chu, Sean Gunn, Paul Yee, Ken Shikaze, Linda Uyehara Hoffman, and Rick **Shiomi**, was a chapbook published through the efforts of the Chinese Canadian Writers Workshop and featured writers who have come to dominate the category of Asian Canadian writing: Sky Lee, Paul Yee, Joy Kagawa, Roy Miki, and Jim Wong-Chu. Cyril Dabydeen edited a specialist poetry anthology, *Another Way to Dance: Asian Canadian Poetry,* in 1990. Further anthologies include *Many Mouthed Birds: Contemporary Writing by Chinese Canadians,* edited by Bennett Lee and Jim Wong-Chu (1991), and *Strike the Wok: An Anthology of Contemporary Chinese Canadian Fiction,* edited by Lien Chao and Jim Wong-Chu (2003). As these titles indicate, the difficulty of formulating an adequate definition of *Asian Canadian* results in anthologies that focus upon the work of one ethnic group, such as Chinese or Japanese Canadians, or deal with only one literary genre, such as poetry. The field of Asian Canadian studies is so diverse, because of the history of Canadian immigration and also because of changing attitudes toward what constitutes the "Asia" from which migrants are emigrating, that it always risks fragmenting into distinct ethnic subcategories. Recent South Asian Canadian writers who have come to prominence, such as Michael **Ondaatje** and to a lesser extent Bharati **Mukherjee**, emphasize this changing profile of Asian Canada. In this respect, Asian Canadian studies confronts the same issues that scholars of **Asian American studies** face. As Tseen-Ling Khoo has persuasively argued, the very existence of the field of Asian

Canadian studies offers a public image of Canada as a nation that is tolerant and successfully multicultural. Invested in programs such as Asian Canadian studies is the management of Canada's image abroad, as well as the management of domestic multicultural communities, through policies of official multiculturalism, which produce particular sanctioned fields of minority or ethnic study. For this reason, the broad category of Asian Canadian studies sustains the value of multiculturalism, even as it draws its existence from that same multicultural policy. **See also** Japanese American Internment; Multiculturalism and Asian America.

Further Reading

Chao, Lien. *Beyond Silence: Chinese Canadian Literature in English.* Toronto: TSAR, 1997.

Deer, Glenn, ed. Special issue: Asian Canadian Writing. *Canadian Literature* 163 (Winter 1999).

Khoo, Tseen-Ling. *Banana Bending: Asian-Australian and Asian Canadian Literatures.* Montreal: McGill-Queen's University Press, 2003.

Miki, Roy. *Broken Entries: Race. Subjectivity. Writing.* Toronto: Mercury Press, 1998.

Mukherjee, Arun. *Oppositional Aesthetics: Readings from a Hyphenated Space.* Toronto: TSAR, 1995.

Ty, Eleanor. *The Politics of the Visible in Asian North American Narratives.* Toronto: University of Toronto Press, 2004.

Ty, Eleanor, and Donald Goellnicht, eds. *Asian North American Identities beyond the Hyphen.* Bloomington: Indiana University Press, 2004.

Watada, Terry. "Go for Broke: The Spirit of the 70s." *Canadian Literature* 163 (Winter 1999): 80–91.

DEBORAH L. MADSEN

✦ ASIAN DIASPORAS

The term *diaspora* refers literally to a "scattering," which, in human terms, signifies the dispersal of people through the mechanism of migration from a single homeland across many continents and nation states. Among the best known historical diasporas are those affecting Jewish and Armenian communities, and the African communities that were dispersed because of the international slave trade. Diasporic groups, while having their origin in migration, also sustain a sense of cultural identity with the homeland that unifies members in a complex international or transnational network of relations. These relations can be more or less formalized; some community groups form into regional organizations that meet regularly to foster relations and to seek mutual economic and other benefits. For example, transnational beauty pageants, such as the Miss Chinese Cosmos competition, formalize transnational relations and promote common cultural identifications, both among diasporic communities and between those communities and the Chinese homeland. It is this ongoing connection with an Asian "homeland," in which the United States is constructed as a "hostland," that Shirley Geok-lin **Lim** identifies as the obstacle to widespread acknowledgment of Asian diaspora writing. Diaspora sustains the backward vision of first-generation immigrants into subsequent generations. Shirley Lim was born into a Malaysian Peranakan family, part of the ethnic Chinese Hokkien-speaking community that was established in the Malacca region centuries ago. Hence, the extent to which diaspora texts can be incorporated into the national canon of "American literature" or the cultural nationalism of "Asian American literature" is compromised. The concept of a distinct canon of Asian diasporic literature is equally problematic.

A diaspora is a product of the historical phenomenon of Asian immigration and, as a result, is geographically, historically, and culturally complicated by the shifting definition of *Asia*. The Asian communities included in the category of "Asian America" are a dynamic group that changes in response to patterns in Asian immigration. The oldest and largest groups are East Asian: Chinese is the largest, the next largest group is Filipino, followed by Japanese. The most recent wave of Asian migrants to the United States comprises Vietnamese, Cambodians, and Laotians; and South Asians, who include immigrants from Pakistan, India, Bangladesh, Sri Lanka, Nepal, Bhutan, and the Maldives. Correspondingly, in recent years Asian America has come to include writers of Vietnamese, Burmese, and Southeast Asian descent. In 1990, 6.9 million Asians were counted by the U.S. Census. Between 1990 and 2000 the diasporic Asian American population, of people born in the United States rather than Asia, had increased by 48 percent. In comparison, the total U.S. population grew by only 13 percent. This diversity is reflected in the very different histories of each Asian group in the United States.

Mass Chinese immigration began in the mid-nineteenth century, coinciding with the California gold rush and with conditions in China that made migration an attractive option for those suffering from famine and violent political unrest. In the 1860s, and increasingly after the abolition of slavery, cheap Chinese laborers (coolies) were imported to fill the labor gap created by the absence of slaves in the American South and to work on the **transcontinental railroad**, the Hawaiian sugar plantations, and in other industries such as logging and mining. These Chinese laborers were seen as sojourners: temporary workers who would eventually return to China. Increasing numbers of Chinese sojourners, however, created public anxiety, particularly in California and the Pacific Northwest. Subsequently, the first of several **Chinese Exclusion Acts** was passed in 1882 and remained in operation until the Immigration Acts of 1943 and 1946 allowed a quota of Chinese immigrants and resident aliens to establish themselves legally in America. During this period, Chinese migrants were forbidden naturalization as U.S. citizens, and so they continued to look to China as a cultural "home." This is not to suggest that Chinese communities in the United States did not strenuously object, in the courts and wherever their voices could be heard, against the range of prejudice they faced. **Chinese American autobiographies**, from the late nineteenth century onward, respond to this racial discrimination, explaining Chinese cultural practices to remove the exotic and threatening otherness of the Chinese community. Texts such as **Lee** Yan Phou's *When I Was a Boy in China* (1887), **Yung** Wing's *My Life in China and America* (1909), and Wu Tingfang's *America through the Spectacles of an Oriental Diplomat* (1914) explain why Chinese lifeways, rituals, ceremonies, and cultural habits are different. Edith Maude **Eaton** (Sui Sin Far), the first Asian American writer of short fiction, published her autobiographical text "Leaves from the Mental Portfolio of an Eurasian" to draw attention to the plight of Eurasians, who were accepted neither by the white community nor by the Chinese during this period of violent anti-Chinese sentiment. Her younger sister, Winnifred **Eaton** (who wrote under the Japanese pseudonym, Onoto Watanna), became the first Asian American novelist when *Miss Nume of Japan* appeared in 1899. Eaton's fictional subject was the impoverished conditions of life imposed upon Chinese immigrants living in ethnic ghettos or **Chinatowns**, often referred to as bachelor societies because of the absence of women. "Oriental" (Chinese and Japanese) women were specifically excluded from immigration to the United States by the terms of the Page Act of 1875. The gender imbalance of these Chinese communities is addressed by Louis **Chu** in his novel *Eat a Bowl of Tea* (1961). Chu sets the novel during the period of transition following the reform of immigration law in the mid-1940s when small numbers of Chinese women could enter the United States.

The 1970s saw the emergence of the Asian American movement and an accompanying Asian American cultural nationalism. Representative of efforts to create an authentic identity for Chinese Americans is the work of playwright, novelist, and scholar Frank **Chin**. Chin has famously claimed that only writers born in the United States and writing in English can be counted as Chinese American writers; this is a radically counterdiasporic perspective that would accept only individuals of the second and subsequent generations as **Asian American**. Frank Chin's views about "authentic" Chinese American identity brought him into a well publicized conflict with Maxine Hong **Kingston**, author of the widely read autobiographical narratives *The Woman Warrior* and *China Men*. Chin accused Kingston, along with other Chinese American writers such as Amy **Tan** and David Henry **Hwang**, of using inauthentic, Western literary forms in their work. More recent writers such as Gish **Jen**, in her novels *Typical American* and *Mona in the Promised Land*, and David Wong **Louie**, in his novel *The Barbarians Are Coming* and stories collected in *Pangs of Love*, explore an experience of Chinese America that exists outside the symbolic space of Chinatown. Instead,

Chinese American identity is explored within the context of contemporary American multiculturalism, though the issues of racism and Oriental stereotyping are also present in these texts.

In contrast to Chinese immigrants, many of whom were temporary workers and were perceived as such in general terms in the United States, Japanese immigrants tended to be permanent settlers rather than sojourners. From the period of the Meiji Restoration in the 1860s, Japan pursued a policy of encouraging greater contact with the West to increase trade and Japanese industrialization. This resulted in some Japanese immigration to the United States, but significant numbers arrived only between 1890 and 1910. These immigrants tended to settle in territories like Hawaii, the Pacific Coast, and the largely undeveloped northwestern United States. The Gentlemen's Agreement of 1907 between the U.S. and Japanese governments allowed Japanese laborers to bring "picture wives" to the United States. This was a form of arranged marriage, brokered by a matchmaker, using only pictures of each of the intended couple. This system allowed for the establishment of Japanese families and permanent communities much earlier than was the case for Chinese immigrants, who felt the full impact of the exclusionary immigration laws. By ensuring that brides were brought to the United States from Japan (Korea, in the case of Korean picture brides), diasporic ties with the culture and lifeways of the homeland were reinforced in each generation. Until the U.S. Immigration Act of 1917, which introduced an "Asiatic Barred Zone" from which migrants were not accepted, Japanese immigrants were not subjected to the same racial hostility as Chinese immigrants. Indeed, a vocabulary developed to distinguish each generation born outside Japan: the first-generation of American-born Japanese are referred to as **issei**, the American-born second generation are **nisei**, and third-generation Japanese Americans are referred to as **sansei**.

From the 1920s, a flourishing Japanese American press enabled writers to publish their work in the United States. A distinctively Japanese American literature emerged in the period following **World War II** and the imprisonment or internment (between 1942 and 1945) by the War Relocation Authority of Japanese Americans residing in the western United States. This internment experience, following Executive Order 9066, uprooted 110,000 Japanese Americans from their homes and sent them to live behind barbed wire fences in inland desert camps. Literary works that explore the internment experience tend to focus upon the distinction between "Japanese" and "American" identities, and the need for U.S.-born individuals to understand their location between these two worlds. John **Okada's** *No-No Boy* and Monica **Sone's** *Nisei Daughter,* for example, seek to distinguish between what is subjectively American from what could be termed Japanese or Japanese American. Internment autobiographies, such as Jeanne Wakatsuki **Houston** and James D. Houston's *Farewell to Manzanar,* record the suffering and sacrifice, in the face of pervasive American racism, of relocated Japanese American families and individuals.

The American annexation of the Philippines occurred after two separate wars: the Spanish-American War of 1898 and the Filipino-American War (1899–1902). After the cessation of the second war, Filipinos began to immigrate to the United States in large numbers, though Filipino migration to the United States can be dated back to the seventeenth century. Direct American colonial rule of the archipelago was modulated with greater self-rule during the Commonwealth Period of 1935–1946, after which the Philippines gained independence. The Philippines constituted a region of free trade for the United States up to and after independence. During the period between 1906 and 1946, 150,000 Filipinos migrated to the United States, mostly to settle in California and Hawaii; the Hawaiian sugar plantations commissioned many Filipino laborers. According to the terms of the 1934 Tydings-McDuffie Independence Act, these migrants occupied the status of "nationals" rather than citizens on the one hand and "aliens" on the other, even though they were traveling from a U.S. colony to the U.S. proper. A quota of 50 Filipino immigrants per year was imposed by the 1934 act. A significant wave of Filipino immigration followed the reform of immigration legislation in 1965, and the political and economic uncertainty of the Marcos regime in the Philippines accounted for increased Filipino immigration during this post-1965 period.

In the early part of the twentieth century, Filipino writers such as Carlos **Bulosan**, José García **Villa**, Bienvenido **Santos**, and N.V.M. **Gonzalez** wrote from the perspective of migrants to the United States. Bulosan's *America Is in the Heart* stands as one of the paradigmatic texts engaging the Filipino American experience of isolation and economic exploitation. Later writers, such as Ninotchka **Rosca**, Linda **Ty-Casper**, and Jessica **Hagedorn**, continue to engage the question of whether the United States provides the opportunity for developing hybrid Filipino American identities and whether, or under what conditions, an "authentic" Filipino identity might be possible.

Korean immigration to the United States was inhibited in the late nineteenth and early twentieth centuries by the exclusionary immigration laws that limited the eligibility of Asian immigrants. In addition, the Japanese annexation and colonial administration of Korea, which ended only in 1945, also limited the size of the immigrant Korean population in the United States. Korean immigration occurred in a number of waves: between 1903 and 1905 Hawaiian sugar planters recruited Korean plantation labor; in the early decades of the 1900s, farm and cannery workers migrated to California and the Pacific Coast; throughout the first half of the twentieth century students and political exiles entered the United States; and the reform of U.S. immigration quotas in 1965 heralded a further wave of Korean immigration.

The effects of Japanese colonization are addressed in various ways in the work of successive Korean American writers: Younghill **Kang**, Richard E. **Kim**, Sook Nyul

Choi, Theresa Hak Kyung **Cha**, and Nora Okja **Keller**. Second-generation Korean American writers such as Mary Paik **Lee** and Ronyoung **Kim** engage the issues arising from the Korean immigrant experience in the United States, not least the diversity and hybridity of Korean Americans. The part-Chinese, part-Korean Hawaiian poet Cathy **Song** exemplifies the multiracial or multicultural condition of individuals who are the product of intersecting migrant "routes" to America, particularly in her affirmation of her own multiple ethnic identities.

Significant numbers of Vietnamese began arriving in the United States not as immigrants but as refugees in the immediate aftermath of the fall of Saigon to the Communist North Vietnamese forces in 1975. Resettlement of Vietnamese refugees continued through the 1979 Orderly Departure Program. Before this period, a small diasporic Vietnamese population, comprised primarily of students and diplomats, resided in the United States, but the contemporary Vietnamese American community is U.S.-born. Much **Vietnamese American literature** reflects a refugee rather than immigrant experience: Le Ly **Hayslip**'s autobiographical works, like Jade Ngoc Quang Huynh's *South Wind Changing* and Nguyen Qui Duc's *Where the Ashes Are: The Odyssey of a Vietnamese Family*, offer Vietnamese perspectives on the military conflict and the place offered to Vietnamese migrants in contemporary U.S. society.

South Asian migrants to the United States include immigrants from Pakistan, India, Bangladesh, Sri Lanka, Nepal, Bhutan, and the Maldives. The earliest immigrants came to North America from the Panjab between 1904 and 1924 and settled in the Pacific Coast region of the United States and Canada. Under the terms of the 1924 Immigration Act, South Asians, like all Asians in the United States, were denied access to citizenship, and this legislative provision contributed to significantly reduced South Asian immigration. The quota system introduced with the immigration reform effort of 1943 reserved half of the quota for immigrants of the professional class. This meant that many South Asian migrants arrived in possession of a British colonial education and fluency in the English language. Largely because of this economic and social positioning, South Asians have been represented as the new **model minority**. However, this stereotype denies the increasing diversity of the South Asian American population. Recent writers grappling with the complexities of belonging, of claiming a heritage within a "hyphenated" cultural identity, include Meena **Alexander**, the poet Agha Shahid **Ali**, Sara **Suleri**, Bharati **Mukherjee**, Chitra **Divakaruni**, and Jhumpa **Lahiri**.

The literature of each of these Asian American groups engages with the difficulties of entrenched U.S. racism and exclusion, together with the impossibility of returning "home." This is the diasporic dilemma: home is both the nation of residence and the culture of birth. The complexity of negotiating this "between world" condition is the consequence of the history of American immigration and the legacy of Asian emigration. **See also** Japanese American Internment; Multiculturalism and Asian America; Racism and Asian America.

Further Reading

Kim, Elaine H. *Asian American Literature: An Introduction to the Writings and Their Social Context.* Philadelphia: Temple University Press, 1982.

Lim, Shirley Geok-lin. "Immigration and Diaspora." In *An Interethnic Companion to Asian American Literature,* ed. King-Kok Cheung. Cambridge: Cambridge University Press, 1997. 289–311.

U.S. Census 2000 Brief. Issued February 2002. The Asian Population: 2000 [Online December 2006] U.S. Census Bureau Web site. http://www.census.gov/prod/2002pubs/c2kbr01-16.pdf.

DEBORAH L. MADSEN

✦ ASIAN PACIFIC ISLANDERS

Based on physical and cultural differences, the Asian Pacific Islands are composed of three main parts. Located in the Southwest Pacific, the Melanesian Islands are clustered around the northeastern part of Australia and cover New Guinea, Fiji, and the Solomon Islands. The history of these islands used to be characterized by European colonization, but now these islands have assumed identities of independence, though some remain parts of Indonesia. More than 3.5 million people living on this part of the islands seldom migrate to the Unites States, so their cultures remain relatively free from the influence of American culture.

The Micronesia Islands are located in the midwestern part of the Pacific, and the largest island is Guam, with a population of about 105,000 and an area of 206 square miles. Its residents became U.S. citizens in 1952, 54 years after the United States assumed control of the island. Around 93 other Micronesian islands, which have a population of about 125,000 and an area of 708 square miles, are "the Trust Territory formed by the United Nations after **World War II**" (Kotchek 1986, 34). As the trustee of these islands, the United States is interested in them mainly for military purposes.

The Polynesian Islands, scattered across the triangular area of the central and eastern Pacific, are made up of Samoa (American Samoa and Samoa), the Cook Islands, French Polynesia (Tahiti and the other Society Islands, the Marquesas Islands, the Austral Islands, and the Tuamotu Archipelago), the island of Niue, the islands of Tokelau, Tuvalu (formerly the Ellice Islands), the islands of Tonga and of Wallis and Futuna, the Hawaiian Islands, and Pitcairn Island. New Zealand's original inhabitants, the Maori, are also known as Polynesian. These islands have suffered from colonization by both European countries and the United States. Tonga used to be colonized by Great Britain, Marquesa and Tahiti by France, and Samoa and Hawaii by the United States.

Before 1941, migration from these islands to the United States was limited. After World War II, however, migration has undergone a great change. The access to Western values and technology made an increasing number of islanders realize that the self-sufficient economy no longer suited them and that a materially comfortable life was more attractive. Therefore, "with the push of population and economics and with the pull of expectations for life in a developed country, Pacific Island migration has increased exponentially" (Kotchek 1986, 34). Nevertheless, the U.S. Immigration Act of 1965, though removing national origin quotas from migration to the United States, stipulated that only those who had certain qualified professional skills and had families in the United States could apply for U.S. citizenship.

It is on the Polynesian Islands, specifically on Samoan Islands, that the transformation of migration to the United States and the corresponding effects on the island culture can be observed. During the late nineteenth century, the rivalry between the United States and Germany for the control of the Samoan islands ended with mutual partition of the islands. Western Samoa was under the control of Germany and New Zealand before and after World War I, respectively. In 1962, Western Samoa won its independence. American Samoa was under dominion by the U.S. Navy until 1952, when the Navy closed its Samoa base. Since then, it has been governed by the Department of the Interior. Economic depression followed the removal of the Navy base in Samoa, and residents began to migrate to Hawaii and the West Coast of the United States. Since the kin network served as the main channel through which migration was made, American Samoans, once settled in the United States, attempted to maintain close family ties. However, the scattered family relatives across the United States found it difficult to sustain such family-centered Samoan culture. The different ethnic groups around them, the difficulties in learning English, and the mainstream values that emphasized competition and success have formed an immense challenge to their ethnic culture. Samoan students in American public schools are "often discomfited by the atmosphere of competition and aggressiveness" (Kotchek 1986, 36).

Despite the slim chance for American Samoans to provide family alliance across scattered states, the Samoans make full use of the opportunity to support each other within the family circle. Such an extensive scale of mutual support in both material and spiritual aspects, however, met with critical observation from employers of these Samoans. To counter the opposition from their employers, the Samoans must form alliances on a larger scale. However, their confinement within the family circle prevents them from being able to achieve the goal of winning more rights. Thus, the advantages and disadvantages of the American Samoan culture of close family ties are exposed.

Similar to Chinese immigrants, the Samoan immigrants in the United States also experience generational differences in their attitude toward their traditional ethnic culture. The first generation tended to cling to their ethnic culture, which provided immense support for their survival. The second generation was inclined to assimilate into the American mainstream culture, at the expense of compromising their ethnic identity. The third generation, however, torn between their ethnic identity and their American identity, experiences ceaseless internal conflicts.

In a similar vein, the culture of Hawaii was also facing the threat of Western values. In fact, since Captain James Cook's discovery of Hawaii in 1778, the islands have been exposed to the West. In the early nineteenth century, American whaling ships had been sailing in Hawaii, and depictions of such experiences of exploration can be seen in Herman Melville's *Typee: A Peep at Polynesian Life* (1846) and *Omoo: A Narrative of Adventures in the South Seas* (1847). The arrival of New England missionaries in 1820 transformed Hawaii in that Protestant and Roman Catholic beliefs were introduced and that written language replaced oral literature. Despite the missionary support for the islands' Kamehameha kingdom in guarding its independence, the sovereignty of the islands had been the target of control by the United States, Great Britain, and France. Such rivalry ended with the Kamehameha kingdom being overthrown in 1893 and Hawaii becoming U.S. territory in 1900.

Although most people identify the culture of Hawaii with warm climate, primitive beauty, and ideal resorts, Hawaii also boasts of a multicultural identity. Since the first indentured Chinese field hands and the first Japanese came to the islands in 1851 and 1868 respectively, the population of the islands has been growing increasingly multiethnic. The earlier generations of these ethnic groups tend to associate life on the islands with that in their native lands, yet successive generations hit a dilemma in which identity crisis becomes increasingly poignant.

Similar to early Asian American literary works on the mainland, the earliest works written by Asian Pacific Islanders are largely autobiographical in nature. Florence Frisbie's autobiography *Miss Ulysses from Puka-Puka* (1948), written in English, was known as the first published work by an Asian Pacific Islander. The first published novel, *Makutu* (1960), by Thomas Davis, a Cook Islander, and Lydia Henderson, his New Zealand-born wife, depicts the cultural conflicts between Pacific and Western values in an imaginary land—Fenua Lei. The Samoan writer Albert Wendt was determined to write a literature characteristic of Asian Pacific Islanders, though, in his novella *Flying Fox in a Freedom Tree* (1974), the protagonist-narrator expresses his wish to be another Robert Louis Stevenson (Oceanic literature 2007). Still, Wendt was a distinct contributor to the establishment of an Asian Pacific Islander literature in that he made extensive use of the images, mythologies, colloquialism, and narrative styles that smack of Asian Pacific Island culture. Wendt's achievement is "his ability to absorb the history, myths, and other oral traditions of his country and to synthesize them with contemporary realities and the idiosyncrasies of written fiction, imposing upon it all a vision that is his own" (Oceanic literature 2007). By setting up Bamboo Ridge Press in Hawaii, the Chinese American poet Eric **Chock** has made monumental efforts to explore the conflicts between Asian traditional values and modern Western values by writing poems in either English or **Hawaiian Pidgin** English. Having crossed the threshold of self-discovery, the literature of Asian Pacific Islanders seems to be developing into a multicultural effort that combines the ethnic root with other subsidiary branches.

Further Reading

Kotchek, Lydia. "Pacific Islanders in the U.S." In *Dictionary of Asian American History*, ed. Hyung-Chan Kim. Westport, CT: Greenwood Press, 1986. 33–38.

"Oceanic literature." *Encyclopædia Britannica*. 2007. Encyclopædia Britannica Online. 8 May 2007. http://search.eb.com/eb/article-14355.

JIN LI

✦ ASSIMILATION/AMERICANIZATION

Raised first by Chicago sociologists led by Robert E. Park, who had been secretary to Booker T. Washington, the concept of assimilation has become essential to one's understanding of the major currents of ethnic studies. According to Michael Omi and Howard Winant, the ethnicity paradigm has passed three stages: a pre-1930s stage, in which the prevalent biologistic view of race was challenged; a 1930s to 1965 stage, in which two "recurrent themes—assimilationism and cultural pluralism—were defined"; and a post-1965 stage, during which "group rights" met the challenge of neoconservative egalitarianism. Social Darwinists, Spencerists, and eugenicists believed that race embodied its hereditary features and that racial intermixture would result in "biological throwbacks" (1986, 14). Such beliefs, however, were questioned by progressive scholars such as Horace Kallen and by other Chicago sociologists such as Robert E. Park. Whereas Kallen advocated a coexistence of multiple racial and ethnic communities, Park proposed assimilationism based on the 1923–1926 Survey of Race Relations on the Pacific Coast that ranged from asking Asian Americans to fill out the questionnaire about intermarriage to accumulating examples of assimilated Asians. Park shared the same belief as the missionaries did: that intermarriage could serve as the evidence of American assimilation. He wrote, "If the Japanese are not permitted to intermarry in the United States, we will always have a race problem as long as they are here" (1921, 61). Park once used "racial uniform" to depict the skin color of Asians and blacks, reflecting his assumption of exotic differences. Such foreignness of Oriental culture, in Park's view, suggested a gap between the Oriental and the Occidental. Such a view revealed Park's assumption of the superiority of American culture to the Oriental, so it was small wonder that he would continue to assert that race consciousness could provide a solution to close the gap. In this sense, the sociological approach to immigrant cultures was similar to that of the missionaries, because both had the same goal of cultural/spiritual conversion in mind.

When the Survey of Race Relations on the Pacific Coast came to its end, Park drew a conclusion that "The race relations cycle—contact, competition, accommodation and eventual assimilation—is apparently progressive and irreversible" (Yu 2001, 70). It is important to note that the race relations cycle has the American culture at the center, with various Oriental cultures to accommodate and accept the dominant culture. Park's complacency was noticeable when he stated, "If America was once in any exclusive sense the melting pot of races, it is so no longer. The melting pot is the world" (71). The ideological implications of the assimilation cycle were that the United States was inclusive and any foreign cultures would be subject to the transformation and become Americanized. Thus, Park presented a structure that emphasized the exoticness of the Oriental culture, which promised integration into American mainstream culture.

The Asians' assimilation, however, was not to be gained without undertaking a process of marginalization. Chicago sociologists, when confronted with narratives of second-generation Japanese immigrants that pointed to a lost identity, invented a new term of *marginal man*. In "Human Migration and the Marginal Man," which was published after the Survey of Race Relations ended, Park described various forms of marginality. He applauded the new cultural phenomenon by suggesting that the marginal man enjoyed more freedom to move between two cultures. The theoretical concept of the marginal man exerted great influence over Chinese and Japanese students in the United States. In 1928, a Chinese student named Ching Chao Wu presented his sociology dissertation in which he studied American **Chinatowns**. He echoed Park's theory about assimilation, whose nature lies in Americanization, by stating that the marginal man's "mind is the real melting pot of cultures" (qtd. in Yu 2001, 114). Nevertheless, as Yu points out, Wu's insufficient firsthand information about the Chinese immigrants and his heavy reliance on the documents from the Survey of Race Relations belies its validity. Ironically, Wu's attempt to contribute to the "Oriental" study proves to be an assimilation into the mainstream American culture represented by Robert Park.

Asian American intellectuals such as Rose Hum Lee, a Chinese American who held a doctorate in sociology from the University of Chicago, only strengthened the theory of assimilation in different ways. Instead of adopting the term *assimilation*, Lee used *integration* to emphasize the importance of integrating into American culture in solving the problem of the marginal man. She argued for closing cultural gaps, which was "brought about by the processes of acculturation and assimilation" (Lee 1960, 127). Different from Park, who made more efforts at confirming the irreversibility of cultural assimilation in the direction of the occidental culture, Lee expanded the concept of assimilation into an ideal state in which no "dissimilar" people exist. By 1960, Lee advocated a complete commitment to integration. In her work *The Chinese in the United States of America* (1960), Lee contended that the only way to build an integrated community was to eliminate both physical and psychological distinctiveness. Her reductive binary distinction of Chinese traditional gender roles and American modern ones, however, became problematic when the women's movement broke out in the United States in the same period. Lee construed American identity as cultural homogeneity, which was, in effect, a renunciation of the traces of Chinese identity.

The American Orientalism's advocacy of assimilation exerted a great influence on the living of Chinese Americans, as can be found in Chinese American writings since the 1850s. **Yung** Wing's autobiographical *My Life in China and America* (1909) challenged the American popular belief that Chinese were unassimilable and was regarded as influential in improving the image of Chinese immigrants. American culture influenced him so greatly that there were tangible evidences, both physical and cultural, of his American identity. He became so assimilated that "he had even almost entirely forgotten his native tongue" (Yin 2000, 72). To a certain extent, the second generation of Chinese immigrants relived the experiences that Yung had. As early as the 1920s, the second-generation Chinese had been striving to assimilate into American culture to such a degree that they were labeled "Orientals in appearance but not in reality" (118). The reason for their full-scale assimilation lies in their receiving American education while losing touch with traditional Chinese ethics. The pursuit of the American dream and the quest for independence and equality became central themes of their writings. Such themes were in keeping with the American mainstream culture. Pardee **Lowe's** *Father and Glorious Descendant* (1943) and Jade Snow **Wong's** *Fifth Chinese Daughter* (1950) are emblematic of Chinese Americans in the early twentieth century. As Xiao-huang Yin asserts, Low "epitomized the second-generation's experience of assimilation as a process of alienation from traditional Chinese culture" (2000, 131). Wong's *Fifth Chinese Daughter,* on the other hand, celebrates traditional Chinese values that had enabled the second-generation Chinese to assume "the role of being the **model minority**" (136).

Despite the dramatic social transformation of the Chinese American experience since the 1960s, it remains uncertain whether Chinese Americans can achieve success without having to undergo an assimilation experience. Contrary to the earlier Chinese American writing tradition of informing the West about Chinese culture, contemporary

Chinese American writers tend to forsake their Chinese identity and maintain an Americanized identity. As Maxine Hong **Kingston** claimed about the influence of American literature on her book *The Woman Warrior:* "My heritage is Shakespeare and Walt Whitman. The first story about the aunt in *The Woman Warrior* is straight out of *The Scarlet Letter.* . . . My experimentation with time and space, straight from James Joyce and Virginia Woolf. I consider the Beat writers—Kerouac, Ginsberg—they are my teachers" (Yin 2000, 259). **See also** Orientalism and Asian America.

Further Reading

Huang, Guiyou, ed. *Asian American Literary Studies.* Edinburgh, Scotland: Edinburgh University Press, 2005.

Kim, Elaine H. *Asian American Literature: An Introduction to the Writings and Their Social Context.* Beijing: Foreign Language Teaching and Research Press, 2006.

Lee, Rose Hum. *The Chinese in the United States of America.* Hong Kong: Hong Kong University Press, 1960.

Omi, Michael, and Howard Winant. *Racial Formation in the United States: From the 1960s to the 1980s.* New York: Routledge, 1986.

Park, Robert E., and Ernest W. Burgess. *Introduction to the Science of Sociology.* Chicago: University of Chicago Press, 1921.

Yin, Xiao-huang. *Chinese American Literature Since the 1850s.* Urbana: University of Illinois Press, 2000.

Yu, Henry. *Thinking Orientals: Migration, Contact, and Exoticism in Modern America.* Oxford: Oxford University Press, 2001.

JIN LI

✦ ASSOCIATION FOR ASIAN AMERICAN STUDIES (AAAS)

The Association for Asian American Studies is a nonprofit organization incorporated in the District of Columbia. Although AAAS currently has over 750 members comprised of faculty, staff, graduate and undergraduate students, publishers, and community organizations interested in the field of Asian American studies, its beginning was discreet. In 1979, Douglas W. Lee, who was a faculty member at the University of Washington at that time, organized the first national conference in Seattle, Washington. "He named himself president, appointed [Sucheng Chan] vice-president, and appointed Edwin Clausen as secretary treasurer." However, Chan writes that Lee became disillusioned with the field of Asian American studies and drove all the way to California from Washington State to make Chan his successor. Chan writes that she consulted with various colleagues at the University of California, Berkeley, about the situation and did not receive much support or enthusiasm for keeping the organization going. However, Chan felt differently and considered the possibility of the association playing a constructive role in developing Asian American studies programs throughout the nation. She recognized that, although UC Berkeley students may not feel a need for such an association, other students in nonprogressive states would benefit greatly from the advocacy of a national organization. Chan became the caretaker president and organized a second conference, where a process allowed the election of new officers for the organization. At that time, Don Nakanishi and Gary Okihiro assumed responsibility for the association (Chan 2005, 28). Since its inception, the association's membership has produced groundbreaking research and community activism in the areas of literature, social sciences, humanities, social justice, ethnic coalition building, and Asian and Asian American transnational/diaspora; the Association for Asian American Studies continues to evolve.

The association has been the center stage for scholars, academics, community leaders, and students to exchange ideas and foster dialogue about what it means to be **Asian American** and what it means to study and teach **Asian American studies**. The mission of the Association for Asian American Studies "is the purpose of advancing the highest professional standard of excellence in teaching and research in the field of Asian American Studies; promoting better understanding and closer ties between and among various sub-components within Asian American Studies: Chinese, Japanese, Korean, Filipino, Hawai'ian, Southeast Asian, South Asian, Pacific Islander, and other groups. AAAS sponsors professional activities to facilitate increased communication and scholarly exchange among teachers, researchers, and students in the field of Asian American Studies. The organization advocates and represents the interests and welfare of Asian American Studies and Asian Americans. AAAS is also founded for the purpose of educating American society about the history and aspirations of Asian American ethnic minorities" (Chan 2005, 29). This interdisciplinary association continues to advocate for social justice issues and has embraced a democratic process of including members from across the nation and the globe.

Since 1980, AAAS has held meetings annually across the nation and in Canada. With a growing membership, the association is currently rethinking the way in which regions are outlined for its membership. As of 2006, the organizational structure consists of a president, president-elect, secretary/treasurer, and board members from Hawaii/Pacific Islands, Southern California, Northern California, Pacific Northwest, and Midwest, South, and East Coast representatives. The regions were established to ensure that there was representation from the regions where Asian Americans studies existed at that time. However, the geographic boundaries of the regions were established in the 1980s, and the state of Asian American studies has changed significantly in the past two decades. The 2000 U.S. Census highlights the fact that Asian Americans are a fast-growing population in the United States. In almost every state, the public and the media are becoming increasingly aware that Asian Americans are an important part of the American mosaic (Danico and Ng 2004). With this rapid demographic growth, there has been an accompanying expansion of university and college courses and programs in Asian American studies. Started at only a few colleges and universities in the 1960s and 1970s, the field has expanded through the continent, reflecting the evolving migration patterns of Asian immigrants and Asian Americans. In addition to promoting better understanding among the various Asian ethnic groups who are examined in Asian American studies: Chinese, Japanese, Koreans, Filipinos, Hawaiians, Vietnamese, Hmong, Cambodians, Laotians, South Asians, Pacific Islanders, and other groups, the association is a resource for college campuses interested in developing an Asian American studies program. As the field grew, criticism surfaced to the California-centricity of the field. In the fall of 1991, on the campus of Cornell University, representatives from 23 colleges and universities established a caucus: "East of California" (EOC), within the Association for Asian American Studies. The EOC caucus has become the heart of Asian Americanists outside of California, often fighting to build Asian American programs unique to their regional needs and separate from California's program models, histories, and legacies. The caucus has successfully helped institutionalize Asian American studies outside of California, promote region-specific research and publications, and serve as a basis of support for individuals and programs in the network. Since 1991, EOC has organized an annual conference held at a member campus and developed a starter kit "to assist in the institutionalization of Asian American Studies on college and university campuses. Recognizing that students are invariably the leaders of such initiatives, the East of California Network has compiled this packet of information to respond to student requests, especially from campuses with no faculty or other resources in Asian American Studies" (AAAS Web site). The EOC also played a critical role in creating a directory of Asian American studies and scholars so that such resources would be available to those seeking information.

The history and information on AAAS are housed institutionally at Cornell University, which has served as host campus to AAAS by offering staff support to manage the association. In addition to managing the association's organizational flow, the AAAS staff helps facilitate the construction of the Web site and Listserv. Other members contribute by editing the newsletter and the association's publication, the *Journal of Asian American Studies* (*JAAS*), through Johns Hopkins University Press. Before the journal took form, the organization published an annual anthology, often with papers and essays drawn from its annual meetings at different sites across the country; however, as scholarship in the area intensified, *JAAS* was created to address the diverse body of scholarship among Asian Americanists. The quarterly newsletters highlight the latest research and news in the field, as well as job, professional, and conference announcements, book reviews, community issues and activism, and public opinions on topics related to Asian Americans in North America. However, as globalization or neoliberalism became more apparent, AAAS looked at how the field has evolved and has been creating opportunities for dialogue and scholarship in the area of Asian American diaspora/transnationalism. The association recognizes the fluidity of Asian American studies and attempts to change as the field evolves.

In addition to disseminating information, the association acknowledges achievement by scholars, community leaders, and Asian Americans who have committed themselves in the area of Asian American studies. The book award committees, comprised of AAAS members, receive nominations from publishers and then select books in the areas of cultural studies, history, poetry/prose, and social science for AAAS Book Awards every year. The awards are given yearly to titles published in the field that deserve special recognition. In addition, the association has given a number of lifetime and community achievement awards to those who have made an impact on scholarship, service, students, and community. In addition to scholars, community leaders, and activists, AAAS also hosts the Anita Affeldt Graduate Travel Fund to support up to two graduate students who are upcoming scholars in the field to attend the national AAAS meetings.

The field of Asian American studies has grown rapidly, with a corresponding increase in the number of publications on Asian American history, contemporary issues, and literature. In addition to groundbreaking research, the association lends its support and resources to the growing demand for Asian American studies programs and departments around the nation. As progress and movement toward a more inclusive curriculum spread throughout the country, the Association for Asian American Studies too repositions itself to become a place where the public can turn for information, resources, and guidance to gain better insight into what *Asian American* means in a changing global world. **See Also** Asian Diasporas; Asian American Political Activism.

Further Reading

Chan, Sucheng. *In Defense of Asian American Studies: The Politics of Teaching and Program Building.* Chicago: University of Illinois Press, 2005.

Danico, Mary Yu, and Franklin Ng. *Asian American Issues.* Westport, CT: Greenwood Press, 2004.

AAAS Web site: http://aaastudies.org/pub.tpl?key=sub&rank=1.

MARY YU DANICO

B

✦

✦ *BAMBOO RIDGE: THE HAWAII WRITERS' QUARTERLY*

A publication dedicated to providing a venue for local Hawaiian literature, *Bamboo Ridge* had its early beginnings in the 1970s, which not only witnessed what many now call the Hawaiian Renaissance in language and music but gave birth to the push for writing in a "local" context—that is, a literature written by the people who grew up on the islands and who recognize the importance of island culture, experiences, and voices in their writing. Named after a famous fishing spot on the island of Oahu, *Bamboo Ridge* has, since 1979, devoted itself to providing a key outlet for a distinctly "local" understanding of writing. The push for local representation can be largely traced to the creation of Talk Story and the first major conference for Hawaiian writers, which took place in Honolulu in 1978. This was followed by Talk Story Big Island in 1979 and the Hawaii Literary Arts Council's Writers Conference in 1980. Among the core group of enthusiasts who were paving the way for the emergence of local literature were John Dominis Holt, Milton **Murayama**, Maxine Hong **Kingston**, Garrett **Hongo**, Stephen Sumida, Arnold Hiura, and Eric **Chock**. Amid such excitement, Chock and fellow writer Darrell H.Y. **Lum** founded Bamboo Ridge Press in 1978.

Bamboo Ridge has published a number of local writers of diverse ethnic backgrounds. The list of contributors includes Eric Chock, Darrell H.Y. Lum, Juliet S. **Kono**, Wing Tek **Lum**, Susan Nunes, Marie Hara, Cathy **Song**, Rodney Morales, Ian Macmillan, Lee Cataluna, Wayne Wang, and Gary **Pak**. Some of the more notable collections are devoted to specific topics or to particular communities: *Ho'i Ho'i Hou: A Tribute to George Helm & Kimo Mitchell* (1984), an anthology devoted to the memory of two Hawaiian activists who were lost during a voyage of the *Hōkūle'a* in 1977;

Mālama, Hawaiian Land and Water (1985); *Poets Behind Barbed Wire* (1985), which features a collection of tanka poems written by interned Japanese Americans during **World War II**; *Kauai Tales* (1985); *Paké: Writings by Chinese in Hawaii* (1989); *Sister Stew: Fiction and Poetry by Women* (1991); *Intersecting Circles* (2000), a collection exploring the issue of mixed-race heritage; *YOBO: Korean American Writing in Hawai'i* (2003); and *He Leo Hou: A New Voice—Hawaiian Playwrights* (2003). Coeditor Darrell Lum has pointed out that the journal is often printed without a glossary or annotations—the reasoning behind such omissions is the desire to preserve readership for a local audience. In other words, as a voice of the islands, *Bamboo Ridge* is not necessarily interested in promoting or printing glimpses of local life for nonlocal voyeurism.

The journal's importance was not lost on scholars in Asian American literature in the 1970s and the 1980s. Stephen Sumida, who was actively involved in the Big Island Talk Story conference and subsequent publication of an anthology by that same title, directed scholarly attention to the press' activities. Sumida's "Waiting for the Big Fish: Recent Research in the Asian American Literature of Hawai'i" was published within a special edition of the journal in 1986. In this essay, Sumida highlights the development of a lengthy canon that is ignored, given the preeminence of James A. Michener's *Hawaii* (1959) and A. Grove Day and Carl Stroven's largely Anglo American collection of writing, *A Hawaiian Reader* (1959). Sumida implies that *Bamboo Ridge* is the culmination of a long struggle to refute the assumption that "in this supposed paradise, hardworking Asians did not write, did not cultivate verbal expression while they cultivated Hawaii's soil, much less indulge in verbal creativity" (1986, 303).

Bamboo Ridge's cause was also championed in the local press. In 1998, the *Hawaii Herald*, a Japanese American periodical in Honolulu, devoted a 27-page special issue to the press. In large part, the *Hawaii Herald's* decision to print the in-depth report came in the wake of scathing criticism leveled at *Bamboo Ridge* writer Lois-Ann **Yamanaka**, whose Book of the Year Award for *Blu's Hanging* was rescinded by the Association for Asian American Studies. In fact, the article goes so far as to cite the national success of many *Bamboo Ridge* writers—such as Lois-Ann Yamanaka and Cathy Song—who were given their first publishing opportunities by *Bamboo Ridge*. The report adds that despite financial difficulty, many valuable collections have been produced, including those devoted to Hawaiian issues.

Nevertheless, the 1990s were a turbulent time for *Bamboo Ridge* as Yamanaka was not the only writer targeted for criticism. At the 1994 Hawai'i Literary Arts Council Conference, Dennis Kawaharada directed heavy criticism at the emerging prominence of Asian writing with its penchant for nostalgic representations of family and homeland. Such views would become clearly linked to an assumed agenda on the part of *Bamboo Ridge* in the minds of scholars, who were quick to expand this line of critical reasoning. Haunani-Kay Trask has been especially keen on challenging the ascendancy of Asians in Hawaii. To Trask, the literature of "settlers"—specifically mentioned are Eric Chock, Darrell Lum, Garrett Hongo, and Ron Takaki—and their claim to represent the islands results in the "falsification of place and culture" (1999, 169). Trask further reproves of the false nostalgia that is inherent in the use of pidgin and the Asian aspiration to dominate as the "unique voice of Hawai'i" (170).

Rob Wilson attempts to contextualize the spate of racialized criticism leveled against *Bamboo Ridge* in his *Reimagining the American Pacific* (2000). For Wilson, the emergence of *Bamboo Ridge* must be understood as a "localist" strategy that confronts the challenges of globalization and transnational capitalism: "within the tormented cultural politics of the literary scene . . . local entrenchment in ethnicity and place-based identity, at times refuses to join in the global flow" (vii). Wilson astutely identifies the murky gray space posited by Hawaii's transition from an independent Pacific nation to an American territory as an environment that on the one extreme nurtures the Native Hawaiian need to "possess and preserve the land as a locus of cultural identity" whereas *Bamboo Ridge* "posits a way of *reimagining* relationship among region, nation, and globe in which difference is not negated nor reified but constructed, negotiated, and affirmed" (179). In other words, *Bamboo Ridge's* celebration and perpetuation of the "local"—which is an idealized amalgamation of different races and cultures—in many ways negates the absolute divisions between what is considered "foreign" and "indigenous."

On the other hand, a particularly telling piece by Dennis Kawaharada indicates that perhaps much of the controversy over racial and ethnic representation stems from internal and highly personal conflicts among the writers themselves. Kawaharada's essay "Local Mythologies" first acknowledges the importance of Lum and Chock, who helped the writer "reconnect with [his] roots and [his] childhood growing up as a pidgin speaker in Kāne'ohe" (2000, 189). Though he himself became managing editor and grant writer for the press, Kawaharada cites a certain "clannishness" permeated the group; he notes that the core members were well-educated, middle-class Asians who rarely, if ever, invited participation from *haole* (whites) or Pacific Islanders (including Native Hawaiians). He also argues that *Bamboo Ridge* became engaged in what many would call "vanity publishing" (217). Such sentiments were also echoed by another former *Bamboo Ridge* writer, Rodney Morales, in his essay "Literature."

For their part, the editors of *Bamboo Ridge* have remained relatively quiet about the imbroglio that dominates the world of Western scholarship and academic discourse. In the Spring 1996 issue, Erick Chock released "The Neocolonization of Bamboo Ridge: Repositioning Bamboo Ridge and Local Literature in the 1990s," within which he admits to upholding a certain ideal, that of the multicultural nation, which he felt Hawaii was a model for. Although he hinted of times that made him consider retiring and dissolving the press (given the perpetual struggle to maintain fiscal solvency), *Bamboo Ridge* remains committed to its vision by continuing to nurture local writing through regular workshops and by publishing a wide range of new talents and voices.

Further Reading

Chock, Eric. "The Neocolonization of Bamboo Ridge: Repositioning Bamboo Ridge and Local Literature in the 1990s." *Bamboo Ridge: The Hawaii Writers' Quarterly* 69 (Spring 1996): 11–23.

Chock, Eric, and Darrell H.Y. Lum, eds. *The Best of Bamboo Ridge: The Hawaii Writers' Quarterly*. Honolulu: Bamboo Ridge, 1986.

Kawaharada, Dennis. "Local Mythologies, 1979–2000." *Hawaii Review* 56 (Spring 2001): 185–225.

Morales, Rodney. "Literature." In *Multicultural Hawai'i, the Fabric of a Multiethnic Society*, ed. Michael Haas. New York: Garland, 1998. 107–228.

Sumida, Stephen H. "Waiting for the Big Fish: Recent Research in the Asian American Literature of Hawaii." In *The Best of Bamboo Ridge: The Hawaii Writers' Quarterly*, eds. Eric Chock and Darrell H.Y. Lum. Honolulu: Bamboo Ridge, 1986. 302–321.

Trask, Haunani-Kay. "Decolonizing Hawaiian Literature." *Inside Out: Literature, Cultural Politics, and Identity in the New Pacific*. Lanham, MD: Rowman & Littlefield, 1999. 167–182.

Wilson, Rob. *Reimagining the American Pacific: From South Pacific to Bamboo Ridge and Beyond*. Durham, NC: Duke University Press, 2000.

SERI I. LUANGPHINITH

✦ BAO, QUANG (1969–)

Vietnamese American author, playwright, editor, and executive director of the Asian American Writers' Workshop (AAWW) in New York City since 1999, Quang Bao has been one of the driving forces and visionary leaders working to enhance awareness of Asian American literature. Moreover, as executive director, he has fostered an emerging community of Asian American writers through the many resources offered at AAWW, articulated as follows on its Web site:

Established in 1991, The Asian American Writers' Workshop, Inc., is a nonprofit literary arts organization founded in support of writers, literature and community.

Operating out of our 6,000 square-foot loft, we sponsor readings, book parties and panel discussions, and offer creative writing workshops. Each winter we present The Annual Asian American Literary Awards Ceremony to recognize outstanding literary works by Americans of Asian descent. Throughout the year, we offer various youth arts programs. In our space we operate a reading room of Asian American literature through the decades.

The only organization of its kind, the Workshop has become one of the most active community arts organizations in the United States. Based in New York City, we have a fast-growing membership, a list of award-winning books and have become an educational resource for Asian American literature and awareness across the nation.

Through his work at AAWW, Bao has advocated vociferously for Asian American experiences to be included in the U.S. mainstream through multiple literary genres. Of particular importance because of his personal history is highlighting the history of the Vietnamese in the United States.

Born on November 17, 1969, in Can Tho, Vietnam, Quang Bao fled with his family to the United States at the age of six in 1975. He and his family relocated to Sugar Land, Texas, and later to Houston, Texas. He received his bachelor's degree in English at Boston University and his Arts Management Certificate at Columbia University in New York City.

Many of Bao's stories involve tales, either fictional or factual, of the narrator's relationship with his mother and/or father. In fact, three works, "Mother" (2005), "Nobody Knows" (1998), and "Memories Are Priceless" (2003), all revolve around the personal revelations of a child about his parents, who are of Vietnamese descent. Underlying each work are the effects that the American phase of the **Vietnam War** has on both the child and his parents, especially in relationship to memory and loss. In "Mother" the personal loss is of economic class and status, as the mother transitions from being someone who can afford to hire housemaids to a refugee who has no home. The ending is the most poignant scene in that it reveals a sense of bittersweet loss when both the narrator and his mother must flee Vietnam in the middle of the night with the help of one of the mother's housemaids, Tai. The narrator details: "Tai said goodbye to me. We hugged. . . . Then, Mother reached into her pocketbook and took out the key to our house and handed it to Tai. And in one moment, however brief, all the maids in Vietnam owned everything. It was time to leave" (Bao 2005). This scene of possibility for the maid and the unknown for the narrator and his mother dramatizes the ambivalence and hardship it takes to leave one's past.

Whereas "Mother" displays the moment of exile, "Memories Are Priceless" recalls the moment of the exile's return to his homeland. Just as there is ambivalence and guilt in leaving, there is as much emotion in the narrative of return and reunion to one's place of origin. In reflecting upon his journey to Vietnam with his father, the narrator recalls, "I was born in Vietnam but I remember almost nothing about it. In returning, I yearned for a clearer picture of a place I had been trying to imagine for so long. At the end of the trip I only felt an overwhelming sense of loss and guilt, not the connections I was searching for" (Bao 2003). What made the trip so psychically exhausting was that the possibility for a better life that was embodied with Tai, the housemaid in "Mother," is not realized. Even with the ousting of the Americans and the French, the hope that the Vietnamese people had of living a better life free from Western imperialism was outweighed by the constant poverty and strife experienced by many of the Vietnamese nationals who did not leave.

Finally, in "Nobody Knows," the narrator recounts his life with his parents in the United States. This story describes the negotiations both the parents and the son must make as they acclimate to a different country. For example, the parents urge their single son to marry and produce children, denying what their son has been struggling to convey to them through his letters—that he is gay. His parents, drawing from their experiences in Vietnam, attempt to convince him that it will be better for all of them if he chooses to get married and have children and that they will be able to assist him in finding a wife if need be. The undercurrent of their conversations, however, is the idea that their lives would be radically different had they not left Vietnam, had there not been a war. Thus, as the narrator points out, neither he nor his parents can fully overcome the mental, emotional, and psychic idea that "the war is over" (Bao 1998, 42).

Besides painting a picture of a devoted son in his few published pieces, Bao also incorporates aspects of sexuality into his narratives. In his support of Asian American writers, Bao focuses on many aspects of Asian American literature, particularly with respect to GLBT literature. As he articulates in an interview with *PersuAsian*, Bao states, "I think that gay Asian American writing pushes the margins. The works grapple with complicated, unspoken issues. I don't hold it to a different standard than what I would just plain old good writing but I think the perspectives are fresh and vibrant. . . . Over the next couple of years, the most interesting Asian American writing will be coming from gays and lesbians, refugees and writers from countries where the U.S. was a colonial power" (2005, 5). To this end, he coedited with Hanya Yanagihara the anthology *Take Out: Queer Writing from Asian Pacific America* (2000), which was a finalist for the 2002 Lambda Literary Foundation Award.

For his contribution to Asian American literature, Bao has received numerous awards and honors. They include the 2006–2007 Revson Fellowship, the 2006 Fiction/Creative Nonfiction Fellow from the Massachusetts Cultural Council, and an honoree of the 2005 M. Jacquie Lodico Distinguished Service Award at the Alliance 2005 Gala.

Bao has also been interviewed on Studio 360, an affiliate of National Public Radio, and has participated in the discussion session of the Search for Asian American sponsored by PBS. Finally, Bao has just completed his first novel, entitled *The Make Believers* (publishing date unknown).

Further Reading

"Asian American Writers' Workshop." http://www.aaww.org.

Bao, Quang. "Memories Are Priceless." *The New York Times* 31 August 2003. http://query.nytimes.com/gst/fullpage.html.

———. "Mother." *Ploughshares* (Spring 2005). http://www.pshares.org/issues/artcle.

———. "Nobody Knows." In *Watermark: Vietnamese American Poetry & Prose*, eds. Barbara Tran, Monique Truong, and Luu Truong Khoi. New York: Asian American Writers' Workshop, 1998. 37–42.

"Quang Bao." *PersuAsian: Newsmagazine for the Gay Asian & Pacific Islander Men of New York*, May/June 2005: 5.

"Quang Bao, Revson Fellow, 2006–2007." http://www.revson.columbia.edu/fellows/alumni/quang_bao.html.

"Quang Bao." http://www.pbs.org/searching/aafr_cc.html.

"Quang Bao." http://www.temple.edu/tempress/authors/x127_qa.html.

Waddell, Robert. "Helping Asian-Americans into Print." *The New York Times* 25 December 1999. http://query.nytimes.com/gst/fullpage.html.

NINA HA

✦ BARROGA, JEANNIE (1949–)

A Filipina American playwright, dramaturge, director, teacher, and literary manager, Jeannie Barroga received a BA in fine arts from her hometown university, the University of Wisconsin at Milwaukee, and moved to California after graduation. She has been teaching playwriting, screenwriting, and theater classes at various schools and universities, mainly in the Bay Area, and has worked as a director. She founded the Palo Alto Playwright Forum in 1983 and was the literary manager for TheatreWorks, a repertory theater in Palo Alto, from 1985 to 2003. Together with Philip Kan **Gotanda**, she has co-mentored Asian American Theater Company's NewWorks Incubator program and currently she also serves as their artistic director. She is the recipient of many awards, including the 1991 Bay Area Playwrights Festival Ten-Minute Play Award, the 1996 Los Angeles Maverick Award, and the 2000 CalArts Award nomination. Her plays have been produced throughout the United States.

Barroga's work includes more than 50 plays as well as several cable TV productions. Her pre-1990 plays range from *Night Before the Rolling Stones Concert* (1981), in which a group of friends reunite for a Stones concert à la Lawrence Kasdan's classic *The Big Chill* (1983); to romantic comedies such as *Gets 'em Right Here* (1983) and *Batching It* (1986); to spoofs such as *In Search of . . .* (1984) and *The Paranoids* (1985); to historical vignettes such as *Wau-Bun* (1983), set in the 1850s, *When Stars Fall* (1985), which features the wife of General Custer, and *Lorenzo, Love* (1986), set in the 1920s in Taos, the New Mexican artist's colony. Barroga's explorations of sociopolitical and cultural issues concerning Filipino immigration and life in the United States and in the Philippines have clearly been an important focus of her dramatic work, as already evident in her early plays such as *Donato's Wedding* (1983), *The Flower and the Bee* (1983), *Adobo* (1987), *Kin* (1990), *Shades* (1992), and the family comedy *Eye of the Coconut* (1991), in which she portrays the problems of different generations within a Filipino American family in the Midwest. Likewise, in her docudrama, one-act play *Kenny Was a Shortstop* (1991), based on an actual killing of an 18-year-old Filipino in Stockton in 1990, Barroga traces the roots of a family tragedy through the character of a Filipina Chinese journalist, Cora, who interviews the dead youth's parents for an article. Barroga's musical *The Bubblegum Killers* (1999), about competing Filipino gangs in San Francisco in the 1930s, was also inspired by a newspaper article. But Barroga has also addressed more general concerns about racial prejudices, national politics, and panethnicity in the context of larger, multiethnic frameworks. A prime example of Barroga's multiperspectival dramatic vision is her play *Walls,* which premiered at the Asian American Theater Company in San Francisco in April 1989. It received its fifteenth anniversary production by the Asian American Theater Company in 2006.

In a century dominated by monumental and controversial warfare, debates concerning the purpose and design of memorial architecture commemorating the unparalleled number of victims of some of the twentieth-century's bloodiest conflicts have been equally controversial. One of the most notorious controversies grew out of the plans for the most prominent American war monument, the Vietnam Veterans Memorial in Washington, DC, which was dedicated in November 1982. Cofounded by the veteran Jan C. Scruggs, the Vietnam Veterans Memorial Fund organized a competition for the memorial's design. Although the winning design convinced the organizing committee unanimously, the design itself and the background of the designer caused one of North America's most notorious controversies over public art. The unexpected winner, Maya Lin, at that time a 21-year-old undergraduate architecture student at Yale, had designed a decidedly anti-monumental, modernistic memorial in the form of a V-shaped wall, consisting of polished black granite panels that rose out of the ground. These were engraved with the names of the more than 58,000 soldiers who died or were missing in action in Vietnam. Not only did veterans and others oppose the design because of its alleged "unheroic" character, but they also objected to Lin's age, gender, and Chinese descent. Eventually, and without Lin's agreement, a flag and a sculpture of three American soldiers (designed by Frederick Hart) were added to the site.

Walls centers around the Vietnam Veterans Memorial controversy and its sensitive issues of loss, community, and national identity. The play is set at the height of the controversy, between 1982 and 1984, and most of the dramatic action takes place directly in front of the memorial. Its intertextual references were mainly inspired by

Jan Scruggs and Joel Swerdlow's classic account, *To Heal a Nation: The Vietnam Veterans Memorial* (1985), with some of the play's characters clearly based on accounts in the book. The play opens with a heterogeneous group of people who are on a visit to the memorial with equally varied expectations. The historical figures of Maya Lin and Jan Scruggs are complemented by allegorical characters such as a news reporter, various veterans of Anglo American, African American, and Asian American descent, war protesters, a nurse, and two young, dead soldiers who appear as ghosts in combat gear. This multiethnic medley of women and men mirrors the conglomeration of daily visitors at the memorial and allows Barroga to present the audience with a multiperspectival view of the contested war and its equally contested memorial. Barroga also draws in the audience by building on the most striking component of the memorial as a visual medium itself, in which visitors can see their reflections in the polished marble and the names of the honored dead. The characters have been marked for life by their experiences of the war: psychologically, as in Stewart's posttraumatic shock syndrome and physically, as in the case of the paraplegic Morris and in the case of the two ghost figures, Dan and Jerry, who have lost their lives. As such, *Walls* functions as a dramatic analysis of war's repercussions and its gradual, traumatic encroachment into everyday life.

The collapse of the borders, framing private and public spaces, cannot be contained within a realist format, and Barroga resorts to a discontinuous time frame, flashbacks, and the use of ghosts. The cacophony of voices is further dramatized in the play's episodic structure. The conversations and arguments between various constellations of characters throughout the play (a veteran versus a nurse, an antiwar protester versus a veteran, Maya Lin versus the press) mirror their deep divisions. Even more importantly, these vignette-like debates essentially re-voice questions of whose version of events or whose perspective of the war dominates historical accounts, who defines public memory, and who shapes a politics of remembrance. Given the play's title, it also reflects the ambiguous function of the memorial itself: on the one side, as a place where pluralist and fragmentary memories are expressed in a moment of communal remembrance, and on the other as a site where the iconic wall reveals the persistence of other, imaginary walls, engendered by race, class, age, and so on. What at times makes the play slightly confusing simultaneously contributes to the play's literary reflection of the monument's "message," which Lin has always emphasized to be psychological, not political, by refusing to dictate or privilege any point of view. This same conception, however, has also been criticized, precisely for its lack of political intent, in that this kind of healing experience may also lead to a sort of national amnesia.

Barroga has realized that the memorial's minimalism allows for all kinds of interpretations and reflects it appropriately in her highly stylized play. Thematically, however, the play offers no healing closure. On the contrary, apart from the character of Maya Lin, the play also foregrounds several other Asian American characters who are forced to face the irony that they resemble the very enemies the United States fought against in the **Vietnam War**. Although the play ends with a meditative gesture, as all characters together read the names on the panels until the lights fade, it becomes clear that, as one character proclaims, wars will go on despite monuments, stones, or statues.

In *Talk-Story*, which was first produced in April 1992 by TheatreWorks in Palo Alto, Barroga also uses the figure of a Filipina American woman journalist, Dee Abano, to explore intergenerational rifts within a Filipino American family and to retrieve Filipino immigration history to the United States by contrasting Dee's contemporary ambitions with her father's past. Barroga's dramatic portrayals of life in the Philippines and in the United States, marked by constant shifts in place and time as well as multilinguality, contribute to a broader mapping of Filipino American transnationality, which is also evident in the productions of the Filipino American Ma-Yi Theatre in New York and in Louella Dizon's play *Till Voices Wake Us*, in particular. Both Barroga and Dizon emphasize the importance of storytelling and the first-generation immigrants' function of bearing witness and of preserving a community's collective cultural memory. At the same time, they also indicate the unreliability of personal stories and the heterogeneity of Filipino identities and experiences. The challenges of establishing a new life in an immigrant context also form the basis for Barroga's Off-Off-Broadway comedy *Rita's Resources*, which premiered at New York's Pan Asian Repertory Theatre in 1995. In *Rita's Resources* Barroga humorously adapts the motif of the American Dream from Arthur Miller's classic *Death of a Salesman* (1949). With *Banyan* Barroga leaves the boundaries of realist theater, although keeping its dreamlike elements, and delves into Philippine folklore and American popular culture, mainly the American musical *The Wizard of Oz* (1939), based on L. Frank Baum's children's book *The Wonderful Wizard of Oz* (1900). First produced at the Asian American Theater Company in San Francisco in 2005, Barroga sends her heroine, the young Filipina American professional Ona, on a return trip to the Philippines. Not unlike Dorothy Gale, Ona has to undergo a heroic journey and is confronted with corruption, terrorism, magic, and evil spirits from Philippine folklore. In *Banyan*, whose title refers to the banyan tree, Barroga not only deconstructs essentialized notions of "home" and myths of easy cultural returns but also situates her characters on the fault lines of intercultural encounters and their specific challenges.

Further Reading

Lee, Josephine. *Performing Asian America: Race and Ethnicity on the Contemporary Stage.* Philadelphia: Temple University Press, 1997.

Lowe, Lisa. "The Power of Culture." *Journal of Asian American Studies* 1.1 (Feb. 1998): 5–29.

Schlote, Christiane. "Monuments of Protest and War: Literary Representations of Memorial Architecture." In *Anglistentag 2005: Proceedings,* eds. Christoph Houswitschka and Anja Müller. Trier: WVT, 2006. 79–91.

————. "Staging Heterogeneity: Contemporary Asian American Drama." In *Asian American Literary Studies,* ed. Guiyou Huang. Edinburgh: Edinburgh University Press, 2005. 225–245.

Srikanth, Rajini, and Esther Yae Iwanaga, eds. *Bold Words: A Century of Asian American Writing.* New Brunswick, NJ: Rutgers University Press, 2001.

CHRISTIANE SCHLOTE

✦ BARRY, LYNDA (1956–)

Graphic novelist, cartoonist, writer, and playwright Lynda Barry is well-known for her comic strip *Ernie Pook's Comeek.* Barry was born in Richland Center, Wisconsin. Her family moved westward, and she grew up in a multicultural neighborhood in Seattle, Washington. Being biracial, part Filipina and part Caucasian, she fit right into the neighborhood. She graduated from Evergreen State College, where she became friends with Matt Groening, who later created the *Simpsons.* He published some of her comics in the school paper. She later moved to Chicago, Illinois, and began her career.

Lynda Barry created a series of online cartoon strips that she collected into the graphic novel *One Hundred Demons,* which captures the angst of her adolescence. Barry tries to define her work as "autobifictionalography," a multigenre text, part fiction and part reality driven. Not only is the book nonconventional, but her multiracial construct is also nonconventional. Constructs or terms like ***Asian American*** do not seem to work when defining Barry. Other multiracial people have similar problems. For example, on the *Oprah Winfrey Show,* Tiger Woods, whose one parent is African American (black/Indian/white) and the other is Asian American (Chinese/Thai) called himself "Cablinasian," a mixture of Caucasian-black-Indian-Asian. African Americans were quick to point out that the white majority only sees him as black. Lynda Barry does not look Filipina with her red hair and red freckles, and the Asian American label does not quite fit her.

In her colorful graphic narrative *One Hundred Demons,* Lynda Barry illustrates her encounters with 17 demons of her childhood, one per chapter. The unconventional dimension of a 6 × 10 book looks more like a photo album or scrapbook with two panels per page. Indeed, the cover appears like a collage of images, cut and pasted onto the page. The bright colors and fanciful images are more feminine in nature than the haunting drawings of ghosts and monsters found throughout *One Hundred Demons.* Each chapter in her narrative album begins with a two-page splash section, creating a montage effect and functioning as a preview and transition. Usually found within the splash sections are preview panels for the chapter, the words *Today's Demon* on top of the panel, and an assortment of added drawings with a multitude of demons of the moment, appearing to be cut and pasted, or ripped and glued onto the pages. In each chapter, she fights demons of her childhood, such as her worst ex-boyfriend, her first job, hate, resilience, and even the Filipino vampire Aswang.

Added to the format of the text, Barry has opening and closing sections that she calls "Intro" and "Outro" that function much like a preface and epilogue. These sections differ visually from the book as she discusses the meta-process of creating the book. She becomes a character as a mature adult, explaining the origins of a Zen exercise. Barry introduces the innovative narrative device for her text: the Zen painting exercise called "One Hundred Demons," developed by the Japanese monk Hakuin Ekaku (1686–1769). Barry mentions her discovery of this artist in Stephen Addiss's book *The Art of Zen* (1989). Hakuin painted these demons as a way to face his own demons. Zen paintings are usually done in black ink contrasted against white paper. Hakuin's paintings, however, are in color, just as Barry's graphic novel is in color.

One chapter or demon she fights is the Aswang, the Filipino vampire. The Aswang tale introduces an important occurrence for all immigrants: the immigration of cultural fables and morals. The Aswang tale by Lynda Barry explores the relationship between mothers and daughters. Lynda is not close to her mother, but neither is her mother close to her own mother (Lynda's grandmother). The grandmother explains to young Lynda, "When your Mommy first arrive in this country, she thought the Aswang did not follow her. Too much ocean! But the Aswang don't care about the Ocean!" (*One Hundred Demons* 2005, 92). Her mother is not free from the clutches of the Aswang as Lynda's grandmother had told her, and the grandmother reminds her mother of this. Her mother is still haunted by the Aswang in America, especially since her own mother continues to remind her of the horror. Lynda's grandmother seems to taunt her daughter joyfully with the horrors of the Aswang tales.

One of the purposes of the Aswang tale is to warn of the consequences, such as unwanted pregnancies, just as the tale of the "No Name Aunt" in Maxine Hong **Kingston's** *The Woman Warrior* functioned in a similar manner. Filipino women warn girls about the *hiya* (shame) that can occur to women who do not maintain respectable practices. Though Aswangs can be males, Aswangs are more often females, who attack pregnant women, sucking the blood of the unborn. Women are taught to fear Aswangs, who come in many disguises. Some are dogs, while others can be handsome men who take young women away from their families, just as Lynda's mother was taken away to the United States.

Though one can kill an Aswang, one cannot kill gossip or the fear of gossip, so Lynda learned not to communicate the truth to her mother. The less her mother knew, the better. Lynda's mother "didn't know about my secret life" (Barry 2005, 164). Perhaps it is normal for most teenagers not to communicate with their parents. However, this can be even more intense for children of Filipino immigrants, where the relationship is meant to be intimate and interactive. Whenever the mother appears in the book, in some 22 out of 162 panels, she is calling someone a name (usually Lynda), screaming at Lynda, or both screaming and calling Lynda a name. For the most part, yelling at Lynda is the norm. On one occasion, Lynda's mother screams and threatens her with the ultimate revenge that she too will one day experience her own hell by having children (Barry 2005, 95). Since her mother is always abusive, the readers become used to it and start to accept the mother on her own terms. With an abusive relationship between the grandmother and the mother, the cycle of maternal suffering and mistrust is complete.

In the chapter called "Dogs" (2005, 170–180), Lynda Barry writes that she has avoided hell by not having any children. However, Lynda did have dogs. If you ask dog owners if their dogs are their children, many would probably say yes. In some ways, dogs are more childlike, never growing up and leaving, staying obedient even as they age. The story about the origins of this dog reveals much. Physically, the adult Lynda now looks like her mother with her hair tied up in a bun and wearing glasses. Lynda, who is married, decided to save a dog, Ooola, who was badly beaten and wounded from the shelter. She decided to treat the wounded dog the same way she had been treated growing up in an effort to make the dog strong and to teach it who was boss. The turning point was when the dog retaliated and bit her. This bite from the dog parallels an incident in Lynda's childhood when she bit her mother in retaliation for not talking about her stuffed bear in a respectful fashion. Then she remembered how different teachers taught her. Those teachers who were tough and relentless only made Lynda, the child, worse. However, one teacher was kind to her and made a positive impact. Being humane and understanding was more effective than being fierce.

With this insight, the husband and wife started to spoil the dog and gave it a second chance. This worked. The angry dog became a "good" dog. Ooola was not an Aswang waiting for the night to segment into two pieces, to fly off, and to find another victim sleeping in bed, sucking up the nutritious inner organs for sustenance. Instead, Ooola was trusted to sleep on their bed in peace. It is critical to note that Ooola is female because the relationship between Lynda and Ooola parallels her own childhood relationship with her mother. Though they were not able to repair the damage of abuse caused by her mother, Ooola became like a daughter who felt love and trust. Thus, love is possible between a mother and daughter.

By telling such stories, using words to fight words and using visual illusions to fight delusion, Lynda Barry breaks the spell of the Aswang, just as Hakuin broke the spell of his childhood hell by cultivating Zen in painting pictures of Hell. Art is salvation. It is not the artifact that has power to cast a spell upon a person. It is the person attached to the delusion that holds the power. Liberation is freedom from the tongue that sucks one's soul dry: vampires or mothers. **See also** Biraciality.

Further Reading

Barry, Lynda. Archive at Salon.com. <http://dir.salon.com/topics/lynda_barry/index.html>

———. *One Hundred Demons.* Seattle: Sasquatch Books, 2005.

de Jesus, Melinda Luisa. "Of Monsters and Mothers: Filipina American Identity and Maternal Legacies in Lynda J. Barry's *One Hundred Demons.*" *Meridians* 5.1 (2004): 1–26.

———. "Liminality and Mestiza Consciousness in Lynda Barry's *One Hundred Demons.*" *MELUS* 29.1 (2004): 219–252.

Jenkinson, Edward. "Will You Climb Up to the Heavens That Enclose Us Above: A Talk with Lynda Barry, 2000." In *Page to Page: Retrospectives of Writers from the Seattle Review*, ed. Colleen J. Mcelroy. Seattle, WA: University of Washington Press, 2006. 167–177.

Tensuan, Theresa. "Comic Visions and Revisions in the Work of Lynda Barry and Marjane Satrapi." *Modern Fiction Studies* 52.4 (2006): 947–964.

WAYNE STEIN

✦ BATES, JUDY FONG (1949–)

Teacher, storyteller, and fiction writer, Judy Fong Bates was born in China and came to Canada as a young child. She grew up in homes above laundries in several small towns in Ontario. She worked as an elementary school teacher in Toronto before devoting herself to writing. Her stories have been broadcast on CBC radio and published in *Fireweed: A Feminist Quarterly, This Magazine,* and the *Canadian Forum.* She has published *China Dog and Other Tales from a Chinese Laundry* (1997), a collection of short stories, and the much-awaited *Midnight at the Dragon Café* (2004), her debut novel. She lives in Toronto and has taught Asian Canadian writing at the University of Toronto.

Fong Bates's two works of fiction are concerned with the lives of Chinese immigrants as they settle in small towns in Ontario during the 1950s and 1960s. Her stories deal with the shock of arrival, the encounter with European Canadians, who are viewed as the "Other" by the Chinese immigrants, and the protagonists' poignant experiences as they cope with seemingly mundane things such as the winter weather, attending school, driving to Toronto for dim sum, the strange foods that *lo fans* (foreigners) like to eat, and finding a suitable marriage partner in the new land. Fong Bates has been compared to Canadian short story writer Alice Munro, who also often sets her narratives in small towns in Ontario. Both authors excavate the hidden lives of outwardly average folks to reveal the often hidden mysteries, the quirkiness, and the strangeness of everyday life in small towns. The difference between them is that Fong Bates often presents racialized dimensions of what it means to be isolated in a town with one main street, one grocery store, one school, one bakery, one drugstore, and so forth.

Like other **Asian American** writers, Fong Bates explores several issues common to first-generation immigrants, including displacement, alienation, and nostalgia. Her works explore the problems of assimilation, differences between first and second generations, and living in a bicultural world. Although these themes are not new to Asian American literature, Fong Bates is able nevertheless to enthrall readers with her attention to particulars and with her sensual and detailed descriptions of the work that happens in the back rooms of laundries and restaurant kitchens. Her tone is controlled and deliberately unexotic and unsentimental. In *China Dog and Other Tales from a Chinese Laundry,* she depicts the lives of a host of Chinese immigrants who arrived in Canada at the turn of the twentieth century and shortly after World War II. Of the eight short stories, six are set in either a Laundromat or a Chinese restaurant in small towns in Ontario. They depict the aspirations of the immigrants who come with high hopes to Gam Sun, or **Gold Mountain**, only to find an inhospitable climate, grueling working conditions, and loneliness. Most of the characters demonstrate resilience, strength, and an attitude of resignation to their uncomfortable or less-than-ideal circumstances. The immigrants console themselves by thinking that they have led better lives in China, and that they can always return there for a life without discrimination. In "Eat Bitter," Hua Fan, who has been working for five years as his uncle's apprentice in a hot Laundromat, pushes back his memories of humiliation and tries to convince himself that this life in Canada is not his "real life." When he is pelleted with ice by a local ruffian and called "Ching, Ching, China-man," he imagines himself back in his home village, "dressed like a gentleman in fine clothes as he presided over the operations of his teahouse" (Bates 2002, 42, 51). However, the story ends with the fantasy unfulfilled, as the longed-for trip to China is deferred because the smooth running of the Laundromat necessitates Hua Fan's constant presence in Canada.

In "My Sister's Love," the newly arrived, elegantly dressed half-sister from Hong Kong looks with amazement and disdain at the meager and working-class atmosphere of the home/workplace of the Laundromat owned by her family. She eyes the washing machine standing like a "monstrous steel barrel," and "swallowed as she looked at the four burner coal stove with an oven" (Bates 2002, 13). The move from cosmopolitan Hong Kong to Cheatley, Ontario, with a population of 2,000, is shown to be a disappointment and a step down for the sister. The Chinese Canadian family is depicted as "coarse, tough, and sinuous" compared to the "tall, elegant, and exquisite" sister (11). The family makes do with old winter coats donated by the ladies from the Presbyterian church, while the sister has a new tailor-made wool coat from Hong Kong. Dallying with a rich, older man with a fancy car, the sister settles by the end of the story for the hollow-chested and severely pockmarked Chinese accountant whom her mother has arranged for her to marry. Through poignant metaphors and nuanced descriptions of their daily lives, Fong Bates reveals the compromises and disappointments of these first-generation Chinese Canadian settlers. However, instead of wallowing in despair or negativity, the attitude of the characters in Fong Bates's stories is usually one of stoic acceptance or quiet resignation. Rather than lamenting the lack of riches in Gold

Mountain, the immigrants find resourceful ways of dealing with their lowly social status in the community and the harsh working conditions they face, whether it is the extreme heat all day in the Laundromats or the unappreciative customers in their restaurants. There are small feuds and economic rivalries between families and immigrant groups, but these are depicted with gentle irony and humor. Generally, the Chinese settlers form strong bonds with other immigrants, help each other whenever they can, and console themselves with the thought that their children will not suffer the same kinds of discrimination as they have, and will not have to work in menial jobs as they do.

Fong Bates's novel *Midnight at the Dragon Café* is once again set in a Chinese restaurant, this time in the fictional small town of Irvine, Ontario. The narrative is told mainly from the perspective of Su-Jen, who arrives in 1957 at the age of six. A child's innocence adds a level of sweetness, sadness, and wonder to this typical story of an immigrant family struggling for a better life in a new land. Su-Jen describes with awe the first time she sees a family with their own refrigerator and electric stove or the first snowfall, and provides a firsthand account of the customers who patronize the greasy spoon with its Formica counters and red vinyl stools. Father and Mother both advise Su-Jen to work hard and to *hek-fuh* (swallow bitterness). At school, Su-Jen goes through a predictable pattern of a second-generation immigrant: she learns to speak English, makes friends with an artistic girl, and encounters a bully, but at home the isolated family lives a tangled life of abnegation and secrecy. While Su-Jen's world expands and develops, her mother's world becomes smaller, as she is unable to make friends easily or to speak to her neighbors with her limited language skills. The mother continues to cook traditional Chinese foods, herbs, and medicines and to pay homage to the spirit of her ancestors. In her desperate loneliness and unhappiness, the mother turns to her stepson (by marriage) for consolation and love, creating more confusion and turmoil in the family. The novel is at once a *bildungsroman*, an ethnographic account of a Chinese Canadian family, and a Gothic tale set in a small town. Fong Bates reveals the family tensions, repressed emotions, and dreams of the seemingly perfect immigrant family who blended so seamlessly into the everyday life of the town and thus remained invisible. **See also** Assimilation/Americanization.

Further Reading

Bates, Judy Fong. *China Dog and Other Tales from a Chinese Laundry*. New York: Counterpoint, 2002.

Cuder-Domínguez, Pilar. "In Conversation with Judy Fong Bates." *Commonwealth: Essays and Studies* 28.1 (Fall 2005): 119–125.

Ng, Maria N. "Chop Suey Writing: Sui Sin Far, Wayson Choy, and Judy Fong Bates." *Essays in Canadian Writing* 65 (Fall 1998): 171–186.

ELEANOR TY

✦ BERSSENBRUGGE, MEI-MEI (1947–)

Chinese American poet, playwright, educator, and collaborator of small press, fine art books, Mei-mei Berssenbrugge was born in Beijing of a Dutch American father and a Chinese mother. Her family immigrated to the United States when she was only one, eventually settling in Massachusetts, where her father pursued a graduate degree in Far East studies at Harvard. The early linguistic shift from Chinese to English produced a vivid childhood imagination of comparison and proportion, which developed an inherent sensibility for the relativity of meaning and expression, a theme that would become central to her work and the insight that drew her at such a young age to poetry.

Berssenbrugge attended Barnard College for a year before transferring to Reed College, where she studied with Galway Kinnell, whose influence with experimental American poetry attracted important American poets Robert Bly and Robert Duncan, both of whom were hosted by the Brussenbrugges, who cooked and threw parties after readings. Completing her baccalaureate degree from Reed College in 1969, she immediately entered Columbia University where she earned an MFA in 1973.

Eager for new experiences after graduate school, she settled in northern New Mexico where she still resides with her husband, artist Richard Tuttle, and her daughter, Martha. The expansive geography and shifting light of the American Southwest has become synonymous with her work. In New Mexico she knew the prominent American painters Georgia O'Keefe and Agnes Martin before teaching at the Institute for American Indian Art in Santa Fe and cofounding the literary journal *Tyuonyi*. She has also taught at Brown University and has been a contributing editor to *Conjunctions* magazine since 1978. Her work has won two American Book Awards, two Asian American Book Awards, and she has received two grants from the National Endowment for the Arts.

Mei-mei Berssenbrugge is prominently known for her critically acclaimed books of poetry, whose long, expansive lines shift and flicker through multiple perspectives, authorial agency, and emotive states, but her early association with the experimental literary, theater, and dance group known as the Multicultural Movement produced the play *One, Two Cups,* which was directed by Chinese American writer/director Frank **Chin**. During this period she also collaborated with the Morita Dance Company, directed by Theodora Yashikama and was anthologized with the *Aiiieeeee!* group. She forged lifelong friendships with its members, which included Leslie Silko, Ishmael Reed, Frank Chin, and his wife, the political activist Kathleen Chang. She has also been an Artist-in-the-School in Alaska and New Mexico, where she taught creative writing workshops.

In the 1970s Berssenbrugge published her first 3 (of 12) books and collaborative projects, which include *Fish Souls* (Greenwood Press, 1971), *Summits Move with the Tide* (Greenfield Review Press, 1974), and *Random Possession* (Reed Books, 1979), which won the American Book Award. Together with *The Heat Bird* (Burning Deck

Press, 1983), her fourth book of poetry, these early books begin her explorations of identity, linguistic alienation, bodily isolation, and femininity and mark the beginning of her deep, philosophic engagement with phenomenology and multiperspectival perception, which have become central concerns of her work. In *Summits Move with the Tide,* with comparatively shorter lines, stanzas, and poems than her later work, Berssenbrugge explores the continuum between the material and immaterial with drastic shifts in scale and stunning parataxis that splice deep personal emotion with vivid and vast geographical descriptions of the indigenous land of the Pueblo and Hopi tribes living on reservations in New Mexico. Performing complex processes of emotive perception that meticulously interrogate the materiality of language as social code, Berssenbrugge's poems compress subject and object relations, exposing language's alienative capacity and yet releasing its aleatory potential to create multiplicities of subjective energy for reception. Her poems also effectively destabilize previous literary models of stable authorship and authority, while simultaneously creating an emotional resonance and a spiritual affinity with the Native Americans whose post-colonial displacement and isolation become charged environments to explore her own cultural duality.

Random Possession is perhaps the book whose title best describes Berssenbrugge's working process, which is a combination of appropriation, collage, and written mediation. Throughout the production of a poem, Berssenbrugge focuses on sustained reading projects engaged with the ideas she wishes to explore. Simultaneously studying a relevant piece of Eastern philosophy and a relevant piece of Western philosophy as part of the research for her poems, she cuts through, transposes, and recalibrates apparent discrepancies between polarities of perception such as East/West, object/subject, and single/multiple and recasts perceived objective limits as emotionally charged temporary states of moving liminality. Within these crafted spaces, subjectivity is more similar in its coming undone than different in its bound individuality. Witnessing the masculine language and privilege of scientific discourse, *Random Possession* encompasses the beginnings of Berssenbrugge's ongoing project of feminizing the language of science and in so doing continually reveals language's often unquestioned social and cultural codes. The poems begin to be serialized over several pages, and the temporal structure of their lyrics starts to become a matter of shifting indeterminacy, overlapping imagery, and emanating syllabic reverberations. Images of animals, humans, geography, and myths repeat over the extending surfaces of Berssenbrugge's lengthening lines, which begin to encroach the standard space of the margin. Paradoxically, the effect is nonlinear and works on the reader perceptually like the points of a constellation.

In *Empathy* (1989) Berssenbrugge's lines reach their longest. The book's physical shape is wider to accommodate the protracted expansions of her multiperspectival sentences, which sometimes wrap through four to five of these extended horizontal spaces.

Much like the wide, open austerity of the landscapes of New Mexico and Alaska that Berssenbrugge is drawn to, her lines shift with the varying intensities of light moving across a wide horizontal space, yet feel intimate like intricately felt subjective states of perception as one risks his or her alterity to become closer to another. Empathy in its extreme form is to become the other, and in *Empathy* Berssenbrugge networks human emotion and intimacy with the expanses of the environment and the elements: from melting ice to jealousy, from fog to desire, from confidence to particles, and what remains is the relativity of intimacy and expression. Perhaps her most visual book, *Empathy* continues Berssenbrugge's active engagement with the history of Chinese culture and poetry through complexities of philosophic inquiry rooted in nature. At these interrogations of the borders and limits of a subject and what it observes, Berssenbrugge is able to explore a poetic ethics of intimacy and engagement. "Alakanak Break-Up" and "Fog" were written in collaboration with the choreography of Theodora Yoshikami for the Morita Dance Company while traveling between the mainland and Alaska. The poem "Honeymoon" appeared in a different form as *Hiddenness* (1987), one of several of Berssenbrugge's collaborations with visual artists, but it was during this collaboration that she met her husband, Richard Tuttle.

In addition to Richard Tuttle, with whom she has collaborated twice, on *Hiddenness* and *Sphericity* (1993), Berssenbrugge has also collaborated twice with the artist Kiki Smith on *Endocrinology* (1997) and *Concordance* (2006).

Hiddenness uses a metaphor to explore the way a material object can hide or hold light and spirituality. The text explores the way light can be hidden or escape through different layers of material and works on three distinct levels. The first level is slightly under the page. The text literally recapitulates the process of light escaping material, as the letters and words are pressed in, or incised into, the surface. Richard Tuttle's highly colorful shapes are *of* the page because they are mixed into the pulp of the paper, forming the intermediary level. And the outer layer is represented by a number of hand-stamped shapes that are pressed on top of the page throughout the book and made from burning different types of wood. Another way the collaboration explores the physical light in the book is by shifting the blocks of text into unusual relationships with the margins, sometimes printing across them, creating varying degrees of spatial fluctuation between and of the text. *Sphericity* is the second of Berssenbrugge's collaborations with her husband. It collects a series of his drawings, which are printed in relation to Berssenbrugge's text.

Endocrinology is Berssenbrugge's first collaboration with the artist Kiki Smith. Continuing her explorations of the continuum between the material and the immaterial, this book literally represents, through the monoprints of Kiki Smith, the human endocrine system, which is responsible for the transference of nearly imperceptible hormones into the undeniable trajectory of behavior. Exploring the transparency and transience of the body, the original book was printed on a rice paper that closely resembles skin. Berssenbrugge, tired of writing in the long hovering lines that she has become known for, approached Kiki Smith with five stanzas of poetry. They proceeded by layering the imagery so that various traces of previous layers could be seen through the thinness of the rice paper, mirroring the way a vein might show through skin. Berssenbrugge proceeded to cut up her stanzas and disperse them throughout the book more or less randomly. *Endocrinology* produces a visual and literary space of transparent mirroring, in which the systems of the human body are equated to the system of writing; but most apparent is that the codes of language exist concretely in the body, and, placed as they are within a system like the endocrine system, the potential for change is ever-present. *Concordance* is the second and most recent collaboration between Mei-mei Berssenbrugge and Kiki Smith, which explores the contingent and parallel worlds of the animal body and the human body with imagery of birds, feathers, pods, and stars interspersed throughout and under Berssenbrugge's poetic texts. The effect is a paradoxical one, when held in relation to dominant modern paradigms of humanism—which hold that culture itself is a progressive and linear process within which the human is continually distancing from the animal. In *Concordance,* however, the human and the animal coexist and in fact merge with each other and with their environment to create a unified perceptual space of multiple subjective registers.

Four Year Old Girl (1998) and *Nest* (2003) explore the relationship between the competing domestic space of motherhood and identity. Using the language of genetic code to explore alterity, *Four Year Old Girl* uses a thin graphic box around the first page of each poem, objectifying it as the original thought or idea for the poem that follows. The box is absent from each proceeding page, or stage of the poem, stressing the serialized nature of what follows. Emphasizing a transitory and copied process while using the scientific language of genetics, Berssenbrugge creates something equitable to a poem species, capturing a literal and objective embodiment of the varying and unstable shifts between the immateriality of idea and the linguistic object.

Nest investigates the differences among Berssenbrugge's several familial mother tongues, audience, and margins. Suggesting that one's mother tongue or identity exists in the unstable, unfixed area of the margins, Berssenbrugge explores the errant and the erring as spaces for productive identity. The poems are serialized but remain distinct from all of her other work in that they emphasize the spaces between their sentences with wide areas of blank space between each line, allowing the book's central concern—the margins—to run through the text and dominate the spaces of the poem. In "Hearing" and "Audience" Berssenbrugge explores the audience as margin and reciprocity, where the social space of the audience and the energy of hearing become a fluid force field of connectivity.

In *I Love Artists: New and Selected Poems* (2006), Berssenbrugge investigates the many collusions of art and life by rendering the working processes of various artist friends with highly descriptive language. Contextualized by her selected poems, the new poems for *I Love Artists: New and Selected Poems* continue to question the separation among subject and object and split consciousness and posit, through long reverberating resonance of line, that meaning is just a temporary place, generally in the human animal, on a plane, moving like a filter, grid, or sieve, and that true differences are in potential.

Further Reading

Alteri, Charles. "Intimacy and Experiment in Mei-mei Berssenbrugge's *Empathy*." January 2008. Electronic Poetry Center Web site. www.epc.buffalo.edu/authors/berssenbrugge.

Bernstein, Charles. "Berssenbrugge in Conversation with Charles Bernstein." January 2008. Close Listening Web site. www.writing.upenn.edu/pennsound/X/berssenbrugge.html.

———. "Mei-mei Berssenbrugge and Charles Bernstein: A Dialogue." January 2008. Electronic Poetry Center Web site. www.epc.buffalo.edu/authors/berssenbrugge.

Hinton, Laura. "Three Conversations with Mei-mei Berssenbrugge, 2003." January 2008. From *Jacket Magazine* 27 (2005). www.jacketmagazine.com/27/hint-bers.html.

Martin, Camille. "Radial Dialectics in the Experimental Poetry of Berssenbrugge, Hejinian, Harryman, Weiner, and Scalapino." PhD Diss., Louisiana State University and A&M College, May 2003.

Zhou, Xiaojing. "Blurring the Boundaries between Formal and Social Aesthetics: An Interview With Mei-mei Berssenbrugge." January 2008. B Net Web site. http://findarticles.com/p/articles/mi_m2278/is_1_27/ai_89929580.

WARREN LLOYD

✦ BIRACIALITY

Biraciality describes those who are of mixed racial ancestries. The seemingly monoracial Asian American community was preserved because interracial marriage was legally banned, and the Asian American community was segregated from the mainstream American society, so it was rare that Asian Americans married outside of the group. However, interracial couples between Asian Americans and non-Asian Americans have existed throughout American history since the first Asian immigrants set foot on the American shore. Biraciality has therefore never been a recent phenomenon. In fact, the first Asian American writer is said to be a Eurasian, Sui Sin Far (Edith Maude **Eaton**). When the antimiscegenation law was abolished in 1967 by the Supreme Court, supported by the **civil rights movement**, more and more Asian Americans outmarried, and now it is reported that 30 to 60 percent of Asian Americans marry non-Asian Americans. The fact that the U.S. Census now allows people to mark more than one racial category proves the increasing number of biracial people in the United States. Biraciality is now conspicuous, not only in the Asian American community but also in Asian American literature. There are many biracial Asian American writers such as Nora Okja **Keller**, Jessica **Hagedorn**, and Velina Hasu **Houston**, to name just a few, and they address issues of biraciality in their works.

There are two main arguments regarding biraciality in Asian American literary studies. One is that biraciality may threaten the unity of Asian Americans. The umbrella term *Asian American* has been controversial, given the diversity of Asian American populations. The term has been criticized because it cannot contain the different experiences that each Asian American individual or group has undergone. Yet, as a minority in America, claiming political and social demands separately is not effective. It is strategically useful for all Asian Americans to unite under the umbrella term *Asian American* and voice together for their existence and demands. As a community, Asian Americans have achieved many political, cultural, and social rights. Asian American literature has become an important American cultural asset. Some are therefore anxious that biraciality may destroy the unity of Asian Americans and make their political, cultural, and social activities ineffective.

In addition to the uneasiness biraciality provokes in the Asian American community, some Asian American writers express identity problems. Kimiko **Hahn**, a biracial poet of a Japanese American mother and a German American father, expresses her anxiety of being biracial in "The Hemisphere: Kuchuk Hanem" in *The Unbearable Heart*. She writes that when she is with her white father, she is afraid that people may think that she is his sexual companion because they do not resemble each other. Kip Fulbeck, a son of a Chinese mother and a Caucasian father, also attests in *Paper Bullets* that he was troubled by a white "rice chaser" woman who wanted to date Asian men. Because the body of Asians is highly eroticized and exoticized in the United States, having a part of Asian blood makes biracial Asian Americans sexually marked, and that gives them a troubling feeling of being biracial. Hahn and Fulbeck's texts illustrate how biraciality is related strongly to the questions of gender and sexuality and how it complicates family relations as Hahn has shown.

Against the negative views on biraciality, some see its positive force. America's racial hierarchy, which holds whiteness at its top, has functioned as the basis of racism and justified it. Asian Americans have been discriminated against because of the white-centered racial setting. Yet, biraciality, the possibility of racial mixing, reveals that race is never a fixed entity but rather contingent and changeable. Thus, biraciality is in a possible position to challenge the white-centered American racial hierarchy. The mixed-race movement is born out of this expectation. People who push this movement believe that biraciality could overcome the racial stratification of American society and enable interracial coalition.

It is however not certain to what extent biraciality really challenges the deep-rooted American racial hierarchy because the degree of social acceptance is different in terms of whom Asian Americans mix with. It is reported that biracial people are divided between a color line. Biracial people who have Asian and black parents tend to associate themselves with African Americans. Since the notorious one-drop rule, which means that a drop of black blood makes a person black, still functions in the American imaginary, biracial Asian Americans with black parents find that they are associated more with blacks than with Asian Americans. Tiger Woods, the internationally acclaimed golfer of a Thai mother and an African American father, is usually referred to as a black golfer in the media, although he identifies himself as Asian American. His case shows the persistence of the one-drop rule. Frank Wu points out that while many Asian Americans try to climb the racial, class, and social ladder by marrying whites, they marry less to blacks. As a result, outmarried Asian Americans are 30 times more likely to have white spouses than black spouses. Some critics, such as Michael Omi, find the mixed-race movement risky, because if racial mixing between white Americans and Asian Americans is preferred, it may create a new dichotomy between blacks and nonblacks, by which blacks remain a lower social class and are left out of the melting pot practice other groups enjoy.

On the other hand, biracial people who have Asian and white parents find it easy to pass as either an Asian American or a white American. Some Asian Americans who have white parents try to pass as white because whiteness grants them more privilege in white-centered American society. Anne Xuan Clark illustrates the internalized racism in her short essay "What Are You?" in *Intersecting Circles: The Voices of Hapa Women in Poetry and Prose.* She writes that at one point of her life, she was ashamed of her Vietnamese mother and was proud of her white father. She confesses that she internalized the racist assumption that white was favorable and nonwhite was shameful.

In both cases, biracial people find difficulty in perfectly belonging to any of their parents' groups. Some feel they belong nowhere. Yet, as Clark has concluded that she is Asian American, biracial Asian Americans may feel attachment to Asian Americans, regardless of the polemic over biraciality.

There are many debates over biraciality, but as the outmarriage rate shows, approximately half of Asian Americans now outmarry, and this trend will continue. As the visibility of biraciality in the Asian American community increases, more biracial writers now address biracial issues. As Asian American literature has expanded its horizon with social and historical changes, biracial Asian American writers open the threshold of Asian American literature beyond the color line. They complicate the already complicated term *Asian American.* They question who Asian Americans are in their works, challenge our fixed notion of Asian American identity, and disclose our/their internalized racial, gender, and class biases. Biraciality thus now takes an important position in the development of Asian American literature. **See also** Racism and Asian America.

Further Reading

Hara, Marie, and Nora Okja Keller, eds. *Intersecting Circles: The Voices of Hapa Women in Poetry and Prose.* Honolulu: Bamboo Ridge Press, 1999.

Williams-León, Teresa, and Cynthia Nakashima, eds. *The Sum of Our Parts: Mixed-Heritage Asian Americans.* Philadelphia: Temple University Press, 2001.

KAORI MORI

✦ BRAINARD, CECILIA MANGUERRA (1947–)

A Filipino American essayist, novelist, anthologist, and short story writer, Cecilia Manguerra Brainard was born on November 21, 1947. She attended St. Theresa's College in Cebu and Manila and from 1964 to 1968 Maryknoll College in Quezon City, from which she graduated with a BA in communication arts. She studied film-making at UCLA in 1969 and 1971 but later concentrated on creative writing. A self-described freelance writer since 1981, she has published, as author or editor, 14 books, some 36 short stories, and over 300 essays. Her work has brought her an array of awards, both Philippine and American. The former include the Makati Rotarian Award (1994), the Outstanding Individual Award from the City of Cebu (1998), the Amazing Alumni Achiever's Award from Maryknoll College (2003), and a Certificate of Recognition from the Cebu Provincial Government through the Provincial Women's Commission (2006). The latter include a Special Recognition Award, Los Angeles Board of Education (1991), a City of Los Angeles Certificate of Appreciation (1992), and a Certificate of Recognition from the California State Senate, 21st District (2001). These accolades denote appreciation for her overall contributions, not just for her literary works, although she has been the recipient of these as well (e.g., a 1989–1990 California Arts Council Artists' Fellowship in Fiction, a 1990–1991 City of Los Angeles Cultural Grant, a 1991 Brady Arts Fellowship, a 1992 Literature Award from the Filipino Women's Network, a 2000 California State Summer School for the Arts Award, and a 2001 *Filipinas Magazine* Achievement Award for Arts and Culture).

Brainard's ability to be multifaceted is revealed in the age range of audiences she is able to serve. She has edited or coedited two anthologies of children's stories: *Seven Stories from Seven Sisters: A Collection of Philippine Folktales* (1992) and *The Beginning and Other Asian Folktales* (1995). For adolescents, she has produced *Growing Up Filipino: Stories for Young Adults* (2003) and her autobiographical *Cecilia's Diary*

1962–1969 (2003). For adult consumption are her novels *Song of Yvonne* (1991, reissued under the title *When the Rainbow Goddess Wept* (1994), and *Magdalena* (2002); and her short story collections *Woman with Horns and Other Stories* (1987) and *Acapulco at Sunset and Other Stories* (1995). Another important contribution to **Filipino American literature** is the fiction anthologies that she has edited or coedited: *Fiction by Filipinos in America* (1993), *Contemporary Fiction by Filipinos in America* (1998), and *A La Carte: Food & Fiction* (2007).

In *Philippine Woman in America* (1991), the reader can glimpse Brainard the person and even sample the background of some of her fiction. All but two of the essays (mostly published in the *Philippine American* between 1982 and 1988) are written in the first person and have the chatty, charming quality of the familiar essay. Some, as Brainard notes, "served as a kind of draft for some stories" (vi). *Cecilia's Diary* also provides autobiographical insights. Although precocious as a writer, Brainard has been cautious about publication. Of the items acknowledged in her curriculum vitae, the earliest to see print was "The Discovery," in *Mr. & Ms. Magazine* in July 1982 and included in *Woman with Horns*. Nominally a short story, it reads as much like an essay as it does a work of fiction and as such may represent a transition from nonfiction to fiction writing. Four years after her first short story collection (*Woman with Horns*), her first novel (*Song of Yvonne*) appeared, and four years after that a second, much larger short story collection, *Acapulco at Sunset*. The even, unhurried interspersing of short story collections and novels has continued with *Magdalena*. The intertwining of the two genres is also manifested in the interconnections between short stories, making the stories resemble chapters in a novel. For instance, "Woman with Horns," the opening selection in the collection of the same name, is narratively related to "Trinidad's Broach" and "The Balete Tree" and "Miracle at Santo Nino Church," which is likewise linked to the next story, "Waiting for Papa's Return." Again, elements of the short stories find their way into the novels (e.g., the mythic quality of a story such as "The Magic Spring" from *Woman with Horns* is a prominent element of *Song of Yvonne*).

Brainard's short stories, with their unitary plots and narrative stances, are often so pellucid that they can appear to lack thematic substance. In particular, the 17 tales in *Acapulco at Sunset,* especially those set in late eighteenth-century Mexico, can come across as mere vignettes, even idylls. Yet these stories raise issues of life and death (through characters from each state conversing), appearance versus reality (Are the dreams of characters a mechanism for enlarging the scope of reality or escaping into fantasy?), and identity versus inauthenticity (What status does a green card bestow?). Even the setting of a story may be an important identity variable rather than a signifier. The 12 stories in *Women with Horns,* for instance, are anchored in Ubec (Brainard's native Cebu spelled backward). This reversal may suggest that stereotypical male/female roles are equally reversed, granted that all but one of the stories revolve around strong, successful women. These stories, with settings at crucial historical junctures, are also reminders that identity is an accretion, both historical and personal, rather than an implantation by a single occurrence.

"1521" involves the battle between Lapu-Lapu and Magellan but revolves around a central character, Old Healer. Her emblematic name is indicative of her universality and sets the chronological stage for other fictional settings—in both short stories and novels—in conquest contexts. "Alba" ("dawn" or "daybreak" in Spanish) is an obviously ironic title, granted that in 1763 the English occupied Manila, but the result was not a new day of freedom resulting from the temporary expulsion of the Spaniards; rather, it was a substitution of one invading European power for another. Another case in point is "The Black Man in the Forest," set in 1901, during the Philippine-American War, the result of which was the U.S. colonization of the country. Brainard's later short fiction is also replete with serious motifs. "Tiya Octavia: 1943," published in 2003, starts out with a palate-appealing description of a kitchen with frying bananas and white rice but quickly changes to a sordid rape scene in which a Japanese officer precedes two enlisted men in violating Octavia. "Romeo," published in 2007, is about a 65-year-old woman and a dog, living by themselves in Manila. Although we enter a world of such settled domesticity that we are privy to the desires of the dog, we are apprised of a mugging in which the woman's earrings are ripped from her ears, and the resultant wounds must be treated by a doctor.

Magdalena has an episodic structure reinforced by the absence of chapter numbers and the presence of looping flashbacks. We open in 1966–1967, flash back to 1930, fast forward to 1939 and then to 1942, before reverting to 1912 and then to 1926. The novel's narrative ends in 1968. Thus, the reader appreciates the family flow chart between the prologue and the first chapter. The structure mirrors the unsettled, if not unstable, nature of relationships articulated in the narrative of the pregnant Juana. Her mother Magdalena (whose name is appropriate to her long-suffering fidelity to an unworthy husband) dies in childbirth. Victor (perhaps a fitting name for a successful womanizer) immediately after their wedding starts living with a mistress and has an infant son (ironically named Inocencio) by her. A parallel plot development involves Tiya ("aunt" in Tagalog) Estrella and her unfaithful husband Esteban. Estrella's daughter withers and dies at age seven. Another juxtaposed marital situation involves Luisa and Nestor a generation earlier. Nestor is another two-timer, eventually marrying Cora, so Luisa lives with Fermin. The latter had been running around with a floozy named Chi-Chi and has, thanks to generations of inbreeding, six physically and/or mentally defective immediate family members. This situation is the most palpable manifestation of the dysfunctional domestic relationships in the novel. Although the plot might seem soap opera-level, Brainard ballasts it, as she does in much of her fiction, with a scene of wartime atrocity: Japanese soldiers invade the house of Fermin's aunt and murder the occupants, including the feeble-minded ones. Another tragedy involves the senseless death, ironically on Good Friday, of Mario Cepeda, who has been goaded by Nestor and Junior Hernandez to descend into an abandoned mine. The boy misses a step on the ladder and plunges to his death. Not long thereafter, a miner who has been talking about organizing a labor union is found dead at the bottom of the same shaft. Later Junior commits suicide by throwing himself down a different shaft. Near the end of the book, a typhoon wreaks havoc, but, though graves in the cemetery are damaged to the point that bodies wash out, the mausoleums of the wealthy and prominent Hernandez and Delgado families sustain only minor damage. These events impress on readers that human existence is as transient as its intimate associations are ephemeral.

Song of Yvonne, however, remains Brainard's pièce de résistance. It is set during the Japanese occupation and narrated by nine-year-old Yvonne Macaraig. This narrative stance—though facilitating some light-hearted moments, as when, at confession, Yvonne numbers "concupiscence" among her sins but of course has no idea what the word means—imposes a sometimes significant restriction. As in *Cecilia's Diary,* Brainard is compelled to endow her child narrator with adult sensitivities and speech patterns to render adult material.

Song of Yvonne attempts to elevate the implications of a crisis period in Philippine history to cosmic proportions; Layden, the family cook, is the principal means of doing so. In recounting ancient myths, Layden assumes the role of the *babaylan* (pre-Hispanic priestess) and thus provides both physical nourishment (food) and spiritual sustenance, but her epic tales undermine narrative credibility, minimize the horror of the atrocities depicted, and are digressive. In the former regard, Layden, who has temporarily lost her bardic voice, dreams that she drinks from a spring and thereby recovers this voice. In chapter 5 of the novel she locates the spring and, having recovered her voice, "sang through the night until dawn." She reports that "I saw Inuk [the prototypical bardic seer] . . . riding a cloud shaped like a boat to heaven" (45). Evidently, we should take this literally. The brutalities of war include an episode in which an American nurse is captured by the Japanese and impregnated, has her tongue cut out, her arms cut off, and her eyes put out—and then she is released. The myths tend to mute the tragedies because the epic hero always triumphs and the dead are frequently reconstituted by magical means. Layden's recital of the legend of the goddess Meybuyan, who has breasts all over her body to nourish the infants too young to cross the underground river into the afterlife, may gloss over the horror of an incident like the immolation of innocent Japanese shopkeeper Sanny and her baby by Filipinos because the legend implies all will somehow be made right in the hereafter. Other myths are not integrated into the plot (e.g., the beautiful maiden who spins rainbows and is rescued by the hero Tuwang or the woman warrior Bongkatolan, who killed a dozen attackers of her brother Agyu). These stories, designed to enrich the consistent Brainard motif of strong, successful women, dilute coherence and impede narrative flow.

Song of Yvonne is a *bildungsroman;* Yvonne grows into adolescence, her menstruation symbolizing not only her own passage into adulthood but also the resurgence of life in the face of death during wartime; her blood starkly contrasts with wartime bloodshed. The novel's universality lies partially in its implication, as a distinguished critic has suggested, that just as a youth grows into independence, so does a country. Filipinos realize that though they welcome American aid, they cannot afford to wait for it or even depend on it; the Philippines must free itself. Although it may be that, in a macrocosmic sense, no one is an island, perhaps in a microcosmic sense a period of peril in a nation of islands requires that everyone be one.

Further Reading

Brainard, Cecilia Manguerra. "Cecilia Manguerra Brainard." www.ceciliabrainard.com.

———. "Introduction." In *Philippine Woman in America: Essays by Cecilia Manguerra Brainard.* Quezon City: New Day, 1991. v–vi.

———. *Song of Yvonne.* Quezon City: New Day, 1991.

Casper, Leonard. "Cause of Birth Undetermined." In Casper, *Sunsurfers Seen from Afar.* Pasig City: Anvil, 1996. 81–84.

———. "Song of Yvonne: Possibilities of Humaneness in an Age of Slaughter." *Philippine Studies* 41 (1993): 251–254; rpt. in Casper, *Sunsurfers Seen from Afar.* Pasig City: Anvil, 1996. 75–80.

Grow, L.M. Rev. of Cecilia Manguerra Brainard, *Song of Yvonne. Heritage* 6.4 (1992): 35–36, rpt. in Grow, *And Quiet Flows the Dawn.* Quezon City: Giraffe Books, 2003. 77–79.

Guerrero, Amadis Ma. "Another Filipina Wins Acclaim for Novel." *Philippine Daily Inquirer* 15 Mar 1996: sec. E: 1.

Villanueva, Marianne. "Realities and Myths of War." *Philippine News* 23–29 Nov 1994: sec. B: 6.

L. M. GROW

✦ BULOSAN, CARLOS (1911–1956)

A Filipino American poet, short story writer, autobiographer, editor, journalist, and novelist, Carlos Bulosan is among the most famous writers of **Filipino American literature.** He is best known for the fictionalized autobiography ***America Is in the Heart*** (1946) and for his consistent political and cultural engagement with issues of racial, class, and ethnic hierarchy. Bulosan was born into a relatively impoverished farming family in the village of Mangusmana near Binalonan, Pangasinan, in 1911. His formal education extended into two years of high school, and in 1930 he migrated to the United States, following the path laid out by his older brothers Dionisio and

Aurelio. Never having the opportunity to return to the Philippines, Bulosan spent most of the rest of his life on the West Coast, often moving from place to place. He worked primarily as a labor organizer of agricultural and cannery workers in the states of California and Washington. Between 1936 and 1938, Bulosan spent two years in the Los Angeles county hospital, being treated for tuberculosis. During his convalescence, he read widely and began writing poetry in earnest. Although the **World War II** years of the 1940s proved to be Bulosan's most prolific period and the height of his popularity, a plagiarism case brought against him in 1944 (which was settled out of court), and the dark turn toward anticommunism in both the United States and the Philippines following the war seem to have contributed to the waning of his reputation. He died in a sanatorium in Seattle in 1956. However, since the republication of *America Is in the Heart* by the University of Washington Press in 1973, along with the publication of previously unseen texts, Bulosan's work has again become known. It now holds a central place within the field of Asian American literary studies.

Bulosan arrived in Seattle during the first period of massive Filipino immigration to the United States. Following the forcible annexation of the Philippines by the United States because of the Philippine-American War (1899–1902), Filipinos were allowed unrestricted entry into the United States due to their colonial status as "nationals." By 1930, there were over 45,000 Filipinos living in the United States, the majority of them working as migrant agricultural laborers on the West Coast. As the depression deepened, anti-Filipino sentiments and xenophobic movements swept through cities and towns in California, targeting Filipinos on the grounds of racial difference, alleged economic competition, and interracial sexual politics. These social and political conditions would have a marked influence on Bulosan's literary production.

Bulosan began his writing career as a poet. Within two years of immigrating to the United States, he published his first poems in the anthology *California Poets* (1932). In 1934, he coedited a small magazine titled the *New Tide: A Magazine of Contemporary Literature*, which included his poem "Cry against Chaos," short stories by his compatriots Chris Mensalvas and José Garcia **Villa**, and stories and poems by other U.S. writers. From the mid-1930s through the World War II period, Bulosan continued to publish poems in such venues as the *Lyric, Frontier and Midland*, the *Tramp, Voices, Saturday Review of Literature,* and *Poetry* magazine. His literary education was aided by Sanora and Dorothy Babb, close friends who brought him books to read while he recovered in the Los Angeles county hospital. As Bulosan describes this episode in *America Is in the Heart,* he averaged a book a day, devouring a plethora of material, ranging from Marxist theory to world history to lyrical poetry. Legendary *Poetry* magazine editor Harriet Monroe also encouraged Bulosan's poetic endeavors, and she published several of his poems before her premature death in 1936.

Many of these early poems were collected in Bulosan's first book, *Letter from America* (1942). Dedicated to his brother Aurelio, the volume consists of five parts, each of which is framed by a "Passage from Life" fragment. The poems themselves cover a variety of topics: recollections of the poet's homeland ("Letter in Exile: I," "Who Saw the Terror," "Patterns in Black and White," "Letter to America: II"), insistent claims on and criticisms of the United States ("American History," "All the Living Fear," "Last Will and Testament," "Interlude of Dreams and Responsibilities"), and lamentations on poverty, loneliness, hunger, violence, and death ("Biography," "These Are Also Living," "Night Piece," "For a Child Dying in a Tenement"). Stylistically, Bulosan's poems are neither formally innovative nor transparently straightforward. He often eschews narrative linearity for odd juxtapositions of images. The ambiguity that results is further reflected in the way that the poetic voice weaves metaphorical descriptions of the outside world with a lyric "I," whose dimensions shift from the personal to the collective. Similarly, Bulosan frequently employs an indeterminate second-person ("you"), whose addressees include the poet's brother, a U.S. figure or reader, or an intimate lover. The volume as a whole is notable in that it shows Bulosan's poetic imagination extending well beyond the prosaic mode of hard-hitting social critique (for which he is best known) and experimenting with diction, metaphor, and the non sequitur.

Bulosan's second book, the poetry collection *The Voice of Bataan* (1943), is quite different from *Letter from America,* having been written in the midst of World War II as a response to the fall of Bataan (the Philippine peninsula where Filipino and U.S. forces made a final stand against the Japanese and eventually surrendered on April 9, 1942). Rather than simply commemorate the military valor of this last defense, Bulosan uses the historic event to comment on the ravages of war through a variety of perspectives. In this regard, the title of the slim book is somewhat of a misnomer. *The Voice of Bataan* contains a multiplicity of voices: Bulosan's own dedication "To Aurelio Bulosan"; a prefatory note by E. Llamas Rosario, secretary and director of research of the American-Philippine Foundation; a foreword by diplomat and statesman Carlos P. Romulo; a prologue consisting of a "metrical paraphrase" of Lieutenant Norman Reyes's farewell radio address from Corregidor; a framing poem laconically titled "Bataan"; and seven poems rendered from the viewpoints of differently positioned soldiers. The first two body poems, "Hospital: First Soldier" and "Prison: Second Soldier," speak of the physical casualties of war and the disillusionment that accompanies fighting for what comes to be seen as lies. The volume takes a surprising turn, though, in "Japan: Third Soldier." This poem sympathetically imagines the position of a Japanese soldier who is first inculcated with martial beliefs of superiority and then is separated from his homeland and his family to wage war in a distant land. Whereas "Escape: Fourth Soldier" alludes to General MacArthur's flight to Australia before the fall of Bataan, "America: Fifth Soldier" elegizes a fallen Filipino peasant. "Philippines: Sixth

Soldier" provides the most resounding declaration of perseverance in the face of momentary defeat and holds out the promise of a rebirth of freedom. However, the book closes not on this hopeful, triumphant note, but with "Epilogue: Unknown Soldier," whose speaker addresses a son and the uncertain future that the next generation will inherit.

During this prolific period in his life, Bulosan also edited an anthology of poetry, *Chorus for America: Six Philippine Poets* (1942), and published several important essays, including "Filipino Writers in a Changing World" (1942) and "Letter to a Filipino Woman" (1943). Perhaps his most famous wartime essay is "Freedom from Want," a piece that was printed alongside Norman Rockwell's artwork in the *Saturday Evening Post* (March 6, 1943) and served as an elaboration of one of President Franklin D. Roosevelt's four freedoms (the others being freedom of speech, freedom to worship, and freedom from fear). In marked contrast to Rockwell's tableau of an abundant Thanksgiving dinner table surrounded by smiling family members, Bulosan's essay uses the refrain "If you want to know what we are" as a means of forcing renewed attention toward farm laborers, urban workers, and the unemployed. Bringing this collective working-class voice into public view, Bulosan calls upon "America" to reassess its democratic ideals to ensure just distribution of resources and proper recognition to those on the margins of society.

In the early 1940s, Bulosan began publishing short stories in such U.S. magazines as the *New Yorker, Town and Country,* and *Harper's Bazaar.* A number of these were collected in Bulosan's third book, *The Laughter of My Father* (1944). Departing in some ways from both his earlier poetry and his essays, these stories combine absurdity with ambiguity, satiric humor with social critique. Presumably set in the Philippine village and town of Bulosan's own childhood, the collection is comprised of 24 stories, arranged in roughly chronological order and told from the perspective of an unnamed child-narrator. The stories center on the exploits of the narrator's father, a poor, largely well-meaning alcoholic who is part trickster (outwitting his wealthy neighbor in "My Father Goes to Court") and part buffoon (giving away the family's house to his nephew as a wedding present in "The Gift of My Father"). As social satire, the stories portray the ludicrous effects of the colonial legal system's move toward land enclosures ("The Tree of My Father"), the morally corrosive consequences of U.S. capital investment ("The Capitalism of My Father"), the bribery and corruption intrinsic to provincial governmental politics ("The Politics of My Father" and "My Father and the White Horse") and to institutionalized Catholicism ("My Father Goes to Church"), and the intrafamilial rivalries that result from gambling and cockfighting ("The Triumph of My Father" and "My Father's Tragedy"). Finally, the element of absurdity arises in the bawdy humor that accompanies some of the stories' treatments of heterosexual eroticism, marriage, and adultery ("The Marriage of My Father," "My Father's Lonely

Night," "The Song of My Father," "My Father's Love Potion"). In fact, the book's concluding story, "The Laughter of My Father," describes how the narrator's father sends his son to the United States to escape from marriage.

In the essay "I Am Not a Laughing Man" (published in the *Writer*, May 1946), Bulosan would subsequently repudiate the notion that the stories in *The Laughter of My Father* are meant to be read solely as humor or comedy. He goes on to assert that his forthcoming autobiography *America Is in the Heart* will put to rest the mistaken idea that he is "a laughing man." Indeed, Bulosan's fourth book, which would eventually secure his place in the Asian American literary canon, moves much more emphatically in the direction of proletarian writing. *America Is in the Heart* (1946) chronicles the life of Allos, Bulosan's mirror image, first-person narrator, from his impoverished childhood in provincial Philippines to his political and cultural work as a labor activist in the United States. Complicating the traditional immigration narrative of assimilation or upward mobility, Bulosan's fictionalized autobiography advances many of the themes taken up in his earlier work—descriptions of poverty and loneliness, criticisms of class hierarchy, depictions of erotic and sexualized relationships, and calls for democracy and equality—but focuses even more emphatically on issues of racial difference and racialized violence in the United States.

Subtitled "a personal history," *America Is in the Heart* furthermore embeds the individual narrator's experiences within a larger framework of social history, documenting the lifeways of peasants in the Philippines and working-class Filipinos in the United States during the interwar period. The book is divided into four parts, with Part 1, the section dealing with Allos's life in the Philippines, constituting nearly a third of the narrative. This section focuses on the struggles of Allos's peasant family to survive in the face of absentee landlordism, the usurious practices of landowners, who keep peasants in debt, and the need for the family to sell their diminishing plot of land to fund his older brother Macario's education. Demonstrating that these difficulties are not exclusive to Allos's family, Bulosan interprets the past through the lens of class-based social history, referring, for example, to the Colorum uprising in Tayug, which occurred in the 1920s. Under these crushing conditions, Allos leaves home and travels to the resort town of Baguio, where he works for an American woman named Miss Strandon at a library. After a brief return home to Binalonan, Allos again departs, this time for Lingayen, where he attends school for a short period. Allos's third departure from his village is his last; he travels to Manila where he boards a steamer headed for the United States.

Although Allos's first impression of Seattle is one of familiarity, he is rapidly disabused of any sense that he and his fellow Filipino immigrant-laborers would be welcomed in the United States. In Bulosan's rendering of this underclass world during the Depression in Part 2 of the book, the overwhelmingly male workers are exploited by

Filipino cannery foremen and Chinese gambling-house owners, hunted down by white vigilantes out of fears of miscegenation and economic competition, victimized by unmotivated police brutality, and fight among themselves over white women. Positioned against this vicious world are the organizing efforts of such characters as the labor leaders José and Felix Razon, the newspaper editor Pascual, and Allos's brother Macario, as described in Part 3. Though often engulfed by this world of cruelty and violence, Allos simultaneously strives to maintain a certain distance from it, a dissociation that becomes literal when he spends two years in an L.A. county hospital recovering from tuberculosis and other ailments. It is during his convalescence that the intermittent moments of Allos's literary and political education (which had begun in the Philippines under the tutelage of his older brothers and the American librarian Miss Strandon) take on a more purposeful direction. Paralleling Bulosan's own life narrative, Allos spends a great deal of time reading the books and progressive magazines brought to him by Alice and Eileen Odell. He continues to pursue his intellectual ambitions once released from the hospital, in part by patronizing the Los Angeles public library. Part 4 also narrates Allos's increasing investment in political radicalism as he visits with and talks to the ethnic migrant laborers along the West Coast, writes essays and pamphlets for various progressive outlets, and organizes informal sessions for the political education of the field workers. The book's historical frame concludes with the bombing of **Pearl Harbor** and the consequent scattering of Allos's brothers Macario and Amado once again. The narrative ends on an ambiguous note, with Allos professing his faith in America, in spite of the atrocities he has experienced and witnessed. Certainly, this seeming contradiction has become a focal point of the critical tradition.

Although Bulosan continued to publish short stories in U.S. magazines until the end of the 1940s, he did not come out with a new book during his lifetime. However, since his death in 1956, a number of posthumously published texts have appeared. Among the most important of these is the novel *The Cry and the Dedication* (1995), edited by E. San Juan, Jr. The book has attracted scholarly attention since it seems to perform a kind of symbolic return to the homeland—a return that Bulosan himself was unable to fulfill in literal terms. The novel is typically read as an allegorical rendering of the Huk Rebellion, a radical peasant organization that first formed in opposition to the Japanese occupation of the Philippines during World War II and later in resistance to U.S. neoimperialism and the collaboration of the Filipino elites. Set in the postwar moment, Bulosan's novel depicts a seven-member guerilla group (known in the novel only as part of the "underground"), whose mission is to travel through the provincial countryside and rendezvous in Manila with Felix Rivas, a Filipino expatriate who has recently returned from the United States and who is to provide the rebels with money, arms, and medical supplies. En route to Manila, the band of guerillas visit their respective hometowns with the leader Hassim to assess the social situation on the ground and to educate the peasants about the underground's political goals of national unity and international working-class solidarity. In the course of the journey, the guerilla band listens to the grievances of the peasants: landlords are demanding increasing shares of the harvest, while the local constabularies and collaborators are seeking to eradicate any signs of communism or radical organizing, often through murderous means. In turn, the group attempts to convince the peasants to join their organization, thereby fending off the lure of competing political groups. The novel ends with Dante, another Filipino expatriate returned from the United States, being killed by his brother, a priest who has gathered a wealth of information about the underground's activities. It is unclear whether Bulosan actually finished the book, given that the remaining members continue on their journey to Manila in its closing pages. The novel is significant, nonetheless, in that it shows Bulosan's continued commitment to Philippine radicalism and its complex connections to Filipinos in the United States.

Other texts published in the wake of Bulosan's death include a volume of letters, *Sound of Falling Light: Letters in Exile* (1960); two collections of short stories, *The Philippines Is In the Heart* (1978) and *The Power of Money and Other Stories* (1990); several anthologies, *Selected Works and Letters by Carlos Bulosan* (1982), *If You Want to Know What We Are* (1983), *Bulosan: An Introduction with Selection* (1983), *On Becoming Filipino: Selected Writings of Carlos Bulosan* (1995), as well as a special issue of *Amerasia Journal* devoted to Bulosan's work (1979); a volume of poetry, *Now You Are Still and Other Poems* (1991); and the novel *All the Conspirators* (1998, 2005). The majority of his papers are currently held in the Special Collections area at the University of Washington–Seattle. **See also** Assimilation/Americanization; Racism and Asian America.

Further Reading

Alquizola, Marilyn. "Subversion or Affirmation: The Text and Subtext of *America Is in the Heart*." In *Asian Americans: Comparative and Global Perspectives*, eds. Shirley Hune, et al. Pullman: Washington State University Press, 1991. 199–209.

Campomanes, Oscar V., and Todd S. Gernes. "Two Letters from America: Carlos Bulosan and the Act of Writing." *MELUS* 15 (1988): 15–46.

Daroy, Petronilo. "Carlos Bulosan: The Politics of Literature." *St. Louis Quarterly* 6 (1968): 193–206.

de Jesús, Melinda Luisa María. "Rereading History/Rewriting Desire: Reclaiming Queerness in Carlos Bulosan's *America Is in the Heart* and Bienvenido Santos' *Scent of Apples*." *Journal of Asian American Studies* 5 (2002): 91–111.

Espiritu, Augusto Fauni. "Suffering and Passion: Carlos Bulosan." *Five Faces of Exile: The Nation and Filipino American Intellectuals*. Stanford: Stanford University Press, 2005. 46–73.

Evangelista, Susan. *Carlos Bulosan and His Poetry: A Biography and Anthology*. Seattle: University of Washington Press, 1985.

Lee, Rachel. "Fraternal Devotions: Carlos Bulosan and the Sexual Politics of America." *The Americas of Asian American Literature: Gendered Fictions of Nation and Transnation*. Princeton: Princeton University Press, 1999.

Libretti, Tim. "First and Third Worlds in U.S. Literature: Rethinking Carlos Bulosan." *MELUS* 23 (1998): 135–155.

Miller, Joshua L. "The Gorgeous Laughter of Filipino Modernity: Carlos Bulosan's *The Laughter of My Father*." In *Bad Modernisms*, eds. Douglas Mao and Rebecca L. Walkowitz. Durham, NC: Duke University Press, 2006. 238–268.

Morantte, P.C. *Remembering Carlos Bulosan (His Heart Affair with America)*. Quezon City: New Day, 1984.

Mostern, Kenneth. "Why Is America in the Heart?" *Hitting Critical Mass* 2 (1995): 35–65.

Ponce, Martin Joseph. "On Becoming Socially Articulate: Transnational Bulosan." *Journal of Asian American Studies* 8 (2005): 49–80.

San Juan, E., Jr. *Carlos Bulosan and the Imagination of the Class Struggle*. Quezon City: University of the Philippines Press, 1972.

———. "Violence of Exile, Politics of Desire: Prologue to Carlos Bulosan." *The Philippine Temptation: Dialectics of Philippines-U.S. Literary Relations*. Philadelphia: Temple University Press, 1996. 129–170.

Slotkin, Joel. "Igorots and Indians: Racial Hierarchies and Conceptions of the Savage in Carlos Bulosan's Fiction of the Philippines." *American Literature* 72 (2000): 843–866.

MARTIN JOSEPH PONCE

C

✦

✦ CAO, LAN (1961–)

Like Monique **Truong**, another Viet Kieu (Overseas Vietnamese) author who is also a lawyer, Lan Cao, an attorney, is well-known for her 1997 novel *Monkey Bridge*. However, unlike Truong, who stopped practicing law to become a full-time writer, Cao is currently a Boyd Fellow and professor of law at the College of William and Mary Marshall-Wythe School of Law, teaching in the areas of corporations, international business transactions, and international trade law. After receiving her bachelor's degree in political science at Mount Holyoke College and her JD at Yale University, Cao became a Ford Foundation Scholar in 1991. According to her faculty page Web site, she also practiced law with Paul, Weiss, Rifkind, Wharton & Garrison in New York City, clerked for Judge Constance Baker Motley of the U.S. District Court for the Southern District of New York, and taught at the Brooklyn School of Law for six years before attaining her current position at the College of William and Mary. A prolific scholar, Cao has been published in a number of reputable law journals, including the *Berkeley Journal of International Law* and the *California Law Review*. Yet her greatest contribution to **Vietnamese American literature** and **Asian American studies** would have to be her novel *Monkey Bridge* and her other work, *Everything You Need to Know about Asian American History* (1996), coauthored with Himilce Novas. In fact, this text was revised and published for a second edition in 2004.

Although it may appear that Cao abandoned the literary elements of her writing style, the subjects that she chooses to engage with in her profession as a law professor still maintain a connection to her personal history and background as a refugee from Vietnam, which she details in her fictional narrative *Monkey Bridge*. For example, her

2007 article, "Culture Change," published in the *Virginia Journal of International Law*, argues for the necessity of international law to actively engage with cultures and different societies. As Cao stresses, "In this Article, I argue that norms matter, or more controversially, culture matters to law and development. The observation, that culture matters, and the proposal, that it be examined and evaluated, run counter to the tradition of public and private international law. Law and development, however, must disassociate itself from this long-standing tradition" (2007, 358). Cao believes that having laws that address only structural issues may not be enough to spur development in countries that are struggling to survive and grow economically. International laws, particularly those dealing with development, must take into consideration the changing cultural norms and the variety of traditions that govern and direct each individual nation. Of particular importance are those countries in East and Southeast Asia, Africa, and the Middle East, in which it is imperative to understand the cultures before implementing laws that may impede economic progress and national prosperity.

As a refugee who immigrated to the United States at the age of 13 in 1974, Cao recognizes the significance of living in two cultures and negotiating between two different worlds or communities. Thus, her articles in various law review journals are just as detailed and informative as her first novel, especially in their understanding and appreciation of those whose lives may radically differ from a Western hegemonic norm. *Monkey Bridge* provides a diasporic lens from which to read a history fraught with death and war and a story about struggle, survival, and the passing down of one's personal stories; Cao's legal articles are just as striking in their ability to convey how globalization and economic development affect not only the nation-state but more importantly the lives of individual people and their respective communities. Examining these issues is of particular import in her article "The Transnational and Sub-National in Global Crimes," which was part of the Stefan A. Riesenfeld Symposium 2003: *International Money Laundering: From Latin America to Asia, Who Pays?* According to Cao's summary: "Human trafficking and money laundering are international problems that have been fueled by globalization." However, the people who are intimately affected by human trafficking are mostly women, whose lives are intertwined not only with local, personal factors but also with the global geopolitical effects that allow for human trafficking to take place.

Thus, it is necessary to place Cao's recent works, which contribute to the study of international law and development, into a context that may have stemmed from the writing of her 1997 novel. Although legal writing could appear to be dry and filled with jargon, Cao's impassioned arguments and insistence in "humanizing" law convey how vital it is to tell a persuasive story that allows change to improve the lives of the people affected by these laws.

In a way, *Monkey Bridge* is an intimate portrayal of what Cao has tacitly deployed in her legal articles, albeit with less personal characterization. Through her novel, the author describes how tragedy affects the protagonist, Mai, and the lives of those around her. In fact, the impact of war, like the effects of globalization and economic development, can incur trauma upon its victims and can indeed propel people to flee their homelands and seek new lives in new lands.

Nevertheless, *Monkey Bridge* is also far from a legal document. It is a *bildungsroman* that employs literary devices such as irony (see Michele Janette's examination of *Monkey Bridge*). Moreover, this text gestures to previous Asian American novels, employing themes around mothers and daughters, such as Maxine Hong **Kingston's** *The Woman Warrior* and Fae Myenne **Ng's** *Bone*. More importantly, it conveys issues such as the passing down of personal histories and memories and negotiating ideas of loss, identity, community, and culture, all subjects that many Viet Kieu authors contend with.

Further Reading

Cao, Lan. Book Review, "The Ethnic Question in Law and Development." *Michigan Law Review* 102 (2004): 1044–1103. (Reviewing Amy Chua, *World on Fire: How Exporting Free Market Democracy Breeds Ethnic Hatred and Global Instability*, 2003.)

———. "Corporate and Products Identity in the Post-National Economy: Rethinking U.S. Trade Laws." *California Law Review* 90 (2002): 401–484.

———. "Culture Change." *Virginia Journal of International Law* 47 (2007): 357–412.

———. "The Diaspora of Ethnic Economies: Beyond the Pale?" *William & Mary Law Review* 44 (2003): 1521–1625.

———. "Looking at Communities and Markets." *Notre Dame Law Review* 74 (1999): 841–924.

———. Note, "Illegal Traffic in Women: A Civil RICO Proposal." *Yale Law Journal* 96 (1987): 1297–1322.

———. Symposium Issue, "The Cat that Catches Mice: China's Challenge to the Dominant Privatization Model." *Brooklyn Journal of International Law* 21 (1995): 97–178; rpt. in *Chinese Law*, ed. Tahirih Lee. New York: Garland Publishing, 1997. Available online at www.wm.edu/law/publications/online/cao-653-6423.pdf (PDF format).

———. Symposium Issue, "Chinese Privatization: Between Plan and Market." *Law & Contemporary Problems* (Autumn 2000): 13–62.

———. Symposium Issue, "Reflections on Market Reform in Post-War, Post-Embargo Vietnam." *Whittier Law Review* 22 (2001): 1029–1057. (By invitation)

———. Symposium Issue, "The Transnational and Subnational in Global Crimes." *Berkeley Journal of International Law* 22 (2004): 59–97. (By invitation)

———. "Towards a New Sensibility for International Economic Development." *Texas International Law Journal* 32 (1997): 209–270.

Cao, Lan, and Himilce Novas. *Everything You Need to Know About Asian American History*. New York: Plume/Penguin Books, 1996.

Cao, Lan, and Spencer Weber Waller. "Law Reform in Vietnam." *New York University Journal of International Law & Politics* 29 (1997): 555–576.

Janette, Michele. "Guerrilla Irony in Lan Cao's *Monkey Bridge*." *Contemporary Literature* 42.1 (2001): 50–77.
Kakutani, Michiko. "The American Dream with a Vietnamese Twist." Aug. 19, 1997. http://query.nytimes.com/gst/fullpage.html.
"Lan Cao." http://lawprofessors.typepad.com/immigration/2007/08/immigrant-of-14.html.
"Lan Cao." http://www.wm.edu/law/facultyadmin/faculty/cao-653.shtml.

NINA HA

✦ CARBÒ, NICK (1964–)

Besides being an acclaimed lecturer at several universities across the United States, Filipino American poet and editor Nick Carbò is primarily known for his poetry, but he has also edited and coedited four anthologies. Born in Legaspi, the Philippines, he was adopted at the age of two, together with his younger sister, by a wealthy Spanish couple of Greek background (his grandfather on his mother's side came from Greece). He was brought up with Spanish, Greek, and Filipino influences in Westernized Manila, where he attended the International School before furthering his education in the United States. He started developing an interest in poetical composition while studying at Bennington College, Vermont, in 1984–1985. In 1990 he received his BA in English from St. Mary's University, San Antonio, Texas, and in 1992 he obtained his MFA in creative writing at Sarah Lawrence College, Bronxville, New York.

His teaching experience has been wide and varied, starting in 1992 as resident poet in the Department of English of Bucknell University, Lewisburg, Pennsylvania. He later taught courses, among others, at the American University, Washington DC (fall 1993); New Jersey Institute of Technology, Newark, New Jersey (fall 1996); Manhattan College, Riverdale, New York (from spring 1997 to spring 1998); Rutgers University, New Brunswick, New Jersey (from spring 1998 to spring 1999); and the University of Miami, Coral Gables, Florida (fall 2000–fall 2003, fall 2004–spring 2005). He is currently teaching poetry at the New College of Florida, Sarasota, Florida.

Nick Carbò has published writings in specialized literary magazines such as *Asian Pacific American Journal, DisOrient, Gargoyle, Mangrove,* and *North American Review*. His poems have been featured in important anthologies such as *Asian American Poetry: The Next Generation* (2004) and *Dark Horses: Poets on Overlooked Poems* (2007). Among his awards are grants in poetry from the National Endowment for the Arts (1997) and from the New York Foundation for the Arts (1999).

Carbò has published two chapbooks of poetry: *Running Amok* (1992) and *Rising from Your Book*, a collection released online in 2003 that includes experimental pieces. In his first volume of poems, *El Grupo McDonald's* (1995), Carbò explores the complexity of the Filipino American identity, the Filipino **diaspora,** and the impact of **colonialism** on his motherland. Moreover, behind his witticism and irony, he subtly conveys political reflections stemming from his personal experience in the Philippines in the 1980s, during the dictatorship of Ferdinand Marcos.

His second book of poetry, *Secret Asian Man*, was published in 2000, won the Asian American Literary Award in 2001, and was an official selection of the Academy of American Poets Poetry Book Club. It is a collection of 35 poems that can be read either individually or as a story, set in New York. The main character, introduced by Carbò in the Foreword, is Ang Tunay na Lalaki, which in Tagalog means the "Real Man." The name leaves aside the languages of the two colonial empires: the Spanish (Spanish language) and the American (English language), choosing Tagalog over both Spanish and English. Thus being fashioned as a sort of postcolonial Everyman, Ang Tunay na Lalaki faithfully mirrors the experiences of every Filipino American eager to partake in the American Dream but at the same time afraid of feeling displaced in an alien and often hostile environment (in almost every poem Carbò seems to feel the reassuring urge to record the exact coordinates of his character). Of the 35 poems, 26 start with "Ang Tunay na Lalaki" and the action he is carrying out in that precise moment; by choosing such a difficult name for a westerner to pronounce and by placing the stress on his character's being *active*, Carbò seems to prompt the readers to reconsider the stereotypes that, for centuries, have undermined Americans of Asian descent, perceived by WASPs as an undistinguished yet mysterious **model minority**, thus showing that the "real" Asian American man is not at all anonymous, passive, or silent.

Andalusian Dawn (2004) is Carbò's most recent book of poems, written during his residency in Spain, which replaces the United States or the Philippines as the setting of his poems. The volume is divided into four sections in which English and Spanish are both used and in which memories of the writer's childhood and adulthood mingle with Filipino folklore (as in the poem entitled "Mal Agueros"). *Andalusian Dawn* echoes Garcia Lorca's compositions, and the contemplation of the Andalusian landscape often overlaps reminiscences of the past with the geography of the mind.

Carbò's activity as an editor has produced four anthologies. The first one is the breakthrough *Returning a Borrowed Tongue* (1996), featuring side-by-side Filipino and Filipino American poets. Carbò decided to put together this anthology when he was studying at Sarah Lawrence College, after realizing that in every course of poetry or world literature he was taught no mention was ever made of Filipino or **Filipino American literature,** despite the fact that Filipino poets had been publishing in the United States since the 1920s (Marcelo de Gracia Concepcion) and writers such as Carlos **Bulosan**, with his *America Is in the Heart* (1943), had been giving voice to the hopes and the disappointments of Filipinos struggling to redefine their identity in the United States.

Carbò coedited his second anthology, *Babaylan: An Anthology of Filipina and Filipina American Writers* (2000) with Eileen **Tabios**, aiming to fill, also in this case, an even deeper gap in world literature. The volume features the writings of over 60 Filipina and Filipina American writers of the diaspora (M. Evelina Galang, Jessica **Hagedorn**, and Marianne Villanueva, to mention a few), composing in different times and different parts of the globe and belonging to different generations. The word *babaylan* means priestess, *curandera*, for the Visayan natives of the Philippines; a *babaylan* is a healer, a woman who performs important ceremonies within the community, a person whose magic words can cure or cause somebody to fall in love. Carbò's choice, therefore, signifies the important and powerful role that women can play in the Philippines.

Sweet Jesus: Poems about the Ultimate Icon (2002) is Carbò's third anthology, coedited with his poet wife, Denise Duhamel. It is a collection of poems inspired by Carbò's and Duhamel's Roman Catholic background and focusing on the figure of Jesus, portrayed from different perspectives: African American, **Asian American**, Native American, lesbian, gay, married, divorced, and even atheist.

Carbò's last anthology, *Pinoy Poetics: A Collection of Autobiographical and Critical Essays on Filipino Poetics* (2004), perfectly follows Carbò's already manifested intention of breaking the silence surrounding Filipino poetry in English. The volume gathers poetic essays and sample poems by writers, university professors, activists, and journalists who are either Filipino or of Filipino descent. The themes the contributors deal with as important strands in their writings range from the aftermath of Marcos's dictatorship to the influx of American imperialism, postcolonialism, and history. **See also** Asian Diasporas; Colonialism and Postcolonialism; Gay Male Literature; Lesbian Literature.

Further Reading

Davis, Rocio G. "The Struggle for Form: A Conversation between Nick Carbò and M. Evelina Galang." *MELUS: The Journal of the Society for the Study of the Multi-Ethnic Literature of the United States, Filipino American Literature Issue* (Spring 2004). http://www.findarticles.com/p/articles/mi_m2278/is_1_29/ai_n6148077.

ELISABETTA MARINO

✦ CHA, THERESA HAK KYUNG (1951–1982)

In her short career as a writer, filmmaker, and visual and performance artist, Theresa Hak Kyung Cha made important contributions to **Korean American literature** and late twentieth-century conceptual art. She experimented with form and language in various media, and her best known work is the book *Dictée*.

Cha was born in 1951 in Pusan, Korea, as the middle child of five. Her parents were Koreans raised in Manchuria and educated as teachers, and her mother's experience as a Korean exile longing for homeland would later be referenced in *Dictée*. In 1962 Cha's family moved from Korea to Hawaii and two years later to San Francisco, where she went to the Convent of the Sacred Heart School, a private Catholic high school for girls. There she studied French, read Greek and Roman classics, and received many scholastic awards. After a semester at the University of San Francisco, Cha transferred to the University of California, Berkeley, in 1969, where she studied art with James Melchert and literature and French film theory with Bertrand Augst. With them, she started her lifelong exploration with the art of sculpture, theatrical performance, film, and poetry. Her reading in her undergraduate years of Korean poetry and such writers as Samuel Beckett, James Joyce, Stéphane Mallarmé, and Marguerite Duras would also show continuing influence in her later art. At Berkeley Cha obtained a BA in comparative literature in 1973, a BA in art in 1975, an MA in art in 1977, and an MFA in 1978. The antiwar events of the 1960s and 1970s at Berkeley and the explosive atmosphere around the Bay Area provided a perfect environment for artistic experimentation for young artists like Cha. The Berkeley years witnessed her development into an outstanding performance and video artist, and she received numerous awards for her photography and video work. Through the university's Education Abroad Program, she attended the Centre d'Etudes Américain du Cinéma in Paris in 1976 for a study with film theorists such as Christian Metz, Raymond Bellour, and Thierry Kuntzel and became involved with European artists and projects. The study in Paris provided a catalyst for Cha's artistic career, and she completed several important performances after she returned to the Bay Area. She moved to New York in 1980, and the following two years saw the debut of her films *Exilée* and *Permutations* and the publication of most of her important writings. She returned to Korea several times between 1979 and 1981, and the experience is centrally referenced in both *Dictée* and *Exilée*. *Dictée* was about to be published officially by Tanam Press when Cha was murdered on November 5, 1982. *White Dust from Mongolia*, the film she went back to Korea to shoot, remained unfinished.

Through works in various media, Cha shows a strong interest in inventive ways to force the audience to reconsider their own role in the process of viewing. She started her artistic experimentation in video and performance around the mid-1970s to explore language and other themes related to immigration experience, and her works require active thinking from the audience. Influenced by her study with Augst, who taught film mainly through frame-by-frame close analysis, Cha's videos, and her later films, are mostly constructed as a series of stills, always black-and-white, one dissolving into another, and often accompanied by voice-over. Among her numerous videos, important works include *Mouth to Mouth* (1975), a piece about an encounter with

Korean language; *Vidéoème* (1976), a work built upon the construction and the inner fractures of its title word; and *Re Dis Appearing* (1977), a piece again fusing visual and audio media by accompanying spare and pure imagery with multiple articulations of enigmatic phrases. The use of text-images, symbolic audiovisual combination, and sequences of stills in Cha's videos also translates into her performances. Readers and critics today can only get a glimpse of her mixed-media performances through the photos and documentation she left. In *A Ble Wail* (1975), for example, her dream-like dancing movement was viewed through an opaque curtain that divided the space between her and the audience, and the consequent viewing of her partially tai chi, partially Korean dance gestures might call to mind the challenges of any cross-cultural encounter. Her later performances show even more thinking about the significance of media in art creation. *Other Things Seen, Other Things Heard (Ailleurs)* (1978), one of her major works, consisted of two slide projectors and one film projector, projected images on the wall, recorded voices, and sandy powder on the floor. She intended to introduce the performance aspect to projection in this piece and to explore the meaning and effect of apparently simple gesture and imagery.

Cha's films further expand into adventurous exploration of language, displacement, and identity. Her 50-minute film *Exilée* (1980) combines film and video projection by embedding a video monitor into a large film screen. Opening with a text-image in which the title is broken into a list of words and word fragments—*exil, exile, ile* (island, isolation), *é* (sign for the female gender), and *ée*—the film makes evident its central concern with women in displacement. Based on Cha's own experience of traveling back to Korea as an American citizen, a significant part of the film comprises a sequence of still images of cloud, shot through the window of a flying airplane, to capture the distance of an exile's travel. The images are shown with Cha's own soft, poetic, and hypnotic voice-over, which counts off the passing minutes of the flight between San Francisco and Seoul. Together with the visual images, the voice-over text creates a melancholic sensation of suspension and rootlessness. Another sequence of stills in the film contains several different designs of the letter X and opens a number of possibilities for interpretation. Visually an intersection of routes, the sign may remind the audience of the cross-cultural encounters an exile has to confront; it is also a sign paradoxically both for deletion and for multiplication. It can point to the complexity of the exile identity, involving both tremendous loss and multiple ways of self-positioning in the world. Another film by Cha, the 10-minute silent *Permutations* (1982), also forces the audience to think actively and to do interpretation for themselves. It features a series of close-up shots of Cha's sister. Quick frames of her face with eyes open—reminiscent of those depersonalized, expressionless identity photos—or closed and frames of the back of her head leave more questions than definitive messages about identity and its transformation.

The theoretical underpinning for Cha's philosophy of active viewing can be found in *Apparatus—Cinematographic Apparatus: Selected Writings*, an anthology of essays on film she edited in 1981, for which she is known among film scholars. The book includes writings by theorists and artists such as Roland Barthes, Maya Deren, and Christian Metz and her own piece "Commentaire." Composed of words, photographs, film stills, and blank and black pages, "Commentaire" is a text that foregrounds its inventive form. In a book about the mechanism of film, it most effectively provides a filmic presentation with its screen-like page arrangement. Most of its pages contain one or two words each, capitalized and placed in the middle or to the margin. Many of these pages present her characteristic play with words by breaking a word into multiple words or word fragments, which calls attention to the variable signification and complicated connotation of any word or any frame in a film. Taking language apart in this way, the text challenges the usual way of reading or viewing that takes meaning for granted. In her preface to the anthology, Cha expresses her hope that the book makes its readers active in thinking about their own position in relation to the film. "Commentaire" is a piece that defies passive, absorptive reading or viewing and instead drives readers to think actively about not merely the text's content or "meaning" but their own commentary and, more importantly, how the text brings that out.

Cha's most famous work, *Dictée* (1982) can be seen as a culmination of the ideas demonstrated in her videos, films, and performances. The book constantly crosses linguistic, textual, and generic boundaries in a postmodern fashion. Its highly avant-garde form resists any conventional form of classification, fusing and confusing poetry and prose, literature and history, text and image. Drawing upon her family's and her own experience of traveling between nations, languages, and cultures, Cha examines a number of interrelated issues, including power and history writing, female subjectivity, and the cultural politics of language.

The book is divided into nine sections designated by the nine classical Greek muses, in which the three major sections—the first "Clio History," the second "Calliope Epic Poetry," and the fourth "Melpomene Tragedy"—center on the modern history of Korea, from its struggle against Japan's colonization in the early twentieth century to the political and military turmoil during and after the **Korean War**. Intentionally discontinuous and sometimes painfully disrupted, the sections foreground a sophisticated way of perceiving history by weaving together various subtexts, including historical and personal photographs, maps, historical documents, personal correspondence, and lyric and prose poems. In so doing, it moves among different languages, voices, times, and geographical spaces and presents the modern history of Korea as multidimensional and contextualized in a variety of political relations. In reference to the recurring war and political uproar in Korea, the text analyzes the United States' complicity in Japan's colonization of Korea and its later role in Korea's severance on the one hand and, on the other, points to the predicament Korean people encountered during the democratic movement against their own government in the early 1980s. The multiple historical references reveal a profound interrogation of how history is conventionally written, specifically how Korea has been missing from the master narrative of the West.

Not just a text about history, *Dictée* is also a woman's text, expressing a feminist idea by questioning and commenting on both Korea's traditional patriarchal culture and the male-centered literary and cultural tradition of the West. Courageous female figures play a significant role in the book: Yu Guan Soon, the patriotic girl who sacrificed her life in Korea's anticolonization movement, and Hyung Soon Huo, the author's mother who retained a deep love for her homeland as an exile, are juxtaposed to female figures famous in Western history such as Joan of Arc and St. Therese. Through the women's stories, the book explores its major themes of exile, displacement, and identity, and the women can be seen as different aspects of the diseuse, the female speaker recurring throughout the book. Giving voices to the women, Cha's text seeks to restore subjectivity in the women who were traditionally silenced and by doing this retrieves what has been missing from the male-dominated record of history.

As the title suggests, *Dictée* is ultimately a work about language. The French word for "dictation," the title reminds one of not only the immigrants' experience of foreign language learning but also the colonizer's systematic suppression of the native language, both described repeatedly in the book. Using multiple languages in the text, Cha shows how language, Japanese, French, and English, can become a colonial tool or a medium for political and cultural suppression. In its intentional fragmentation, disruption, abundant historical references, and untranslated multilingual presentation, the book draws attention to the mechanisms and structures of language and the political and cultural implication hidden inside language. It forces the reader to contemplate what lies behind the text for a more complete understanding and, in possible discomfort and frustration, to witness linguistic exchanges as deeply rooted in and shaped by imbalanced political powers.

Published first with a small press in 1982, *Dictée* did not elicit much criticism until a panel discussion at the meeting of the **Association for Asian American Studies** in 1991 addressed the book's significance as an Asian American literary text. The four papers presented at the panel were later collected into a book, *Writing Self, Writing Nation*, and published in 1994, in which critic Shelley Sunn Wong attributes the increasing attention to *Dictée* 10 years after its initial publication to the major shifts in social, political, and cultural coordinates since the late 1980s. These major shifts include the demographic changes in the Asian American community and the consequent broadening of Asian American identification, the growing concern with gender issues, and the development of postmodernist and poststructuralist theories. *Dictée* has been widely studied in university poetry, ethnic studies, and postmodern literature classes over the past decade and is now embraced by many artists and scholars as a significant work of contemporary literature, both in Asian American context and beyond.

After Cha's tragic and untimely death, her family entrusted the Berkeley Art Museum with the Theresa Hak Kyung Cha Archive. In addition to unpublished writings, the photographs and documentation of her video, film, and performance works, the archive also contains many of Cha's less known works of visual art. Handmade artist books, such as *Earth* (1976) and *Father/Mother* (1977), incorporate photographs, paintings, and writings to emphasize the physical book as a work of art. Pieces of concrete poetry such as *The Missing Page* (1976) arrange poetic elements on paper for certain pictorial and typographical effects. There are also works of intermedia art and mail art. Two exhibitions of Cha's oeuvre were held in the early 1990s in the Berkeley Art Museum and the Whitney Museum of American Art respectively. From 2001 to 2005, an exhibition built upon the previous two titled *The Dream of the Audience: Theresa Hak Kyung Cha (1951–1982)* was held in Korea, Austria, Spain, and the United States.

Further Reading

Chang, Julia. "'Transform This Nothingness': Theresa Hak Kyung Cha's *Dictee*." *Hitting Critical Mass: A Journal of Asian American Cultural Criticism* 1.1 (1993): 75–82.

Cheng, Anne Anlin. "History in/against the Fragment: Theresa Hak Kyung Cha." In *The Melancholy of Race,* Cheng. New York: Oxford University Press, 2000. 139–168.

Guide to the Theresa Hak Kyung Cha Collection 1971–1991. Online Archive of California. January 2007. http://oac.cdlib.org/findaid/ark:/13030/tf238n986k.

Kim, Elaine H., and Norma Alarcon, eds. *Writing Self, Writing Nation: A Collection of Essays on* Dictée *by Theresa Hak Kyung Cha.* Berkeley, CA: Third Woman Press, 1994.

Kim, Sue J. "Apparatus: Theresa Hak Kyung Cha and the Politics of Form." *Journal of Asian American Studies* 8.2 (2005): 143–169.

Lewallen, Constance M. *The Dream of the Audience: Theresa Hak Kyung Cha (1951–1982).* Berkeley, CA: University of California Press, 2001.

Spahr, Juliana. "'Tertium Quid Neither One Thing Nor the Other': Theresa Hak Kyung Cha's DICTÉE and the Decolonization of Reading." In *Everybody's Autonomy: Connective Reading and Collective Identity,* Spahr. Tuscaloosa, AL: University of Alabama Press, 2001. 119–152.

XIWEN MAI

✦ CHAN, JEFFERY PAUL (1942–)

With Frank **Chin**, Lawson Fusao **Inada**, and Shawn **Wong**, Chinese American author, editor, and professor of **Asian American studies** Jeffery Paul Chan coedited the groundbreaking anthologies of Asian American literature *Aiiieeeee!: An Anthology* *of Asian American Writers* and *The Big Aiiieeeee!: An Anthology of Chinese American and Japanese American Literature.* He is also known for his many short stories, plays, and his 2004 novel *Eat Everything Before You Die: A Chinaman in the Counter Culture.* Born in Stockton, California, Chan graduated from the University of California, Berkeley, and received a master of arts degree in creative writing from San Francisco State University. In 1970 he helped create the School of Ethnic Studies at San Francisco State University and cofounded the Department of Asian American Studies. He spent the bulk of his career there in a joint appointment with the Department of English. He retired from teaching in 2006 to focus more on his writing. Since the late 1990s Chan has spent part of the year in Rome, where he has been witnessing and writing about the Chinese diaspora in Italy.

Chan's paternal grandfather immigrated to the United States around the turn of the nineteenth century; his maternal grandmother may have been Chinese and Ute Indian. Chan's father spent his childhood roaming Nevada. Eventually his parents left him in Carson City, where he attended high school. As an herbalist and merchant, Chan's maternal grandfather was exempt from exclusion. He brought his wife and first daughter to San Francisco also around the turn of the nineteenth century. Five more daughters, including Chan's mother, and three sons were born and then raised in San Francisco's **Chinatown**. Chan himself spent his early years living near his maternal grandparents. Later, his family moved to the suburbs, becoming the first Chinese family in El Cerrito, California. Chan has one brother, Michael Paul Chan, an actor known for his roles in television and film.

Chan began writing and publishing short stories while still a student at UC Berkeley. By the late 1960s, Chan was among a handful of young Asian American writers struggling to articulate the terms of this newly coined identity. From the beginning, Chan took as his subject what he calls the process of acculturation and the crisis of identity in the lives of Chinese Americans. Characteristics of these early stories, such as a sharp focus on detail and a poet's attention to language, can be found throughout his work. In such stories as "Auntie Tsia Lays Dying" (1972) and "The Chinese in Haifa" (1974), Chan plunges the reader into the mundane realities of a central character's day-to-day existence. Chan's willingness to allow the smallest actions of his characters to tell the larger story makes these stories fiercely antiromantic. The intricate prose meanders almost lyrically until it is caught up short by a discomfortingly explicit aspect of personal hygiene. The subjects of Chan's stories are old, young, tired, maybe angry, and trying to work out what it means personally for them to be Chinese American. China itself appears only occasionally—in a popular song, a news story, a memory—as a place one should, but does not, call home. Taken together, these early stories function like a mosaic, each story a complex and independent tile working together to characterize a distinctly Chinese American sensibility.

As an undergraduate in the early 1960s, Chan witnessed the student strikes at Berkeley, where he learned that political action could result in real change. The tone of his early fiction was not particularly political. His insistence, however, that Chinese Americans were a worthy and interesting literary subject was in and of itself radical. In the late 1960s Chan met Frank Chin. Together they began to follow a lead established by such scholars as Him Mark Lai, Philip Choy, and Thomas Chinn—the founders of San Francisco's Chinese Historical Society. Chan and Frank Chin began to look for texts to add to this archive, helping to identify and shape the literary legacy of Chinese in America. They sought work written by an earlier generation—texts that had long been out of print or were never recognized by the mainstream. Among the earliest of these identified was an English-Chinese phrase book from 1875 (partially reprinted in *The Big Aiiieeeee!*). Chan and Chin noted the ironic, insider jokes and linguistic twists residing in this seemingly nonliterary vehicle. They credit the author or authors with surreptitiously demonstrating point of view, humor, and an understanding of the situation they were in as immigrants in the United States. More significantly, Chan was instrumental in the rediscovery and republication of Louis **Chu's** *Eat a Bowl of Tea* (1961, 1979). Both texts are notable for their dexterous use of language. According to Chan, Chu created a literary language that operates simultaneously in English and the Toisan dialect of his 1950s Chinatown. This language, Chan argues, is a particularly Chinese American dialect—the words of individuals simultaneously Chinese and American. In his introduction to the 1979 edition, Chan identifies Louis Chu as the first Chinese American novelist. According to Chan, earlier works pandered to white readers, providing a sanitized version of Chinese America explicitly for white consumption. In contrast, Chu created a more realistic vision of a Chinatown community. It was a vision that recognized the challenges of an immigrant society as it was transitioning from the bachelor ghetto to a family-based community. Chan's introduction functions as a geographical inscription of Chinese America as an almost concrete place with social, political, and historical roots. This inscription recurs in all of Chan's work, as, in the face of Orientalism and reductionism, he insists on the complexities of the Chinese American landscape.

In 1973 Chan, Chin, Lawson Fusao Inada, and Shawn Wong published *Aiiieeeee!* The anthology collected many of the texts the editors had rediscovered alongside the work of contemporary Asian American writers. *Aiiieeeee!* insists on the status of Asian American literature as a literary genre worthy of attention. A product of the activism of its time, the book's fiery, rhetorical introduction, coauthored by the editors, blasted white racism. A polemic, the introduction angrily condemned a genre of Orientalized writing that constructed and upheld Asian stereotypes. They called instead for serious writing about the complicated realities of the Asian American experience.

Since its publication, the book has been extremely influential in the field of Asian American studies. It has been praised for identifying some of the key structures of anti-Asian discrimination in the United States. It influenced and inspired a genera-tion of Asian American writers, artists, and activists. At the same time, the editors have also been criticized, in particular for promoting what has been called an ultra-masculinist vision of what Asian America should be. This vision is given its clearest articulation in an essay cowritten by Chan and Chin prior to the publication of *Aiiieeeee!* In the frequently cited "Racist Love" (1972), the coauthors write of the emasculation of the Asian American man. They claim anti-Asian bias feminizes Asian American men, making them weak and womanly. Stereotypical Asian American men are not courageous, daring, or original—all qualities the authors identify as par-ticularly masculine. Most contemporary scholars agree that the particular workings of racism emasculate Asian American men. At the same time, scholars such as King-Kok Cheung have criticized the authors for the misogyny and homophobia that seems to underpin Chan and Chin's argument; the authors seem to argue that women and homosexuals are weak, derivative, and fearful.

Known first as a writer and editor, Chan spent the bulk of his career as a teacher and activist at San Francisco State University. He began teaching in the English department while still a master's student. In 1968 he became involved with what would become known as the **Third World Students' Strike**. The strike resulted in major institutional changes and curriculum reform. The School of Ethnic Studies (which included a department of Asian American studies) created as a consequence of the strike was among the first program of its kind in the country. The success of the strike sent a clear signal to American universities that institutional change and curricu-lum reform recognizing the needs of minoritarian students would be required. Chan joined the faculty of Asian American Studies at its inception. For the next 38 years, he would continue to shepherd and shape the department, serving twice as chair.

In 2004 Chan published his first novel, *Eat Everything Before You Die: A Chinaman in the Counter Culture*. As the title indicates, the novel is a gustatory whirlwind, as it rev-els in the pleasures and pitfalls of sex, drugs, and, of course, food. Novelist and scholar George Leonard identifies the book's metaphor of eating as another way of understand-ing assimilation. Eating-as-assimilation emphasizes assimilation as a complex process of consumption. Rather than tamely melting into the American status quo, the Chinese American characters of the novel experience assimilation as pleasurable, painful, nau-seating, transgressive, and, most of all, compulsory. A transformational process, it alters both eater and eaten, while blurring the boundaries between the two.

True to his roots as a scholar of Chinese America, the novel is very much about remembering, though not in the stultifying form of memorial. Remembering instead becomes a form of digestion, a way of processing and understanding the past. Memory provides the narrative spine of the book. The novel follows Christopher Columbus Wong as he journeys back in his mind over the first 50 years of his life. Raised in San

Francisco's Chinatown by a coterie of figures who may or may not have been his parents, Wong is a product of what Chan identifies as a lost generation. For the most part this is not the post-1965 Chinatown in which husbands know their wives and grandparents their grandchildren. Instead, this is a Chinatown populated by Chinese bachelors and the few women, children, and white folk who have stumbled into the long shadow of exclusion.

In a loosely chronological narrative, the novel finds Wong as a boy piecing together the fragments of the history of one possible father, his uncle Lincoln. At the same time, the young Wong must face his ambivalent feelings toward another father figure, the Reverend Candlewick, a white missionary who turns out to be a pedophile. Later, Wong goes to college. In discovering women, he also discovers the distance between himself and "real," that is, Chinese-born Chinese. By the late 1960s and 1970s, Wong has become a hippie. He finds himself living in a Marin County commune, where he encounters yet another way of being Asian in America: his fellow residents include a number of preliterate Hmong, one of whom is reinventing himself as a spoken word performance artist. By the end of the novel, we recognize that the nominal orphan, Christopher Columbus Wong, has been parented by the last 50 years of the Asian American experience.

As with his earlier works, Chan's imploding use of language is central to the novel. If, however, his early work used language as an appetizer, the novel features a five-course meal with wine pairings. Chan is a master of the never-ending sentence, the many-paged paragraph. This is not to call him long-winded. Rather, these long descriptions and observations evoke a complexity of sensual experience made tangible on the page. There is something literally gluttonous in his language, as though the language is in and of itself the "everything" of the title. Chan's masterful balance between linguistic exactitude and abundance recalls the experience of living as both carefully contained and fundamentally uncontainable. Reading itself becomes the titular act of consumption.

This sentiment is reiterated by the structure of the novel. Rather than following a strict chronological narrative, for the most part the novel is a series of intimate scenes. Working against the strictures of conventional plot, Chan seems to place these scenes almost randomly, forcing the reader to draw his or her own conclusions as to the relevancy and meaning of their adjacency. As with his earlier works, the effect is mosaic. By resisting the simplification of linear narrative, Chan's readers must step back to contemplate the entire design. Again, Chan exercises just enough narrative control to allow for a greater freedom of meaning and consequence.

The narrative of the novel recounts the particular experience of Christopher Columbus Wong as he is embedded in the context of circumstance. The novel as a whole, however, can be understood as a response to the legacy of **Chinese American literature** Chan has spent his career reading. The title itself invokes both Louis Chu's *Eat a Bowl of Tea* and Frank Chin's 1974 play *The Chickencoop Chinaman*. In one

respect, the novel can be read as a parody of the canon of Chinese American literature, taking on such familiar themes as autobiography/history, food, and sexual identity. At the same time, Christopher Columbus Wong's ironic perspective and wry tone
allow the novel to veer sharply between a satire and a real warmth of feeling. Chan's
gentle mockery of his literary predecessors betrays gratitude, respect, and a genuine
appreciation for those who have come before.

Eat Everything Before You Die was produced in part by a California Arts Fel-
lowship and the Marin County Writers-in-Residence Award. It also won the
American Pen Oakland Literary Award for fiction in 2005. Parts of the novel, as
well as Chan's other work, have been translated into Italian. **See also** Asian
Diasporas; Asian American Political Activism; Asian American Stereotypes;
Assimilation/Americanization; Chinatowns; Orientalism and Asian America;
Racism and Asian America.

Further Reading

Cheung, King-Kok. "The Woman Warrior Versus the Chinaman Pacific: Must a Chinese
American Critic Choose Between Feminism and Heroism?" In *Conflicts in Feminism,* eds.
Marianne Hirsch and Evelyn Fox Keller. New York: Routledge, 1990. 234–251.

Daniels, Roger. "*Aiiieeeee!: An Anthology of Asian-American Writers* by Frank Chin, Jeffery Paul
Chan, Lawson Fusao Inada, Shawn Hsu Wong." Book Review. *The Pacific Historical Review*
44.4 (November 1975): 571–572.

Leonard, George. "Review of *Eat Everything Before You Die: A Chinaman in the Counter Culture.*"
San Francisco Humanities Review (November 14, 2005). See humanities.sfsu.edu/san-
francisco-humanities-review/.

Mochizuki, Ken. "This Is Our Literature, and They Have Stood Up: Twelve Quintessential
Asian American Works." *International Examiner (1976–1987)* 14.11 (June 3, 1987): 6.

Partridge, Jeffrey F.L. "Aiiieeeee! and the Asian American Literary Movement: A Conversation
with Shawn Wong." *MELUS* 29.3/4 (Fall 2004): 91–103.

———. "Eat Everything Before You Die: A Chinaman in the Counterculture/The Love Wife."
MELUS 30.2 (Summer 2005): 242–253.

Wenger, Deutcha. "After 38 Years of Teaching Professor Jeffery Paul Chan Reflects on His
Career." Golden Gate Xpress Online (September 29, 2005). See xpress.sfsu.edu/archives/
news/004399.html.

Whitson, Helen, and Wesley Kyels. "On Strike! Shut It Down!" J. Paul Leonard Library Web
site (accessed May 2007). www.library.sfsu.edu/exhibits/strike/case7-text.html.

JENNIFER CHAN

✦ CHANG, DIANA (1934–)

Chinese American novelist, poet, and painter Diana Chang is best known for her
first novel *The Frontiers of Love* (1956), considered the first novel published by an

American of Chinese origin in the United States. Born in New York City in 1934, she moved as an infant to China with her Chinese father (an architect) and U.S.-born Chinese American mother. During her childhood, she lived in various Chinese cities, including Beijing, Nanjing, and Shanghai—the city that became the setting for *The Frontiers of Love*. At the end of **World War II**, Chang returned to New York and completed a baccalaureate degree at Barnard College in 1949. After graduating, she worked as a full-time junior editor until she decided to pursue a writing career while working various part-time jobs such as answering telephones and freelance copyediting. Between 1956 and 1978, she produced six novels, including *A Woman of Thirty* (1959), *A Passion for Life* (1961), *The Only Game in Town* (1963), *Eye to Eye* (1974), and *A Perfect Love* (1978). Chang has also published three volumes of poetry and placed numerous short stories in literary journals and anthologies. As an accomplished painter, she has exhibited paintings in solo and group shows as well. In 1979 she returned to Barnard College to teach creative writing in the English department, a position she held for many years. She served for a time as the editor of the *American Pen*, a journal of the international writers' association PEN, and she has received a Fulbright and the John Hay Whitney Fellowship. A member of the Asian American Writers' Workshop, Chang continues to give readings of her work. She currently lives in Manhattan and Water Hill, Long Island.

Critical attention to *The Frontiers of Love* was revived through an influential introduction by Asian American author and critic Shirley Geok-lin **Lim** when the University of Washington Press reissued the novel in 1994. Chang's other novels, with the exception of *The Only Game in Town*, primarily feature white characters and have generated less scholarly interest. In interviews, Chang has explained her choice of white characters as an attempt to speak to universal issues such as existentialism, love, and the role of the artist in society. Critics such as Frank **Chin** have read her later works as a betrayal of her Chinese heritage, despite Chang's engagement with the "hyphenated condition"—a term she coined in 1976—in two novels, much of her poetry, and the short story "The Oriental Contingent," published in *The Forbidden Stitch: An Asian American Women's Anthology*. More recent critics such as Carol Spaulding have argued that Chang's white characters are acutely conscious of their racial identity, and so whiteness is challenged as an invisible subject position in U.S. society. In all of Chang's fiction, characters face crises of ethnic, national, gender, and artistic identity, whether they are biracial Chinese Americans living in Shanghai or white Protestants residing in New England.

The Frontiers of Love (1956), Chang's first and most influential novel, focuses on the love affairs and identity crises of three Eurasian characters in Shanghai, a "Eurasian" city during the final months of its Japanese occupation in 1945. The novel uses a limited third-person narration, focalized through particular characters in each chapter to create a nuanced and multivocal discourse (Lim 1994). The three major

Eurasian characters—Sylvia Chen, Feng Huang, and Mimi Lambert—strive to resolve the contradictions of mixed race and bicultural identities, and they each represent a different resolution of these issues. Sylvia, 20, has a belligerent American mother and an intellectual Chinese father, and she does not feel comfortable in Western or Chinese dresses. Hinting at her eventual acceptance of a self-constructed identity, she declares in the novel, "I shall have to design my own kind of clothes, a modified Chinese dress" (Chang 1956, 4). Feng is a 26-year-old lawyer with brown hair and freckles, and he has a Chinese father and an English mother. In contrast to Sylvia, he seeks an essentialist Chinese identity, particularly through his ideological involvement with the Communist Party. Mimi, a 19-year-old orphan of an Australian father and a "Chinese socialite," is the most cosmopolitan of the three main characters, and her trajectory is toward integration into Western society; she is dating Robert Bruno, 34, the son of a Swiss businessman who owns a printing company, and her character is trapped by a stereotypical gender role.

The novel opens with Sylvia, Mimi, and Feng attending a cocktail party at the home of Bill and Julie Jastrows, a Jewish couple who host regular gatherings of the cosmopolitan crowd in transnational Shanghai. Mimi argues with Robert about his tardiness because he was at the Chinese opera, and Feng explodes in a tirade, accusing those gathered of looking down on Chinese culture. Later that night, Feng conspires with a communist cell leader, Tang, who secretly prints political pamphlets in the Bruno's printing press after hours and who is planning a strike at the plant. Feng reveals that he overheard the Bruno heir discussing his father's plans to expand control of printing and the media in China after the war. He is assigned to cultivate a relationship with Sylvia, whose father, Liyi, is the plant manager.

The next day, Sylvia moderates a disagreement between her parents, a role she is accustomed to playing and one that is symbolic of her identity dilemma. She takes her mother, Helen Ames Chen, on a walk in the city, and they remember a previous visit to New York City through the sights and sounds of Shanghai. Sylvia contemplates how uncomfortable she felt in the United States and how much she envies her father and cousin Peiyuan because of their well defined Chinese identities. She considers the cosmopolitan character of Shanghai, a city with European enclaves superimposed on a Chinese backdrop and where cultural relativism rules the day.

In the evening Feng arrives for an unannounced visit to determine Liyi's knowledge of the Brunos's plans. Like Sylvia, he also is drawn to Peiyuan, who is a 16-year-old country boy who comes to represent an essential Chineseness, unvarnished by Western colonialism. During the visit Feng launches into a political diatribe against Chinese liberalism, a position advocated by Sylvia's Western-educated father. A few days later, Sylvia and Mimi spend an afternoon together at Mimi's house. Mimi reveals that she may be pregnant with Robert's child, and she asks for Sylvia's help to hide a secret rendezvous from her aunt. Sylvia cannot help her that night, however, because she has agreed to go on a date with Feng. Feng and Sylvia's first date is disastrous because he scolds her throughout the dinner for being spoiled, and she calls his political ideas romantic. Sylvia cuts the evening short and tells Feng she has promised to meet Mimi even though she has not.

On the evening of August 4, 1945—a date recognizable to the novel's readers as being on the cusp of the first U.S. nuclear attack on Japan—Soviet radio breaks the news that the war in the Pacific is about to end in the defeat of the Japanese. The cosmopolitan crowd gathers at the Jastrows to celebrate, as they had long planned to do. However, when Robert Bruno does not arrive, Sylvia, Feng, Mimi, and their Irish friend Larry Casement venture out into the nighttime city streets to find him. After they discover that Robert has passed out at his father's house, they decide to celebrate the victory in the streets, only to be picked up by a Japanese patrol and imprisoned.

In one of the novel's most significant scenes, the characters are sorted according to nationality by the armed Japanese soldiers, who are extremely drunk. Sylvia and Feng are both identified as "white Chinese" while Mimi—despite being phenotypically similar to Sylvia—identifies herself as Australian and is designated as a white foreigner. During the ordeal, Feng protects Sylvia while they are all forced to stand throughout the night. After a night of humiliation, they are released. Sylvia and Feng form an attachment that eventually turns into a love affair.

In the following days Mimi reveals to Robert at a garden party that she is pregnant. He wants her to get an abortion so they can remain lovers, eventually revealing that he can never marry her because of his father's prejudices. The strain of this rejection causes Mimi to faint, and she loses the baby in a spontaneous miscarriage. Meanwhile, Sylvia seems to lose herself in her affair with Feng, attracted to his idealism and social conscience.

As the war ends and American GIs begin to arrive in Shanghai, Sylvia's mother, Helen, grows increasingly eager to leave China for the States, and at the same time she is increasingly irritated with Peiyuan living in her home. When she demands that Peiyuan leave the house, Liyi arranges a job for him at the Bruno printing plant, despite his initial objections to nepotism. From his new apartment near the plant, Peiyuan observes Feng entering the building and follows him to a meeting of the secret communist cell. Peiyuan is discovered by Tang, the communist leader, and imprisoned in the factory for several days. When he attempts to escape, he is killed by Tang on the street in the climax of the novel. Peiyuan's murder ends the romance between Feng and Sylvia because Feng had confessed to Sylvia that Peiyuan was being held because he discovered Feng's secret activities. The communist strike is also averted because Sylvia reports what she knows about Peiyuan's death to Mr. Bruno, her father's boss.

The novel concludes with Feng leaving Shanghai on a train for an inland assignment for the communists. Mimi adopts a promiscuous lifestyle after being jilted by Robert and takes up with the Americans. The last glimpse of her in the novel is in the city streets in a sexually compromising position. In the final chapter, Sylvia's family is on vacation at a beach house, where she feels reborn as a whole self.

While *The Frontiers of Love* explicitly addresses Asian American identity through Eurasian characters, the rest of Chang's novels do not deal overtly with Asian American characters and themes, with the exception of a short satirical work *The Only Game in Town*. However, critics such as Carol Spaulding contend that the emphasis on class, gender, artistic, and religious identities in Chang's remaining novels may in fact represent a transmutation of underlying questions of ethnic identity and, as a result, draw attention to the construction of racialized selves even in white Protestant characters (3024–3025).

Chang's second novel, *A Woman of Thirty* (1959), is set in the high-class world of publishing in New York City, where Emily Merrick becomes infatuated with a married architect, David Sansom, whom she meets at a cocktail party hosted by her boss. Recently divorced, Emily seeks to escape the narrow confines of her morally rigorous, white Protestant rearing in New England through an extended vacation in Florida and later by embarking on an affair with David. However, Emily discovers the instability of basing her identity on a romantic relationship. David sporadically breaks off their relationship for weeks at a time, only to begin wooing her again, full of apologies and with renewed passion. Emily learns that her quest to explore the widest ranges of possibilities in life cannot be fulfilled by marriage.

A Passion for Life (1961), Chang's next novel, continues her exploration of white Protestant morality, in this case in the claustrophobic atmosphere of a small New England town. Barbara and Geoffrey Owens find their conventional life in Kingsbridge, Massachusetts, turned upside down when Barbara is raped during a break-in at her home by an escapee from a mental institution. Driven by duty and social obligations, the couple believe they must keep the rape and the resulting unwanted pregnancy secret from their narrowly moralistic neighbors. Set in a period when abortions were illegal and extremely dangerous, Barbara and Geoffrey are forced to entrust the town's newest doctor with their secret. Since Dr. David Bergman is Jewish and a new arrival to Kingsbridge, he has been socially isolated in the white Protestant town, and the Owenses feel his outsider status makes him a safe ally. He agrees to help the couple find an adoption agency, in part to gain acceptance, and in the end the Owenses and the Bergmans form a friendship. Eventually, Barbara persuades Geoffrey to keep the child, and the new parents move to Boston, leaving behind the restrictive morality of the small town.

In Chang's fourth novel, *The Only Game in Town* (1963), she returns to a portrayal of ethnic identity in what has been called an East-West spoof. This short satiric novel—originally composed as a film script—is "a slight, farcical piece of political satire" in the form of a love story between a white Peace Corps volunteer and an attractive Chinese dancer who is a communist (Ling 1980, 74).

Eye to Eye (1974), Chang's fifth novel, deals most explicitly with her vision of the artist in society. George P. Safford is a respected visual artist who—although he is happily married and a father—becomes smitten with an unattainable Jewish woman who works in the same building. The woman, Nan Weil, is a novelist, and she attempts to discourage George's attentions by telling him that she has three children although she has none. George thinks Nan is a "foreign princess" who makes his wife Edith seem to be even more the epitome of the average Protestant American woman. To deal with his obsession, George enters psychotherapy with Dr. Yale H. Emerson, an analyst who is intrigued with the "Orient." Throughout the novel, George also produces immense dioramas, or mood scenes, which come to symbolize his progress toward self-awareness. In addition, he seeks advice from his friend, Bob Meachum, a free-spirited poet who ends up having an affair with Nan at a writers' retreat. In an unexpected twist, Nan is revealed to be Dr. Emerson's wife, who has kept her maiden name, and the analyst abruptly ends his work with George. As George uncovers the link between his obsession with Nan and his desire to break out of Protestant conventionality, he is able to move forward to greater self-understanding, and a persistent cough that plagues him throughout the novel vanishes.

Chang's sixth novel, *A Perfect Love* (1978), continues her familiar theme of the love affair as a mechanism to break free of social conventionality. This novel's protagonist, Alice Mayhew, is a middle-aged married woman who feels confined by her 20-year marriage to an emotionally unavailable man. For a time she is able to contain her discontentment because of her daughter's promise. However, when her daughter drops out of college and begins an affair with a much older man, Alice is thrown into an identity crisis. She begins her own love affair with an intense younger man, David Henderson, who disrupts her tidy world. Alice's relationship with David terrifies her, and at the same time she feels herself opening up to exhilarating possibilities in life.

After the publication of her last novel, *A Perfect Love,* Chang shifted her literary attention toward the production of poetry and short stories. She published three volumes of poetry: *The Horizon Is Definitely Speaking* (1982), *What Matisse Is After* (1984), and *Earth, Water, Light* (1991). She was also involved in two translated volumes of poetry by Chinese women, *Approaching* (1989) and *Saying Yes* (1991). In fact, after *The Frontiers of Love,* Chang's clearest examination of her ethnic identity is found in poems such as "An Appearance of Being Chinese," "Second Nature," "Saying Yes," "Otherness," and "Allegories," as well as her short stories "The Oriental Contingent" and "Falling Tree." Critics have also praised her poems dealing with the visual arts such as "Plunging into View: Inspired by the Art of James Brooks" and "A Double Pursuit."

Chang's best known short story "The Oriental Contingent" directly engages Asian American identity, in particular questions of authenticity and assimilation. The story centers on the fraught relationship between two Chinese American women—Lisa Mallory and Connie Sung—who each secretly feel inferior to the other because neither woman feels she is authentically Chinese. At the same time, the well assimilated women are labeled as the "Oriental continent" in their elite social circles. Chang's short story, like much of the rest of her fiction, explores the inner conflict of characters in "the hyphenated condition" as they seek both to form an individual identity and to find a place within their immediate communities and the wider U.S. society. **See also** Assimilation/Americanization; Colonialism and Postcolonialism.

Further Reading

Baringer, Sandra. "'The Hybrids and the Cosmopolitans': Race, Gender, and Masochism in Diana Chang's 'The Frontiers of Love.'" *Mixed Race Literature*, ed. Jonathan Brennan. Stanford, CA: Stanford University Press, 2002. 107–121.

Chang, Diana. *The Frontiers of Love*. 1956. Seattle: University of Washington Press, 1994.

Fink, Thomas. "Chang's 'Plunging into View.'" *Explicator* 55.3 (1997): 175–177.

Grice, Helena. "Face-Ing/De-Face-Ing Racism: Physiognomy as Ethnic Marker in Early Eurasian/Amerasian Women's Texts." In *Re/Collecting Early Asian America: Essays in Cultural History*, eds. Josephine Lee, Imogene L. Lim, and Yuko Matsukawa. Philadelphia, PA: Temple University Press, 2002. 255–270.

Hamalian, Leo. "A Melus Interview: Diana Chang." *MELUS* 20.4 (1995): 29–43.

Lim, Shirley Geok-lin. "Introduction." *The Frontiers of Love*. Seattle: University of Washington Press, 1994. v–xxiii.

Ling, Amy. "Writer in the Hyphenated Condition: Diana Chang." *MELUS* 7.4 (1980): 69–83.

Lynch, Joy M. "'A Distinct Place in America Where All Mestizos Reside': Landscape and Identity in Ana Castillo's 'Sapogonia' and Diana Chang's 'The Frontiers of Love'" *MELUS* 26.3 (2001): 119–144.

Spaulding, Carol Vivian. "Blue-Eyed Asians: Eurasianism in the Work of Edith Eaton/Sui Sin Far, Winnifred Eaton/Onoto Watanna, and Diana Chang." *Dissertation Abstracts International*, Section A: The Humanities and Social Sciences 57.7 (1997): 3024–3025.

Wu, Wei-hsiung Kitty. "Cultural Ideology and Aesthetic Choices: A Study of Three Works by Chinese-American Women—Diana Chang, Bette Bao Lord, and Maxine H. Kingston." *Dissertation Abstracts International* 50.12 (1990): 3956A.

ERIC MARTINSEN

✦ CHANG, LAN SAMANTHA (1965–)

Author of *Hunger: A Novella and Stories* (1998) and the novel *Inheritance* (2004), Lan Samantha Chang, one of four daughters of Chinese immigrant parents, was born and raised in Appleton, Wisconsin. She has a BA in East Asian studies from Yale University, an MA from Harvard University's Kennedy School of Government, and an MFA from the University of Iowa Writers' Workshop. Chang was awarded the Bunting Fellowship at Radcliffe Institute and fellowships from Princeton University, the National Endowment for the Arts, Stanford University, Harvard University, and the Iowa Writers' Workshop. *Hunger* won a California Book Award Silver Medal and the *Southern Review* Prize, and *Inheritance* was awarded a PEN Beyond Margins Award in 2005. Chang was Briggs-Copeland Lecturer in Creative Writing at Harvard University until 2005, when she was named director of the Iowa Writers' Workshop, the first **Asian American** and the first woman to occupy this position.

Chang's fiction focuses on the dynamics of family relationships, most often in the context of the Chinese American immigrant experience. She portrays the tension of family dissonance through elegant prose that reflects the nuances of dialogues that hide more than they reveal. As her characters deal with separation from their homeland and the need to fit in a new country, they willingly make the ultimate sacrifice to belong: forgetting. In "Pipa's Story," a woman recalls how years before in China she took revenge upon the man who killed her father on behalf of her mother, a story her present family in the United States does not know. Tian, in "Hunger," puts his family, who did not support his dream of becoming a violinist, and the past behind when he moves to the United States. Ming, in "The Unforgiving," tells his wife they will forget the past to make room for the space required by the present. These deliberate rejections produce in Tian and Ming an obsessive hunger to belong to the American Dream. When this dream is denied them—Tian and the father in "The Eve of the Spirit Festival" are passed over for promotion at the music school and lab where they work, respectively, and Ming, who dreamed of being a scientist, works as a Xerox machine technician—they channel their fierce regret through their children. Unable to deal with their fathers' dreams for them, the children eventually leave. The balance between what the characters choose to forget and the hunger produced by what they remember becomes the hinge upon which the tension in the stories turns.

Many of the stories in *Hunger* are told from the perspective of women and center on the ways they deal with preordained roles and expectations. Min, the narrator of "Hunger," lives in a state of controlled anxiety as she helplessly observes how her husband's frustration leads him to drive his daughters—tone-deaf Anna and talented Ruth, who leaves home to escape the pressure of becoming a violinist—to a perfection they neither want nor can achieve. Ming's wife, Sansan, tries to arbitrate between her husband's dreams for their son and the youth's ambitions, realizing how similar they are. Chang's female characters appear fragile, but that fragility is generally accompanied by a hint of hidden passion or the strength to hold on when hope has diminished. Children often find themselves caught between familial obligations, inherited cultural norms, and personal identity. In "Hunger" and "The Eve of the Spirit Festival," two daughters react differently to their fathers' needs and impositions: one struggles to please him while the other breaks free. Caroline, the narrator of "San," chronicles her father's slide into gambling and his abandonment of the family. Using the riddles of mathematics that her father has taught her, she understands that she will never learn what he was seeking when he left them. These children cope with their parents' hunger for adaptation, success, and love and their subsequent regrets and frustrations as they define their own positions in relation to the family, the buried past, and possibilities for the future.

The opposing positions of two sisters that Chang explored in stories in *Hunger* are taken up in *Inheritance*, the story of a family in China from the 1920s to the United States in the 1990s. The novel describes the Japanese invasion of China, the nationalist movement, the communist revolution, and the inevitability of immigration. Hong, the narrator, recounts the story of her mother, Junan, and aunt, Yinan, sisters bound by the tragedy of their mother's suicide because of their father's rejection. As she explains how their love for the same man, her father Li-Ang, shattered their bond, Hong also connects the political upheavals in China to the family story. The novel is about fragmentation on many levels: the ruptures in the family mirror the divisions in China. The estrangement between Li-Ang and his brother because of opposing political loyalties reflects the split between China and Taiwan, just as the final rupture between Junan and Yinan is a paradigm for the separation between families caused by the diaspora. These ruptures will haunt the family for generations.

The novel explores forms of love: sisterly love, brotherly loyalty, romantic love, and daughterly devotion motivate the characters to make difficult choices in complex situations. Against her better judgment, Junan, a calculating and possessive woman, falls passionately in love with her husband. Pregnant with her second child and hoping for a boy, she sends her timid sister to attend to him when he is stationed in Chongqing, the wartime capital of China. The two fall in love, and Yinan bears Li-Ang a son. Junan eventually leaves China with her two daughters. Many years later, Hong travels back to China to reunite with her father and aunt and to try to heal the wounds of separation and betrayal. Chang shows in *Inheritance* how attitudes toward family responsibility and loyalty are generationally transmitted or revised. Hong's relationship with her sister Hwa, for instance, is colored by their different perspectives on their mother's story. Hong's narrative then becomes an attempt to reconnect with her family and her own past in an act of compassionate understanding that seeks forgiveness for errors made in the name of passion.

Chang's fiction examines the intergenerational experiences of Chinese immigrant families and explores how individuals negotiate multiple inheritances, adapt to changing situations, and fulfill ambitions. As her characters struggle to sate the hunger—

for freedom, for control, for economic opportunities, for another chance—that led them to make choices, they deal with the elusive nature of the dream they sought, as well as their children's unique dilemmas. These narratives widen our perspectives of Asian American engagements on the connection between history and personal stories. **See also** Asian Diasporas.

Further Reading
Ellis, Sherry. "Memories That Reach Back into Consciousness: An Interview with Lan Samantha Chang." *Iowa Review* 36.2 (Fall 2006): 157–167.

ROCÍO G. DAVIS

✦ CHANG, VICTORIA (1970–)

Victoria Chang is a Chinese American poet and anthologist who wrote an award-winning volume of poetry and edited a pioneering anthology of contemporary Asian American poetry. She has also written reviews and essays for the *Boston Review, Southern Review, Slope,* and others. Her *Asian American Poetry: The Next Generation* (2004) is considered a groundbreaking anthology because it brings together Asian America's most recent poetic talents, including Lisa Asagi, Nick **Carbó**, Suji Kwock Kim, Srikanth Reddy, Brenda Shaughnessy, and Paisley Rekdal. Due to the multitude of styles and subjects, this anthology does away with previous uniform perceptions of Asian American poetry and culture. Her own volume of poetry, *Circle* (2005), won the Crab Orchard Review Award Series in Poetry and the **Association for Asian American Studies** Book Award. It was a finalist for both the 2005 *ForeWord* magazine Book of the Year Award and the 2005 PEN Center USA Literary Award.

Chang's poetry has appeared in journals such as *Poetry,* the *New England Review,* the *Paris Review,* the *New Republic, Ploughshares, Triquarterly,* and *Threepenny Review.* Her poem "Seven Changs" is included in *Best American Poetry 2005,* guest-edited by Paul Muldoon. She is the recipient of a John Atherton Scholarship in Poetry from the Bread Loaf Writer's Conference, a Kenyon Writer's Workshop Taylor Fellowship, the Hopwood Award from the University of Michigan, the Holden Minority Fellowship from the MFA program at Warren Wilson College, and a Peter Taylor Fellowship from the Kenyon Review Writer's Conference.

A second-generation Chinese American, Chang was born on December 3, 1970, in Detroit, Michigan, and grew up in West Bloomfield, Michigan. She has a bachelor's degree in Asian studies from the University of Michigan, a master's degree in Asian studies from Harvard University, and an MBA from Stanford Business School. Chang is currently in the PhD program in literature and creative writing at the University of

Southern California and works as a business researcher and writer for the Stanford Graduate School of Business. She lives in Los Angeles with her husband Todd and their daughter.

Chang's poetry collection *Circle* explores an array of subjects. The first part, "On Quitting," focuses on wanting, the wish to possess, and the difficulty of ending a relationship. In "Five-Year Plan," the second subdivision of the volume, her Chinese American identity and family take center stage. In the third section, "Limits," themes such as violence and crime are contrasted with poems about finding a home and about mortality and the self (selves). *Circle* is about the progress of the human mind, be it personal progress in matters of love, temporal progress from one generation to the next, or general progress through human evolution. Chang doubts the mind's capacity for progress, especially in the subsection "Limits," which shows that its relationship to aggression and cruelty have not advanced but regressed.

The collection's title, *Circle*, alludes to many aspects touched on in the poems. A circle stands for repetition, such as the recurrence of violence in humankind; it is a symbol of transformation (e.g., from "Gertrude" to bombshell); and it represents perfection such as that which the speaker's family and social stereotypes demand of her but which she cannot provide. There can also be a circle of experiences and emotions, such as being single, falling in love, being jealous, being bored, splitting up; and history can be circular, as described in the beheading of people from the Middle Ages to now. It must not be forgotten that a circle can also refer to the area inside the circle line. In this context, the circle designates her closest companions: her sexual partners and her family. At the center of this circle is of course the poetic persona herself. The exploration of her subjectivity and of the world surrounding her is the core of this poetry collection.

Other major images in *Circle* include food, birds, the garden, and the ocean. Food, a vital necessity in the lives of all creatures, also has a social dimension, as meals are often shared with loved ones, be they partners or parents. Chang gives credit to the importance of food by featuring it in numerous poems. Mentioned are not only Chinese American dishes like chicken feet ("Hong Kong Flower Lounge") and winter melon soup ("Seven Reasons for Divorce"), but also European American food such as Bundt cake ("Preparations") and meringue ("Edward Hopper Study: Hotel Room"). Birds also appear frequently in Chang's poems. Their ability to fly and enjoy infinite freedom of movement ("Flight") and their natural instincts ("Instinct") are envied. According to the speaker's father in "The Laws of the Garden," birds are allowed to have sex—unlike people. Ravens can feel at home where humans are killed ("The Tower of London"), and larks move while humankind is static: *"we have always been this way*—a thousand young larks/mount the sudden breeze"* ("Meditation at Petoskey," 2005, 63). The garden, nature cultivated by humans, is another recurring image in

Circle. The cultivation of beautiful or useful plants (including tulips and vegetables) and the elimination of weeds relates to morality and the attempt to develop one's good sides while giving up bad habits (cf. "The Laws of the Garden," "To Want," and "On Quitting").

The image of the ocean is also prominent. It stands for separation, loneliness, and being far from rescue ("Seven Reasons for Divorce"); for impossible or very difficult tasks ("On Sameness"); and for absence of a sense of belonging ("Mostly Ocean"). In "Mostly Ocean" the poetic persona's racially marked body is described by Chang as an ocean. The Pacific Ocean, situated between the United States and China, symbolizes the perception of the speaker as culturally in-between. As she tries to reach land, raging hounds and soldiers attempt to scare her off. When she goes ashore, she is inspected and interrogated. A look back at the sea painfully reminds her that she does not really belong to this land: "As I look // back at the sea, I know my body/will always be mostly ocean, // a disease stitched into me" (2005, 42).

There are many unusual metaphors, such as comparing a woman during a (imagined) sex scene to a washrag spreading in a basin ("Edward Hopper Study: Office at Night") or linking Shang Yuan lanterns to human heads, hung in a line during the Japanese Nanking invasion: "they hang in a row for decoration, foreheads bumping/into each other, // glowing like a galaxy of holiday lights" ("Lantern Festival," 2005, 47). The conversational language describes atrocities and emotional disappointments in a forthright way, so that the intensity of the turmoil reaches the reader unhindered. Some poems start with an epigraph explaining the historical or political background of a poem (i.e., "Grooming," "Sarah Emma Edmonds," and "Yang Gui Fei"). References are made to history, art, and films.

Most of the poems in *Circle* are couplets and tercets. This form echoes the poet's concern with societal regulations, moral rules, and limits to freedom and life. The fact that the couplets and tercets are unrhymed signifies a break with tradition. There are beautiful sound clusters (for example in "Mostly Ocean" and "Before"). Anaphora, repetend, parallelism, and lists are frequent (e.g., in "Chinese Speech Contest," "$4.99 All You Can Eat Sunday Brunch," "Holiday Parties," and "Five-Year Plan"). These repetitions are the formal expressions of thematic repetitions such as disappointment in love, generational difficulties, and brutality. The harmony between form and content, along with the originality of the poems and their inner correspondence, prove Chang's position as an outstanding new voice in Asian American poetry. **See also** Racism and Asian America.

Further Reading
Chang, Victoria. *Circle.* Carbondale: Southern Illinois University Press, 2005.
———. "Victoria Chang." January 2007. http://www.victoriamchang.com.

Worra, Bryan Thao. "An Interview with Victoria Chang." Voices from the Gaps. The University of Minnesota Web Site. January 2007. http://voices.cla.umn.edu/vg/interviews/aap/chang_victoria.html.

BRIGITTE WALLINGER-SCHORN

✦ CHARLIE CHAN

The fictional Chinese American detective Charlie Chan is a creation of the Ohio-born white American writer Earl Derr Biggers, who is said to be inspired from the career of the Hawaiian police detective Chang Apana. Between 1925 and 1932, Biggers wrote six novels in which Charlie Chan was the hero. Realizing that "[s]inister and wicked Chinese are old stuff, but an amiable Chinese on the side of law and order has never been used" (Lackman) Biggers created the character of Charlie Chan in contrast to Sax Rohmer's Dr. **Fu Manchu.** In his novels, Charlie Chan lives in Honolulu with his large family. His sons are known as son No. 1 and son No. 2, who support their father but often cause him troubles. Charlie Chan is described as a man who is courageous, intelligent, amiable, patient, and characteristically modest. Although he is very fat, he moves gracefully. He speaks English fluently and often quotes Confucius. All the six novels were serialized and published, winning immediate success from the time they appeared. Before his death in 1933, Biggers saw all his Charlie Chan novels except the last one adapted into films.

After that, Charlie Chan continues to be a great charm to the American audience. He is the hero of 49 movies, 47 of them shot before 1950. The Charlie Chan movies are mostly produced by Fox Film Corp, which was later succeeded by 20th Century Fox and by Monogram Pictures. Of the three white actors who successively starred Charlie Chan, Warner Oland has acted in 16 Charlie Chan movies, Sidney Toler in 22, and Roland Winters in 6. Most of the movies were favorably received and were popular. Although in Biggers's novels Charlie Chan stays in Honolulu and never travels anywhere except to California, in the movies he is constantly on the road to various places around the world, solving one mysterious murder case after another and making himself a widely known celebrity.

Besides movies, Charlie Chan also appears as the hero in a Broadway play in 1933, on radio during the 1930s and 1940s, in comic strips from 1938 to 1942, in TV series in 1957–1958, in a theatrical play during the 1970s, and in books by several other writers. The only occasion in which a Chinese starred as Charlie Chan was in an animated series in the 1970s in which Keye Luke, who acted as Charlie Chan's eldest son in some of the previous films, got the chance to act as Charlie Chan. With his name gaining popularity in American society, Charlie Chan is more famous than his creator, Earl Derr Biggers, who brought him into literature. He is probably the most popular ethnic detective ever created in the United States.

Despite the fact that he was created to be the opposite of the evil Orientals who incarnated the **Yellow Peril** and that he was popular in American society, Charlie Chan and his movies have become targets of criticism and protest from militant Asian and African Americans since the 1960s. African Americans complained against the description of frightened blacks in the Charlie Chan movies. Asian Americans were upset about the stereotypical portrayal of Asians as inscrutable and inassimilable Orientals. They felt that the Charlie Chan image has reinforced white preconceptions about Asians, and the Charlie Chan movies have misrepresented or underrepresented Asian culture. The most scathing criticism comes from the Chinese American writer Frank **Chin**, who produced articles, short stories, essays, and novels to dispel the Hollywood stereotype of Charlie Chan. He identified Charlie Chan as a representative of racist love, and for Chin racist love was as harmful as racist hate. Chin and the characters in his novels tried hard to escape from the specter of Charlie Chan. Chin was not alone in fighting the Charlie Chan stereotyping. In 1993, the Filipino American poet, playwright, novelist Jessica **Hagedorn** edited an anthology titled *Charlie Chan Is Dead: An Anthology of Contemporary Asian American Fiction.*

It should be mentioned that, praise or criticism, the Charlie Chan movies have experienced a resurgence of interest in recent years. Cable television and videotapes of the 1980s connected younger generations with the Charlie Chan movies. In 2003, Fox Movie Channel showed Charlie Chan movies shot before 1950. In 2004 MGM released six of the Monogram movies. In 2006 Fox released some of the Charlie Chan movies on DVD.

Further Reading

Armato, Douglas M. "Charlie Chan in Books and in Motion Pictures." *Armchair Detective: A Quarterly Journal Devoted to the Appreciation of Mystery, Detective, and Suspense Fiction* 7 (1974): 97–99.

Breen, John L. "Who Killed Charlie Chan?" *Armchair Detective: A Quarterly Journal Devoted to the Appreciation of Mystery, Detective, and Suspense Fiction* 7 (1974): 100–127.

Chin, Frank. *Gunga Din Highway.* Minneapolis: Coffee House Press, 1994.

———. "Racist Love." *Seeing Through Shuck*, ed. Richard Kostelanetz. New York: Ballantine Books, 1972. 65–79.

———. "The Sons of Chan." *The Chinaman Pacific & Frisco R.R. Co.* Minneapolis: Coffee House Press, 1988. 131–165.

Cohen, Michael. "The Detective as Other: The Detective versus the Other." In *Diversity and Detective Fiction*, ed. Kathleen Gregory Klein. Bowling Green, OH: Popular, 1999. 144–157.

Ellman, Neil. "Charlie Chan Carries On." *Armchair Detective: A Quarterly Journal Devoted to the Appreciation of Mystery, Detective, and Suspense Fiction* 10 (1977): 183–184.

Godfrey, Thomas. "Charlie Chan for Rent." *Armchair Detective: A Quarterly Journal Devoted to the Appreciation of Mystery, Detective, and Suspense Fiction* 22.4 (Fall 1989): 352–364.

Hagedorn, Jessica, ed. *Charlie Chan Is Dead: An Anthology of Contemporary Asian American Fiction.* New York: Penguin Books, 1993.

Hanke, Ken. *Charlie Chan at the Movies: History, Filmography, and Criticism.* Jefferson, NC: McFarland & Company, Inc., 1989.

Lachman, Marvin S. "Earl Derr Biggers." *Dictionary of Literary Biography,* ed. George Parker Anderson. Gale, 2005. Feb. 25, 2007. <http://galenet.galegroup.com/servlet>.

Mitchell, Charles P. *A Guide to Charlie Chan Films.* Westport, CT: Greenwood, 1999. xiii, 260.

Piazza, Tom. "The Great Escape: The Pleasures of Charlie Chan in Post-Katrina New Orleans." *BookForum: The Review for Art, Fiction, & Culture* 13.3 (Sept.–Nov. 2006): 23–24, 35.

KUILAN LIU

✦ CHEE, ALEXANDER (1967–)

Alexander Chee, a Korean American novelist, essayist, short story writer, book reviewer, activist, and professor of creative writing, was born in South Kingston, Rhode Island. Because of his parents' affinity for traveling, Chee had either lived in or visited the states of California and Maine as well as Korea, Kauai, Truk, Guam, Mexico, Canada, and the Canary Islands, all before attending college. After this itinerant upbringing, Chee attended Wesleyan University from 1985 to 1989, devoting time to creative writing, primarily under the tutelage of Annie Dillard. Subsequent to undergraduate studies, Chee moved to San Francisco, becoming heavily involved with queer activist organizations ACT UP and Queer Nation. He then left for New York, where he worked as the assistant editor of *Out* magazine. From 1992 to 1994 he attended the Iowa Writers' Workshop and received an MFA in fiction writing. Since completing his schooling, he has taught creative writing at a number of institutions, including New School University, Goddard College, Wesleyan University, and, as of 2006, he teaches at Amherst College.

Chee's first novel, *Edinburgh* (2001), was published by Welcome Rain to glowing reviews in the *New York Times,* the *New Yorker, Kirkus Reviews, Publisher's Weekly* (where his novel was named Best Book of the Year), and *Lambda Book Report,* among others. Due in large part to its critical acclaim, *Edinburgh* was picked up by a larger publishing company, Picador, soon after its debut. Chee has received numerous distinctions related to his writing, including a National Endowment of the Arts Fellowship in fiction writing (2004), a MacDowell Colony Fellowship, the Whiting Writers' Award, the Asian American Writers' Workshop Literature Award, a Lambda Editor's Choice Prize, and a Michener/Copernicus Prize.

Edinburgh is a lyrical novel set in Maine. It is structured in four primary sections. The first, "Song of the Fireflies," centers on the early life of Aphias Zhe (nicknamed Fee), a biracial Korean American adolescent who is one of a number of boys molested by a choir director, ominously named Big Eric. Complicating this sexual abuse, Fee develops a passionate attachment to a fellow choirboy named Peter. The second part,

"January's Cathedral," follows Fee as he grows older and unacknowledged trauma resurfaces. Some of the choirboys, including Peter, commit suicide. Fee attempts suicide but does not succeed. The third section, "And Night's Black Sleep Upon The Eyes," is narrated from the viewpoint of Warden, a high school student and swim team member, who bears a ghostly resemblance to Fee's childhood love, Peter. At this point, Fee has returned to Maine, after having briefly lived in both San Francisco and New York for a number of years subsequent to his college schooling. When Fee takes a job as a swimming coach, his relationship to Warden takes a problematic turn as Warden becomes strongly infatuated with him. The final portion, "Blue," investigates how the complicated web of desire and loss entangling Fee and Warden forces Fee to confront the cyclical and destructive nature of melancholic love. Warden discovers that his father was the one who had molested Fee and kills him as an act of love. The novel is framed by a Korean folktale of the fox-woman, Lady Tammamo, who transforms into a human after falling in love with a man. After the man dies, she throws herself on his funeral pyre, even though she could have lived for centuries. Using this particular fable, Chee makes clear the ways in which Fee must consider his racial and ethnic identity as being constitutive of and informing his sexual experiences.

Chee's shorter writings (comprising short fiction, essays, and autobiographical sketches) have been widely anthologized or published in a variety of literary venues from 1990 onward. These pieces include "Memorials" (1990) in *Literature of Tomorrow: An Anthology of Student Fiction, Poetry, and Drama*; "A Queer Nationalism" (1991) in *Out/Look*, a journal of LGBT studies; "These Trees Were Once Women" (1996) in *Boys Like Us: Gay Writers Tell Their Coming Out Stories*; "A Pilgrimage of You" (1999) in *His 3: Brilliant New Fiction by Gay Writers*; "Burn" (2000) in *Take Out: Queer Writing from Asian Pacific America*; "After Peter" (2001) in *Loss Within Loss: Artists in the Age of AIDS*; "13 Crimes Against Love, or, the Crow's Confession" (2002) in *Lodestar Quarterly*; "Self-Quiz" (2002) in *The Man I Might Become: Gay Men Write About Their Fathers*; "Best Friendster Date Ever" (2005) in *Best Gay Erotica*; "Before, During, and After" (2005) in *Blithe House Quarterly*; and "Dick" (2006) in *From Boys to Men: Gay Men Write about Growing Up*. Although these writings are quite divergent in genre and narrative details, Chee has been consistently interested in themes related to loss, trauma, desire, queer identity, activism, AIDS/HIV, race, ethnicity, and/or Asian American identity. He is one of a select group of queer Asian American writers that include Timothy Liu, Justin Chin, Lawrence Chua, Russell **Leong**, Nina Revoyr, and Ginu Kamani who have received strong critical attention within literary studies. He also is part of a growing contingent of Korean American novelists whose works have been favorably reviewed in the last decade, such as Marie Myung-Ok Lee, Don **Lee**, Chang-Rae **Lee**, Suki **Kim**, Susan **Choi**, Nora Okja **Keller**, and Caroline Hwang.

Chee has written book reviews for *Wilson Quarterly* and *Lambda Book Report* and contributed articles for various magazines. He is currently at work on two novels and an autobiography. He is working on his next novel, *The Queen of the Night*, which chronicles the experiences of a nineteenth-century Paris opera singer. **See also** Asian American Political Activism.

Further Reading

Cooper, Michael L. "Alexander Chee's Childhood Feels like 'A Long Trip by Car, Plane, and Boat." *Lambda Book Report* 10.8 (March 2002): 14–15.

Sarkessian, Juliet. "Artful Story about the Victims of Child Molestation." Rev. of *Edinburgh*, by Alexander Chee. *Lambda Book Report* 10.8 (March 2002): 16–18.

Spinella, Michael. Rev. of *Edinburgh*, by Alexander Chee. *Booklist* 98.6 (Nov. 15, 2001): 550.

STEPHEN HONG SOHN

✦ CHENG, NIEN (1915–)

A Chinese American author and survivor of the Cultural Revolution (1966–1976), Nien Cheng is known internationally for her memoir *Life and Death in Shanghai* (1987), which describes her victimization, imprisonment, and torture for six and a half years in communist Shanghai. Born in Beijing, Cheng was educated at Yanjing University and the London School of Economics. She married Kang-Chi Cheng, diplomat for the Kuomintang (nationalist) regime. On the establishment of the People's Republic of China in 1949, Cheng's husband became general manager of Shell Oil's Shanghai office until his death in 1957. After he died, Cheng was employed by Shell as an advisor to its British managers in China. She worked in this capacity until 1966. Before the Cultural Revolution, Cheng had lived a privileged lifestyle in communist Shanghai. She had been permitted to keep servants, had a large bank account in Hong Kong to draw from, was allowed to travel outside China, and had managed to avoid involvement in the political campaigns preceding the Cultural Revolution. In 1966, this privilege, taken as evidence of counterrevolutionary sympathies, made her an inevitable target for the Red Guards who, in August 1966, ransacked her home and held her hostage while they destroyed her books, pictures, and many priceless pieces of Chinese porcelain from her collection. This was followed a month later by her arrest and detainment at No. 1 Detention House in Shanghai on the trumped-up charge that she was a British spy. Jailed in solitary confinement for nearly seven years, refusing to make a false confession, Cheng also lost her only child, her daughter Meiping, to the horrors of the Cultural Revolution. The official explanation offered Cheng was that her daughter, a prominent Shanghai film actress, had committed suicide while under interrogation by throwing herself out the window of a high building. Later, after persevering at some personal risk to uncover the truth of Meiping's death, Cheng learned that she was murdered by Maoists for refusing to denounce her mother.

Cheng was released from prison unexpectedly in 1973 because of a misdiagnosis of cancer made by an unqualified Cultural Revolution "physician." Like many other victims of the Cultural Revolution, Cheng was rehabilitated after the Gang of Four was arrested; she was permitted to leave China in 1980. She moved first to Ottawa, Canada, where she began writing her memoir. She wrote in English with the aim not only of documenting the atrocities of the Cultural Revolution and her personal suffering but also of educating the West on the brutal facts of life in communist China. In the Author's Note, Cheng explains that her memoir provides a reliable factual account, a product of her need, during long confinement, to repeatedly recall events and dialogue to memory to evaluate their significance to her case. *Life and Death in Shanghai* was completed in Washington DC, where Cheng eventually settled. In 1988 she became an American citizen.

Life and Death in Shanghai is divided into three parts. The first part, which is the shortest, describes the events leading up to her arrest. We are introduced to Cheng's daughter, several friends, and her ever loyal house servants. The peace of this household is shattered by the arrival of the Red Guards, Mao's youth army. The night when her home is ransacked is vividly narrated, the education and sophistication of Cheng exposing the ignorance and blind fanaticism of her young opponents. This is best exemplified when she manages to dissuade them from smashing more of her porcelain, arguing that the value of the pieces will help them finance their world revolution. In this first section, Cheng is also forced to attend two "struggle meetings"; she is a reluctant observer at the first (denouncing a colleague from Shell) and the unfortunate subject of the second. Such meetings, which took place all over China during the Cultural Revolution, were public persecutions of counterrevolutionaries, capitalist-roaders, and intellectuals, who were paraded, beaten, and humiliated before large crowds until they confessed their "guilt." Cheng refuses to confess and is promptly taken to prison.

Cheng continues to refuse to confess throughout her long imprisonment, detailed in the central section of her memoir. In a clear and understated manner, Cheng describes the conditions of her solitary confinement in Shanghai's No. 1 Detention House. Her lonely and squalid existence is punctured by occasional interrogations. Cheng maintains her sanity partly by keeping her brain active; and her study of Mao's writings in her cell enables her, under interrogation, to use the language of the revolutionaries in her own defense. The intelligence and skill by which she holds to her principles also highlight the dulling effects of ideological fanaticism. The language of her interrogators, full of clichés and quotations from Chairman Mao's *Little Red Book*, are no match against her manipulative and tactical expertise. At one point, when a picture of her dancing with a Swiss friend is produced as evidence of her lack of patriotism, she counters that in dancing with foreigners she was serving the revolutionary cause by making her dance partners unpatriotic to the capitalist West. Though such moments of wit may thrill the reader, her interrogator was not amused. She was punished on this occasion by being forced to read aloud from Mao's collected works for three consecutive days.

Frustrated in their attempts to extract a confession, her enemies resorted to methods of physical torture. At one point, she was locked in a tiny dark cell, her hands cuffed behind her back so tightly that her wrists and arms oozed with pus. But her mind never breaks. When she is eventually informed that she is free to leave as a beneficiary of proletarian magnanimity, she is enraged. Refusing to leave until she is issued an official apology for wrongful arrest and a declaration of her innocence, Cheng is eventually dragged out of the detention house by two female guards.

The final section of *Life and Death in Shanghai* records Cheng's experience living as a proletariat after her release from jail. She is provided with modest quarters but is quickly made aware of the suspicion and hostility of her new neighbors. Although she was still under surveillance, Cheng investigates the circumstances of her daughter's death, teaches private English lessons, and stubbornly sustains her attachment to old China in, for example, her continued study of poetry from the Tang dynasty and her resistance to wearing the standard proletarian navy blue drill clothing. Her description of China in the 1970s depicts a malaise of cynicism and political disillusionment in the context of general social disorder. Her account of the "back door" system, whereby regulations were circumvented through negotiation of personal favors, exemplifies the political and moral breakdown of this period of Chinese history.

Cheng assesses the Cultural Revolution as a disaster for China, deliberately caused by unscrupulous leaders embroiled in factional conflicts. *Life and Death in Shanghai*, with its combination of riveting memoir and historical evaluation, takes its place with a number of other autobiographical accounts of the Cultural Revolution and its aftermath. *Born Red: A Chronicle of the Chinese Revolution* (1987) by Gao Yuan and *Red Scarf Girl* by Ji Li Jiang, both written by former members of the Red Guards, create an interesting contrast with Cheng's book. Swept up by the revolutionary excitement as teenagers, Yuan and Jiang explain how their indoctrination in the cult of Chairman Mao prepared them to root out counterrevolutionaries with enthusiasm and little conscience. Their zeal, however, was considerably compromised when members of their own families became targets. Such accounts show that less privileged people than Cheng also suffered greatly from a campaign that encouraged widespread paranoia and suspicion, and that most people were ill equipped to combat the immorality and cruelty that resulted.

Cheng's gender, age, and physical frailty render her courage all the more impressive. Undoubtedly, her tormentors did not expect such stubbornness and bravery from a woman. Her memoir is important, then, as a record of female strength and intelligence under extreme duress. It belongs with a number of other memoirs by Chinese women who tell the recent history of China from their female point of view. Nien Cheng and writers like Jung Chang, Adeline Yen **Mah**, and Hong Ying document extraordinary female resistance and courage through searing accounts of lives affected not only by the turbulent and violent history of twentieth-century China but also by the long legacy of Chinese oppression of women.

Further Reading

Bennett, Gordon A., and Ronald N. Montaperto. *Red Guard: The Political Biography of Dai Hsiao-ai.* Garden City, NY: Doubleday, 1971.

Chang, Jung. *Wild Swans: Three Daughters of China.* New York: Simon and Schuster, 1991.

Jiang, Ji Li. *Red Scarf Girl.* New York: Scholastics, 1997.

Liang, Heng. *Son of the Revolution.* New York: Alfred A. Knopf, 1983.

Ling, Ken. *The Revenge of Heaven.* New York: G.P. Putnam's Sons, 1972.

Mah, Adeline Yen. *Falling Leaves: The True Story of an Unwanted Chinese Daughter.* London and New York: Penguin, 1997.

Wong, Cynthia F. "Remembering China in *Wild Swans* and *Life and Death in Shanghai.*" In *Women Writers and the Politics and Poetics of Home,* eds. Catherine Wiley and Fiona R. Barnes. New York and London: Garland, 1996. 115–133.

Ying, Hong. *Daughter of the River: An Autobiography.* New York: Grove Press, 1999.

Yuan, Gao. *Born Red: A Chronicle of the Cultural Revolution.* Stanford: Stanford University Press, 1987.

LINDSAY DAVIES

✦ CHIANG, MONLIN (1886–1964)

Also known as Jiang Menglin, American-educated Chinese writer and educator Monlin Chiang was born in Zhejiang Province, China. Chiang received his traditional Chinese education from private tutoring when he was very young. Later he went to Hangzhou, the capital city of Zhejiang province, and attended Qiu Shi College, the precursor of the present Zhejiang University. From 1908 to 1917 he studied in the United States, taking his undergraduate work at the University of California, where he received a bachelor's degree and later a PhD from Columbia University in 1917 under John Dewey's guidance. For three years he wrote editorials for the *Chinese Free Press*, Dr. Sun Yat-sen's revolutionary organ in San Francisco. His impressions of the revered revolutionary leader both in the United States and later in China are valuable source materials for his contributions to the press. On his return to China in 1917, he edited an educational magazine entitled *New Education*. From 1923 to 1926 he was the acting chancellor of National Peking University, and from 1930 to 1935 he became its president. As the head of Peking University, he moved with his university to Southwest Associated University in Kunming, Yunnan province. He was also asked to be the head of Zhejiang University and later the Minister of Education during Chiang Kai-shek's administration. Before the founding of the People's Republic of China, he moved with Chiang Kai-shek's administration to Taiwan and died there in 1964.

Chiang is known mainly as an educator who was instrumental in the establishment of a modern education system in China. Being well educated in the traditional Chinese school, to the extent of having attained the first honor in the imperial examination, while at the same time having studied in westernized institutions in China and in the West, Chiang is well versed in two cultures and their educational differences. In his early life he witnessed the political vicissitudes and educational changes in China. His meditations on education culminated in a book, *Tides from the West: A Chinese Autobiography,* which was written in English in an air-raid shelter during the difficult years when he was teaching at Southwest Associated University in Yunnan. The book was accepted and published by Yale University Press in 1947. The title of the book is a pun, alluding not only to the famous tides near Hangzhou Bay but also to the flood of Western influence on China. The book is called an autobiography, but it is more than an autobiography, as it gives a panoramic view of the changing political, social, and cultural structure of China at that time; it describes sincerely and perhaps a bit whimsically the author's keen diagnosis of China's ills and offers shrewd analysis of the Chinese and Western outlook on life.

Tides from the West consists of seven parts. Part I begins with the description of Chiang's early life in his hometown, then narrates his education and the examination system in China. Part II is devoted to his study in the United States and also his comparisons between Chinese and American cultures. Part III focuses on the intellectual awakening in the whirlwind of changes in modern China. Part IV narrates his relation with Dr. Sun Yat-sen and also constitutional experiment in China. Part V is a description of the social and cultural aspects of Chinese life. Part VI tells of the war in China and its devastation to Chinese people and education, and the last part reflects on China's position in the modern world. Chapters such as "China and Japan—a Comparison," "Characteristics of Chinese Culture," and "Modern Civilization" are the result of his mature opinions. The author explains the fundamentals of the Chinese outlook on life and the principles that have always guided China in her appropriation of alien ideas. Having received a sound education both in China and in the United States, Chiang knows clearly what Chinese people have been interested in and feels that he has the duty to articulate the interactions between China and the West. After enumerating some of the gifts that China has received from the West, he adds that the West has also learned a great deal from China, maintaining a comparatist stance with regard to Eastern and Western cultures.

Straddling both Chinese and Western cultures, Chiang likes to compare and contrast the origin and development of Chinese and Western cultures. In his early days he was pro-West during China's intellectual debates about the relationship between Chinese and Western cultures, maintaining that China should take Western culture as essence and Chinese culture as application, that is, first, pay attention to Western culture; second, make a good study of Chinese culture; and third, give attention to natural science. Later he moderated his view by trying to reconcile Chinese and Western cultures.

Issues of education in China are Chiang's lifelong concern. In the United States Chiang studied under John Dewey and obtained his PhD in 1917 with a dissertation entitled *A Study in Chinese Principles of Education*, analyzing Chinese educational systems since Confucius's time, with cross-references to Western culture and educational practices. On his return to China, he edited *New Education* monthly and prepared a *John Dewey Special*, introducing Dewey's ethics and moral education to Chinese readers. He compared Dewey's ethical views to ancient Chinese Confucian philosopher Wang Yangming's moral attitude toward learning. Through comparison and contrast between Chinese and Western ways of education, Chiang hoped that he could put what he had learned in the United States into practice in China. But he lived in a turbulent period in modern Chinese history, and it was difficult for him to realize his dream.

Further Reading

Hsu, Francis L.K. "Review of *Tides from the West: A Chinese Autobiography* by Chiang Monlin and *Autobiography of a Chinese Woman* by Buwei Yang Chao." *Journal of American Folklore* 62.243 (Jan.–Mar. 1949): 76–77.

Hummel, Arthur W. "Review of *Tides from the West: A Chinese Autobiography*." *Far Eastern Survey* 16.10 (May 1947): 120.

Marlone, Carrol B. "Review of *Tides from the West: A Chinese Autobiography*." *The Far Eastern Quarterly* 7.1 (November 1947): 103–104.

GUANGLIN WANG

✦ CHIANG, YEE (1903–1977)

A Chinese American poet, writer, painter, calligrapher, and professor of Chinese, Chiang Yee was best known for the series of Silent Traveller books, in addition to his introductory volumes on Chinese painting and calligraphy. Born in Jiujiang, Jiangxi province, China in 1903, Chiang grew up in an affluent household that valued Confucianism and Chinese classical education. Under the tutelage of his father, a traditional Chinese intellectual/poet/painter, Chiang had been immersed in Chinese painting and literature since early childhood. Before attending public high school, he received a family education with his cousins in the Chinese classics. Caught in the tumultuous developments of modern China when economic interests in the early Chinese republic were being divided by militant Japanese and colonial Western powers, Chiang believed Western science and technology would help improve his country, and so he decided to study chemistry instead of art in college. After obtaining his bachelor's degree, he worked as a chemistry teacher, a journalist, and subsequently a county magistrate in three different counties along the Yangtze River. As county magistrate, Chiang witnessed firsthand the suffering of the commons at the hands of corrupt politicians and Japanese invaders. He was determined to implement reforms to better the living conditions of his compatriots; however, his idealism was not appreciated by his superiors and colleagues. In 1933, out of frustration and fear of persecution by his power-hungry superiors, Chiang chose to leave China for Britain, leaving his wife and four children behind.

Initially Chiang intended to study foreign government at the University of London, but he ended up teaching Chinese there instead, and later on worked at the Wellcome Museum of Anatomy and Pathology. During this period, Chiang's expertise in Chinese painting and calligraphy brought him publishing opportunities, and he began to assume the role of self-appointed ambassador of Chinese culture in the West. The year 1935 saw the publication of his first book, *The Chinese Eye: An Interpretation of Chinese Painting*, whose lucid and humorous explication of Chinese philosophy and painting was so well received that the book was soon sold out and reprinted. In 1937 Chiang published his first travel book, *The Silent Traveller: A Chinese Artist in Lake Land*, also an immediate success. His English audience found his interpretations of English landscape and social practices from a unique Chinese perspective and his renditions of them in Chinese-style painting refreshing. Chiang would continue to produce in the same fashion, illustrating his prose with his own pen-and-ink drawings and Chinese-style paintings, accompanied by the poems he composed in traditional Chinese lyric form and penned in Chinese brushes. He would publish eleven more books in the Silent Traveller series, including those about Edinburgh, London, Oxford, the Yorkshire Dales, Dublin, Paris, New York, San Francisco, Boston, Japan, and wartime in general. In 1938 Chiang published *Chinese Calligraphy: An Introduction to Its Aesthetic and Technique*, in which he explains the composition of Chinese characters and their strokes and draws on Chinese legends and stories for illustration. In 1940 he published *A Chinese Childhood*, his memoir of adolescence in Jiujiang. From his recollections of well-ensconced childhood and prelapsarian formative years in the

Chiang mansion, the reader can see how the larger sociopolitical climate affected the welfare of the Chiang family. In his explications of Chinese customs and culture in the book, Chiang tried to make the Chinese understandable to his Western audience, and hence dissipating the stereotype of the "inscrutable" Chinese. His persistent efforts to dispel negative stereotypes about the Chinese and to focus on the similarities between the East and the West established him as one of the earliest bridge builders between East and West. Chiang is mostly remembered today for his Silent Traveller series and books on Chinese painting and calligraphy, but he also wrote and illustrated several children's books during his sojourn in England.

In 1945, at the suggestion of his publisher, Chiang took a trip to New York at the end of **World War II** and later published his first American travel book, *The Silent Traveller in New York*. In 1955 he resettled in the United States, serving first as a lecturer of Chinese at Columbia University and later became professor emeritus. Some time in between, he received a two-year fellowship at Harvard University and then served as a visiting professor at the University of California, Berkeley. His stay in these places resulted in two more American travel books, *The Silent Traveller in Boston* (1959) and *The Silent Traveller in San Francisco* (1963). Despite his success in publishing and probably due to the cold war, Chiang never got a chance to return to his motherland until 1975, when he was finally able to reunite with his family on a trip arranged by the Chinese government. In his travel impressions *China Revisited: After Forty-Two Years*, published posthumously in 1977, Chiang was uncharacteristically emotive; he raved about the changes and reconstructions he witnessed in communist China. Along with his unexamined admiration for the "new China" was his long overdue critique of European and American imperialism and the devastation it inflicted on China. Such explicit disapproval was rarely detected in his other books. In 1977 Chiang took another trip to China and was planning to write another book about Chinese art before he fell seriously ill in Beijing. He was hospitalized and died shortly thereafter.

With the rise of **Asian American studies** and its transnationalist approach, Chiang's contributions to diasporic Chinese literature are being reevaluated, and several volumes of his Silent Traveller series are being republished. Chiang's travel experience in the West presents an exceptional case of Chinese American mobility. Unlike many of his contemporary Asians in America, most of whom were laborers and hence economically and geographically immobilized, Chiang as an artist/writer could afford frequent leisure travels. Although his initial journey out of China was dictated by necessity, to borrow critic Sau-ling Cynthia Wong's term, his subsequent travels in Europe and America were more for extravagance; he embarked on the journeys both for pleasure and for collecting materials for his books.

Chiang's travel books can be placed in the tradition of both Chinese and Western travel writing. On the one hand, his travelogues reiterate the Western ideal of the voyage as progress, liberation, salvation, and expansion of knowledge. On the other, his adoption of the pseudonym Silent Traveller, his fusion of various genres in his books—prose, poetry, and painting, and his allusions to Chinese art, literature, and history hark back to the conventions of travel writing by Chinese literati, whose political visions and social critique are embedded in their depictions of natural surroundings and native customs. Perhaps aware of his position as a cultural other in the West, especially during the cold war, Chiang was not vociferous about social and political injustices in Britain or the United States. His evasiveness on political issues could have resulted from his identity as a Chinese exile striving for recognition in the West. His travel books mostly offered his good-natured appreciation of Western social practices, complemented by his unique stylized renditions of Western landscapes. Contemplating Western natural scenery, Chiang often evokes Chinese poets and painters, such as Du Fu, Su Dongpo, Tao Yuanming, and so on, to enhance his sentiments. His allusions to Chinese art and literature may imply his masked homesickness and his attempts at bridging Chinese and Western cultures. Ultimately, Chiang upheld a universalist humanism that leveled differences between Chinese and Westerners; such universalism may inadvertently result in cultural indifference. Critic Elaine Yee Lin Ho warns against the ahistorical and apolitical undertone in Chiang's universalizing strategy. His books paint a picture of a solitary world where race and culture are erased, and hence neither conflicts nor struggles seem to exist. **See also** Asian American Stereotypes.

Further Reading

Ho, Elaine Yee Lin. "The Chinese Traveller in the West." *Mattoid* 52–53 (1998): 316–333.

Huang, Su-ching. "'I Do Not Mind Placing Myself in a Melting Pot So Long As I Do Not Get Boiled': Mutual Authentication of the 'Silent Traveller' and the American Landscape." *Crossings: Travel, Art, Literature, Politics*, ed. Rudolphus Teeuwen. Taipei, Taiwan: Bookman, 2001. 233–254; rpt. in Huang, *Mobile Homes: Spatial and Cultural Negotiation in Asian American Literature*. New York: Routledge, 2006. 15–38.

Liu, Esther Tzu-Chiu. "Literature as Painting: A Study of the Travel Books of Chiang Yee." Diss. University of Northern Colorado, 1976.

Zheng, Da. "Chiang Yee." *Asian American Writers*, ed. and with an introduction by Deborah Madsen. Detroit, MI: Gale, 2005. 36–43.

———. "Double Perspective: *The Silent Traveller in the Lake District*." *Mosaic: A Journal for the Interdisciplinary Study of Literature* 36.1 (2003): 161–178.

———. "Home Construction: Chinese Poetry and American Landscape in Chiang Yee's Travel Writings." *Journeys* 1.1-2 (2000): 59–85.

———. "The Traveling of Art and the Art of Traveling: Chiang Yee's Painting and Chinese Cultural Tradition." *Studies in the Literary Imagination* 37.1 (2004): 168–190.

———. "Travel Writing and Cultural Interpretation: Chiang Yee's *Silent Traveller* Books and His American Experience." *Crossings: Travel, Art, Literature, Politics*, ed. Rudolphus Teeuwen. Taipei, Taiwan: Bookman Books, 2001. 211–231.

SU-CHING HUANG

✦ CHIN, FRANK (1940–)

A Chinese American playwright, actor, novelist, literary critic, literary historian, and activist, Frank Chin is best known for his two groundbreaking anthologies of Asian American writings coedited with Jeffery Paul **Chan**, Lawson Fusao **Inada**, and Shawn **Wong**. He has also written two widely acclaimed novels, several plays, and a collection of short stories. Besides, he has contributed numerous critical essays on Asian American literature, identity, and culture. For his contributions, Chin has sometimes been considered the godfather of Asian American literature. Yet for his radicalism, poignancy, and freewheeling imagination, Chin has been nicknamed the Ayatollah or a literary gangster. Born on February 25, 1940, in Berkeley, California, a fifth-generation Chinese American, Frank Chin attended the University of California at Berkeley as an English major from 1958 to 1961, when he won a fellowship that took him to the Writers' Workshop at the University of Iowa. In 1965, he received his bachelor's degree from the University of California at Santa Barbara. In the 1960s, Chin worked for two years as a clerk at Western Pacific Railroad in Oakland, California, and one year as a brakeman on the Southern Pacific Railroad, and he claims to be the first Chinese American brakeman in the company's history. In 1966 he left the railroad and started writing and producing documentaries for King Broadcasting Co., in Seattle, Washington. In 1969, he left his job and became a part-time lecturer in **Asian American studies** at the University of California, Davis. In the early 1970s, Chin began his dramatic career and wrote two plays, *The Chickencoop Chinaman* (1972) and *The Year of the Dragon* (1974), which were produced Off-Broadway by the American Place Theatre. The success of these two plays made Chin the first Asian American to have work presented on a mainstream New York stage. Chin was also the first Chinese American playwright to produce plays about the Chinese American experience. In 1973 he established the Asian American Theatre Workshop in San Francisco and remained as its artistic director for four years. Since the 1980s, instead of focusing on theatre, Chin started writing fiction and essays on Chinese and Japanese history, culture, and literature. He has taught courses on Asian American subjects and creative writing at San Francisco State University; the University of California at Berkeley, Davis, and Santa Barbara; Western Washington University; and the University of Oklahoma at Norman. He has also received a number of awards and fellowships throughout his career, such as the James T. Phelan Award in Short Fiction and East West Players Playwriting Award in 1971, the Rockefeller Playwright Grant in 1974, and three American Book Awards, respectively in 1982 for *The Chickencoop Chinaman* and *The Year of the Dragon*, in 1989 for his collection of short stories, *Chinaman Pacific and Frisco R.R. Co.*, and in 2000 for Lifetime Achievement. Currently, he resides in Los Angeles, California.

Frank Chin's important contribution to the development of Asian American literature has been acknowledged by critics such as Ishmael Reed, Elaine Kim, and King-Kok Cheung. His writings and polemics have influenced and inspired major Asian American writers, including David Henry **Hwang** and Russell **Leong**. Some of his works have also been excerpted in American literary anthologies such as *Heath Anthology of American Literature*. In his publications, Frank Chin explores issues related to Chinese American history, community, and family, especially the father-son relationship. The Asian American sensibility, racial stereotypes, Chinatown, Chinaman, and railroads have been key themes for Chin. Influenced by the **civil rights movement** and the cultural nationalist movements, in the 1970s, Chin endeavored to preserve the cultural and historical integrity of Chinese America and form the cultural identity of Chinese Americans by distinguishing them from both white America and China and exposing the falsity of racial stereotypes established by white supremacists. He also developed a pidgin language exclusively for Chinese America and called himself "Chinaman" to distinguish himself from assimilated Chinese Americans.

In the early 1970s, together with Jeffery Paul Chan, Lawson Fusao Inada, and Shawn Wong, Frank Chin founded the Combined Asian American Resources Project to preserve the cultural and historical integrity of Asian ethnic groups. They rediscovered the ignored writings of Asian American writers such as Louis **Chu** and Toshio **Mori** and compiled the foundational anthology, *Aiiieeeee!: An Anthology of Asian American Writers* (1974). Its preface and introduction have been regarded as the declaration of intellectual and linguistic independence of Asian America. In the preface, Frank Chin and his comrades condemned the prevailing racism and white supremacy in the United States and dissected the false and effeminate Oriental stereotypes of racist love and racist hate, respectively represented by **Charlie Chan** and **Fu Manchu**. By means of reduction to absurdity, they created a new term *Asian American sensibility*, which they claimed to be authentic and distinguish Asian America from both Asia and white America, though they failed to provide a substantial definition to the term. With the publication of this anthology, they intended to show the real Asian American communities and real Asian Americans their "dual personality identity crisis." *Aiiieeeee!* also excerpts act I of Frank Chin's own *Chickencoop Chinaman*.

Frank Chin first gained fame as a playwright with the production of *The Chickencoop Chinaman*. This two-act play won the 1971 East West Players Playwriting Award for Chin. The play debuted at the American Place Theatre, New York City, on May 27, 1972, and became the first Asian American play performed in New York stage history. The play's protagonist Tam Lum is a Chinese American writer and filmmaker who is making a documentary of his idol—Ovaltine Jack Dancer, an African American prizefighting champion. To find more information about Ovaltine, Tam goes on a trip in search of Charley Popcorn, Ovaltine's father. The play traces Tam

Lum's trip from Oakland, California, to "Oakland," a black ghetto in Pittsburgh, Pennsylvania, where he unites with his childhood friend, Kenji, a Japanese American, and meets Lee, a possible Eurasian or Chinese American passing for white, and Tom, a Chinese American writer and one of Lee's ex-husbands. In Pittsburgh, Tam interviews Charley Popcorn. However, to his great disappointment, Charley is not Ovaltine's father but his former boxing trainer, now an owner of a porn movie house. The inspiring father-son story told by Ovaltine is a mere lie. Back from the interview, Tam has a fight with Lee and Tom. Tam attacks Lee for pretending to be white and Tom for being the Americanized **model minority** and a brownnoser of white culture. Lee and Tom, in return, attack Tam for his imitation of African Americans and not being positive about his Chinese American identity. The play ends with Tam's monologue about his grandmother hearing the legendary Iron Moonhunter, a train made by Chinamen, which repeatedly appears in Chin's writings as a symbol of masculinity, heroism, and the pioneering spirit of Chinese America. The production of *The Chickencoop Chinaman* caused a great stir and aroused controversy because of its theme of Chinese American history, genealogy, and identity, its experimental combination of the scenes of dream and reality, and its language of synthesis and hybridity. The play apparently is about Tam Lum's quest for a heroic father figure to replace his own effeminate and absent father. However, underneath, the play centers on Chinese Americans' struggle with their identity problem and their search for their missing history and genealogy. The combination of surrealistic and realistic scenes presents various elements that constitute the hybrid experience and broken memory of Chinese Americans. The Pidgin English in the play is full of slang, black American vernacular, obscenities, Cantonese, and unusual grammar, which presents difficulty for the audience to fully understand the play. However, Chin argues that with the bold and unconventional linguistic experimentation, he follows the Asian American sensibility and truly represents Chinese America.

Two years later, Frank Chin again displayed his talent with *The Year of the Dragon* produced at the same place on May 22, 1974. In 1975, the play was videotaped for the PBS program *Theatre in America* and broadcast nationally. In 1977 Chin also starred in a San Francisco production of the play. Compared with *The Chickencoop Chinaman*, *The Year of Dragon* is more traditionally structured and better received by the public. The play is set in an apartment in San Francisco's **Chinatown**. The story is about a Chinese American family, the Engs. Father, Wing Eng, is the respected "mayor" of Chinatown. The young Wing immigrated to the United States and left in China his first wife, China Mama, mother of Fred Eng. In the United States, Wing married Hyacinth, a Chinese American girl, who later gave birth to Mattie and Johnny. Now that Wing is in his sixties and is dying of a lung disease, he can only depend on Fred to support the family. Fred works as a Chinese American travel agent and tour guide in Chinatown. Though he hates this job and wishes to be a writer, he cannot quit, so he stays for the sake of his family. Mattie married Ross, a China-crazy white American, after her college graduation and is determined to leave Chinatown forever. Johnny is a rebellious Chinatown street kid in his late teens. During the Chinese New Year, fully aware that death is approaching, Wing Eng brings China Mama to the United States and calls back Mattie to have a family reunion. Though old and dying, the autocratic father insists that the whole family remain in Chinatown and rejects Fred's proposal to let Hyacinth and Johnny leave Chinatown and go to Boston with Mattie for a new beginning. Wing Eng dies in a fierce argument with Fred.

The play centers on the disintegration of the Chinese American family in Chinatown. In it, for white American tourists, Chinatown is a museum of "ornamental Orientalia" and their "private reserve" to appreciate the exotic culture; however, for Chinese Americans, it is poverty-stricken, degenerating, and suffocating. The Eng family is a microcosm of Chinese American community, and the conflicts within the family reflect the problems of the community at large: The old generation of Chinese immigrants is dying, and thus, the connection with China and Chinese traditional culture is fading. The second and later generations of Chinese Americans have been trapped in Chinatown under the imposed aura of "model minority" and suffer from economic exploitation and institutional racism.

Besides two plays, in 1988 Frank Chin compiled eight stories mostly written in the 1970s into an award-winning collection, *The Chinaman Pacific & Frisco R.R. Co.* Throughout these stories, Chin attacks racial stereotypes and indicts white supremacy and imperialism. He also attempts to synthesize the myths and history of Chinese America based on the legends of early Chinese railroad builders and miners to empower and restore masculinity to Chinese American males. However, most male protagonists in these stories are still ironic and tragic antiheroes such as Tam Lum and Fred Eng, without any positive features.

In the 1980s Frank Chin also published several critical essays. Around the mid-1980s, after years of reflection, Chin changed his negative views on Chinese culture. Instead, he started reading Chinese classics including *Romance of the Three Kingdoms, the Water Margin*, and Sun Tzu's *The Art of War*, based on which he made efforts to claim a new literary and racial authenticity for Chinese America. This change is seen clearly in *The Big Aiiieeeee! An Anthology of Chinese American and Japanese American Literature* that he coedited with Jeffery Paul Chan, Lawson Fusao Inada, and Shawn Wong, published in 1991. In its introduction, Chin and his comrades explain that their early misunderstanding of Asia and Asian culture was caused by the white social Darwinist philosophers and fictionists who, through teaching and various ways of propaganda in mass media, forced Asian Americans to accept as both fact and stereotype their Christian vision of Asia as a remote area with a brutish and sadomasochistic culture.

Therefore, they felt the urge to revive Asian history and culture to differentiate the real from the fake and claimed to offer an authentic literary history of Asian American writing. At the beginning of this anthology, Chin contributed a 92-page-long essay, "Come All Ye Asian American Writers of the Real and the Fake," which summarizes his reflections and research in the 1980s. In this essay, Chin criticizes many Asian American writers, including Jade Snow **Wong**, Maxine Hong **Kingston**, Amy **Tan**, and David Henry Hwang for being Christianized, assimilating, and contributing to the stereotyping of Asians by faking Chinese culture and history. In the essay he even inserted the original "Ballad of Mulan" both in Chinese and in English translation to prove that Kingston distorted the legend of Fa Mulan in *The Woman Warrior*. Chin also introduced a number of Chinese classics, including *Romance of the Three Kingdoms, the Water Margin,* and *Journey to the West,* to demonstrate the heroic tradition in Chinese culture and cited historical documents on the tongs in Chinatowns to show their inheritance of this tradition. Moreover, Chin selected a few heroic figures out of these classics such as Kwan Kung, Song Jiang, and Lin Chong as masculine models and representatives of Chinese Americans to replace the effeminate and demonized Oriental stereotypes. *The Big Aiiieeeee!* also excerpts Chin's own short story "The Only Real Day."

The 1990s is another productive period for Frank Chin, within which he shifted his focus from the theatre to fiction and published two novels, *Donald Duk* (1991) and *Gunga Din Highway* (1994) as well as a collection of essays, *Bulletproof Buddhists and Other Essays* (1998). *Donald Duk* is Chin's first novel. Compared with his early writings, *Donald Duk* is less poignant and more tolerant. It demonstrates Chin's transformation of his attitude from rejection to recognition of Chinese culture and heritage. Donald Duk, the protagonist of the novel, is a twelve-year-old Chinese American boy who grows up in Chinatown and studies in a private school where the majority of students are Caucasians and Chinese American students are discriminated against. While dreaming to be the "Chinese Fred Astaire," Donald feels embarrassed and self-contemptuous of being Chinese American, especially when his history teacher devalues Chinese traditional culture and philosophy. When the Chinese New Year approaches, Donald's father makes 108 paper planes on which he paints the 108 outlaws from *the Water Margin*. These planes make Donald continuously dream about outlaws from Liang Shan (Mount Liang) and Chinese American forbears who defeated the Irishmen in the tracklaying contest and broke its world's record. The vividness of his dreams forces Donald to do research in the library to find out whether what went on in his dreams actually happened in history. The historical facts he finds fill him with pride in his Chinese American identity and Chinese culture. Hence, when his imperialistic teacher misrepresents Chinese railroad workers in class, Donald daringly points out his mistake and forces him to apologize. On the Chinese New Year's Day, Donald joins the dragon team in the parade and lights the planes with his father on Angel Island to commemorate the heroes in Chinese history and culture, as well as the Chinese American railroad workers. Being Chin's first novel, this *bildungsroman* is considerably different from his early works.

Unlike Chin's past antiheroes in their doomed search for identity and genealogy, Donald Duk finds his cultural root in Chinese classics and Chinese American forebearers' contribution to the building of the **transcontinental railroad**, and now he firmly establishes his identity based on the Chinese legacy. Through the young protagonist's dreams and research, Chin unearths the silenced, heroic history of Chinese American ancestors and glorifies Chinese traditional culture and classics. The novel is also filled with hypermasculine personae such as traditional Chinese heroes Kwan Kung and Lee Kuey, as well as upright Chinamen like King Duk and Kwan the Foreman to replace emasculated Oriental stereotypes. Furthermore, Chin even changes his attitude toward white Americans and becomes more objective and tolerant, which can be evidenced in his different portrayals of white characters. In his early writings, white characters were all white supremacists who looked down upon Chinatown and Chinese Americans with prejudice like Ross in *The Year of the Dragon*. However, in *Donald Duk*, Azalea was portrayed as Donald's best friend, who even helps to search for the hidden history of Chinese railroad workers. In short, Frank Chin wrote this novel not only to restore Chinese Americans' pride in their cultural heritage, but also to give white American readers an opportunity to gain a fair understanding of the real Chinaman, Chinatown, and China.

In September 1994, Frank Chin published *Gunga Din Highway*, his longest and most complex novel to date. It is an encyclopedic saga of late and contemporary Asian American experience, which takes on plots and characters that have appeared in Chin's early writings. The major characters of the novel are Longman Kwan, a Cantonese opera heartthrob in China and now an actor in Hollywood, his son Ulysses Kwan, and Ulysses's cousins and best friends, Benedict Han and Diego Chang. The story, told by four first-person narrators, centers on Kwan's family history from the 1940s to the 1990s. Its major conflict lies in the tense relationship between Longman and Ulysses Kwan. Longman Kwan has acted in many movies as the Chinaman Who Dies and Charlie Chan's Number Four Son, which he proudly claims to be the most Americanized and thus the most legitimate son of Charlie Chan. His lifelong dream is to play Charlie Chan in the movies and to set an example for future generations. In opposition to his father and furious about racial discrimination and cultural imperialism in the United States, Ulysses Kwan resists being assimilated into a model citizen. Instead, he forms his cultural identity as a Chinaman and obtains his personal integrity by identifying with Chinese history and the heroic tradition and then by working as a brakeman on the Southern Pacific and Western Pacific railroads built by Chinese laborers. In *Gunga Din*

Highway, as the novel's title implies, Frank Chin uses parody to attack Oriental stereotypes such as Charlie Chan and assimilated Chinese Americans such as Pandora Toy and Benedict Han, who are fictional counterparts of Amy Tan, Maxine Hong Kingston, and David Henry Hwang. Chin accuses them of betraying their people like Gunga Din in Rudyard Kipling's poem "Gunga Din" and being ignorant of their cultural heritage. Chin uses collage and intertextuality to combine their Chinese heritage with American experience to portray a cultural identity of Chinese America, which, as the name Ulysses Kwan indicates, is a combination of East and West—Kwan Kung, Chinese God of War, and Ulysses, the famous Western mythological hero. In the end, the death of Longman Kwan and Ulysses driving the pregnant housekeeper in labor to the hospital symbolize the end of the era of assimilation and the further development of the Chinaman's genealogy.

In 1998 Frank Chin published *Bulletproof Buddhists and Other Essays*, a critically acclaimed collection of six best essays written from 1972 to 1995. Though the locales for these essays vary from Castro's Cuba to the California-Mexico border, from Singapore to Interstate 5, the collection centers on Chinese heritage, racial authenticity, and the formulation of cultural identity. The latest publication of Frank Chin's is *Born in the USA: A Story of Japanese America, 1889–1947* (2002), a critical cultural study of Japanese American histories before **World War II** and **Japanese American internment** during the war, presented through in-depth interviews, diaries, novels, popular songs, and newspaper articles. **See also** Asian American Stereotypes; Racism and Asian America.

Further Reading

Cheung, King-Kok. "Re-viewing Asian American Literary Studies." *An Interethnic Companion to Asian American Literature*, ed. King-Kok Cheung. New York: Cambridge University Press, 1997. 1–36.

Chin, Frank, et al., eds. *Aiiieeeee!: An Anthology of Asian American Writers*. Washington DC: Howard University Press, 1974.

Chu, Patricia P. "*Tripmaster Monkey*, Frank Chin, and the Chinese Heroic Tradition." *Arizona Quarterly* 53.3 (Autumn 1997): 117–139.

Goshert, John Charles. "Frank Chin." *Boise State University Western Writers Series*. Boise: Boise State University Printing and Graphic Services, 2002.

Huang, Guiyou. "Frank Chin." In *Asian American Novelists: A Bio-Bibliographical Critical Sourcebook*, ed. Emmanuel S. Nelson. Westport, CT: Greenwood Press, 2000. 48–55.

Kim, Elaine H. *Asian American Literature: An Introduction to the Writings and Their Social Context*. Philadelphia: Temple University Press, 1982.

Li, David Leiwei. "The Formation of Frank Chin and Formations of Chinese American Literature." In *Asian Americans: Comparative and Global Perspectives*, eds. Shirley Hune, et al. Pullman: Washington State University Press, 1991. 211–223.

Lim, Shirley Geok-lin. "Twelve Asian American Writers: In Search of Self-Definition." *MELUS* 13.1 (1986): 57–77.

Ling, Jinqi. "Performing the Margins: Ethics and the Poetics of Frank Chin's Theatrical Discourse." *Narrating Nationalisms: Ideology and Form in Asian American Literature.* New York: Oxford University Press, 1998. 79–109.

McDonald, Dorothy Ritsuko. "Introduction." *The Chickencoop Chinaman* and *The Year of the Dragon: Two Plays by Frank Chin.* Seattle: University of Washington Press, 1981.

JINGJIE LU

✦ CHIN, MARILYN MEI-LING (1955–)

A Chinese American poet and professor of English, Marilyn Chin was born in Hong Kong on January 14, 1955. She immigrated to the United States while a child and was reared in Portland, Oregon. Chin received her BA in classical Chinese literature from the University of Massachusetts at Amherst in May 1977, her MFA in creative writing from the University of Iowa in May 1981, and was a Stegner Fellow at Stanford University from 1984 to 1985. She has been working at San Diego State University since 1989 as a professor in the English and Comparative Literature Department, teaching literature and codirecting the master of fine arts program in creative writing. While at San Diego State, she also took opportunities to work as a visiting scholar worldwide: visiting associate professor in English/**Asian American studies** at the University of California, Los Angeles, in spring 1990; visiting professor at the University of California, San Diego, in 1993; the University of Hawaii, Hilo, in 1997; visiting professor at the University of Technology, Sydney, Australia, in fall 2001; and visiting Fulbright professor at National Dong Hua University, Taiwan, from 1999 to 2000.

Marilyn Chin is a widely acclaimed and recognized poet and social activist. Her books have become Asian American classics and are taught and read internationally. She is the author of three individual collections of poetry: *Dwarf Bamboo, The Phoenix Gone, the Terrace Empty,* and more recently *Rhapsody in Plain Yellow.* Her poems have been published in numerous journals and featured in a variety of anthologies, including the *Paris Review,* the *Iowa Review,* the *Washington Post,* the *Columbia Anthology of Women's Poetry, Norton Introduction to Poetry,* the *Writer's Chronicles,* the *Best American Poetry 1996, Pushcart Prize Anthology,* the *Open Boat,* and the *Oxford Anthology of Modern American Poetry.* While studying at the University of Iowa, Chin participated in the International Writing Program from 1978 to 1982, co-translating *The Selected Poems of Ai Qing* (1982) with Peng Wenlan and Eugene Eoyang. She also co-translated the poetry collection *Devil's Wind: A Thousand Steps or More* (1980), with the author Gozo Yoshimasu. In addition to writing and translating, she coedited *Dissident Song: A Contemporary Asian American Anthology* (1991), and *Writing from the World: An Iowa Translation Series* (1985).

Marilyn Chin has won numerous honors for her writing. She is the recipient of a Paterson Book Prize (2003), a Senior Fulbright Fellowship to Taiwan (1999–2000), PEN Josephine Miles Award (1994), four Pushcart Prizes (1994–1997), the Best American Poetry of 1996, Blue Mountain Colony (1996), the Gjerassi Foundation Fellowship (1989), Bay Area Book Review Award (1987), two fellowships from the National Endowment for the Arts in Poetry (1985, 1991), the Stegner Fellowship in Creative Writing, Stanford University (1984–1985), the Mary Robert Rinehart Award in Poetry (1983), Virginia Center for the Creative Arts Fellowship (Summer 1983), Centrum Fellowship (1987), MacDowell (1987), Reader's Digest Award, Yaddo (1990–1994), and Villa Montalvo Artist Residency (1992, 1999), among others.

One of the leading voices of contemporary Asian American poetry, Marilyn Chin has been invited to read her poetry and teach workshops all over the world. She was guest poet at universities and poetry festivals in Hong Kong, Taiwan, Sydney, Singapore, Berlin, Wellington, and elsewhere. She is also judge for the Ruth Lake Memorial Award (Poetry Society of America, 1994), panelist for the National Endowment for the Arts (Translation Division), poetry selection panelist for the Corporation of Yaddo (1993–present), and panelist for the National Book Award in the category of poetry.

Chin's study in classical Chinese literature and practice in translating modern Chinese and Japanese poetry make her poetic style distinct. The crisp images and rhythms she creates are worth repeated savoring. She relates the Chinese immigrants' American experiences with ancient Chinese allusions and in the tradition of Chinese verse. The titles of her poems and the names of Chinese places and those of important figures in Chinese history are all ethnic markers that show her immersion in Chinese culture. In fact, there are new lyric forms in each of Chin's books, which are often hybrids of both Chinese and English forms indicated by the poet's voice impressively moving from pleasant tenderness to searing irony. She dwells on the themes of race, history, gender, culture, love, nature, and politics, and her poems are of various kinds: long meditations, hymns, blues poems, ballads, and political anthems.

Different from many Chinese American writers writing about assimilation, Chin sticks to her cultural identity as a bicultural and bilingual person. She stresses the perpetual struggle and tension of assimilation and the tragic loss of one's culture, language, religion, and sense of self. In an interview with Bill Moyers, Marilyn Chin said: "I am afraid of losing my Chinese, losing my language, which would be like losing a part of myself, losing part of my soul. Poetry seems a way to recapture that, but of course the truth is we can't recapture the past. The vector only goes one direction and that is toward the future. So the grandeur of China—the grandeur of that past of my grandfather's, of my grandmother's, of my mother's and so forth—that will be all lost to me. I lose inches of it every day. Sometimes I think I lose a character a day" (Moyers 1995, 70).

Critics have praised Chin's work for its unshrinking examination of the contradictory feelings brought about by immigration in general and for Asian Americans specifically. Throughout her work, Chin expresses her earnest concerns for social issues. Growing up in an era of vast sociopolitical changes, Chin was greatly influenced by the activist poets and developed an activist voice of her own. She deals with such particular issues as bicultural identity and assimilation. Her dedication to feminist issues within the Asian American community is also strongly voiced in many of her poems, notably in pieces like "Homage to Diana Toy." There are images of Asian women as exotic and doll-like in her poems, so her poetry exemplifies a complex intersectionality between race and gender identity. Chin's boldness about female sexuality and the social roles of women of color and her frequent references to the revolutionary movement in China have earned her a reputation as an important political feminist poet.

Just as Denise Levertov points out in her review of Chin's poetry on the back cover of *Dwarf Bamboo*, Marilyn Chin "draws on ancient cultural sources and at the same time reflects something wholly Western, urban and contemporary—so that we have here two kinds of sophistications combined" (1987). This assessment can be underpinned by most poems in Chin's three published collections.

Dwarf Bamboo is Chin's first book and a winner of the Bay Area Book Reviewers Award in 1987. It was dedicated "to Ai Qing, Chinese revolutionary and poet." The title of the book suggests Chin's interest in Po Chu-yi (Bai Jüyi), a Tang dynasty Chinese poet who wrote many poems about the dwarf bamboo. The collection consists of three long sections and an abbreviated fourth, containing numerous poems that focus on the immigrant experience in the United States. It is a product of artful irony and satire, infused with the pains of cultural assimilation.

"A Chinaman's Chance" is one of the well-known poems in this collection. The influence of both traditional Chinese culture and contemporary American society on the poet is apparent when her poetry moves from Plato and Socrates to Confucius: "If you were a Chinese born in America, who would you believe/Plato who said what Socrates said/Or Confucius in his bawdy way: 'So a male child is born to you/I am happy, very, very happy" (Chin 1987, 29). The quotation and the question meant for the Chinese American women to answer evidently reveal Chin's feminist inclinations. Then Chin reminds those who would choose Plato over the history of the Chinese Americans, demonstrating the pains of assimilation with bold and stunning words: "The railroad killed your great-grandfather/His arms here, his legs there . . . /*How can we remake ourselves on his image?*" (Chin 1987, 29)

Chin's second book, *The Phoenix Gone, the Terrace Empty*, winner of the PEN Josephine Miles Award in 1994, has been more critically acclaimed than her first collection. The title is a literal translation from the work of Li Po (Li Bai), another Chinese poet of the Tang dynasty, with a typical Chinese syntax. The pains of cultural assimilation are seen here as more strongly expressed. The collection is divided into six titled sections, beginning with "Exile's Letter." Here multiple exiles—political, cultural, linguistic, and familial—haunt Chin's poems with brilliance. The most anthologized and quoted poem of this part is "How I Got That Name," subtitled *an essay on assimilation.* To shake off the specific binds that they had to face after arriving in the United States, Asian women immigrants must change in every possible way to be accepted as Americans. Chin fights against culture and gender displacement with severe mockery and incisive humor: "Of course/the name had been changed/somewhere between **Angel Island** and the sea,/when my father the person/in the late 1950s/obsessed with a bombshell blonde/transliterated 'Mei Ling' to 'Marilyn'./And nobody dared question/his initial impulse—for we all know/lust drove men to greatness,/not goodness, not decency./And there I was, a wayward pink baby,/named after some tragic white woman/swollen with gin and Nembutal" (Chin 1994, 16). Chin criticizes changing Asian women immigrants' names and customs and cutting off their links with the old culture to assimilate more easily into the new one. She also explores group identities and stereotypes imposed upon Asian Americans by the mainstream American culture and accuses American politicians who use Asian "success" to erase the inequality and poverty caused by exclusion, racism, and oppression: "Oh, how trustworthy our daughters,/how thrifty our sons!/How we've managed to fool the experts/in education, statistics and demography—/We're not very creative but not adverse to rote-learning./Indeed, they can use us./But the **'Model Minority'** is a tease" (Chin 1994, 17).

The second section, "The Tao and the Art of Leavetaking," foregrounds the themes of loss and elegy. There is obvious experimenting with hybrid forms. The one-line stanzas of "Reggae Renga," the longish elegant lines of "Autumn Leaves," and the aphoristic leaps of "The Tao and the Art of Leavetaking" impress the reader in both emotion and style. Chin's elegies, dealing with loss and identity politics, are also in gorgeous lyric forms, such as "Altar" for a grandmother, "Elegy for Chloe Nguyen," and "Leaving San Francisco" for "Master Weldon Kees." While mourning her brilliant friend in "Elegy for Chloe Nguyen," Chin relates the fatality of the cultural assimilation experience with a touching ironic voice: "Bipedal in five months, trilingual in a year;/at eleven she had her first lover." At thirty-three, she was dead. The last line reads: "Chloe, we are finally Americans now. Chloe, we are here!" (Chin 1994, 37–38).

A third section, "The Phoenix Gone, the Terrace Empty," is the most significant, consisting of five poems including the title poem of both the section and the book. The poem relates death and the regeneration of identity and contains more powerful cultural elements. Here are many meaningful images and allusions, supernatural in a Chinese way. While walking in a Chinese garden, the Chinese American speaker seems to be inhabited by the spirit of an ancestor. In the presence of the unnamed spirit, she dialogues with several spirits, her father, grandfather, grandmother, and aunt, together recalling their suffering and ruin in China. At the end of the poem, they accompany her to an American garden where she meets her boyfriend secretly. Her ancestors are quick to point out all the bad omens in the garden. "The snake bites her own tale,/meaning harmony at the year's end./Or does it mean/she is eating herself into extinction?" The poem ends like a fairy tale, with the speaker crying out like a doomed princess: "Oh dead prince, oh hateful love/shall we meet again/on the bridge of the magpies" (Chin 1994, 51).

The center section, "Homage to Diana Toy," is a chilling portrayal of the life and death of a psychiatric inpatient. The eight little poems that make up the section are moving and wrenching, in a tone of great tenderness and high tragedy. Toy, a patient Chin tutored, commits suicide when denied citizenship in the United States and sexually taken advantage of by an administrator. Chin blames herself as an "unworthy tutor" who "failed to tell her about the fifty paltry stars" (Chin 1994, 63).

The fifth section, "Love Poesy," adds more charm to the collection with tender emotion. The poems here bring the reader to face an intersection of love, sex, family, and politics. Like her other poems, Chin's love poems are full of lexical rewards and they explore what Chin refers to as love's "postcolonial subtext" (qtd. in Weisner). For her, love always means assimilation in the Chinese American context, and one must learn to erase one's former identity to merge into the new culture, language, and religion. "His Parents' Baggage" portrays the colonized landscape of a lover's psyche, while the excellent "Composed Near the Bay Bridge" opens with a psychocultural tango. The segment ends with the appealing "Summer Love."

The last section, "Beijing Spring: *for the Chinese Democratic Movement*," shows Chin's concern for China. The series of poems present a glimpse into the complex world of cultural contestation and negotiation of a Chinese American. Chin politicizes her purposes in relation to her most personal themes as in her other poems. The political homage to the Chinese democratic movement is interwoven with portraits of cousins, mothers, and self. "The Floral Apron," an accomplished closed-form lyric homage to Chin's mother and her ancestresses—women of both a literal and a mythical past—shows Chin's attempt to bridge two cultures. Her mother's knowledge of cooking and the floral apron are both symbolic. Significant are the lessons her mother is trying to pass down through the process of cooking: "patience, courage, forbearance, on how to love squid despite squid, how to honor village, the tribe, that floral apron" (Chin 1994, 86).

Rhapsody in Plain Yellow, Chin's third collection of poetry, won the Paterson Book Prize in 2003. The book continues to focus on the struggle between heritage and the New World, exploring her relationship with her parents and her grandparents. In this volume, Chin drew inspiration for the forms and rhythms from Chinese music, Persian ghazals, and American blues music. The book is distinguished for its fusion of the East and the West, and of popular culture and ancient Chinese history. The song-like poems cover a terrain of emotional nuance and postmodern experimentation—from homage to Li Po to polyphonic samplings of Emily Dickinson, from ballads of eternal love to lamentations. With her intercultural singing, Chin elegizes the loss of her mother and maternal grandmother and tries to unravel the complexities of her family's past. She narrates the trials of immigration, of exile, of thwarted interracial love, and of social injustice. "Blues on Yellow," an angry poem in blues rhythm, is put before the title page to set the tone for the book. In the first part, Chin turns her critique inward and laments the loss of her "Chinese half," focusing on her family and bringing their experiences into continuum of a Chinese past and an American present. Then Chin works outward from her own life with the sarcastic fable-like "The True Story of Mr. and Mrs. Wong." The volume ends with the title poem "Rhapsody in Plain Yellow," referencing the Han dynasty and taking in everything that has come before. It is dedicated to "my love, Charles," starting as a love poem with the collection's rhythmic theme and a repeated word—*say*: "I love you, I love you, I love you, no matter/your race, your sex, your color. Say:/the world is round and the arctic is cold./say: I shall kiss the rondure of your soul's/living marl. Say: he is beautiful, serenely beautiful, yet, only ephemerally so" (2002, 96). After moving through her personal wants and desires, the history from both hemispheres, the relation of life to fable, and quotations from poetry and philosophy, the poem ends in silence: "Hills and canyons, robbed by sun, leave us nothing" (2002, 103).

Marilyn Chin is finishing a book of stories that will be published by Norton in 2008. The *Indiana Review* has published her two short fiction pieces: "The Parable of the Fish" in volume 24.1 and "The Parable of the Cake" in volume 25.1. **See also** Assimilation/Americanization; Racism and Asian America.

Further Reading

Altieri, Charles. "Images of Form vs. Images of Content in Contemporary Asian American Poetry." *Qui Parle* 9.1 (Fall–Winter 1995): 71–91.

Chin, Marilyn. *Dwarf Bamboo*. Greenfield Center, NY: Greenfield Review Press, 1987.

———. *The Phoenix Gone, the Terrace Empty*. Minneapolis, MN: Milkweed Editions, 1994.

———. *Rhapsody in Plain Yellow*. New York: Norton, 2002.

Huang, Guiyou. "Marilyn Mei Ling Chin." In *The Columbia Guide to Asian American Literature Since 1945*, Guiyou Huang. New York: Columbia University Press, 2006. 180–182.

Li, Guicang. "The Literature of Chinese American Identity." PhD Diss., Indiana University of Pennsylvania, 2002. 178–193.

Marquart, Lisa. "The Zen of Irony and Wit: Poet Marilyn Chin Strikes a Balance between East and West." *Daily Aztec* 2 (March 1994): 9.

Moyers, Bill. "Marilyn Chin." *The Language of Life: A Festival of Poets*. New York: Doubleday, 1995. 67–79.

Slowik, Mary. "Beyond Lot's Wife: The Immigration Poems of Marilyn Chin, Garrett Hongo, Li-Young Lee, and David Mura." *MELUS* 25.3–4 (Fall–Winter 2000): 221–242.

Tabios, Eileen. "Marilyn Chin's Feminist Muse Addresses Women, 'The Grand Victims of History.'" In *Black Lightning: Poetry-in-Progress*, Eileen Tabios. New York: Asian American Writers' Workshop, 1998. 280–312.

Uba, George. Rev. of *Dwarf Bamboo*. *MELUS* 15.1 Ethnic Women Writers V (Spring 1988): 125–127.

———. "Versions of Identity in Post-activist Asian American Poetry." In *Reading the Literatures of Asian America*, eds. Shirley Geok-lin Lim and Amy Ling. Philadelphia: Temple University Press, 1992. 33–48.

Wang, Dorothy Joan. "Necessary Figures: Metaphor, Irony, and Parody in the Poetry of Li-Young Lee, Marilyn Chin, and John Yau." PhD Diss., University of California, Berkeley, 1998. 72–120.

Weisner, Ken. "Review of *The Phoenix Gone, the Terrace Empty* by Marilyn Chin." *American Book Review Online*.

Zhou, Xiaojing. "Breaking from Tradition: Experimental Poems by Four Contemporary Asian American Women Poets." *Revista Canaria de Estudios Ingleses* 37 (November 1998): 199–218.

———. "Marilyn Mei Ling Chin." In *Asian American Poets: A Bio-Bibliographical Critical Sourcebook*, ed. Guiyou Huang. Westport, CT: Greenwood Press, 2002. 71–82.

AIQIN LIU

✦ CHIN, VINCENT (1955–1982)

The Vincent Chin case catalyzed the unification of Asian Americans against anti-Asian violence in the United States. The motivation to mobilize was caused by the lenient sentencing of two white Detroit autoworkers, Ronald Ebens and Michael Nitz, who brutally murdered Chin on June 19, 1982. The autoworkers pleaded down from second-degree murder to manslaughter, which is a lighter charge, hence a lighter sentence — no jail time, probation for three years, and fines of $3,780 for each person. His case inspired the founding of the American Citizens for Justice (ACJ), which was the first explicitly pan-Asian American community advocacy group that offers assistance nationally against anti-Asian violence. Because this hate crime highlighted the failures of the justice system, in recognizing the severity of Chin's murder and race as key motive, the case became the blueprint for how Asian American communities should organize to ensure that future crimes against Asians received fair treatment and the full attention of the justice system.

Vincent Chin was the only son of Lily and David Bing Hing Chin. The Chins adopted Vincent from Guangdong Province, China, in 1961. David Chin died in

1981, one year before Vincent was killed. Vincent was an active teenager. He was a high school track athlete and wrote poetry. Friends and family describe Vincent as friendly, yet tough and outspoken. Helen Zia, an award-winning journalist who worked tirelessly with the ACJ to pursue justice for Chin, describes him as an "energetic, take-charge guy who knew how to stand up for himself on the tough streets of Detroit" (2000, 63). After high school, Chin worked as a draftsman in Oak Park, Michigan. He was happily engaged and planned to wed on June 26, the week after he was killed.

On June 19, 1982, Chin's pals took him out to a bachelor party. They went to Fancy Pants, a striptease bar, the place in which the downward spiral would begin. Chin's three friends, including another **Asian American**, Choi, and two white men, Koivu and Sirosky, were tipping the dancers generously and frequently to entertain the husband-to-be. The exchange began with Ebens's annoyance with the dancers' attention directed toward an Asian American. According to a white dancer at Fancy Pants, Racine Colwell, Ebens shouted across the dance stage at Chin: "It's because [of] you little mother fuckers that we're out of work" (*United States v. Ebens*, No. 83-60629-CR, Vol. 299, 226). This racially motivated comment became the smoking gun that transformed Chin's murder into a hate crime. In response to Ebens, Chin yelled, "I'm not a little mother fucker." Ebens countered, "Well, I'm not sure if you're a big one or a little one," which caused Chin to go around the stage to confront Ebens (*United States v. Ebens*, No. 83-60629-CR, Vol. 299, 226). Other accounts indicate that Chin's friends overheard Ebens say, "Chink," "Nip," and "fucker" (*United States v. Ebens*, 800 F.2d, 1427). This shouting exchange resulted in a scuffle. Both groups were ejected from the bar.

Fighting words continued in the parking lot. Chin yelled, "Come on, you chicken shits, let's fight some more." Ebens retrieved a baseball bat from his vehicle, and Chin and his friend, Choi, ran away while his white friends stay put, unthreatened by the two autoworkers. Ebens and Nitz started their search. They recruited a stranger, a black man named Jimmy Perry, by paying him $20 to help them "find a Chinese guy" and "bust his head" (*United States v. Ebens*, 800 F.2d, 1428). While most of this sequence was disputed or denied by defense witnesses, including Ebens and Nitz, Ebens did admit that he told Perry that he "was looking for two Orientals," a deeply racist term rooted in Western imperialism used to reinforce the foreignness of Asian Americans (*United States v. Ebens*, Vol. 299, 179).

Eventually, they spotted Chin and Choi outside a McDonald's restaurant. Ebens and Nitz approached them. Choi escaped, but Chin was grabbed and held by Nitz while Ebens beat Chin with the bat. After several blows, Chin escaped and ran out into the street before falling to the ground. Unsatisfied, Ebens followed Chin. Standing over him in a golf stance, Ebens took several homerun swings at Chin's head. Two off-duty police officers at the McDonald's stopped and arrested Ebens and Nitz. An ambulance arrived. The driver saw Chin's injuries and parts of his brain matter on the street. At the hospital, Chin was declared brain dead. Four days later, the life support was unplugged, and he died.

The Wayne County prosecutor opted for second-degree murder—homicide with no premeditation. Ebens and Nitz struck a plea bargain in which they pleaded down from second-degree murder to manslaughter, which carries a maximum sentence of 15 years in prison. On March 18, 1983, almost nine months to the day, Wayne County Circuit Court Judge Charles Kaufman, who is white, sentenced Ebens and Nitz to three years probation, fines of $3,000 each (and court costs to be paid over three years), with no imposed prison time for either of them. This sentence shocked Detroit. In response to the lenient sentence, local press printed scathing headlines and cartoons criticizing the decision. The Asian American community remained silent. Even if the community wanted to protest, there was no advocacy or watchdog group to turn to for assistance.

After the news of the sentences of her son's murderers, Lily Chin wrote a letter in Chinese to the Detroit Chinese Welfare Council: "This is injustice to the grossest extreme. I grieve in my heart and shed tears in blood. My son cannot be brought back to life, but he was a member of your council. Therefore, I plead to you. Please let the Chinese American community know, so they can help me hire legal counsel to appeal, so my son can rest his soul" (Zia 2000, 64).

On March 31, 1983, the council met, which eventually led to the creation of the American Citizens for Justice advocacy group. The formation prompted Liza Chan, the only Asian American woman practicing law in Michigan, to take the lead in pursuing Chin's case. On April 15, ACJ held its first news conference at the Detroit Press Club. Shocking numbers of Asian Americans gathered along a strong presence of local and regional media. The goal was to educate the community about anti-Asian violence, Asian American history in the United States, and the need for justice in the Chin case. In May 1983 ACJ started a mass rally in downtown Detroit to protest Kaufman's lenient sentences. The protest was the first to have broad representation of Asian American communities involved. The growing prominence of the case gave Asian Americans the first direct entry on the national level into the white-black race dynamic, complicating many people's notion of race and oppression in the United States. The *New York Times* picked up the story, which catalyzed other national media interest, including TV news magazine specials and Lily Chin's appearance on the *Phil Donahue Show*. With public pressure mounting and after meeting with Chan and other ACJ representatives, Judge Kaufman responded in June 1983 by defending his lenient sentence. He asserted that Ebens and Nitz were incapable of committing such a crime under normal circumstance and viewed it as an accident rather than a brutal murder. He further defended his decision by pointing out the defendants' "stable working backgrounds and lack of criminal records" and to make the punishment fit the criminal (Espiritu 1992, 141). Kaufman asserted, "Had this been a brutal murder, of course, these fellows would be in jail now" (Ma 2000, 80). He would not reverse his decision.

With the news, Chan and the ACJ pursued a civil rights case using the racial reference from Colwell's testimony, indicating that Ebens mistakenly blamed Chin for the U.S. auto industry demise. In November 1983 a federal grand jury indicted Ebens and Nitz for violating Chin's right to enjoy a place of public accommodations. Judge Anna Diggs Taylor, one of the first African American woman judges to serve on the federal bench, presided. On June 28, 1984, the federal jury found Ebens guilty, but Nitz was acquitted. The case won a retrial by appeal in 1986 due to procedure errors and suspicion that attorney Chan allegedly coached Chin's three friends in preparation for trial. The trial was held in Cincinnati, and jurors were interrogated about their familiarity with Asians to eliminate biases while no questions addressed possible favoritism toward whites. The jury was mostly white, male, and blue-collar, a striking resemblance to Ebens's background. On May 1, 1987, the jury found Ebens not guilty. In the civil suit against the autoworkers for the loss of Chin's life, a settlement of $1.5 million was levied in September 1987 against Ebens. He stopped making payments toward the judgment in 1989.

More than any other incident, the beating death of Vincent Chin epitomizes the racism of lumping together all Asian Americans stamped primarily with an East Asian phenotype, wrongfully affirming, for many, the stereotype that all Asians look alike and are blamed for Japan's economic competitiveness. It also instills fear in Asians and Asian Americans that this violence could happen to them due to anti-Asian attitudes and stereotypes of Asians being passive and silent. Scholars assert that Chin's case empowered many Asian Americans to speak out against injustices. His case catalyzed the formation of many community groups combating anti-Asian violence, pan-Asian social services, and educational organizations at the local, regional, and national level. The case inspired the joining of Asian Americans and other marginalized groups to actively lobby for the passage of the Hate Crime Statistics Act in 1990. This act requires the U.S. attorney general to collect and publish statistics on crimes motivated by prejudice against race, religion, sexual orientation, or ethnicity. Chin's case is a monumental stepping-stone in Asian American history. **See also** Asian American Stereotypes; Racism and Asian America.

Further Reading
Choy, Christine, and Renée Tajima-Pena. *Who Killed Vincent Chin?* Documentary film, 1987.
Espiritu, Yen Le. *Asian American Panethnicity: Bridging Institutions and Identities.* Philadelphia, PA: Temple University Press, 1992.
Ma, Sheng-mei. *The Deadly Embrace: Orientalism and Asian American Identity.* Minneapolis, MN: University of Minnesota Press, 2000.

"Racial Violence against Asian Americans." *Harvard Law Review* 106.8 (June 1993): 1926–1943.

United States v. Ebens, No. 83-60629-CR, Vol. 299.

United States v. Ebens, 800 F.2d 1427, 1428 (6th Cir. 1986).

Zia, Helen. *Asian American Dreams*. New York: Farrar, Straus and Giroux, 2000.

DANIEL HIROYUKI TERAGUCHI

✦ CHINATOWNS

Chinatowns are ethnic communities established by Chinese immigrants since the nineteenth century. There are three main types of Chinatowns in the United States: the frontier and rural, urban, and suburban Chinatowns. The first two types were typically established by Chinese immigrants from the nineteenth century to the mid-twentieth century, whereas the third has developed because of the arrival of the comparatively wealthier and better educated Chinese immigrants since the 1970s. In the beginning, Chinatowns were established out of the necessity for self-protection and a sense of security against the hostile environment and for mutual assistance in life and business in an alien country. Early Chinatowns were isolated from white residential districts or other ethnic enclaves. With the gradual lessening of discrimination and hostility toward Chinese, many Chinese, especially American-born Chinese such as Nina in Fae Myenne Ng's novel *Bone* or some recent immigrants, moved out of Chinatowns to suburban areas.

Although it is recorded that Chinese came to the United States as early as 1785, the first wave of Chinese immigrants, mainly from Guangdong Province, arrived in this country around 1850 because of the discovery of gold in California in 1848. As more Chinese immigrants migrated into California in search of fortune and work, those who were working in frontier and rural areas banded together and established their own distinct communities, which eventually became the frontier and rural Chinatowns.

Early Chinese immigrants established a reputation for hard work—they did mainly farm work, or built the railroads, or did hard labor in the gold mines, so their initial arrival was generally welcomed, although prejudice against them existed. With increasing numbers of Chinese immigrants in the job markets, initial acceptance and tolerance gave way to animosity, especially during the 1870s, when the United States was in a nationwide depression. The Chinese immigrants were loathed by whites, whose hatred eventually led to the passage of the **Chinese Exclusion Act** in 1882, which banned immigration of Chinese laborers to the United States and prohibited Chinese from becoming naturalized citizens. The anti-Chinese sentiment and the deteriorating situation made it necessary for Chinese immigrants in the United States to leave farms, mines, railroads, and other places where they worked to retreat into cities to make a living. Their arrival greatly increased the population, community, and service business in Chinatowns in the cities.

Urban Chinatowns have gradually developed from the districts where the Chinese who remained in the cities crowded together and were later joined by rural or new immigrants. In the United States, some of the largest and most significant urban Chinatowns are those in San Francisco, Los Angeles, and New York. San Francisco Chinatown was the oldest and was once deemed by city officials as a health hazard. In 1906 the earthquake and fires reduced old San Francisco Chinatown into smoldering ashes; the present Chinatown was in fact reconstructed in the outer reaches of the Richmond district. It is one of the most beautiful Chinatowns in the United States today, with each of its streets possessing its own unique characteristics and charming cultural heritage. With anti-Chinese hostility rising on the West Coast in the 1870s, Chinese immigrants began to move to the East Coast, arriving in significant numbers in the New York area in the late 1870s and beginning to create enclaves for existence and self-protection. New York City Chinatown in Manhattan was thus founded. As the largest Chinatown in the United States today, it provides tourists and visitors with a unique historical and cultural experience not found anywhere else in the world. Like many other urban Chinatowns in the United States, it has become a site of a rich history that tells the story of the Chinese American experience.

Suburban Chinatowns were established as a result of the relaxation of Chinese immigration restrictions, the passage of laws that forbade racial discrimination in real estate, and, most importantly, the improved relationship of China and the United States. As better educated immigrants arrive from mainland China, Hong Kong, and Taiwan, along with younger generations leaving old urban Chinatowns, suburban Chinatowns have sprung up. Unlike old Chinatown populations, which are mainly middle-aged or senior working-class citizens, most people living in suburban Chinatowns are younger generations of middle or upper class. The aging infrastructures in old Chinatowns have been replaced by modern residential buildings and shopping malls in suburban Chinatowns.

Chinatowns used to be close-knit communities with unique organizations and management systems. The Chinese who came from the same region in China formed district benevolent associations, and those with the same family names formed family associations. These associations were first set up to serve the social and personal needs of the Chinese immigrants. The success and survival of early Chinatowns depended a great deal on these benevolent associations, which served as political, social, and economic support systems to old immigrants and newcomers. The members strove to meet the basic needs of the community and represented a united voice in the fight against discriminatory legislations. Today, these benevolent associations, though less influential than they used to be, still play the role of social and welfare institutions that provide the Chinese community with job information and opportunities, monetary aid, and opportunities to express opinions in public affairs.

Since the Chinese usually consider education as the most important asset of life and an important way to glorify the family, they established many Chinese schools in Chinatowns, the first of which was set up in 1884 in old San Francisco Chinatown. Chinese children were schooled in many subjects, among which the learning of Chinese language was the most important. In the minds of older generations, the Chinese language was a significant channel to preserve the Chinese culture and maintain ties with their homeland. With children attending American public schools, most of them were gradually whitewashed and thus became unwilling to learn anything Chinese, an issue that is best reflected in Frank **Chin's** *Donald Duk*. Recently, there has been a revival of Chinese schools in Chinatowns, and these schools play more roles to meet the needs of Chinese parents and their children.

Chinatowns used to have a negative image in the past, with dirty streets, brothels, and opium dens, especially during the period of the Chinese Exclusion Act when Chinatowns became bachelor societies because of the absence of women and children. This situation is vividly caricatured in Louis **Chu's** *Eat a Bowl of Tea,* where most Chinese mainly entertained themselves by playing Mahjong, visiting brothels and opium dens, and spreading rumors. In addition, there was real threat from societies like the tongs, secret groups formed by outcasts who either lacked clan ties or were expelled by their associations. These tongs were involved in operating brothels, gambling parlors, opium dens, and even the extremely lucrative business of importing thousands of Chinese women and girls to the United States to serve the Chinese bachelor population. The tongs were fighting incessantly among themselves for control over territories and profits, which are described in some detail in Pardee **Lowe's** novel *Father and Glorious Descendant.*

With the passing of time, especially with the appearance of new urban and suburban Chinatowns like the ones in Los Angeles and New York City, the images of Chinatowns have changed greatly. Today, Chinatowns remain self-sufficient communities with vibrant businesses, which mainly consist of grocery stores, laundries, shops, restaurants, and banks. Almost everything that a Chinese person needs in daily life can be obtained there. There are also many cultural and recreational activities, including theatrical performance, poetry clubs, and art collectives. Meanwhile Chinese restaurants offer Chinese and non-Chinese visitors delicious Chinese food, and Chinese theatres and joss houses provide them with a glimpse of Chinese culture and religion. These sights and unique customs have turned many old urban Chinatowns into tourist attractions. In addition, there are increasing connections between Chinatowns and the home country. Although many Chinese do not live in Chinatowns anymore, Chinatowns still serve as centers of social, economic, cultural, and business activities for Chinese in the United States today.

Further Reading

Chang, Iris. *The Chinese in America*. New York: Penguin Group, Inc., 2003.

Fong, Timothy P. *The First Suburban Chinatown: The Remaking of Monterey Park, California*. Philadelphia: Temple University Press, 1994.

Towne, Robert. *Chinatown and the Last Detail: 2 Screenplays*. New York: Grove Press, 1997.

Zhou, Min. *Chinatown: The Socioeconomic Potential of an Urban Enclave*. Philadelphia: Temple University Press, 1992.

AIMIN CHENG AND JUN LU

✦ CHINESE AMERICAN ANTHOLOGY

Chinese American literature, which dates back to the late nineteenth century, finally came of age in the 1970s. The publication of Chinese American anthologies was, therefore, symbolic of this maturation. Since Chinese American literature, as a minority literature, fits into the more inclusive, more diverse label — Asian American literature, its anthology more often than not jointly appears with other Asian American literature. This has been a general trend to date, which to a certain degree reflects the interdependent status of Chinese American literature. A clarification is necessary here, however, in that Chinese American literature holds a dominant standing within the larger category of Asian American literature.

The first ever Asian American literature anthology, *Asian-American Authors* (1972), was edited by Kai-yu Hsu and Helen Palubinskas, both of whom had profound knowledge of Chinese, and it included eight writers of Chinese descent (five of Japanese descent, nine of Philippine descent), namely, Pardee **Lowe**, Jade Snow **Wong**, Virginia Lee, Frank **Chin**, Diana **Chang**, Jeffery Paul **Chan**, Shawn Hsu **Wong**, and Russell C. **Leong**, and covered autobiography, novel excerpts, short stories, and poems. In 1974 another anthology, entitled *Asian American Heritage: An Anthology of Prose and Poetry* edited by David Hsin-Fu Wand, made its debut. But the most influential yet highly controversial anthology of this period was *Aiiieeeee! An Anthology of Asian American Writers* (1974), coedited by Frank Chin, Jeffery Paul Chan, Lawson Fusao Inada, and Shawn Hsu Wong. The 14 writers included in this anthology are arranged alphabetically, instead of being categorized according to their ethnic label like Hsu and Palubinskas's. The scope of its collection of Chinese American literature includes six writers, namely, Jeffery Paul Chan, Diana Chang, Frank Chin, Louis Chu, Wallace

Lin, and Shawn Hsu Wong, covering fiction, nonfiction, poetry, and miscellaneous writings. The *Aiiieeeee!* introduction, "Fifty Years of Our Whole Voice," condemned white racism and rejected the Asian American writers who mirrored "white standards." Based on the editors' philosophy, both aesthetical and political, the anthology went as far as to promote the yet unknown writer Louis **Chu**, while excluding the highly respected Jade Snow **Wong**.

If we regard the early 1970s as the first prosperous period for literary anthologies, the next productive period did not occur until the late 1980s, but it lasted throughout the 1990s to date. The major anthologies published during this time include *Pake: Writing by Chinese in Hawaii* (1989), edited by Eric **Chock** and Darrell H.Y. **Lum**; *The Forbidden Stitch: An Asian American Women's Anthology* (1989), coedited by Shirley Geok-lin **Lim** and Mayumi Tsutakawa; *Between Worlds: Contemporary Asian-American Plays* (1990) by Misha Berson; *Home to Stay: Asian American Women's Fiction* (1990) by Sylvia Watanabe and Carol Bruchac; *The Big Aiiieeeee!: An Anthology of Chinese American and Japanese American Literature* (1991) by Jeffery Paul Chan, Frank Chin, Lawson Fusao Inada, and Shawn Hsu Wong; *Dissident Song: A Contemporary Asian American Anthology* (1991) by Marilyn **Chin** and David Wong **Louie**; *Chinese American Poetry: An Anthology* (1991) by L. Ling-chi Wang and Henry Yiheng Zhao; *Charlie Chan Is Dead: An Anthology of Contemporary Asian American Fiction* (1993) by Jessica **Hagedorn**; *Growing Up Asian American* (1993) by Maria Hong; *The Open Boat: Poems from Asian America* (1993) by Garrett **Hongo**; *The Politics of Life: Four Plays by Asian American Women* (1993) by Velina Hasu **Houston**; *Unbroken Thread: An Anthology of Plays by Asian American Women* (1993) by Roberta Uno; *American Dragons: Twenty-five Asian American Voices* (1993) by Laurence **Yep**; *Under Western Eyes: Personal Essays from Asian America* (1995) by Garrett Hongo; *On a Bed of Rice: An Asian American Erotic Feast* (1995) by Geraldine Kudaka; *Asian American Literature: A Brief Introduction and Anthology* (1996) by Shawn Hsu Wong; *Asian-American Literature: An Anthology* (2000) by Shirley Geok-lin Lim; *Bold Words: A Century of Asian American Writing* (2001) by Rajini Srikanth and Esther Yae Iwanaga; and *Asian American Poetry: The Next Generation* (2004) by Victoria M. **Chang**.

In comparison with the first prosperous period, this period witnessed a considerable increase of genre-specific collections, such as plays, poetry, fiction, and collections dedicated to women writers. It sufficiently reflects a shift of research to poetry and plays as well as feminism. *The Big Aiiieeeee!* editors have maintained their endorsement of "Asian heroic tradition" and "authenticity" in *Aiiieeeee!*, and willfully relegated the widely acclaimed writers such as Jade Snow Wong, Maxine Hong **Kingston**, David Henry **Hwang**, and Amy **Tan** into the "fake" category. Wang and Zhao's *Chinese American Poetry: An Anthology*, as one of the few exclusively dedicated to Chinese American poets, is noteworthy here. The 22 poets collected represented multiple geographic locales (including Massachusetts, Hawaii, Alabama, New Mexico, California, Jakarta, Hong Kong, and Malacca), diverse aesthetic perspectives (such as traditional, experimental, and postmodern), and different cultural and linguistic backgrounds (e.g., some have Chinese as their mother tongue, whereas some may only speak English). Considering that many of the selected poets were familiar names, such as Marilyn Chin, Carolyn Lau, Li-Young Lee, John Yau, Laureen Mar, and Stephen Liu, one should not expect to discover the lesser known yet talented poets by looking through this collection. Unlike Wang and Zhao's poetry anthology, Chang's *Asian American Poetry* is dedicated to the up-and-coming poets, making it a good companion to Wang and Zhao's collection. *Bold Words*, on the other hand, covers Asian American writing of all genres and 60 authors from the early years of the twentieth century to the present, with a balanced split between male and female writers. Maxine Hong Kingston, Li-Young Lee, Frank Chin, and Sui Sin Far, among several others, are selected.

Apart from specific Chinese American and Asian American anthologies, Chinese American literature successfully knocks on the door of other anthologies and ultimately comprises a good proportion of them. The historical moment for many Chinese American writers came when Chinese American literature (alongside other Asian American literature) found its way into the American literary cannon. *Columbia Literary History of the United States* (1988), edited by Emory Elliott, was a pioneer in presenting Chinese American literature to a broader audience. Therein, Elaine H. Kim contributed a passionate and thought-provoking introductory essay on Asian American literature. An array of Chinese American writers and other Asian American writers made their grand collective debut. *The Norton Anthology of American Literature* (first published in 1979 and edited by Ronald Gottesman, with sequent editions edited by Nina Baym) overlooked Chinese American writers in its first two editions, but included four of Cathy Song's poems in its third edition released in 1989 and then added Maxing Hong Kingston and Li-Young Lee in its fourth (1995) and fifth editions (1998). *The Heath Anthology of American Literature* (first published in 1990), edited by Paul Lauter, collected works by Edith Maude Eaton (Sui Sin Far), Maxine Hong Kingston, and Cathy Song, as well as poetry by early Chinese immigrants, carved on the walls of the wooden barracks on Angel Island, which were marked by intense footnotes in its very first edition. The latest, fifth edition (2006) has added three more Chinese American writers, namely, Frank Chin, Gish Jen, and Li-Young Lee. By so doing, *The Heath Anthology* presents a more inclusive, more diversified collection of American literature.

Anthology is selective and exclusive, and thus making a value judgment becomes part of its nature. Whatever set of standards it adopts, conservative or liberal, an anthology has to rule out a certain number of works that could inevitably trigger serious debate on its selection criteria. Although a literary debate over anthology selection is not an uncommon occurrence, it is conspicuously visible and loud concerning Chinese American anthology compilation. The complete and unrelenting rejection of some critically favored Chinese American writers by some anthology editors (represented by Frank Chin) can hardly find its repetition in another literature. Despite the argument, conflict, and verbal rhetoric, the increasing number of published Chinese American anthologies forcefully demonstrates the remarkable energy a minority literature is now carrying on its way forward. **See also** Feminism and Asian America; Racism and Asian America.

Further Reading
Cheung, King-Kok and Stan Yogi, eds. *Asian American Literature: An Annotated Bibliography.* New York: Modern Language Association of America, 1988.
————, ed. *An Interethnic Companion to Asian American Literature.* New York: Cambridge University Press, 1997.
Huang, Guiyou. "Narrative Overview." *The Columbia Guide to Asian American Literature since 1945.* New York: Columbia University Press, 2006. 1–29.

LINGLING YAO

✦ CHINESE AMERICAN AUTOBIOGRAPHY

Chinese American autobiography has become a controversial literary form, focusing on debates concerning the authenticity or "Chineseness" of writers in this tradition, as well as the social or political function of **Chinese American literature**. Technically, this is a subcategory of ethnic autobiography within the wider category of life writing. In contrast to biography, autobiography presents the story of a life by the person who has lived that life. Consequently, narrator and narrated are assumed to be identical, and the events narrated are assumed to be historically and objectively true. This latter characteristic distinguishes autobiography from memoir, for example, which relies more explicitly upon remembrance that might not possess the same objective character as autobiography or, the third-person form of life writing, biography. These assumptions of historical verisimilitude and authorial authenticity comprise what Philippe Lejeune has famously described as the "autobiographical pact" in the title of his book, *Le Pacte autobiographique* (1975): a contract or assumed agreement between reader and writer that text comprises a historically true story that has been lived by the narrator.

Autobiography has become a controversial genre in Chinese American literature since Frank **Chin** launched a scathing criticism of writers such as Maxine Hong

Kingston and Jade Snow **Wong** for writing in what he sees as a compromised Eurocentric autobiographical form. Chin's essay "Come All Ye Asian American Writers of the Real and the Fake" was published in the groundbreaking anthology *The Big Aiiieeeee! An Anthology of Chinese American and Japanese American Literature*, coedited by Chin with Jeffery Paul **Chan**, Lawson Fusao **Inada**, and Shawn **Wong**. In this essay, he accuses particular, popular Chinese American writers of using a literary form— autobiography—that is not part of the native Chinese cultural tradition but represents the incursion and negative influence of European missionaries upon traditional Chinese culture. He calls for a style of writing that is neither Chinese nor Euro-American but is specifically Chinese American and that resists the assumption that the lives of Chinese immigrants to the United States can be simply and unproblematically accessed, in their specificities, through autobiographical texts.

Chin's criticism of Chinese American autobiography and its practitioners arises from the history of this literary genre in the United States. Some of the earliest Chinese American autobiographical texts were written in response to and as a gesture against the legislative actions that heralded the period of Chinese exclusion in North America. The first **Chinese Exclusion Act** was passed by the U.S. Congress in 1882. It was preceded by various legislative restrictions on the freedom of Chinese to enter and to move around the United States. For example, the 1870 Nationality Act excluded Chinese from those racial groups authorized to apply for naturalization, whereas in 1878 the Californian Constitutional Convention prohibited Chinese from entering California. Between 1882 and 1943, when the Chinese Exclusion Act was repealed, Chinese immigration was restricted to teachers, students, merchants, and diplomats on temporary visas. Among the many effects upon the Chinese community in the United States was the polarization between an educated migrant class, entering with temporary visas, and the existing class of laborers whose migration to the United States had preceded the exclusion laws. Many early Chinese American autobiographies are written in an apologetic style that attempts to engage the racial assumptions and prejudices that motivated these restrictive laws. Such texts provide an ethnographical account of Chinese culture, which has been likened to Mary Louise Pratt's concept of "auto-ethnography," to dispel American racial anxieties. These autobiographical writings attempted to represent the Chinese perspective on American racism by recognizing, and responding to, white fears and prejudices. To do this, writers often adopted the narrative point of view of racially prejudiced Americans to demonstrate that these prejudices were groundless.

Autobiographical texts such as *My Life in China and America*, written by Wing **Yung**, the first Chinese student to graduate from a U.S. university when he completed his studies at Yale College in 1854, and later texts such as Yee **Chiang**'s Silent Traveller series, attempted to take the mystique out of Chinese customs, habits, and rituals by explaining the purpose and history of these cultural practices. The intention of the autobiographical writers was to reveal the superficiality of cultural differences between Chinese and Americans and to demonstrate that in their common humanity both groups are the same. Jade Snow Wong, in the introduction to her autobiography, *Fifth Chinese Daughter*, explains that: "At a time when nothing had been published from a female Chinese American perspective, I wrote with the purpose of creating better understanding of the Chinese culture on the part of Americans. That creed has been my guiding theme through the many turns of my life" (vii). Sau-ling Cynthia Wong has characterized these texts as "guided Chinatown tours," which emphasize the continuities between middle-class Chinese and American cultures. Not only do these texts create and emphasize false commonalities, Wong argues, they also place Chinese superstition and American racism on the same logical footing, assuming that if one can be explained away, so can the other.

These apologetic texts assume a set of stable and fixed national, ethnic, and cultural differences. They argue not for assimilation but for cultural pluralism and mutual tolerance. However, the autobiographical self in these narratives is treated as the site of socialization into the dominant U.S. culture. Consequently, the explanation of and apology for Chinese cultural difference cannot fully accommodate the demands of Euro-American "normality" or normative values, and as a result texts such as *Fifth Chinese Daughter*, Pardee Lowe's *Father and Glorious Descendant*, and Maxine Hong Kingston's *The Woman Warrior* reveal a necessarily incomplete socialization of the autobiographical "I." Sidonie Smith has written extensively and persuasively about the assumed "universal" subject of autobiography, which complicates all attempts by the ethnic subject to appropriate this literary form. The universal autobiographical subject, against which the ethnic or female subject must be distinguished, is represented as normative in the form of male, white, and European. This, Smith argues, is the culturally sanctioned subject of autobiography, a subject that is able to enact particular experiences that have been sanctioned for autobiographical representation. As a "universal," this self is "desocialized" and consequently is defined not by specific material social roles and relations but by an interior essence that is congruent with maleness, whiteness, and European identity. It is in this context that the early Chinese American autobiographies attempt to engage with American racism and anti-Chinese sentiment. The exclusion of non-European and nonmale subjects may be, Smith suggests, the very cause of their engagement with autobiography as a literary form, to write or talk back to the universal self that is the cause of their exclusion. Writing in an earlier study, *A Poetics of Women's Autobiography* (1987) about Kingston's *The Woman Warrior*, Smith argues that this text "exemplifies the potential for works from the marginalized to challenge the ideology of individualism." If the "universal" subject of European individualism is undermined by the racialized and gendered autobiographical ethnic subject, then the entire autobiographical genre is placed in question. Chinese American autobiography does challenge the European tradition of first-person life writing in this way (Smith 1987, 150).

The internal contradiction of Chinese American autobiography, which attempts to bring together in a condition of mutual tolerance or cultural pluralism the distinct cultures of Chinese and European America, is a direct consequence of the hybrid nature of the literary form. Chinese American autobiographies bring together the origins of the form in European tradition with the details of daily Chinese American experience. In contrast, in his 1985 essay, significantly titled "This Is Not an Autobiography," Frank Chin complains that the dominance of the autobiographical genre within the Chinese American literary tradition has generated the assumption among European or Western readers that all Chinese American writing is life writing, and therefore it necessarily offers authentic insight into the reality of Chinese American culture and experience. He argues that autobiographers "characterize Chinese history and culture in terms of Christian stereotypes and tell of the same Cinderella story of rescue from the perverse, the unnatural, and cruel Chinese into the one true universe" (109). However, autobiographies like *Fifth Chinese Daughter* and *Father and Glorious Descendant* use the conventions of Euro-American autobiography, in the style established by Benjamin Franklin, to tell an American rags-to-riches story. These texts focus upon the narrator's struggles to achieve an education and a successful career and to triumph against all odds, including racial prejudice and inherited Chinese values. Jade Snow Wong and Pardee Lowe both describe at length the circumstances that permit them to benefit from an American college education: the former at Mills College and the latter at Stanford University. Their autobiographies culminate in the story of their individual career triumphs. These writers seek to authenticate both an ethnic Chinese self and a claim to American nationality or citizenship within the context of the autobiographical narrative.

Chinese American autobiographies are perhaps uniquely compromised in the capacity to tell an objectively true story because of the impact upon community and family formation by the history of exclusion. For example, Pardee Lowe expresses early in his autobiography the suspicion that his father was a fake. By this, he means to suggest that his father was a so-called paper son, someone who had falsely purchased the identity of a legitimate Chinese American to claim U.S. citizenship. This practice of inventing or buying personal identities and personal histories was the direct consequence of the Chinese Exclusion Laws. After 1881, Chinese who were resident in the United States but who left the country could then reenter only by producing a Certificate of Return. All Certificates of Return were declared void in 1888; the Scott Act of that year stipulated that returning Chinese residents had to produce their Certificates of Residence upon demand or be deported. This legislative move had the effect of stimulating a market in false identity papers, but it also institutionalized the location of ethnic identity in these papers. Autobiographers like Pardee Lowe use the life narrative to place in question the authority of paper documents to legitimate identity, which then becomes a constitutive part of the autobiography. In *China Men*, the sequel to *The Woman Warrior*, Maxine Hong Kingston describes her father's experience at the **Angel Island** immigration station as a game based on these false, paper identities. What is effectively tested by U.S. immigration officials is not the "real" or objective identity of these immigrants but their ability to construct a self-consistent narrative, a fictive autobiography that is consistent with the paper lives they are presenting as their own. In the period following the 1906 earthquake and fire, which destroyed documents such as birth certificates and citizenship records, the numbers of paper sons claiming U.S. citizenship increased significantly. The legacy of this history for Chinese American autobiography is a tradition of secrecy concerning the origins of families and communities, which is reflected in the radical epistemological uncertainty of autobiographical texts such as *The Woman Warrior* and more conservative texts such as *Father and Glorious Descendant*. **See also** Asian American Stereotypes; Assimilation/Americanization; Racism and Asian America.

Further Reading

Chin, Frank. "Come All Ye Asian American Writers of the Real and the Fake." In *The Big Aiiieeeee! An Anthology of Chinese American and Japanese American Literature*, eds. Frank Chin, Jeffery Paul Chan, Lawson Fusao Inada, and Shawn Wong. New York: Meridian, 1991. 1–92.

———. *Ethnic Autobiography*. Special Issue of *MELUS* 14 (1987).

———. "This Is Not an Autobiography." *Genre* 18.2 (1985): 109–130.

Huang, Guiyou, ed. *Asian American Autobiographers: A Bio-Bibliographical Critical Sourcebook*. Westport, CT: Greenwood Press, 2001.

Kingston, Maxine Hong. "Cultural Mis-Readings by American Reviewers." In *Asian and Western Writers in Dialogue: New Cultural Identities*, ed. Guy Amirthanayagam. London: Macmillan, 1982. 55–65.

Lejeune, Philippe. *On Autobiography*. Minneapolis: University of Minnesota Press, 1989.

———. *Le Pacte autobiographique*. Paris: Seuil, 1975.

Smith, Sidonie. *Subjectivity, Identity and the Body: Women's Autobiographical Practices in the Twentieth Century*. Bloomington: Indiana University Press, 1993.

Wong, Jade Snow. *Fifth Chinese Daughter*. Seattle: University of Washington Press, 1989.

Wong, Sau-ling Cynthia. "Autobiography as Guided Chinatown Tour? Maxine Hong Kingston's *The Woman Warrior* and the Chinese American Autobiographical Controversy." In *Maxine Hong Kingston's "The Woman Warrior": A Casebook*, ed. Sau-ling Cynthia Wong. New York: Oxford University Press, 1999. 29–53.

———. "Immigrant Autobiography: Some Questions of Definition and Approach." In *American Autobiography: Retrospect and Prospect*, ed. Paul John Eakin. Madison: University of Wisconsin Press, 1991. 142–170.

DEBORAH L. MADSEN

✦ CHINESE AMERICAN DRAMA

Compared to other genres of **Chinese American literature**, Chinese American drama started late. The earliest dramas with "Chinese motif" were those traditional Chinese operas translated into English or those written by Americans that dramatized their exotic imagination about China. As for the latter, the Chinese played the role of servants of the whites and functioned dramaturgically only as comic clowns to amuse the audience (Jiang 2006, 115). The caricatured image of Chinese was sustained in dramas with Chinese motif well into the 1950s. The unprecedented success in Chinese American drama came in the 1960s. C.Y. **Lee's** novel *Flower Drum Song* (1957) presented euphemistic portraits of **Chinatown** and quickly earned popular and financial success (Kim 1988, 814), winning a Commonwealth Club Award. In 1958 the novel was revised by Rodgers and Hammerstein into a musical and brought to Broadway. It was the first Chinese American drama presented on Broadway. As a play concerned with Chinese American community, it comically dramatized issues like racial discrimination, the generation gap between FOB (Fresh off the Boat) and ABC (American-Born Chinese), and bachelorhood due to severe disproportion of men to women. The growth of Chinese American drama in the real sense began in the 1970s with the emergence of theater companies particularly concerned with Asian American themes—the Asian American Theater Workshop, the East West Players, the Pan Asian Repertory, and the Northwest Asian American Theatre Company (Vena and Nourgeh 1996, 945). However, only a small part of the dramatic works of this period found their way to publication, which included a one-act play, *One, Two Cups* (1974) written by Mei-mei **Berssenbrugge** and *Points of Departure* (1977) by Paul Stephen Lim. The 1980s and the 1990s witnessed the publication of works by a group of young Chinese American playwrights, such as Merle **Woo's** *Balancing* (1980), Diana W. Chou's *An Asian Man of a Different Color* (1981), Darrell H.Y. **Lum's** *Oranges are Lucky* (1981) and *My Home Is Down the Street* (1986), Laurence **Yep's** *Daemons* (1986) and *Pay the Chinaman* (1990), Genny Lim's *The Only Language* (1986), *Pigeons* (1986), *Paper Angels* (1991), and *Bitter Cane* (1991), and Deborah Rogin's *The Woman Warrior* (1994), which was a dramatic revision of two of Maxine Hong **Kingston's** novels, *The Woman Warrior* and *China Men*. These plays present realistic pictures of early Chinese immigrants' hardship as manual laborers and of the racial, cultural, or generational conflicts encountered by these immigrants. *Bitter Cane* is concerned with the Chinese labor immigrants cultivating sugarcane in Hawaii. *Paper Angels* presents the internment of early Chinese immigrants on **Angel Island**. Mei-mei Berssenbrugge's *One, Two Cups* describes mother-daughter relationships among Chinese Americans. Diana W. Chou's *An Asian Man of a Different Color* is concerned with racial and cultural conflicts.

Today the most influential Chinese American playwrights are Frank **Chin** and David Henry **Hwang**. Established as a man of letters with his collaboration in editing

Aiiieeeee!: An Anthology of Asian American Writers (1974), Chin also stands out by being the first Chinese American dramatist who drew attention from American mainstream critics. Chin's first play *The Chickencoop Chinaman* won the top prize in a playwright contest sponsored by the East West Players in Los Angeles. However, due to financial problems encountered by the company, the play was not produced until it found its way to the American Place Theater in New York in 1972 under the direction of Jack Gelber. It was the first production of its kind in the history of the legitimate American stage and was a landmark event in the history of Chinese American drama in its connection with the Asian American dramatic prosperity that followed (Vena & Nourgeh 1996, 944). After the premiere of *The Chickencoop Chinaman*, Chin's second play, *The Year of the Dragon*, was produced at the same theater in 1974 and then was filmed for *Theater in America* on public television, where it was aired in 1975 (943–945). This play was the first Chinese American drama aired on American television. *Gee, Pop!* a real cartoon in two acts, was produced by the American Conservatory Theater in 1974, while *Flood of Blood*, a one-act play, was published in the *Seattle Review* in 1988. Failed father-son relationships and Chinatown as a place of death are favorite themes in Frank Chin's plays. Both *The Chickencoop Chinaman* and *The Year of the Dragon* portray the prisoner-like life of Chinese Americans in Chinatown. Confining themselves in Chinatown, presented as a place of internment, the inhabitants lose their will and courage to experience life in the outside world, which results in a loss of assertiveness and even in the disintegration of the self and family. Flight becomes the only possible way to establish a self-identity. However, the young protagonists find it impossible because of the older men's clinging to illusions that limit their lives and stifle their opportunity to be real men, hence the conflict between fathers and sons and the image of failed fathers (Kim 1988, 819). After the premiere of *The Chickencoop Chinaman*, Clive Barnes of the *New York Times* commented that Chin showed in this play "an ethnic attitude [he] never previously encounter" (Vena and Nourgeh 1996, 948), for the reason that the play was "the first Asian American work to confront crucial cultural issues that has long been repressed in the theatre and other performance media" (944). It conveys sociopolitical messages about Asian Americans that audiences could not possibly learn from C.Y. Lee's *The Flower Drum Song*. The groundbreaking theme of *The Chickencoop Chinaman* is backed up by Chin's unconventional style with incisive language, biting humor, and nonconformist characters (946).

One of the major issues of the play is the failed father-son relationship that leads to the protagonist's search for an ideal father and selfhood. The protagonist Tam Lum, a Chinese American writer and filmmaker, comes to Pittsburgh to interview Charley Popcorn, the father of a black ex-champion boxer, Ovaltine Jack Dancer, for a documentary movie Tam is shooting. With his actual father being a timid and cowardly old man who is unable to set a model of manhood for his own son, Tam's search for Dancer's father, whom Dancer describes as a model of masculine assertiveness and heroism, is actually a quest for a surrogate father he can be proud of and follow as an example of manhood. After his encounter with his black friend, Kenji, a culturally dichotomized limbo like Tam himself, Robbie, and Robbie's mother, who endeavors to pass for white, Tam finally meets Charley Popcorn, only to discover that Charley is not Dancer's father at all. Nevertheless, Tam pleads with the old man: "[Dancer] needs you to be his father . . . you gotta be his father." Charley turns down the request. The contrast between a needy son desperate for an adorable father and a father failing to or refusing to act out that expectation goes on throughout the play. In the end, his search for a surrogate father ends in failure, and Tam refuses to let go of the feelings of anger and pride engendered by his ancestral heritage with the sound of the train as its symbol. The failed father-son relationship signifies the failure of Asian American manhood to express itself in the former, as its simplest form (Vena and Nourgeh 1996, 947), which is a theme preoccupying Chin in most of his works.

The Year of the Dragon is also concerned with father-son conflict and disintegration of selfhood. The play begins with the imminent death of the father, Pa Eng. The old man is an authority both in Chinatown, as "mayor" of Chinatown, and in the family by demanding unconditional obedience. He removes the protagonist Fred, his eldest son, from college, chooses a despised tour guide business for him, stifles his ambition to be a writer, and forces him to promise he will stay in Chinatown. For Fred, Chinatown is the whites' private preserve for an endangered species. However, as the tour guide of Chinatown, repeating set spiel in line with the white tourists' expectation, Fred is forced to reinforce the American stereotypes of Chinese Americans. Though the job turns him into a self-loathing person, Fred is proud of his success in shouldering family responsibilities by being the income-earner and for his loyalty he expects respect and affirmation from his father. However, his sacrifice is not acknowledged or rewarded by the father, for the old man declares Fred to be a "flop," unable to take care of the family outside Chinatown. Torn between his desire to live as an independent individual and his responsibility to the family and loyalty to a selfish and despotic father, Fred finds himself maimed as an individual.

David Henry Hwang's success as a playwright surpasses Chin's in terms of popularity and finance. Hwang establishes his fame as a playwright with his *Chinese American Trilogy: FOB* (1979), *The Dance and the Railroad* (1981), and *Family Devotions* (1981), which are concerned with the cultural and political experience of Asian Americans. First staged in a dormitory at Stanford University where he was pursuing his BA, *FOB* was later produced in New York in 1980 and won an Obie Award for Best Play. Since then, prolific in writing, Hwang has addressed similar issues in a series of powerful plays, including *The Sound of a Voice* (1983), *The House of Sleeping Beauties* (1983),

Rich Relations (1986), *As the Crow Flies* (1986), *1000 Airplanes on the Roof* (1988), *M. Butterfly* (1988), *The Voyage* (1992), *Bondage* (1992), *Trying to Find Chinatown* (1996), and *Golden Child* (1996). The peak of his career came in 1988 with the production of his masterpiece *M. Butterfly* on Broadway. Not only winning box office success, the play established Hwang as the most renowned Asian American dramatist of the twentieth century, making him the first Chinese American dramatist to win a Tony Award. Beside the Tony Award for Best Play, *M. Butterfly* also won an Outer Critics Circle Award, a John Gassner Award, and a Pulitzer Prize nomination. Ten years later, the Off-Broadway production of his *Golden Child* received an Obie Award, and the Broadway staging earned Tony Award nominations for Best Play, Best Actress, and Best Costume Design (Trudeau 1999, 151).

Since his first play *FOB*, Hwang has been interested in exploring how people of different cultures and genders perceive and react to each other. As a result, fluidity of identity is a favorite theme in Hwang's plays (Bryer and Hartig 2004, 231). The theme is most elaborately explored in his masterpiece *M. Butterfly*. Combining a modern-day political and sexual scandal reported in the *New York Times* with Puccini's opera *Madama Butterfly*, Hwang exposes the illusionary nature of stable identity, consolidated by man/woman and West/East dichotomies. Rene Gallimard, a junior-level French diplomat, develops a relationship with a Chinese opera actress, Song Liling, after watching her performance in *Madama Butterfly*. After a 20-year-long affair, the actress Gallimard loves turns out be a man and a Chinese spy. Not only subverting the stereotyped image of the Oriental woman and the East, the play also questions the stability of identity purported by that political/sexual stereotype.

Despite the successes achieved by individual playwrights, Chinese American drama has a long way to go before its presence in either performance media or critiques is more adequately recognized. As a category of works highly stressing artistic beauty and presenting directly to the audience Chinese American experiences, Chinese American drama deserves greater recognition and support. **See also** Asian American Stereotypes.

Further Reading

Bryer, Jackson R., and Mary C. Hartig. *The Facts on File Companion to American Drama*. New York: Facts on File, Inc., 2004.

Cheng, Aimin. "Preface." In *A Study of Chinese American Literature*, ed. Cheng Aimin. Beijing: Beijing University Press, 2003.

Hwang, David Henry. *M. Butterfly. Modern Drama: Plays, Criticism, Theory*, ed. W.B. Worthen. Fort Worth, TX: Harcourt Brace College Publishers, 1995.

Jiang, Mengmeng. "From Assimilation to Search for Selfhood: a Research into Chinese American Drama." *Foreign Literature Quarterly* 1 (2006): 115–120. (In Chinese)

Kim, Elaine H. "Asian American Literature." In *Columbia Literary History of the United States*, ed. Emory Elliot. New York: Columbia University Press, 1988. 811–821.

Trudeau, Lawrence J. *Asian American Literature: Reviews and Criticism of Works by American Writers of Asian Descent.* Detroit: Gale Research, 1999.

Vena, Gary, and Andrea Nourgeh, eds. *Drama and Performance: An Anthology.* New York: HarperCollins College Publishers, 1996.

XUEPING ZHOU AND AIMIN CHENG

✦ CHINESE AMERICAN LITERATURE

Chinese American literature emerged as an area of academic study with the publication of the first anthologies of Asian American literature in the early 1970s, which had the consequence that literary works produced by writers of Chinese heritage were not clearly distinguished from texts written by members of other Asian cultural groups. Chinese American literature has generally been discussed under the wider rubric of Asian American literature. Early collections included *Asian American Authors* (1972), edited by Kai-yu Hsu and Helen Palubinskas; David Hsin-fu Wand's *Asian-American Heritage: An Anthology of Prose and Poetry* (1974); and the groundbreaking anthology edited by Frank **Chin**, Jeffery Paul **Chan**, Lawson Fusao **Inada**, and Shawn **Wong**, *Aiiieeeee! An Anthology of Asian American Writers* (1974). These anthologies brought Asian American literary texts together to form a new category of literature, within which Chinese American works formed a distinct subcategory.

The first English-language book published in America appeared in 1887, when Yan Phou **Lee**, a Chinese student who graduated from Yale in 1897, published *When I Was a Boy in China.* Whether this constitutes the first work of Chinese American literature is, however, debatable. Indeed, the exact definition of Chinese American literature is the subject of considerable controversy. Yan Phou Lee's autobiographical work was published in the United States but deals only with the author's experiences in China. In content, then, this is a Chinese book, though technically it is American. The "Chineseness" of Chinese American literature is complex, whether a definition is approached in terms of the ethnicity of the author, the literary subjects, or settings featured in the texts, or the language in which the text is written. Perhaps most ambiguous of all is the body of poetry written at the beginning of the twentieth century by Chinese immigrants, awaiting admission to the United States and detained at the **Angel Island** immigration center in San Francisco Bay. These poems were carved into the walls of the barracks to which the writers were confined. Written in Chinese but expressing the savage disappointment concerning their reception in the United States, these poems were written in the liminal space of the detention center, neither inside nor outside the United States. These poems were translated into English only in the

1970s by Him Mark Lai, Genny Lim, and Judy Yung for publication as *Island: Poetry and History of Chinese Immigrants on Angel Island, 1910–1940* (1980).

Edith Maude **Eaton**, known also by her pseudonym Sui Sin Far, is often hailed as the first Chinese American writer. She was in fact Eurasian, born of an English father and a Chinese mother, and raised in Canada. It was Eaton's decision to identify with the cultural heritage of her mother and to write explicitly about the experience of the Chinese in North America in the 1880s that accounts for her status as the earliest pioneer of Chinese American literature. The editors of *Aiiieeeee!* (1974) offered a definition of Chinese American writers that was restricted primarily to those who are American-born of Asian parents, though with an exception for those like Eaton who migrated to America in early childhood. To limit Chinese American writers to those born in America excludes the first generation of immigrants who traveled from China to the United States and who wrote in Chinese. In part because of the exclusion laws in operation in the late nineteenth and early twentieth centuries, these immigrants did not think of themselves as "American" but rather as *huaqiao,* meaning "Overseas Chinese." Only after the repeal of the exclusion laws in 1943 did it become possible to conceptualize a Chinese American class of U.S. citizens and to formulate a category of Chinese American literature.

Those Chinese writers who were living in the United States in the late nineteenth century were either descendants of earlier immigrants or belonged to permitted categories of migrants: students, merchants, and diplomats, for example. Many were Christian and some, like Yan Phou Lee; **Yung** Wing, who wrote *My Life in China and America* (1909); and Huie Kin, the author of *Reminiscences* (1932), were sent from China as students to the United States by Christian missionary organizations. These writers responded to the anti-Chinese prejudice they encountered by writing apologetic autobiographical accounts of their lives in China. It is to this tradition of Chinese American autobiography that the work of later writers such as Jade Snow **Wong** and Maxine Hong **Kingston** belongs. However, it is also to this autobiographical tradition of Chinese American literature that Frank Chin has famously objected. In the introduction to *The Big Aiiieeeee! An Anthology of Chinese American and Japanese American Literature*, Chin and his coeditors describe two kinds of Chinese American literature: the real and the fake. By "fake" Chinese American literature, Chin and his colleagues refer to this Christianized autobiographical tradition, observing that autobiography is not a genre found in the Chinese literary tradition. Chin further objects to the apologetic nature of these early autobiographies, which sought to respond to racism by appealing to the rationality of white American readers. This style of autobiography, which explains and justifies aspects of Chinese cultural tradition that may seem alien and aggressive to Americans of European descent, is seen to underlie a "fake" literature. Chin accuses writers like Wong and Pardee Lowe, and later writers like Maxine

Hong Kingston and David Henry **Hwang**, of internalizing anti-Chinese prejudices that are reproduced in the texts that take these prejudices as their starting point. Also included in this category of "fake" Chinese American writing are Wu Tingfang's *America through the Spectacles of an Oriental Diplomat* (1914), **Lin** Yutang's *Chinatown Family* (1948), and **Chiang** Yee's Silent Traveller series. These educated and privileged Chinese saw themselves as quite distinct from the laboring classes of Chinese immigrants upon whom racist stereotypes as either ignorant buffoons (in the style of **Charlie Chan**) or scheming villains (like **Fu Manchu**) were often based. The effort to contradict Chinese stereotypes by explaining the true character of Chinese and Chinese American experience is seen as based on a false motivation. What Frank Chin sees as the true tradition of Chinese American literature arises out of the Chinese fairy tale, Cantonese opera, and the Confucian heroic tradition. However, because this tradition is fundamentally oral, Chin admits that these texts are notoriously difficult to retrieve. The work to salvage the early sources of the oral tradition occupies contemporary scholars who seek to establish the complex beginnings of Chinese American literature.

The talk-story tradition of oral storytelling that Maxine Hong Kingston describes in *The Woman Warrior* and *China Men* belongs to this oral peasant tradition of the immigrant Chinese. Two collections of the folk rhymes that would have been known to the early Chinese immigrants have been published: Chen Yuanzhu's *Taishan Geyao Ji* (1929) and Hu Zhaozhong's *Meizhou Guangdong Huaqiao Liuchuan Geyao Huibian* (1970), respectively, collect Taishan and Cantonese folk rhymes. Marlon K. Hom's *Songs of Gold Mountain: Cantonese Rhymes from San Francisco Chinatown* (1987) is a selection of poems that Hom has translated from Chinese. These poems are not transcriptions of oral works but were written by members of early twentieth-century **Chinatown** poetry societies. Membership of these societies was composed primarily of educated merchants, though the authors of the poems are anonymous.

From the time of the repeal of the Chinese exclusion laws in the mid to late 1940s, a small group of Chinese American women began publishing literary works: Helena Kuo, Lin Yutang's daughters Adet and Anor Lin (or Lin Tai-yi), Mai-mai Sze, and Han Suyin. Also at this time, the second generation of Chinese Americans, those who were American-born of Chinese immigrant parents, began to write and publish. Jade Snow Wong and Pardee **Lowe** are the most prominent of these second-generation writers. Like the early autobiographers, among whom Wong and Lowe are counted, these writers adopt the stance of a cultural guide who describes and explains to a white American readership the significance of Chinese American customs, rituals, and cultural practices. Sau-ling Wong has famously called these texts "guided Chinatown tours" (1992, 249). Pardee Lowe's *Father and Glorious Descendant* (1943) and Jade Snow Wong's *Fifth Chinese Daughter* (1945) address both a new mainstream readership for texts that concern Chinese American lifestyles and also the conflicts that characterized this transitional period in Chinese American history. Both Pardee Lowe and Jade Snow Wong depict conflict with their fathers as their attitudes change toward the traditional values that are enforced from within the Chinese American family. Such conflicts focus on the shift from Chinese tradition to American modernity, from conformity to individualism, that takes place largely through the dynamics of education. This is particularly true of Jade Snow Wong's experience of growing up in a traditional Chinese family but with the expectations of a modern Americanized woman. Specifically, she expects to go to college, but her father refuses to support her financially and so she must find a way to support herself throughout her college education, an experience that further promotes her commitment to individualism. Other Chinese American women writing at this time expressed their ambivalent experience as Chinese Americans. Though American culture valued women more highly than did Chinese culture, America devalued Chinese people and so was not experienced necessarily as a place of liberation. Helena Kuo's autobiography, *I've Come a Long Way* (1942), Su-ling Wong's *Daughter of Confucius* (1952), and later Katherine Wei's *Second Daughter* (1984) all express this ambivalence.

The changes brought about in the Chinese American community by the repeal of the exclusion laws, in the wake of China's role as an American ally during **World War II**, are dramatized in Louis **Chu's** novel *Eat a Bowl of Tea* (1961). Before the war, the most significant demographic effect of the exclusion laws was the development of male-dominated bachelor societies. The restrictions placed on migrant Chinese women were so severe that few women were able to settle in the United States. Consequently, Chinatowns developed as almost exclusively masculine communities. After the war, and with the relaxing of restrictions on Chinese women migrants, these male-dominated bachelor societies were radically transformed. Chu's novel focuses upon anxieties surrounding Asian male emasculation because of racial discrimination and disempowerment that were identified by the editors of the landmark anthology *Aiiieeeee!* (1974) and elaborated by later critics such as David Eng in his book *Racial Castration* (2001). Frank Chin, Jeffery Paul Chan, Lawson Inada, and Shawn Wong attack the racial stereotype of the Chinese American man as delicate, effeminate, and emasculated. Louis Chu's novel deals with the sexual impotence of the narrative's newly married protagonist, Ben Loy. This private problem quickly becomes a matter of concern for the community. Indeed, Chu represents impotence as a political issue, arising from a history of womanless communities, where prostitutes provided the only female company available to Chinese men. Ben Loy cannot approach his new wife sexually without recalling those encounters with prostitutes, and the memories unman him. The dysfunctionality of Ben Loy's sexuality, his marriage, and his community is diagnosed as a symptom of the history of American racism.

Chu's novel has been described as introducing a strain of gritty realism to Chinese American literary expression. The language, characterization, and setting are all realistic, in particular Chu's deployment of Chinatown slang and the particular verbal idiom of Chinatown. In contrast to Chu's work, other writers of this period persisted in representing a sanitized version of Chinese American culture that would appeal to white stereotypes, while representing a sympathetic portrait of Chinese American life. For example, Virginia Lee's *The House that Tai Ming Built* (1963) uses Chinese stereotypes to present a positive image of Chinese culture. The narrative is sentimental and lacking in analysis of the characters' motivation; rather, it focuses upon the cultural artifacts that surround the characters to create an exotic and tasteful milieu in which they can move.

Louis Chu's effort to bring the Chinatown vernacular language into the domain of literary works is continued by Frank Chin's "Chinaman" language, a form of verbal expression that is particular to Chinese American life by combining Cantonese slang with an urban black idiom (inspired by the Black Power movement) and English. This effort alienated some reviewers of Chin's early play *The Chickencoop Chinaman* (1971). Chin's protagonist Tam Lum responds to the question of where he was born with a tirade that culminates in the exclamation: "I am a Chinaman! A miracle synthetic!" Tam refuses to be identified as either Chinese or American; instead, he is a hybrid of both. Chin's work is highly hybridized, combining the heroic Chinese tradition with American popular culture. Frank Chin's writing in drama, fiction, and prose is a form of protest literature. Chin attacks those Chinese Americans he calls racists, who internalize inauthentic ethnic identities by accepting stereotypes of Chinese Americans.

Many post-1960s writers struggle with the difficulty of being culturally hybrid—Chinese and American but neither Chinese nor American—and the search for an authentic identity. David Henry Hwang's play **M. Butterfly**, which explores the force of Orientalism and racialization through the figure of the emasculated Asian man who passes for a woman, caused controversy when it was first performed in 1988. This concern harkens back to the issue of Asian male sexuality and the force of anti-Asian racism in *Eat a Bowl of Tea*, but the attention that the play attracted is a powerful indication of the concern among contemporary writers with interconnected relations between sexual and gender identity, on the one hand, and personal and ethnic identity, on the other. Catherine Liu's novel *Oriental Girls Desire Romance* (1997), for example, explores interconnections between sexual and ethnic stereotypes through the figure of a bisexual and biracial protagonist negotiating her hybrid Chinese and American cultural identity.

The negotiation of racial stereotypes and the pursuit of alternative ethnic and sexual identities is a theme engaged by contemporary Chinese American writers. Many of this generation of writers are the children of immigrant parents, who deal with the cultural pressures confronted by ethnic communities in the contemporary United States. Maxine Hong Kingston's early works, *The Woman Warrior* and *China Men*, describe the difficulties she encountered dealing with her mother and father, the traditional stories they would tell, the Chinese cultural practices to which they introduced her, and the American cultural artifacts, not least movies, that complicated the formation of her identity as a Chinese American. Gish **Jen's** novels *Typical American* (1991) and *Mona in the Promised Land* (1996), while engaging the tension between American-born children and their Chinese-born parents, focus on the immigrants who came to America in the wake of the Chinese communist revolution rather than the earlier generations of economic migrants who came predominantly from southern China. The relationship between Chinese-born mothers and American-born daughters has become a popular theme in texts written by Chinese American women: Ruthanne Lum McCunn's *Thousand Pieces of Gold* (1981), Alice Lin's *Grandmother Had No Name* (1988), Fae Myenne **Ng's** *Bone* (1993), and Amy **Tan's** best-selling novels *The Joy Luck Club* (1989), *The Kitchen God's Wife* (1991), and *The Bonesetter's Daughter* (2001) all deal with this theme. Amy Tan's work focuses not so much on the life experience of American daughters as the history of Chinese mothers in the novels that have followed publication of *The Joy Luck Club* in 1989.

This body of work produced by contemporary Chinese American writers is marked by a significant shift away from the social and cultural concerns of the "guided Chinatown tours" offered by early twentieth-century writers. Recent Chinese American literature explores the complexity of the subjective life in the context of a post-civil rights culture of identity politics and its aftermath. Writers such as Kingston, Ng, Tan, Liu, and others offer a more psychologically oriented approach to contemporary Chinese American experience that opens up to transnational or diasporic perspectives on the migrant context, out of which Chinese American literature has emerged as a category of study and analysis. Writers such as Shirley Geok-lin **Lim**, a Peranakan Chinese American of Malaysian birth, reveal the complexity of a literature that has developed out of the historical dispersion of Chinese culture into Southeast Asia and across the globe, where the United States is but one point of intersection in an intercultural network of extraordinary complexity and richness. As Chinese American literature advances and increases the critical mass of writings that comprise the canon of this literature, it looks back to the history of Chinese writing in English as it has developed over the course of the past century and a half. In this perspective, Chinese American literature is not simply a subcategory of Asian American literature regionally conceived; rather, Chinese American literature enjoys a relationship with the literatures of other diasporic Chinese communities in Canada, Australia, Southeast Asia, and across the world. **See also** Asian American Stereotypes; Chinese American Autobiography; Chinese Exclusion Act; Orientalism and Asian America; Racism and Asian America.

Further Reading

Chan, Jeffery Paul, Frank Chin, Lawson Fusao Inada, and Shawn Wong, eds. *The Big Aiiieeeee!: An Anthology of Chinese American and Japanese American Literature*. New York: Meridian, 1991.

Eng, David. *Racial Castration: Managing Masculinity in Asian America*. Durham, NC: Duke University Press, 2001.

Kim, Elaine H. *Asian American Literature: An Introduction to the Writings and Their Social Context*. Philadelphia: Temple University Press, 1982.

Li, David Leiwei. "The Production of Chinese American Tradition: Displacing American Orientalist Discourse." In *Reading the Literatures of Asian America*, eds. Shirley Lim and Amy Ling. Philadelphia: Temple University Press, 1992. 320–323.

Madsen, Deborah L. *Chinese American Writers*. Farmingham, MI: Gale, 2002.

Wong, Sau-ling Cynthia. "Autobiography as Guided Chinatown Tour? Maxine Hong Kingston's *The Woman Warrior* and the Chinese-American Autobiographical Controversy." In *Multicultural Autobiography: American Lives*, ed. James Robert Payne. Knoxville: University of Tennessee Press, 1992. 249–279.

———. "Chinese American Literature." In *An Interethnic Companion to Asian American Literature*, ed. King-Kok Cheung. Cambridge: Cambridge University Press, 1997. 39–61.

Yin, Xiao-Huang. *Chinese American Literature since the 1850s*. Urbana, IL: University of Illinois Press, 2000.

DEBORAH L. MADSEN

✦ CHINESE AMERICAN NOVEL

It is the achievement of the Chinese American novel that brings **Chinese American literature** as an essential component of American literature into factual existence. The Chinese American novel in English, either by the first-generation Chinese immigrants or by America-born Chinese Americans, is a relative newcomer, with its debut in the twentieth century.

The development of the Chinese American novel roughly undergoes three stages, each with distinct thematic concerns under changing social circumstances: the decades before the 1960s witnessed the sprouting of Chinese American novels which appealed to little critical concern and a limited reading community because of the unsteady Sino-American relationship, especially when the new communist China is concerned; from the 1960s to the early 1990s, Chinese American literature established the undoubted position in American literature through some notable works, accumulating most of its creative impetus from the increasingly flourishing African American literature inspired by the **civil rights movement** of the 1960s; from the mid-1990s to the present Chinese American novels manifest a kaleidoscopic vision far beyond what American readers have ever expected, owning to

Chinese Americans' assimilation into American culture and, to some extent, the effects of multiculturalism.

In the pre-1960s, critical self-awareness of Chinese American identity and literary tradition had not been a conscious concern of Chinese American writers. The earliest Chinese American novel, though lacking Chinese American sensibility, came into being as early as the beginning of the twentieth century. As the precursor of Chinese American literature, Sui Sin Far (Edith Maude **Eaton**) published her collection of short stories *Mrs. Spring Fragrance and Other Writings* (1912), and her sister, Winnifred **Eaton**, gained fame with the novels *Miss Numè of Japan* (1899), *A Japanese Nightingale* (1901), and *Tama* (1910) under the Japanese pseudonym Onoto Watanna. Her avoidance of Chinese American identity and her catering to the popular stereotypical images of Oriental women in the exclusion era also exclude her from consideration by some Chinese American critics who are more loyal to their ethnic identity.

Another early Chinese American novel that also fails to appeal to critics is **Lin** Yutang's *Chinatown Family: On the Wisdom of America* (1948). Among the many books written by this sophisticated Chinese immigrant who introduced Chinese culture to the Western readership, this novel is an inconspicuous work, relating the story of a working-class Chinese American family that settled in New York City in the 1940s. The lack of real experience in **Chinatown** and his being spared of the pains of exclusion turn the book into a deduction of Lin's Chinese philosophy about balance, tolerance, and harmony, even though he touches, if not empathically, some Chinese American concerns, such as interracial marriage, cultural assimilation, and cultural differences.

C.Y. **Lee's** *Flower Drum Song* (1957) is a novel by a Chinese-born elite. As the best-selling 1957 novel, it has been adapted into a successful musical on Broadway and a movie. It narrates the love story between Wang Ta, a second-generation Chinese American who seeks freedom from his father, and Li Mei, a girl who enters San Francisco illegally with her father from China. Lee's observation of the generation gap and his recognition of the class differences among Chinese Americans are portrayed in a comic, even farcical way, which compromises its influence on Chinese American novels.

Diana **Chang's** *Frontiers of Love* (1956) is among the first few Chinese American novels almost free of critical controversy. Chang's novel deals with a group of Eurasians in search of love and cultural identity in Shanghai during the last days of the Japanese occupation in 1945. The protagonist Sylvia effortlessly explores the issue of cultural identity in a Chinese metropolis dominated by Western colonialism. Chang uses psychological delineation, historical narrative, and sociological observation to achieve a multidimensional view of both the city and the divided self of Eurasians.

Chinese American experience finds the most vocal and steadfast expression for the first time in Louis **Chu's** *Eat a Bowl of Tea* (1961), a novel that portrays the life of a young couple, Ben Loy and Mei Oi, in the bachelor society of Chinatown in the 1940s. Ben Loy's impotence after his marriage gives Ah Song, a gambler in Chinatown, the opportunity to seduce Mei Oi, whose pregnancy excites revenge from Ben Loy's father, Wah Gay. After an ear was sliced off by Wah Gay, Ah Song is forced into exile for five years under the pressure of the local tongs. The two fathers of the couple choose to leave to avoid facing the scandal. The couple makes a new start: the husband finds a job and restores his sexual vitality by drinking a bowl of herbal tea prescribed by an herb doctor; the wife gives birth to a son, whose "haircut party" is held in the parents' hope that a family reunion will be realized at the next party. The novel reveals explicitly the highly patriarchal society of Chinatown resulting from immigration restrictions, establishes an idiosyncratic ethnic Chinese American experience as a legitimate literary subject matter for future generations of Chinese American writers, and impresses readers with authentic Cantonese dialect translated directly.

Most of the pre-1960s Chinese American novels reacted to the social milieu dominated by racial discourse by resorting to Chinese culture, *Eat a Bowl of Tea* being the only remarkable exception. Nevertheless, the Chinese American novels of this time paved the way for later writings by providing a background for more creative and critical awareness of identity politics.

The 1960s, marked by the **Vietnam War** and the civil rights movement, was an era permeated with cultural and racial sensitivity. The increasing ethnic consciousness of Chinese Americans raised by the success of African Americans procured the legitimate existence for the Asian American movement, under the impact of which Chinese American novels widened their thematic scope. Maxine Hong **Kingston** and Frank **Chin**, both tempered by the 1960s, are two outstanding writers of novels who help to shatter stereotypical images of Chinese in their own distinct ways and redefine the Chinese American experience.

Maxine Hong **Kingston's** first book *The Woman Warrior* (1976) means many things to readers, fitting in several labels: nonfiction, autobiography, novel, and memoir. It became a best seller instantly and won the 1976 National Book Critics Circle Award for nonfiction. The book delineates in a nonlinear narrative the growth of a Chinese American girl against patriarchal and racial oppression in an immigrant family in Stockton, California. Of the five chapters, only chapters 2 and 5 feature the first-person narrator as the protagonist. The appropriation of Chinese allusions, especially the story of Fa Mulan; the inheritance of Chinese "talk-story" tradition; and the insightful discovery of Chinese American reality surrounded by the white "ghosts" enrich the book's literary and political significance.

After establishing the place of Chinese American women in her first book, Kingston's second book *China Men* (1980) concentrates on the stories of males in her family: her father, grandfather, great-grandfathers, uncles, and her brother. The narrative strategy is similar to that of *The Woman Warrior*, being saturated with talk-story and allusions appropriated from both the East and the West. Kingston's ambition to reinscribe the history of Chinese Americans is reflected in a chapter entitled "The Laws," in which she encapsulates chronologically restrictions imposed on Chinese immigration to the United States from 1868 to 1978. For some, this section disrupts the flow of the stories with nonliterary materials, but it is these historical facts ignored by most Americans that weigh most for the readers' understanding of the Chinese American experience. The suffering, lonely Chinese men emasculated by American society echo strongly the predicament of Chinese American women silenced by racism and sexism.

Nine years after *China Men*, Kingston published *Tripmaster Monkey: His Fake Book* (1989), unmistakably her only novel to date. Though Chinese myths and intertextuality still occupy the heart of the book, the novel is narrated by an omniscient female narrator with a fictional protagonist, Wittman Ah Sing, who is a rebellious poet and playwright wandering in San Francisco in the 1960s. As a fifth-generation Chinese American, Ah Sing distinguishes himself from the Chinese Americans the readers expect to see. He identifies himself with the mischievous Monkey, a trickster in the classical Chinese novel *Journey to the West* by Wu Cheng'en; Ah Sing ruminates about his being a Chinese American by combining Chinese culture and Western literature into his own theatrical work. Ah Sing succeeds in producing a three-day theatrical event staging Chinese legends, which brings him out of the war in Vietnam and transforms him from a cynic into a pacifist.

Frank Chin's observation of the contemporary Chinese American experience on the other hand seems to be audaciously frank, unveiling Chinese Americans' hard struggle in the suffocating American society. His two novels, *Donald Duk* (1991) and *Gunga Din Highway* (1994), together with his plays, combine to show his resolve to fight racial stereotypes and restore Chinese American males' masculinity by reclaiming the nineteenth-century history of Chinese America, which he values so much because of their contribution to the construction of the railroad in the American West.

Chin's *Donald Duk* is closely tied with this phase of American history. A 12-year-old boy who lives in San Francisco's Chinatown, Donald Duk hates his eccentric name almost as much as his disdain of his Chinese heritage. A series of magical dreams about Chinese Americans who constructed the Central Pacific Railroad with himself as a worker among them transform the boy's attitude about his ethnic identity and kindle his love for Chinese culture, represented by Kwan Kung, the Chinese god of war. The story unfolds against the background of the Chinese Spring Festival, which is delineated from an insider's perspective with the pops of firecrackers and the sound of gongs in the Cantonese opera resonating with Chin's forceful and unaffected prose.

Whereas *Donald Duk* aims to reconstruct a history of early Chinese Americans' heroic deeds performed during the construction of the railroad, *Gunga Din Highway* deals with the Hollywood film industry's deliberate, distorted representation of Chinese Americans and their culture, and it alludes to an array of Eastern and Western artistic traditions. In this provocative novel, Ulysses Kwan, a young artist and son of Longman Kwan, who is famous for his role as **Charlie Chan's** son No. 4, has a poor relationship with his self-absorbed father and finds his father's Hollywood role insulting. The narrative alternates among the points of view of Longman Kwan, Ulysses, and Ulysses's two childhood blood brothers, spanning from the early 1940s to the present. Though somewhat alienated, Ulysses molds himself into a Chinatown cowboy who incarnates Chin's ideal Chinese American male in his refusal to be a passive Chinese American hampered by the Chinatown ghetto.

Kingston and Chin have both received a good deal of critical attention among Chinese American writers, while Amy **Tan** appeals more to the common American readers with novels that feature Chinese culture, mother-daughter relationships, and Chinese American women's experience. Tan's first novel, *The Joy Luck Club* (1989), immediately became a best seller and brought the Chinese American experience to a wide audience. *The Joy Luck Club* details in 16 interwoven stories the complex relationship between four sets of mothers and daughters, whose stories are told in turn from the first-person point of view. Each Chinese immigrant mother adheres to her own view of the world based on her experiences in China to counterbalance her Americanized daughter. The reconciliation between the mothers and the daughters, Chinese culture and American culture, is symbolically achieved through Jing-mei Woo's delving into her deceased mother's history and her reunion with two half-sisters left in China by her mother in a time of war.

Tan's second novel, *The Kitchen God's Wife* (1991), is located primarily in China, again focusing on the relationship between a Chinese immigrant mother (Winnie) and her American-born daughter (Pearl). The heart of the novel is Winnie's recounting of her secrets in war-torn China in the 1940s, when she endures a childhood of loneliness and a nightmarish arranged marriage. When her secrets are uncovered, the gap between Winnie and Pearl is bridged, and Pearl attempts to accept her identity as an American of Chinese ancestry. *The Hundred Secret Senses* (1995), Tan's next book, appeals to readers with Tan's distinctive trademarks: Chinese culture, family history, supernatural elements, and the interwoven narratives. The mother-daughter relationship prevalent in the previous novels is replaced by the more complex relationship between the America-born Olivia and her China-born half-sister Kwan, who comes to the United States when she is 18 and is never assimilated into American culture. *The Bonesetter's Daughter* (2001) is Tan's last novel that focuses on family heritage and fascinates readers with her sensitive portrayal of another mother-daughter relationship. In this novel, after having her mother's autobiographical manuscript translated into English, Ruth begins to reevaluate everything about her mother and get out of the shadow of being a "ghostwriter."

Tan's fifth novel, *Saving Fish from Drowning* (2005), writes about 11 Americans' expedition into southern Burma where they encounter a tribe in the jungle waiting for the return of their leader, who will protect them from destruction by the Myanmar military regime. The novel, narrated from a ghost's satirical first-person viewpoint, is a true departure from Tan's familiar themes and looks into the unexpected consequences of good intentions and the responsibilities individuals must assume for others' sake.

The same year Tan's *The Kitchen God's Wife* enchanted American readers with Chinese myths and family secrets, Gish **Jen** published her *Typical American* (1991), which, in contrast, relates the story of a Chinese immigrant's efforts at assimilating into life in the United States. As "an American story" against ethnic essentialism, the struggle of Ralph Chang's family is portrayed honestly, lacking the usual sentimentality with respect to the Chinese American experience. The book's sequel, *Mona in the Promised Land* (1996), is a first-person account of Mona Chang, Ralph Chang's daughter, who chooses to convert to Judaism. The novel demonstrates the flexibility of ethnic identity and is acclaimed for its recognition of cultural diversity. Jen's more ambitious third novel, *The Love Wife* (2004), explores the themes from her earlier works: racism, cultural identity, the American dream, assimilation, and occasional tensions among ethnic communities. The focus is on the racially mixed Wong family, the stability of which is threatened by a female relative from mainland China, Lan, who helps Carnegie Wong rediscover his Chinese identity. In Jen's novels, the sadness of Chinese American experience is tinged with wit and humor, in keeping with her antiessentialism attitude.

Another Chinese American woman novelist Fae Myenne **Ng's** *Bone* (1993) wins tremendous praises for its contribution toward establishing a Chinese American literary tradition through the poignant story of a family of three daughters in Chinatown, San Francisco. The title, disliked by the publisher, is used to commemorate the Chinese Americans whose bones were sent back to China because they considered themselves displaced sojourners in a foreign country. The focus is not so much on the middle daughter Ona's suicide as on the sense of alienation and displacement among the Leong family or the Chinese American immigrants in a country that they feel reluctant to claim as home. As the narrator and the oldest daughter, Leila feels repugnant about her parents enslaved by their years of humiliating life in the United States, and wistful about the settlement of Chinese Americans in American history. The protagonist's dislocation within her family and her community is also captured in Mei **Ng's** *Eating Chinese Food Naked* (1998).

Since the 1990s, American narratives that represent the Chinese American experience in the United States rather than racism and issues of identity become the uniting theme of Chinese American novels. The contemporary scene of Chinese American novels is marked by multiplicity in subjects and perspectives, conditioned by minority discourse, feminism, postmodernism, and multiculturalism. Some male writers seem more willing to resist the temptation of Chinese culture and disengage themselves from the past. Gus **Lee**, for example, is adept at presenting his character's struggle of reconciling Chinese heritage with American reality and has won critical acclaim for his two autobiographical novels *China Boy* (1991) and *Honor and Duty* (1994). In *China Boy*, in a Chinese community in California in the 1950s, a seven-year-old Chinese American boy Kai Ting learns how to defend himself in the face of the local bully and his stern stepmother. Its sequel, *Honor and Duty*, continues to tell Kai Ting's story after he enters West Point in the 1960s. The expectation of his father and stepmother that he be a "real" American collides with the moral codes imparted by some other figures equally important to Kai Ting, who has to strive to reconcile these values. Lee's third novel, *Tiger's Tail* (1996), is another best seller, featuring Jackson Kan, a military lawyer who struggles between love and duty, while frequently disturbed by his flashbacks of service in Vietnam. Lee's next books are a legal thriller *No Physical Evidence* (1998) and a memoir *Chasing Hepburn* (2003).

The publication of Chinese American novels in unprecedented numbers since the mid-1990s encourages some writers who worked in other literary genres to turn to novel writing, and they have produced some unforgettable novels, such as Shawn **Wong's** *American Knees* (1995) and David Wong **Louie's** *The Barbarians Are Coming* (2000). The Chinese American experience in their works is filled with relatively more chaos, absurdity, and muddled narrative, which seems to reflect the authors' ambition to present the Chinese American experience by narrative itself, instead of appealing to readers with sociological or anthropologic elements. **See also** Asian American Stereotypes; Assimilation/Americanization; Colonialism and Postcolonialism; Feminism and Asian America; Multiculturalism and Asian America; Racism and Asian America; Sexism and Asian America.

Further Reading

Chan, Jeffery Paul, Frank Chin, Lawson Fusao Inada, and Shawn Wong, eds. *The Big Aiiieeeee! An Anthology of Chinese American and Japanese American Literature*. New York: Penguin Books USA Inc., 1991.

Chang, Chiung-Huei Joan. "Neither-nor or Both-and: A Study of Chinese American Writers." PhD Diss., University of Oregon, 1994.

Chun, Gloria H. *Of Orphans and Warriors: Inventing Chinese-American Culture and Identity*. New Brunswick, NJ: Rutgers University Press, 2000.

Ling, Amy. *Between Worlds: Women Writers of Chinese Ancestry*. New York: Pergamon Press, 1990.

Wong, Shawn, ed. *Asian American Literature: A Brief Introduction and Anthology*. New York: HarperCollins College Publishers, 1996.

Yin, Xiao-huang. *Chinese American Literature since the 1850s*. Urbana: University of Illinois Press, 2000.

SHAO YI

✦ CHINESE AMERICAN SHORT STORY

The Eaton sisters are believed to be the pioneers of Chinese American short story writing (Ling 2001, 35; G. Huang 2006, 25). As early as the late nineteenth century, Edith Maude **Eaton** (1865–1914) began to publish short stories in major literary journals and newspapers under the Chinese pseudonym Sui Sin Far, and in 1912 she published *Mrs. Spring Fragrance*, the first short story collection in Chinese American literary history. Born to a family with an English father and a Chinese mother, Sui Sin Far identifies with her Chinese ancestry and challenges the stereotypical representations of Chinese in American popular culture at the time in her stories. However, her younger sister Winnifred **Eaton** (1875–1954) adopted a different racial and cultural position in her writing: by using a Japanese pen name Onoto Watanna, Winnifred wrote novels, screenplays, and short stories, mainly romances between Caucasian men and Asian women. According to Amy Ling, the Eaton sisters have "created paradigms followed by their successors," the "inner-directed" ("existentialist") narrative by Edith Eaton and the "other directed" ("exotic") narrative by Winnifred Eaton (1999, 137, 142).

The decades following the Eaton sisters' careers were a quiet period for Chinese American short story writing. Then, under the influence of the **civil rights movement** and the Pan-Asian movement, Asian American literature started booming, which accordingly brought about the development of the Chinese American short story. In the 1970s, Jeffery Paul **Chan** (1942–), a leading figure in the *Aiiieeeee* group and one of the pioneers in pursuing the Chinese American patriarchal heroic tradition, published several influential short stories, mainly dealing with the Chinese American male identity. In 1975, Monfoon Leong's (1916–1964) short story collection, *Number One Son*, was posthumously published, 11 years after his death; many of the stories are based on his life experience of growing up in San Diego's **Chinatown** as the eldest son in the family. Also during this decade, the prolific writer Diana **Chang** (1934–) published short stories to explore the theme of racial "otherness" in the bicultural or multicultural context.

Then came the noteworthy era of the 1980s for the publication of short stories and collections by well-known Chinese American writers. Alex Kuo (1939–), Shirley Geok-lin **Lim** (1944–), Russell **Leong** (1950–), Darrell H.Y. **Lum** (1950–), Gish **Jen** (1956–), and Fae Myenne **Ng** (1956–) published short stories in magazines, journals, and newspapers. Darrell H.Y. Lum's short story collection *Sun: Short Stories and Drama* came out in 1980. Frank **Chin**, primarily known as a Chinese American playwright and critic, put forward the short story collection *The Chinaman Pacific & Frisco R.R. Co.* in 1988, which "dazzles readers with his intense love/hate reaction to the Chinese American identity" (Ling 2001, 37). And if we take Amy **Tan's** *The Joy Luck Club* (1989) as a short story cycle, it is safe to say the Chinese American short story reached its first major flowering period in 1989.

According to Guiyou Huang, "Asian American short fiction did not fully flower until the 1990s. This decade was characterized by not only a great number of writers working in this genre but also a variety of themes and styles never seen before" (2006, 26). This is also true of Chinese American short story writing. Darrell H.Y. Lum produced a new volume, *Pass On, No Pass Back*, in 1990, and it was awarded the Outstanding Book Award in Fiction by the **Association for Asian American Studies**. David Wong **Louie's** *Pangs of Love* came out in 1991 and has won several notable awards since its publication. In his stories, David Wong Louie tries to go beyond the problems of ethnicity and identity and to show general concerns about human life, such as love, family, divorce, and so on. In 1993, Evelyn **Lau** (1971–) published her first collection of short stories, *Fresh Girls and Other Stories*, reflecting her life as a teenage prostitute and exploring the theme of male domination and masochists. Her second collection, *Choosing Me: A Novella and Short Stories* (1999), centers on women from different social status who are still passively waiting to be chosen by men. Then Shirley Geok-lin Lim published two short story collections, respectively in 1995 and in 1999, which portray the life experience of a diasporic Chinese woman from a colonized Third World (Malaysia). Coincidently, Kathleen Tyau's (1947–) two short story collections, *A Little Too Much Is Enough* and *Makai* also came out in 1995 and 1999, and the former was chosen as the 1996 Best Book of the Year by the Pacific Northwest Book Sellers Association and the latter was a finalist for the 2000 Oregon Book Award. Both of these two collections focus on the development of Hawaii, especially the peculiarity of the physical environment in Hawaii. John **Yau** (1950–), who was born to a Eurasian family, explores the theme of multiethnic identity in his first collection *Hawaiian Cowboys* (1995) and deals with the sexual liberation of a Caucasian woman in the second collection *My Symptoms* (1998). Also in 1998 Lan Samantha **Chang** (1965–) put forth *Hunger: A Novella and Stories*, a short story cycle that has won warm acclaim from academia home and abroad because of its thematic concerns with Chinese American family dynamics and because of its elegant prose style. In 1999 the already well-known Chinese American writer Gish Jen (1956–) published her first short story collection *Who Is Irish*, which explores the themes of "assimilation, identity, displacement, generational conflict, interracial relationships, and the American dream" (Shuchen Susan Huang 2003, 103). According to many critics, Jen's *Who Is Irish* is a breakthrough in **Chinese American literature** because it has transcended the Asian American background and turned to other hyphenated minorities in the United States, such as Jewish Americans and African Americans.

In the twenty-first century, the Chinese American short story continues to thrive. Russell Leong's (1950–) *Phoenix Eyes and Other Stories* (2000) marked a strong beginning in the new era. This collection of short stories portrays the so-called marginalized groups of Asian Americans—the gay Asian male, the Asian prostitute, people who suffer from AIDS, and so forth. Alex Kuo's (1939–) *Lipsticks and Other Stories* (2001) tells of his life in China and the United States and was nominated for the American Book Award. Christina Chiu's *Trouble Maker and Other Saints* (2001) provides a bigger picture of the Chinese American family living in a changing and globalizing society—the ever-present cultural and generation gaps between parents and children, heterosexuality and homosexuality, and the dynamic immigration between the host country and the home country.

Moreover, the so-called new immigrant writers from the mainland of China have contributed a great deal to short story writing since the 1990s and in the new century: Wang Ping's *American Visa* (1994) is about the Cultural Revolution in China and a new immigrant's experience in New York. Ha **Jin** (1956–), the National Book Award winner, published three short story collections within five years: *Ocean of Words* in 1996, *Under the Red Flag* in 1997, and *The Bridegroom* in 2000, which portray the social upheavals in the Cultural Revolution in China and Ha Jin's personal experience as a soldier in the Chinese army. In 2005 Yiyun Lee's *A Thousand Years of Good Prayers*, a short story collection set in and around China, has received high praises from Chinese American critics and won *Guardian* First Book Award along with many other honors.

It is worth noting that Chinese American short story writing in the 1990s was increasingly diverse in thematic concerns and in writing styles. Instead of directly protesting the discrimination and unfair treatment Chinese Americans have suffered from mainstream society as the pioneers have done, writers of the younger generation tend to reflect their diverse life experiences in a more subtle, artistic, and complicated way, and as such they have achieved more in terms of aesthetic contributions to Chinese American short story writing.

It is worth mentioning that the list of short story writers discussed herein is limited to authors who published short stories or collections in English in the United States. Some famous Chinese American writers, such as Hua-ling **Nieh** and Ge-ling Yan, are not mentioned in this entry because their short story collections were published in Chinese and outside of the United States. If the short stories written in Chinese were taken into account, the list of the authors would be much longer. **See also** Assimilation/Americanization.

Further Reading

Huang, Guiyou. *The Columbia Guide to Asian American Literature since 1945*. New York: Columbia University Press, 2006.

Huang, Guiyou, ed. *Asian American Short Story Writers: An A-to-Z Guide*. Westport, CT: Greenwood Press, 2003.

Huang, Shuchen Susan. "Gish Jen." In *Asian American Short Story Writers: An A-to-Z Guide*, ed. Guiyou Huang. Westport, CT: Greenwood Press, 2003. 101–108.

Ling, Amy. "The Asian American Short Story." In *The Columbia Companion to the Twentieth-Century American Short Story,* eds. Blanche H. Gelfant and Lawrence Graver. New York: Columbia University Press, 2001.

———. "Chinese American Writers: The Tradition behind Maxine Hong Kingston." In *Maxine Hong Kingston's The Woman Warrior: A Casebook,* ed. Sau-ling Wong. New York: Oxford University Press, 1999.

RUOQIAN PU

✦ CHINESE EXCLUSION ACT (1882)

This federal act was approved by the U.S. Congress on May 6, 1882. The declared intention of the act was to prohibit the coming of Chinese laborers to the United States for a period of 10 years. This act codified a number of changes to previous legislative instruments that regulated travel, including immigration, between China and the United States.

At the conclusion of the Opium Wars, a number of treaties, known collectively as the Treaties of Tientsin (1858), were ratified by the emperor of China in the Beijing Convention of 1860. These treaties permitted, among other things, the establishment of legations in the previously closed city of Beijing by Britain, France, Russia, and the United States. Further treaty ports were opened, according to the terms of these treaties, and foreigners were permitted to travel freely within China. The Burlingame Treaty of 1868 amended the Treaties of Tientsin by establishing reciprocal conditions for travelers in China and the United States. In particular, reciprocal legal status and protections were accorded U.S. citizens in China and Chinese citizens in the United States.

It was during this period, from 1849, that a significant stream of economic migrants from China began entering the United States. Although there had been some Chinese immigration before this date, the numbers were small. After the discovery of gold in California in 1848 and with worsening political and economic conditions in China, the United States became one of several destinations for many Chinese migrants. Floods followed by drought, starvation, banditry, and the chaos brought about as a consequence of the Tai-ping Rebellion against the Manchu dynasty were important contributing factors. It was also during this time that the imperial government allowed Chinese workers to travel abroad as contract laborers or coolies for the first time, and foreign governments were granted the right to recruit Chinese laborers. In the aftermath of the abolition of slavery throughout the British Empire and the cessation of the transatlantic slave trade, there was a considerable global demand for cheap labor.

Most Chinese migrants to the United States traveled as coolie laborers or on a credit ticket system. The latter involved the payment of the passage by a broker, often located in Hong Kong, and the assistance of a local labor agent in the Unites States; these costs plus interest were repaid in monthly installments. Coolies were required to work for the person who had paid for their passage. In 1852 there were approximately 20,000 Chinese in San Francisco. Between 1848 and 1855, the high point of the Gold Rush, some 47,200 Chinese passed through U.S. Customs in San Francisco. Increasing numbers of Chinese workers, sojourners who had no interest in assimilating to American customs, led to resentment of the money that was remitted to China, to fears of economic competition, and to the hysteria of the **Yellow Peril**. Violence against ethnic Chinese in California and elsewhere escalated, especially in the period immediately following the completion of the **transcontinental railroad** and the economic depression of the 1870s, when the need for cheap labor appeared to have ended. Politicians seeking public favor and newspapers fueled the anti-Chinese sentiment.

The Angell Treaty (1880) modified the terms of the Burlingame Treaty, by allowing the U.S. government to limit and regulate Chinese immigration while separating trade issues from immigration. The Angell Treaty prepared the way for a complete prohibition on Chinese immigration, which came two years later. The Chinese Exclusion Act of 1882 suspended the Burlingame Treaty, which had promised both legal protection and the right to immigration to Chinese citizens in the United States. The Exclusion Act allowed for the detention and deportation of ineligible Chinese immigrants. Subsequent acts of legislation codified the practices authorized by the 1882 Exclusion Act. The Scott Act of 1888 prevented the readmittance into the United States of Chinese persons who traveled abroad, perhaps to visit family in China, by denying the validity of their Certificates of Return. The act authorized the establishment of a detention center, the forerunner of the **Angel Island** Immigration Station in San Francisco Bay, where Chinese immigrants could be held while their documents were checked. The Scott Act also prohibited the courts from granting U.S. citizenship to any person of Chinese ethnicity. Only officials, teachers, students, tourists, and merchants could enter the United States. United States citizens who married a Chinese national lost their U.S. citizenship. In 1892, Congress passed the Geary Act, which extended the 1882 act for another ten years and required all Chinese living in the United States to apply for a Certificate of Residence within a year and carry it wherever they went. The McCreary Amendments of 1893 added an additional six months to the deadline for registration but at the same time narrowed the definition of what constituted a "merchant" to exclude the industries in which most Chinese worked.

The Chinese Exclusion Extension Act was approved on April 27, 1904. This further act of Congress extended the provisions of the 1882 Chinese Exclusion Act indefinitely, with its various amendments. The last of these amendments was passed in 1902 and intended to prohibit all Chinese immigration and to regulate the residence of Chinese migrants and people of Chinese descent in the territories and possessions controlled by the United States.

The United States was not the only nation to act against large-scale Chinese immigration in this period. Similar acts of legislation were introduced in Australia (the Immigration Restriction Act or so-called White Australia Policy of 1901), New Zealand, and Canada. Like Australia and New Zealand, Canada imposed upon all Chinese immigrants a head tax, authorized by the Canadian Chinese Immigration Act of 1885. Initially set at 50 dollars, in 1900 the fee was raised to 100 dollars and in 1903 the amount was raised further to 500 dollars. Later, and again in keeping with Australian practice, legislation was introduced to limit the number of Chinese immigrants who could disembark from a single ship. One Chinese immigrant was permitted to enter Canada for every 50 tons of the ship on which they were traveling, for that one voyage. The Chinese Immigration Act of 1923 authorized a complete ban on Chinese immigration to Canada, including British nationals of Chinese descent.

These discriminatory legislative acts did not go without protest from Chinese communities, both within China and abroad. Strategies ranging from calls for the Chinese government to intervene, to boycotts of U.S. goods, to legal challenges in the U.S. courts were used as Chinese immigrants fought for their civil rights. Organizations such as the Native Sons of the Golden West, later known as the Chinese-American Citizens Alliance, campaigned to change these exclusionary laws. In 1943 the Chinese Exclusion Acts were repealed in the United States, and the McCarran-Walter Act of 1952 removed all racial bars to U.S. citizenship. In 1965 a new immigration law based on hemispheric quotas finally removed racial qualifications from U.S. immigration requirements.

Further Reading

"Angell Treaty" (1880). Transcribed by Cassandra Bates, 2006. November 2006. http://web.pdx.edu/~lorz/texts.htm.

Barde, Robert. "An Alleged Wife: One Immigrant in the Chinese Exclusion Era." National Archives, *Prologue Magazine* Spring 2004, Vol. 36, No. 1. Online November 2006. http://www.archives.gov/publications/prologue/2004/spring/alleged-wife-1.html.

"Burlingame-Seward Treaty" (1868). Transcribed by Cassandra Bates, 2006. November 2006. http://web.pdx.edu/~lorz/texts.htm.

Chan, Sucheng, ed. *Entry Denied: Exclusion and the Chinese Community in America, 1882–1943.* Philadelphia: Temple University Press, 1991.

"Chinese Exclusion Act." November 2006. http://www.cetel.org/1882_exclusion.html.

Pfaelzer, Jean. *Driven Out! Roundups, Resistance, and the Forgotten War against Chinese America.* New York: Random House, 2007.

Yung, Wing. *My Life in China and America.* Online November 2006. http://web.pdx.edu/~lorz/My%20Life%20in%20China%20and%20America.pdf.

DEBORAH L. MADSEN

✦ CHOCK, ERIC (1951 –)

A Chinese American poet and cofounder and coeditor of Bamboo Ridge Press in Hawaii, Eric Chock majored in English during his undergraduate years in Pennsylvania and became involved in activism. He developed a strong sense of social responsibility in his various attempts to participate in local community activities. Later he studied in the graduate program at the University of Hawaii. His teaching and coordination in the Hawaii Poets in the Schools program since 1973 has guided many teachers and students to write poems. Chock was awarded the 1996 Hawaii Award for Literature by Lieutenant Governor Mazie Hirono for his work on *Bamboo Ridge*. The award came from the State Foundation on Culture and the Arts and the Hawaii Literary Arts Council. Currently, he is the writing program director and visiting distinguished writer in the English Department at the University of Hawaii.

The purpose of founding Bamboo Ridge Press, Chock once explained, was "not just to publish, but to help define 'local' literature" (Burlingame 2008). He added that with Darrell H.Y. Lum, the cofounder and coeditor of the press, "We wanted it to be both a showcase and a vehicle. In a way, we were riding on the coattails of other ethnic movements around the United States. We were trying to help create a sense of community, at least a sense of literary community" (Huang 2002, 84). Such efforts are rewarding in that many local writers claimed to have found their space through the literary journal of *Bamboo Ridge: The Hawaii Writers Quarterly* for development in their poetry writing.

In 1978 Chock's first collection of poems *Ten Thousand Wishes* was published. "Ancestry" and "Papio" stand out for their distinct concerns with the root of one's identity, the tracks of growth, recollections of the past, interactions between memory and the present, and prospects for the future. The first lines of "Ancestry" articulate the significance of identity both to the addresser and to the addressee. On the one hand, the question indicates the speaker's curiosity about the first-person persona whose identity might engender a possible friendship or remove such a possibility; on the other hand, the reply suggests the long history of his culture and the dire material background. Chock integrates his observations about the transience of age, the youth of human existence, and the eternality of nature into the process of creating poetry. Similarly, in his other two poems about Chinese ancestry, "Chinese New Year" and "Farmers in the Field Return at Dusk," the young descendants' link to and their departure from the ancestors are closely examined. The mixed feelings about the traditional culture and contemporary culture are derived from the complex mentality of the poet as an individual standing between two cultures and two generations. As he states, "I believe that this social function of poetry is part of the give and take between life and art which ideally makes the two indistinguishable, exciting, and mutually beneficial" (Cheung 2000, 215).

Chock's second collection of poetry *Last Days Here* appeared in 1990. Covering the cycle of childhood, adolescence, and adulthood and structured in four parts, the collection chronicles both the personal and historical repertoire of experiences in Hawaii. It further explores the various aspects of life and dilemmas that modern individuals face.

Recent poems collected in *The Quietest Singing* point to Chock's social concerns as well. "For George, Our Neighbor" overflows with the guilty recollection of the first-person speaker about his old and neglected neighbor George. The indifference to old George arises not just from his neighborhood but also from his family. Chock employs the technique of repetition, which takes the form of a series of "because" clauses. And by beginning most stanzas with "Because," the poem highlights the nonchalance that spreads like a plague among communities. This explains why the title "Our Neighbor" is used instead of "My Neighbor." Satire is also obvious in the poem, when human closeness to animals is contrasted with human isolation. Fortunately, however, the speaker, in inserting his current thoughts into his backward glance over the past, undergoes an awakening to the fact that mutual respect and reciprocal care help to cement a good and healthy human relationship. "After Hurricane Iniki, Kaua'i 1992" reflects the speaker's thoughts and observations of the impact of natural disasters on human beings. The good values about family and community are reemphasized, while people have to face disasters such as hurricanes. Like the poem "For George, Our Neighbor," this poem illuminates the importance of harmonious human relationships, very much in keeping with Chock's principles of poetry writing: "I believe in the function that poetry performs in reflecting and shaping the people and culture which give it life, which sustain it" (Cheung, 215).

While establishing a natural local voice by adopting the first-person speaker, Chock also resorts to **Hawaiian Pidgin** English to convey his philosophy of life. Written in a housewife's voice, "Snacks" illustrates with humor a woman's inner thoughts about her husband and her justification for craving snacks. Beneath the veneer of complaint and light-hearted humor, the reader is guided to perceive the impact of poverty upon local Hawaiian families. In the meantime, the lack of communication between the husband and the wife also points to the mystery of human relationships. It might be that the housewife resorts to snacks to seek consolation from life's pressure.

In exploring the theme of cultural differences and experimenting with the language, Chock has made significant contributions to Hawaiian literature in that the Bamboo Ridge Press has nurtured writers such as Nora Okja **Keller** and Lois-Ann **Yamanaka**, who have received national acclaim. **See also** Asian American Political Activism.

Further Reading

Burlingame, Burl. "'Bamboo' Thriving: 'Bamboo Ridge' Editors Win a State Award." *Honolulu Star-Bulletin*. Available at: http://starbulletin.com/97/06/23/features/story2.html. July, 2008.

Cheung, King-Kok, ed. *Words Matter: Conversations with Asian American Writers*. Honolulu: University of Hawaii Press, 2000.

Chock, Eric. *Last Days Here*. Honolulu: Bamboo Ridge Press, 1990.

———. *Ten Thousand Wishes*. Honolulu: Bamboo Ridge Press, 1978.

Huang, Guiyou, ed. *Asian American Poets: A Bio-bibliographical Critical Sourcebook*. Westport, CT: Greenwood Press, 2002.

Lum, Darrell H.Y., ed. *The Quietest Singing*. Honolulu: University of Hawaii Press, 2000.

JIN LI

✦ CHOI, SUSAN (1969–)

A Korean American fiction writer and lecturer in creative writing, Susan Choi is the author of two well-received novels, *The Foreign Student* and *American Woman*; the latter was a finalist for the Pulitzer Prize in 2004. Born in South Bend, Indiana, to an immigrant Korean father who came to the United States to study at the University of the South in Sewanee, Tennessee, and a second-generation Russian Jewish American mother, Choi initially grew up in the Midwest and moved to Houston, Texas, after her parents divorced. She earned a BA in literature from Yale University, where she had early success with writing, winning the Wallace Prize for fiction, and, upon graduation in 1990, she drifted aimlessly before finding herself working at a health food store while trying to figure out what to do next. In a self-described panic, she applied to graduate school and was admitted to Cornell University's dual PhD/MFA in English and creative writing program. Deciding to drop out of the PhD program but staying on for the master of fine arts degree, she remained at Cornell for three years teaching creative writing courses, writing several short stories that were published in literary journals such as *Epoch* (Cornell's literary journal) and the *Iowa Review*, and forming a rough sketch for what would become her first novel. After graduating, she moved to New York to work as a fact checker for the *New Yorker* magazine while writing during her spare time until shortly after her first novel was published. Choi has since moved on to several writing fellowships and lectureships to pursue writing full-time.

Alongside writers like Chang-Rae **Lee**, Choi has been hailed as part of a vanguard of an emerging generation of Asian American novelists. Coincidentally, both she and Lee published their first novels at the relatively young age of 29, and both studied literature at Yale University, overlapping each other by one year (Lee being three years her senior), even sharing some similar themes in their first novels. In *The Foreign Student* (1998), she explores issues touching on immigration, the legacies of both Japanese and American imperialism, isolation, and especially language, to form a meditation on the linkages between people despite historical, geographic, political, and social barriers. Her second, most recent novel, *American Woman* (2003), takes a different turn in concentrating on issues of homegrown disenfranchisement rooted in class and race, the trauma associated with it, and the multitude of possible responses, signaling a sense of irony in the title. Common to both novels is a fairly developed sense of poetic, elliptical prose whose quietude belies the raw emotional and explosive events that punctuate critical points.

Choi's first novel, *The Foreign Student*, negotiates the difficult task of massaging connections between postwar Korea and the American South in the 1950s to facilitate an unconventional romance. Centering on Chang "Chuck" Ahn, a political refugee from South Korea who comes to a small Southern college on an evangelical church's academic scholarship to earn a degree, Choi jumps back and forth several years between the United States and Korea, unwrapping Chang from a reticent, timid student to his origins as a U.S. Army-employed interpreter and political refugee. He arrives to meet Katherine, a beautiful young woman who also lives in exile, of sorts, because of a sordid affair with a popular college professor, named Charles Addison, that began when she was 14 years old and he was considerably older. As an iconoclast of the Old South, Katherine is estranged from her family and the rest of proper society for returning to Sewanee as Charles's mistress. In Katherine, Chang discovers a fellow journeyman in search of a place to call home after both of their homes had been ravaged by personal and political turmoil, and they turn to each other when it seems that they are utterly alone. Although most critics tend to gravitate toward the American South narrative, *The Foreign Student* really has two threads, the other being situated in another South (Korea). If Chang's life in Sewanee is about a formation of a home, his life in Seoul and Pusan is about the loss of that home. His former social status as the son of a highly respected scholar is reduced to nothing during the war and the military occupation of Korea by the United States. When Seoul falls, his job as a translator for the American wire services cannot protect him, he flees to Pusan, where his family is separated, and he eventually is captured and tortured, even as the country is divided along ideological lines. Throughout the novel, Choi manages to strike a balance between a universal tale of romance and a commentary on the legacy of political and religious imperialism.

American Woman (2003), based on events surrounding the kidnapping of Patty Hearst by the Symbionese Liberation Army in 1974, portrays a Japanese American woman's struggle to come to terms with being relegated to the periphery in every possible portion of American society. Jenny Shimada, loosely based on former-activist-turned-painter Wendy

Yoshimura, is hiding out in upstate New York after her leftist collaborator and boyfriend has been arrested for bombing military draft offices. Lonely and mournful of her solitary situation, she lives out her days questioning her own disillusionment with the radical movement and the violence of their tactics. Meanwhile, two blundering radicals in their early twenties and their newly converted kidnappee, the teenage daughter of a famous media mogul, hide out in a Berkeley apartment after the rest of their organization has been decimated by the police. Eventually, Jenny agrees to look after the three of them by taking them into an isolated farmhouse, while they halfheartedly attempt to write a book detailing their underdeveloped ideologies. She eventually forms a strong connection with Pauline, the kidnapped recruit, whom she looks after; their solitude on the farm is cut short by a botched robbery attempt. Jenny's quiet self-reflection and intellectualism contrast strongly with the knee-jerk reactions of both the mainstream media and the fugitives under her care, but she does share in their paranoia. Hers seems rooted in some part with her estranged father, who was incarcerated at a **Japanese American internment** camp during **World War II**. Choi thus depicts Jenny as having to deal with two layers of conspicuousness: her status as a fugitive and as an **Asian American** who cannot escape the consciousness of race, something that she is reminded of repeatedly, even though she shies away from directly addressing it. Only after she is liberated of her status as a criminal by serving time and in some part paradoxically ignored because of her race by the media, does she begin, alongside her father, to reform herself.

Further Reading

Andriani, Lynn. "Antiwar Activism, Starring Patty Hearst: PW Talks with Susan Choi." *PublishersWeekly.com*. 23 June 2003. Accessed 10 Dec. 2006. http://www.publishersweekly.com/article/CA306495.html.

Birkerts, Sven. "The Safe House." *New York Times* 5 Oct. 2003, late ed.: sec. A: 9.

Dressel, Jenny. "American Woman." *Mostly Fiction Book Reviews*. 28 Nov. 2003.

Eder, Richard. "Books of the Times; When a Receding Tide Leaves Lives Behind." *New York Times*. 12 Sept. 2003, late ed.: sec. E: 2.

Hong, Terry. "Building Character." *AsianWeek.com*. 29 Aug. 2003. http://news.asianweek.com/news/view_article.html?article_id=807373eee04a4c4e3bb1e013f58a77a3.

Lee, Don. "Rev. of *The Foreign Student*." *Ploughshares* 25.1 (1999): 193–194.

Lipman, Elinor. "Rev. of *American Woman*." *Boston Globe* 5 Oct. 2003: third ed. Sec. Books: H8.

Marlowe, Kimberly B. "Chang Chuckified." *New York Times* 18 Oct. 1998: late ed. Sec. 7: 29.

McMichael, Barbara Lloyd. "Shaky flashback to '70s radicalism, feminism." *Seattle Times* 5 Oct. 2003: Sunday fourth ed. Sec. Books: K9.

Nahm, H.Y. "Shadow Novelist." *Goldsea.com*. 10 Dec. 2006. http://goldsea.com/Personalities/Choisusan/choisusan.html.

Press, Joy. "I was an Asian American Fugitive." *The Village Voice*. 8 Aug. 2003. http://goldsea.com/Personalities/Choisusan/choisusan.html.

Stephenson, Anne. "'American Woman' Revisits Era That Bred Hearst Kidnapping." *USA Today*. 18 Sept. 2003, final ed. Sec. Life: 4D.

"What to Read." *Salon.com*. 12 Sept. 2003. Accessed 8 Dec. 2006. http://dir.salon.com/story/books/review/2003/09/12/choi/index.html.

DAVID ROH

✦ CHONG, DENISE (1953?–)

A Chinese Canadian economist, memoir and fiction writer, editor, and biographer, Denise Chong's literary career began with the publication of the memoir of her mother's family, *The Concubine's Children: Portrait of a Family Divided* (1994), which won the City of Vancouver Book Award, the Edna Staebler Prize for Creative Non-Fiction, and the Vancity Book Prize and was on the best seller list of *The Globe and Mail* for 93 weeks. Born in Vancouver, Chong grew up in Prince George, British Columbia. She worked as an economist with Canada's Department of Finance. From 1980 to 1984, she served in the prime minister's office as an economics advisor to Pierre Trudeau. She lives in Ottawa with her husband, CTV reporter Roger Smith and their two children, Jade and Kai.

Originally written as the cover story to the October 1988 issue of *Saturday Night Magazine*, Chong's narrative about her trip to Kwangdong (Guangdong) to meet her relatives in China and the discovery of the history of the earlier sojourner generation prompted numerous offers for her to write a book within a week of the work's publication. *The Concubine's Children* tells the story of her maternal grandmother, May-ying, who was sold as a concubine at 17 to Chan Sam, an immigrant who left his family in China in search of wealth in *Gum San*, or **Gold Mountain**. The book was highly successful, in part, because of its crossover quality, appealing to readers interested in history, biography, Asian American and Asian Canadian literature, and to those who enjoy multigenerational stories about women. Chong combines meticulous research in social and political history, an eye for domestic detail, and an unsentimental but evocative style of narration that earned the book praise. Book reviewers described it as "an utterly absorbing tale" (*The Globe and Mail*), "a gripping story" (*The Vancouver Sun*), and "a wonderfully engrossing family saga" (*The London Free Press*) (*Concubine's Children* 1994, back cover). It has been compared to works by Asian American and Asian British writers such as Maxine Hong **Kingston**, Amy **Tan**, and Jung Chang.

Like other Asian North American writers who write about a previous era, Chong challenges dominant culture's account of the past by documenting the lives of people who have largely been forgotten by traditional versions of history. Her book focuses on first-generation Chinese immigrants who settled in Vancouver's early **Chinatown**, on their poverty, the lack of education, and their exclusion from the larger white society, breaking what Lien Chao calls "silences" about these pioneers (1997, x). In the foreword to her book, Chong writes, "There are as many different versions of events as there are members of a family. The truth becomes a landscape of many layers in an ever-changing light; the details depend on whose memories illuminate it" (*Concubine's Children* 1994, xiii). The story of *The Concubine's Children* spans two continents, two worlds, and two halves of one family with competing versions of the past. The story of her grandmother, May-ying, the concubine who came to Canada in 1924 only to find out that she had to work as a teahouse waitress for at least two years to pay for her passage from China, is one that takes up much of the book. In an even-handed and factual manner, Chong narrates May-ying's life, including her early efforts to work as a waitress and to be a dutiful second wife to Chan Sam, the birth of her three daughters, her eventual habits of gambling, prostitution, and her struggles with alcohol. At the same time, she presents her readers with a concise and useful account of Asian Canadian social history at the turn of the twentieth century: the conditions in China that pushed men to leave their country for California and British Columbia, the discriminatory practices in Canada against hiring men with pigtails during the second half of the nineteenth century, the **Chinese Exclusion Act** of 1882 in the United States, the imposition of the head tax in Canada for Chinese immigrants in 1885 ($50) and then in 1904 ($500), and the Chinese Exclusion Act of 1923 in Canada. She uses various kinds of records—oral history, government documents, and photographs—to represent her grandmother's life in all its facets.

The 36 photographs included in the book add an immediacy and authenticity to her grandmother's, her mother's, and her own life stories. Yet, critics such as Teresa Zackodnik and Eleanor Ty have pointed out that the photographs are public performances, as they are often posed and formal, taken on happy or auspicious occasions. They do not tell the whole story about the family, about the pains and the loneliness experienced by May-ying and later by her daughter, Hing (Chong's mother), who was often left unattended while May-ying worked or entertained her secret male friends. Chong's narrative supplements the public narrative told by these photographs and paints the unexotic and often difficult moments of living in Chinatowns in Vancouver and Nanaimo in the first half of the twentieth century. At the same time, the book acts as a vindication of her grandmother's life. For it was from her hard-earned wages as a waitress that Chong's grandfather, Chan Sam, was able to send money back home to China to support his first wife and the children he left behind there and to build his house. Upon meeting her relatives during her trip to China with her mother in 1987, Chong discovers that their version of the family past was much different from hers. For them, the grandfather, Chan Sam, was the one who held the family together, and May-ying was the troublemaker and the alcoholic whom he could not tolerate. Out of respect for their memories and the grandfather, Chong does not tell her Chinese relatives her version of their family history.

Aside from the book version of *The Concubine's Children*, Denise Chong has contributed a short piece also called "The Concubine's Children" to *Many-Mouthed Birds:*

Contemporary Writing by Chinese Canadians (1991), edited by Bennett Lee and Jim Wong-Chu. She has edited *The Penguin Anthology of Stories by Canadian Women* (1998) and has contributed to the anthology *Who Speaks for Canada: Words that Shape a Nation* (1998), edited by Desmond Morton and Morton Weinfeld. Her second book, *The Girl in the Picture: The Story of Kim Phuc, the Photograph, and the Vietnam War* (1999), is again a work of creative nonfiction. This book is a biographical account of Kim Phuc, the Vietnamese girl who was photographed naked, running away from a napalm bomb attack in June 1972. Similar to her first book, Chong's narrative focuses on a woman's life, her aspirations, desires, struggles with day-to-day difficulties—this time mainly from her physical condition—set against a backdrop of historical and political events. The book, a project suggested by two editors from Penguin Canada, is constructed from interviews with the subject, Kim Phuc, her family members, reporters who covered the **Vietnam War** some 25 years ago, and from newspapers, books, and film sources.

Chong's biography of Kim Phuc renders her human, rather than an icon of suffering or a symbol of the evils of violence and war. The book supplements the story of horror told by the photograph and makes Kim Phuc more than another spectacle of the Vietnam War. She generates interest not only in Phuc but also in the Vietnamese people, their daily lives, their ways of worship, their food, and their family lives by giving details and textures of everyday life. By resituating Kim Phuc in the specificities of history and into South Vietnamese culture, politics, and religion, Chong gives voice to Kim Phuc, who had largely become as still as her photograph, in spite of her apparent public presence in the media. She also describes the events surrounding the taking of the photograph from multiple perspectives: from the viewpoint of the average peasant, from the American government, and from the perspective of the photographer, Nick Ut. These perspectives supplement the captions that had accompanied the picture when it appeared and add different angles and layers not only to the napalm bomb incident but also to the Vietnam War itself. Hence, through these biographies, Chong participates in the rewriting of cultural memory and in the foregrounding of the stories we remember when we think of our history and our collective past.

Further Reading

Chao, Lien. "The Collective Self: A Narrative Paradigm and Self-expression in Three Prose Works." In *Beyond Silence: Chinese Canadian Literature in English*, Lien Chao. Toronto: TSAR, 1997. 88–121.

Chong, Denise. *The Concubine's Children: Portrait of a Family Divided.* New York: Viking, 1994.

Soo, Jacalyn. "Interview with Author Denise Chong." *Chinacity.* http://www.asian.ca/media/chinacity/jsoo.htm.

Ty, Eleanor. "Reconstructing the Woman behind the Photograph: Denise Chong's *The Girl in the Picture*." In *Ethnic Life Writing and Histories: Critical Intersections*, ed. Rocío G. Davis. Münster: LIT Verlag, 2008.

————. "Writing Historiographic Autoethnography: Denise Chong's *The Concubine's Children*." In *The Politics of the Visible in Asian North American Narratives*. Toronto: University of Toronto Press, 2004. 33–53.

Zackodnik, Teresa. "Suggestive Voices from 'the Storeroom of the Past': Photography in Denise Chong's *The Concubine's Children*." *Essays on Canadian Writing* 72 (Winter 2000): 49–78.

ELEANOR TY

✦ CHONG, PING (1946–)

Chinese American playwright, theatre director, choreographer, and video and installation artist, Chong did not feel being a member of a minority group until he was in high school, though he was born in Toronto and raised in New York City's **Chinatown**. He started looking at the United States as an outsider, yet when he passed the phase where his early works were disguised autobiography, he realized that "the role of the outsider was more universal" (Berson 1990, 3).

Ping Chong has written numerous plays. Since *Nuit Blanche*, Chong's work has, according to himself, fallen into two categories, "the conventional scenes, like *Kind Ness*, and the more choreographic works like *Angels of Swedenborg*, which is almost textless" (Ibid). In 1975 Chong founded Ping Chong & Company, a nonprofit art organization. The company, working in partnership with theaters, museums, and community organizations, has created over 30 works of theater and art for audiences around the world. His works include *Humboldt's Current* (1977, Obie Award), *Anna into Nightlight* (1982), *A Race* (1984), *Nosferatu* (1985, 1991), *Kind Ness* (1986, Playwrights USA Award from Theatre Communications Group and Home Box Office), *Plague Concrete* (1988, a triad of outdoor multimedia installations for the Three Rivers Festival in Pittsburgh), *Noiresque: A State of Being* (1989), *Brightness* (1989; two Bessie Awards, 1990), *Elephant Memories* (1991), *Deshima* (1993), *Interfacing Joan* (1996), *After Sorrow* (1997), *Kwaidan* (1998), and *Pojagi* (2000). In 2002, La MaMa presented *SlutforArt, a.k.a. Ambiguous Ambassador*, a collaboration of Ping Chong and choreographer Muna Tseng, as a sequel to their collaboration *After Sorrow*. The ongoing series of community-specific works *Undesirable Elements* beginning in 1992 explore the effects of history, culture, and ethnicity on individuals in a community. The more than 28 productions of *Undesirable Elements*, also known as *Secret History*, as Chong once stated in an online chat, are "both a communication with a community and a testimonial of lives lived" (2005).

Ping Chong has garnered two National Endowment for the Arts Fellowships, a Guggenheim Fellowship, and a National Institute for Music Theatre Award.

Chong's first performance piece, *Paris,* was successfully made in 1972 in collaboration with Meredith Monk, but *Lazarus* was his independent work, which was his "most uncompromising" (Berson 1990, 3) in his entire career. The third play *Nuit Blanche* (1981) shows the influences of Shiva Naipaul and V.S. Naipaul on Chong, who claimed that it was "the first show I did with the theme that has echoed over and over again in my later works: the vulnerability of human beings and the recurrence of destruction" (Berson 1990, 4).

Nuit Blanche explores the destructive effects of alienation and racial discrimination on human beings. As the author makes clear in his comments on the play, it is "really about human history, about the way history evolves vis-à-vis the two characters in the plantation who wind up in their respective worlds later on" (Berson 1990, 5). The play begins with the early nineteenth-century South American ranch owner Señor Ortega giving his daughter Gloria birthday presents—a tea set, a dangerous-looking knife, and a magic lantern that projects a film in which a chimpanzee is hunted and slaughtered by a tiger. These presents point to the paternalistic principle of educating his daughter into a feminine and obedient woman whose rebellion, if any, will certainly result in severe punishment. Berenice, the maid of the house, serves as both a victim of slavery and a victimizer of Gloria, in that the former attempts to keep the latter within the patriarchal domain.

As the scenes unfold, the story develops into the latter half of the nineteenth century. The abolition of slavery in South America enables Berenice to gain freedom, yet her life is torn between hard labor and her unrequited love for her husband. The patriarchal oppression from both her husband and the white man Franklin, who Berenice is subjected to, proves to be no different from that experienced by Gloria. Hence, women's fate under patriarchy seems universal regardless of time, skin color, or living spaces.

When the hotel, the Haven of Peace, located in South Africa, begins to host an increasing number of tourists, the conflicts are ironically intensified. Apparently, the hotel-owner Papa Willie is the ranch owner, only in a different era and place. The Oriental, though unnamed and appearing mysterious, assumes the identity of the indomitable. It is he who plots a number of deaths and who remains the only person alive to witness the funeral scene. The author skillfully adopts both audio and visual techniques to dramatize the dark theme of destruction. With every sound of gunshots, the reader/viewer is informed of the death of a certain character. The successive slides of characters switch from ancient to modern times, to the effect that human emotions, conflicts, and ways of survival or death prove to be universal despite the time difference.

Human history is shown as fluid and repetitive. Ping Chong sends a warning to all human beings: unless individuals rid themselves of alienation and begin to accept each other on an equal standing they will end in destruction. Since his performance of the play, Chong claimed that he has "always come back to [the theme], to the cyclical nature of destruction" (Berson 1990, 4).

Chong once wrote that his works were characterized by "a kind of magic realism" like that of the South American writers (Berson 1990, 4). The increasing concern of his works is with individuals' spiritual journeys and spiritual longings. He has committed to the belief that "we are all together on this one little planet" and that "it's more and more important for us not to feel so foreign with one another" (Berson 1990, 5). When asked about the most rewarding thing about the creative process in creating new works in an online chat, Chong answered, "To create is its own reward" (2005).

Further Reading
Berson, Misha, ed. *Between Worlds: Contemporary Asian-American Plays*. New York: Theatre Communication Group, 1990.
Chat transcript with Ping Chong, author-director of "Native Voices—Secret History." April 28, 2005. http://www2.ljworld.com/news/2005/apr/28/chat_transcript_with/.
Chong, Ping. *Nuit Blanche: A Select View of Earthlings*. In *Between Worlds: Contemporary Asian-American Plays*, ed. Misha Berson. New York: Theatre Communication Group, 1990.
Huang, Guiyou. *The Columbia Guide to Asian American Literature since 1945*. New York: Columbia University Press, 2006.
Miles, Xian Liu, ed. *Asian American Playwrights*. Westport, CT: Greenwood Press, 2002.

JIN LI

✦ CHOY, WAYSON (1939–)

A Chinese Canadian novelist, memoirist, and professor of English, Wayson Choy is best known as the author of three award-winning novels of Chinese immigrant life in Vancouver in the early part of the twentieth century. *The Jade Peony* (1995) shared the Trillium Book Award for Best Book of 1996 with Margaret Atwood and won the 1996 City of Vancouver Book Award. Begun as a short story in 1977, *The Jade Peony* has been anthologized more than 25 times. His memoir, *Paper Shadows: A Chinatown Childhood* (1999), won the Edna Staebler Creative Non-Fiction Award; it was nominated for a Governor General's Award, short-listed for the inaugural Drainie-Taylor Prize, and was a 1999 Toronto *Globe and Mail* Notable Book of the Year. Choy's second novel, *All That Matters*, the sequel to *The Jade Peony*, won the 2004 Trillium Book Award, was short-listed for the 2004 Giller Prize, and was long-listed for the 2006 Impac Dublin Literary Award. In 2005 Choy was named a member of the Order of Canada.

Choy attended the University of British Columbia, where he studied creative writing with such teachers as Earle Birney, Jacob Zilber, and Jan de Bruyn, whom he later named as early influences. His first story, "The Sound of Waves," was published in *PRISM* magazine and anthologized in *Best American Short Stories for 1962*. Choy has explained in interviews that he could not envision a career as a writer because he felt that he had nothing of relevance to write about. At that time, in the early 1960s, his experience of growing up as a child of immigrants in Vancouver's **Chinatown** did not seem to represent the kind of "Canadian" experience that proponents of Canadian literature were then promoting. Choy moved to Toronto in 1962 and taught English at Humber College and the Humber School for Writers from 1967 to 2004. During the sabbatical leave he was granted in 1977, following the death of his mother, Choy returned to UBC, where Carol Shields was leading a short story writing course within the creative writing program. With her encouragement, he wrote the story "The Jade Peony" and submitted it to the UBC *Alumni Chronicle* writing contest. The story won and was published the following year. However, a contract for the novel was agreed upon only in 1992.

Wayson Choy's work is frequently compared with that of Sky **Lee** and the Chinese American novelist Amy **Tan**. He shares their interest in the complexities of the "between worlds" condition of first- and second-generation immigrants to North America. Choy's writing is praised for his sensitive portrayal of childhood experience in Vancouver's Chinatown during the period of exclusion. Particularly, his ability to adopt the narrative point of view of the child is noted by critics, along with his delicate balance between adult and child perspectives.

The Jade Peony tells the story of the Chen family, through three interconnected narratives, each narrated by one of the family's three Canadian-born children. The fourth child, first son Kiam-Kim, who was born in China and traveled to Vancouver with his grandmother Poh-Poh and his father at the age of three, narrates his own story in the sequel *All That Matters*. Choy has explained that originally Kiam-Kim's narrative concluded *The Jade Peony*; however, upon the advice of his editor, he removed that section from the novel with the intention of writing a separate text. His reasoning was that, as the only child born in China and as the First Son who was raised more by patriarchal authorities than by the women in the family, Kiam-Kim's experience was of a different order and so required separate telling. Each of the child-narrators of *The Jade Peony*, however, occupies a distinct position within the family and the Chinatown community: Jook-Liang is the only daughter; Jung-Sum is Second Brother, but he has been orphaned and adopted into the family; finally, Sek-Lung or Third Brother tells his story around his gradual realization that he is gay. As critics have noted, the novel is based upon the notion of transformation; each of the three narratives involves a moment of significant, transformative change, which symbolizes the coming together of the Canadian and Chinese identities of these characters. In his delicate blending of fiction with historical fact (and his work is exhaustively researched in archives and libraries as well as oral histories and personal reminiscences), Choy introduces a subtle, symbolic texture to the novel that works by bringing together the mundane and the mythical. The grandmother, called Poh-Poh or sometimes simply the Old One, will tell stories of Old China to the children who sit peeling vegetables or shelling peas. Choy's novelistic strength lies in his ability to interweave stories of the China that was left behind with histories of Canada, and Vancouver in particular, during the period up to **World War II**. Conflicts between the Chinese and Japanese communities of Vancouver, for example, provide Choy with the occasion to explore the possibilities of multicultural citizenship but within the context of pervasive discrimination.

Like Sky Lee's pioneering novel of Chinese Canadian immigrant experience, Choy's fiction is informed by the culture of secrecy that developed within Chinese communities in the wake of the exclusion laws. As the title of his memoir suggests, "paper" relationships supported by false documents gave rise to a culture of suspicion, where illegal immigrants feared that the falsity of their documents might be exposed and they would be deported. As Choy emphasizes, the first Canadian-born generation was especially suspect because these children may inadvertently betray the true nature of family relationships. The Chen family migrated to Canada to provide a "paper" family for Third Uncle, whose own wife and son died in China. Stepmother is brought from China using the papers of her future husband's dead wife. Even the adoption of Jung-Sum is kept confidential. The keeper and fiery guardian of the family's secrets is the matriarch Poh-Poh; throughout *All That Matters* Kiam-Kim tells of his attempts to navigate the complex maze of truth and falsehood about which Poh-Poh tries to educate him, all the while mistrusting his ability to keep these necessary secrets. This novel returns to many of the situations and events of *The Jade Peony*, but this theme of secrets and silence is emphasized more because Kiam-Kim is the only child old enough to remember such turning points in family history as the arrival of Stepmother and the adoption of Jung-Sum.

This same secret history also informs Wayson Choy's memoir, *Paper Shadows*: he begins by telling of his surprise when a listener of a radio interview he had just broadcast telephoned to inform him that Choy himself was adopted, not unlike his character Jung-Sum. This information, received by the writer in his middle age, caused Choy to reevaluate his recollections of his earlier life, particularly his childhood in Chinatown. He refers to this book as a work of creative nonfiction rather than an autobiography and is clear about the complex relationship between this text and his novels: the one based on memory, the others on fiction. But Choy describes his approach to his writing as the pursuit of a truth that lies somewhere between truth and fiction. Through his lyrical, movingly symbolic, yet profoundly realistic style, he achieves a balance between the present and the past, Canada and China, that speaks to his many readers. **See also** Multiculturalism and Asian America.

Further Reading

Choy, Wayson. Interview by Rocío G. Davis. "Intercultural, Not Multicultural." In *Tricks with a Glass: Writing Ethnicity in Canada,* eds. Rocío G. Davis and Rosalia Baena. Amsterdam & Atlanta: Rodopi, 2000. 269–286.

Davis, Rocío G. *Transcultural Reinventions: Asian American and Asian Canadian Short-Story Cycles.* Toronto: TSAR, 2001.

Lee, Christopher. "Engaging Chineseness in Wayson Choy's *The Jade Peony.*" *Canadian Literature* 163 (Winter 1999): 18–33.

Ty, Eleanor. *The Politics of the Visible in Asian North American Narratives.* Toronto: University of Toronto Press, 2004.

DEBORAH L. MADSEN

✦ CHU, LOUIS HING (1915–1970)

With John **Okada**, Louis Hing Chu was the Chinese American writer to whom *Aiiieeeee* was dedicated. Chu became known for his one book *Eat a Bowl of Tea*. Published in 1961, the book is now acclaimed as a classic in Asian American literature. Born in Toishan, China, in 1915, Chu immigrated at nine with his family to New Jersey, where he completed his high school education. He obtained a BA from Upsala College in 1937 and an MA from New York University in 1940. During **World War II**, between 1943 and 1945, he was stationed in Kunming, China, as a member of the Army Signal Corps. After the war he became owner of a record store in New York City. Chu was also a popular social worker, and for many years he was the only Chinese American disk jockey in New York, hosting a program entitled *Chinese Festival* from 1952 to 1962. He was executive secretary of the Soo Yuen Benevolent Association for 16 years, until 1970, and worked as director of a day center for the New York Department of Welfare. Chu was well-known in New York's **Chinatown** and thoroughly familiar with the bachelors whom he portrayed vividly in his novel, *Eat a Bowl of Tea*.

This novel is considered a landmark in Asian American literature. It truthfully depicts New York's Chinatown in transition after World War II, and, unlike Jade Snow **Wong's** *Fifth Chinese Daughter* and Pardee **Lowe's** *Father and Glorious Descendant*, it is written in a language with many idioms and expressions familiar to and used by the males in the Chinese community. Set in the late 1940s in New York's Chinatown, whose inhabitants are mostly bachelors produced by the racist **Chinese exclusion acts**, the novel develops around Ben Loy and his war bride Mei Oi. The young couple's marriage is arranged by their fathers, Wang Wah Gay and Lee Gong, who came as teenagers to the United States on the same ship, returned to China to marry, and left their pregnant wives at home in the 1920s. Now Wah Gay runs a basement mah-jongg club, symbolically described as a dungeon, where Lee Gong and other old bachelors frequent to kill time and ease their loneliness. Ben Loy and Mei Oi's happy married life soon ends when Mei Oi finds her husband impotent, a consequence of Ben Loy's regular visits to prostitutes. The middle-aged Ah Song takes the opportunity to seduce Mei Oi and makes her pregnant. Wang Chuck Ting, president of the Wang Association, is irritated when he finds cousin Wah Gay involved in the scandal spreading in Chinatown, an incident causing all Wangs "to lose face." He informs Wah Gay of the affair and at the same time asks Ben Loy and Mei Oi to leave New York for Stanton to help Uncle Chuck Ting out in his restaurant, which, he says, is in desperate need of hands. When Wah Gay is wanted by the police for cutting off Ah Song's left ear, Wang Chuck Ting again intervenes and settles the case privately out of court. Taking advantage of his prestige and authority among Chinese, Wang Chuck Ting manipulates Ping On Tong, an organization to which both Wah Gay and Ah Song belong, to order Ah Song to withdraw the charges filed against Wang Wah Gay and keep away from New York for five years. Also leaving the city are Wang Wah Gay and Lee Gong, who are too ashamed to stay, and Ben Loy and Mei Oi, who decide to leave for San Francisco. Free from the elders' control, the young couple begins a new life. Ben Loy not only accepts Mei Oi's son but is now also willing to discuss his physical condition with his wife. Mei Oi in turn feels "both a desire and a responsibility of sharing her husband's problems" (Chu 1979, 242). With the help of Mei Oi and bowls of bitter tea prescribed by a Chinese herb doctor, Ben Loy finally regains his manhood, and the young couple talks happily of inviting their fathers to the haircut party of their second child.

Eat a Bowl of Tea exposes many problems of New York's Chinatown, typical of the Chinese communities in the United States in the late 1940s. Patriarchy reigns, but the fathers' authority is undermined—the old bachelors are reduced to taking insignificant jobs as cooks, waiters, laundrymen, and barbers, and their activities limited within the bounds of Chinatown. Even there they do not feel secure, as "Immigration people . . . hang around out in the streets and all of a sudden they would walk up to you and ask you for your papers" (Chu 1979, 192). They have no contact with the white world except with immigration officers, the police, and prostitutes. With their families away and no home to return to after work, they gather in tea, coffee, or barber shops, mah-jongg clubs, or association buildings to gossip like the "long-tongue women" (common Chinese phrasing) they despised back at home in China. They talk about Lao Lim fighting Lao Ying for taking his wife out, Lao Tsuey running to South Carolina with Lao Ning's wife, Wang Wah Gay's daughter-in-law having "no big belly yet" after she has been in New York for almost a year, and Wang Wah Gay "[sending] his son to a small town to work so as to keep him from the evils of the big city," unaware that "the son used to come to New York several times a week for women" (Chu 1979, 101). Their gossip invariably ends with such conclusions as "[w]omen nowadays are not to be trusted" (Chu 1979, 15), and "[t]his generation of girls is not what it used to be" (Chu 1979, 19). What they appreciate are their "rice cookers" back in China, grass widows who take care of their parents without bitterness and wait patiently for their return year after year.

The old bachelors' living conditions have not improved in their dozens of years' stay in the United States. Wang Wah Gay's basement lodging is crudely equipped, and Lee Gong shares a room with another Lee; both still sleep in folding beds. As husbands, they merely manage to send money to support their families in China; as fathers, they fail to perform their responsibility to look after and provide guidance to their children. As Ben Loy and Mei Oi see Wah Gay and Lee Gong for the first time at 17 and 18, they feel alienated from and find it difficult to communicate with their fathers. However, the fathers have the right to make important decisions for their children in matters such as jobs and marriage. While they see it as their obligation and concern for their children, they have also made the young people dependent and miserable by denying the latter's freedom of choice and impeding their development.

New York's Chinatown is a closed, rigidly stratified patriarchal society, in which the son obeys the father, and the father in turn obeys the head of the family association. This can be seen clearly from the role Wang Chuck Ting plays in the lives of Wah Gay and Ben Loy. In such a society, a person's lot is very much controlled by the patriarch of the family, and the latter's character and personal qualities determine to a great extent the success or failure, rise or fall, of the clan. In the novel, led by Wang Chuck Ting, who skillfully exploits what seem to be perfectly legal and democratic procedures, the Wangs are able to save face and defend their cousin Wah Gay against Ah Song, the only Jo in New York with no family association to support him. In this society, one's identity is defined by one's relationship with others, especially with someone more important or powerful than oneself. Thus Ben Loy is known in Chinatown only as Wang Wah Gay's son, and Mei Oi as Lee Gong's daughter or Wang Wah Gay's daughter-in-law. Because one exists as a member of a group, closely related to others, what one does also affects others; and one's business becomes the business of everybody related to him or her. Consequently, Mei Oi's adultery not only brings shame to Ben Loy but causes all the Wangs in the association to lose face, and, when Wang Wah Gay is in trouble, his cousin Wang Chuck Ting readily comes to his rescue. Thus, an individual's freedom of choice is limited, for one needs to consider the community's interests before taking any action.

Face is important to the Chinese, so important that when the scandal breaks out and the young couple is in great distress and in urgent need of comfort and advice, everyone else, including their fathers, is concerned about their own loss of face. Even

Ben Loy himself, when first learning about the scandal from his father, is "most concerned about any publicity over the cause of his wife's infidelity" (Chu 1979, 144). However, face may not be a negative element in Chinese culture as is presented in *Eat a Bowl of Tea* if we consider that it may keep people from improper conduct and wrongdoing. Far different from the Western culture, which is a guilt culture, Eastern/Chinese culture is a shame culture; and Chinese fear shame and loss of face as much as Christians fear sin and God's punishment. The crux of the issue is whether behaviors bringing about loss of face are truly shameful, and, since one feels loss of face only when one's wrongdoing is exposed, face is not dependable as a sure guarantee against misconduct.

Discrimination against women is prevalent in New York's double-standard bachelor society, in which, as in feudal China, the women's main role is to continue the family line. As the Chinese believe that "There are three things which are unfilial, and to have no posterity is the greatest of them" (Mencius, chapter xxvi), young people have the obligation to marry, and it is unforgivable for a woman not to have "a big belly" soon after marriage. That is why Mei Oi is greatly relieved to find herself pregnant, and Ben Loy too feels somewhat relieved, even though he is not sure whether he is able to become a father. It also explains why Wang Wah Gay begins to bring chicken, pork chops, and herbs to visit his daughter-in-law.

Eat a Bowl of Tea is a truthful and vivid depiction of New York's bachelor society, a deformed Chinese community produced by racist exclusion laws and bearing marked features of feudal China. Because of the lack of a normal family life in the United States, the four great Chinese social vices of eating, drinking, whoring, and gambling, especially whoring, are further aggravated. Ben Loy and Mei Oi's move to San Francisco is significant in that it marks the beginning of the new Chinese American family. At the end of the novel, Louis Chu presents to the reader a bright picture of hope—"New frontiers, new people, new times, new ideas unfolded. [Ben Loy] had come to a new golden mountain" (Chu 1979, 246). Without their fathers' interference, the young couple is able to start a new life; husband and wife are equal, and they make joint efforts to raise a new generation of Chinese Americans.

However, a close reading of the book shows that they move simply from one Chinatown to another, and there is no fundamental change in their situation. Besides, Ben Loy and Mei Oi can hardly be entrusted with the task of bringing up a new generation of Chinese Americans. Ben Loy is regarded as a "good boy" by Wang Chuck Ting, who sees "some phase of Chinese culture" on the young man: "To be obedient when practice and tradition demand it" (Chu 1979, 176). It is true that compared with the double-standard, older generation of men, who themselves whore at home and abroad but demand chastity and fidelity of their wives in China, he is lenient and open-minded in his attitude toward Mei Oi's infidelity. He is able to self-criticize, as he admits to his close friend, "In a way I have myself to blame. I have ruined my health" (Chu 1979, 232). Later in San Francisco he takes Mei Oi as his equal and shares his problems with her. But it is also true that Ben Loy does not have the caliber and makings of one who can bring about a radical change in the situation, his greatest hope and ambition being to rise from a "regular waiter" to "become number one cook at the restaurant" (Chu 1979, 245).

Mei Oi is no doubt Louis Chu's instrument with which to end the bachelor society. However, this female character presented from a male perspective is a flaw in the much praised book. Mei Oi has the looks of a traditional Chinese beauty with an "oval face," soft skin, smooth like ivory, eyebrows like "the crescent of the new moon," and "cherry-red" full lips (Chu 1979, 50). Though she has a secondary education and used to attend the Wah Que School of English before marriage, she has not developed the consciousness of a new woman. Moreover, all her changes in the United States are superficial—with her "make-up technique improved," her skin becomes "softer, smoother, whiter," and her body is "more fully developed" (Chu 1979, 154). She is different from her mother's generation in that she demands rightfully both love and sex in marriage. However, Louis Chu overemphasizes her sexual desire, to the extent that virility seems to be the only quality she wants in a husband. If the impotent Ben Loy is not good enough for her, Ah Song, who is involved with many women, is by no means a wise choice. Mei Oi impresses the reader as a vain, shallow woman with little self-respect, pleased with her attractiveness to men. Feeling the scorn of cousin Wing Sim's wife, she retorts, "Some women would like to have a baby by another man but they don't get the opportunity because no one else would have them" (Chu 1979, 168), thus reducing herself to a sex object. To be true, in the end, Ben Loy regains his masculinity with the help of Mei Oi and bitter tea; nevertheless, most of the time she is seen as a destructive rather than a constructive force.

The title of the book, *Eat a Bowl of Tea*, is well chosen. As is universally known, the Chinese have been drinking tea for over 4,000 years, and tea has become an integral part of Chinese culture and daily life. The function of tea is mentioned time and again in the book—first and foremost, it is the Chinese herb doctor's bitter tea that cures Ben Loy of his impotence; when Lee Gong goes to the restaurant in Stanton to find out more about Ben Loy, the prospective husband he has chosen for his daughter serves him jasmine tea in the hopes of earning a sizable tip. Ben Loy and Mei Oi first meet in a teahouse, arranged by the matchmaker; at the wedding banquet in New York, the bride offers guests tea to show her gratitude; and it is by asking for a cup of tea that Ah Song manages to stay in Mei Oi's apartment and finally succeeds in seducing the young woman. Clearly, tea, as a representative of traditional Chinese culture, can serve purposes both positive and negative; it depends on how the Chinese receive their cultural heritage. To survive, Chinese Americans must be willing to alter old Chinese ways and give up certain Chinese values; obstinate refusal to change will never work. Nor is it advisable to reject totally traditional Chinese culture; after all, it is the Chinese herb tea that restores Ben Loy to health and enables him to start a new life. Base oneself on traditional Chinese culture, discard the dross, and assimilate the best of Western culture: this is perhaps the message conveyed in Chu's *Eat a Bowl of Tea*.

Further Reading

Chu, Louis. *Eat a Bowl of Tea*. Seattle and London: University of Washington Press, 1979.

Hsiao, Ruth Y. "Facing the Incurable: Patriarchy in *Eat a Bowl of Tea*." In *Reading the Literatures of Asian America*, eds. Shirley Geok-lin Lim and Amy Ling. Philadelphia: Temple University Press, 1992.

Ling, Jinqi. "Reading for Historical Specificities: Gender Negotiations in Louis Chu's *Eat a Bowl of Tea*." *MELUS* 20.1 (1995): 35–51.

Mencius. *The Works of Mencius*. Book IV, Part I: Li Lau, Chapter XXVI. 4 July 2008 <http://nothingistic.org/library/mencius/mencius14.HTML>

Shih, David. "*Eat a Bowl of Tea*, by Louis Chu." In *A Resource Guide to Asian American Literature*, eds. Sau-ling Cynthia Wong and Stephen H. Sumida. New York: The Modern Language Association of America, 2001. 45–53.

BING WU

✦ CIVIL RIGHTS MOVEMENT AND ASIAN AMERICA

The emergence of the Asian American movement in the mid-1960s had three major direct influences: the civil rights movement, the critical mass of American-born college students of Asian descent, and the burgeoning antiwar movement. The civil rights movement brought to public consciousness racial inequalities embedded in American institutions and social practices within a black-white paradigm. By the mid-1960s, after the 1964 Civil Rights Act and the 1965 Voting Rights Act were passed, a new generation of leaders emerged. Many of them, who had been radicalized by the intense struggles domestically and by the anticolonial wars internationally, began to articulate political agendas based on their identification with Third World peoples abroad through the similarities in their experiences of oppression at home. The birth of the Asian American movement developed out of the legacy of activists from the previous generations who found voice through the historical period of racial consciousness in African American liberation movements.

The evolution of the civil rights movement into the Black Power movement galvanized young Asian American activists across the country. Asian Americans who had participated in the civil rights movement began to strengthen the movement's infrastructure in their own communities, particularly on the West and East Coasts. On campuses nationwide, the growing number of Chinese and Japanese American students formed organizations mirroring African American, Chicano, and American Indian groups. The movement's crystallization dovetailed with the height of the antiwar movement. In addition to exhaustive community organizing, Asian Americans joined the demand for comprehensive representation on college campuses and an end to U.S. imperialism in Third World countries abroad.

The name "**Asian American**" begot a message that expressed the political orientation of this generation of leaders in contrast to their predecessors. In previous generations, the political orientation of Asians in the United States at large and organizationally was directed toward their respective Asian "homelands." However, by the 1960s, the demographic shift increasing the American-born population of Asian descent recentered the political focus on the rights, contributions, and entitlements of Asian Americans. The energy from the civil rights movement and the growing criticism of American intervention in Southeast Asia stimulated this new generation to think about the similarities of their racial oppression as a monolithic "Asian Other" at home and the oppression of Asian peoples in general in the context of European colonialism and American imperialism. Moreover, unlike many of their predecessors, their lives were situated unproblematically in the United States, to the degree that historic national divisions could more easily be overcome through the commonality of an American identity. To them, the term *Asian American* accurately represented their unique experience of a dual identity that essentially manifested in a different identity that was neither simply Asian nor American. Moreover, the political viability of such a claim complemented the developing notions of similar identity formations in other racialized communities that furthered the concept of Third World solidarity.

As a vibrant social movement, the Asian American movement found expression in numerous ways. Movement activities fell within four general categories: education, social service, political organizing, and artistic creation. The birth of **Asian American studies** on college campuses is often viewed as the origins of the movement itself. Although this is not the case, Asian American studies programs on college campuses are a foundational pillar for the education, politicization, and knowledge production for the Asian American movement. The struggle for Asian American studies manifested as part of the Third World Liberation Front (TWLF) demand for ethnic studies at San Francisco State in November 1968. Students of color, supported by faculty and community, wanted a curriculum that spoke of their contributions and represented their lived experiences. By the spring of 1969, they were victorious in creating the first ethnic studies program in the United States. That fall, the struggle continued at the University of California. By the mid-1970s the movement on college campuses to win ethnic studies programs would move from campus to campus over the next three decades. The fight for these programs precipitated major student organizations, such as Asian American Political Alliance (AAPA) and Philippine-American College Endeavor (PACE). These organizations bonded campus organizing with community and movement campaigns.

For many American-born organizers, the issues facing ethnic communities in geographically bound sites such as **Chinatowns** played a much more critical role in their politicization than the desire of previous generations to intervene in politics of "the homeland." Organizations formed that dealt with local issues, such as street gangs and neighborhood violence, feeding and supporting the poor, or providing job-training courses for community members. However, radical activists and students from the Chinese diaspora came to see the People's Republic of China (PRC) as embodying the strength and spirit of the Chinese people. The alignment with the PRC symbolized the reconfiguration of Asian American priorities in Asia not so much as citizens in exile but as allies in solidarity with anti-imperialist or proletariat struggles in the region. They initiated political educational events to offer people news, perspectives, and propaganda from mainland China. In this light, the Asian American presence represented a radical injection in the predominantly middle-class, white antiwar movement that focused on bringing American troops home rather than the right of self-determination for Southeast Asian peoples.

While direct action tactics and militant strategies were often employed within the context of the antiwar movement, the overlap of participants in community organizing and movement work resulted in similar strategies, tactics, and allies in both spaces. A quintessential example would be the campaigns to fight the demolition of International Hotel and eviction of its elderly Filipino residents in San Francisco's Chinatown. Numerous organizations and coalitions were formed over the I-Hotel, and, on the night of the eviction, the door to the building was barred by hundreds of supporters of all races to create a human wall against local law enforcement.

Moreover, the Asian American movement was not without soundtrack and backdrop. Spaces like Kearny Street Workshop and the Basement Workshop served as exciting laboratories for the creation of Asian American experiences expressed through the arts. Publications like *Gidra* and albums like *A Grain of Sand* by Yellow Pearls offered a medium through which Asian Americans across the country could form a unifying, imagined community. Young Asian Americans in the late 1960s became increasingly involved in interethnic formations, not only in movement activities but also in the expression of a hybrid cultural identity that borrowed extensively from other ethnic groups. Nonetheless, with all the strengths of a multifaceted movement, the recurring shortcoming cited by many scholars and pundits is the movement's lack of a clear unifying voice, personified in a charismatic leader such as Martin Luther King Jr. or Cesar Chavez.

Yet the movement did have strong leaders. For example, Yuri Kochiyama has become an inspirational figure across generations. Yuri is a second-generation Japanese

American (nisei) woman born in San Pedro, California, on May 19, 1921. Like thousands of Japanese Americans, her life was profoundly impacted by the injustice she experienced during **World War II**. On December 7, 1941, she witnessed her father taken into custody by the FBI and held on Terminal Island with no due process, visiting rights, or medical treatment, and soon thereafter she and her family were relocated to **Japanese American internment** camps. After the war, she and her husband Bill raised a family in New York, marking the beginning of their careers as radical political activists.

In the 1960s Yuri dedicated herself to deepening her political education, participating in community organizing, and broadening her alliances to interracial and international solidarity activities. Recognizing her lack of knowledge of the struggles of other people of color in the United States, she studied extensively with the Harlem Freedom School, Malcolm X Liberation School, and Organization of Afro-American Unity among others. Simultaneously, she worked on community-building projects in her Harlem neighborhood and in Asian American and Third World unity coalitions. She worked with Harlem parents' and women's organizations in addition to developing relations with the left-wing forces in Japan. During the civil rights movement, she joined masses of college students and activists who traveled to Southern states to support the organizations in the South.

In 1968 Yuri participated in the fight for ethnic studies in New York, and she was one of the first to respond to Kazu Iijima's call for participants in the pan-Asian group, Asian Americans for Action. At this point, her work began to shift into antiwar and anti-imperialist movement organizing, as was the reflection of the radicalism expressed by the Black Power movement. In the 1970s she supported antiapartheid in South Africa, Puerto Rican independence, and the rights of indigenous peoples in America, and Palestine as a result of U.S. imperialism. Since this period, Yuri has dedicated her life to fighting for the freedom of political prisoners. She has actively participated in numerous legal defense committees for people of color across the United States, including Black Panthers, Assata Shakur, Leonard Peltier, Marilyn Buck, Vincent **Chin**, and Chol Soo Lee. Yuri continues to organize tirelessly for the release of political prisoners and against American imperialism in solidarity with people of color at home and abroad. Her life's work is one of the legacies that will remain with the movement for generations to come.

Although many Asian Americans recognize the emergence of the Asian American movement as a phenomenal moment in American history, its legacies in contemporary Asian American communities have been underplayed. The organizational infrastructure built from the emergence of this movement continues to serve thousands of people and is reproduced in almost every major city in the United States. The new generation of movement leaders also continues to construct a movement based in interracial and pan-Asian solidarity, a positive and complex Asian American identity, and strong voices and representation in the political processes in the United States. **See also** Asian Diasporas; Colonialism and Postcolonialism.

Further Reading

Ho, Fred, et al. *Legacy to Liberation: Politics and Culture of Revolutionary Asian Pacific America.* San Francisco: AK Press and Big Red Media, 2000.

Kochiyama, Yuri. *Passing It on—A Memoir,* eds. Marjorie Lee, Akemi Kochiyama-Sardinha, and Audee Kochiyama-Holman. Los Angeles: UCLA Asian American Studies Center Press, 2004.

Louie, Steve, and Glen Omatsu, eds. *Asian Americans: The Movement and the Moment.* Los Angeles: UCLA Asian American Studies Center Press, 2001.

Omatsu, Glenn. "The 'Four Prisons' and the Movements of Liberation, Asian American Activism from the 1960s to the 1990s." In *The State of Asian American Activism and Resistance in the 1990s,* ed. Karen Aguilar-San Juan. Boston: South End Press, 1994.

Wei, William. *The Asian American Movement.* Philadelphia: Temple University Press, 1993.

LOAN DAO

✦ COLONIALISM AND POSTCOLONIALISM

The question of postcolonialism has surfaced in and out of **Asian America**. In respect to academic scholarship, **Asian American studies** has concerned itself most centrally with questions of racialization and has long worked to expose how norms of citizenship exclude certain bodies from membership within the nation. This emphasis on racial formations has often placed the subject of empire as secondary to the material and epistemological contradictions of the nation-state. However, questions of war, empire, and colonialism have always been prevalent in Asian America, for example, in protests against the **Vietnam War**, literature by Filipino authors, and South Asian activism surrounding the Ghadar movement.

Recent scholarship in Asian American studies has attempted to bring a postcolonial approach to bear on the concerns of the discipline by exposing the imperial practices of the United States and theorizing the colonial structure of "America" as a concept and territorial entity. Postcolonial interventions have most notably pointed to the erasure of the Philippines and Hawaii within Asian American studies, the tensions of which are captured most famously in the Yamanaka awards controversy. As the 1997 recipient of the **Association for Asian American Studies** Best Fiction award, Lois-Ann **Yamanaka's** *Blu's Hanging* sparked a series of impassioned debates over the novel's representation of the central Filipino character and the absence of Native Hawaiians. The contestations elicited by Yamanaka's novel illustrate the tensions between racialized identities brought together under the category "Asian American" but unequally formed by colonialism, imperialism, and capital. Exposing the ways in which Filipino Americans and Central Pacific Islanders are continually positioned as the Other within Asian American studies, the *Blu's Hanging* controversy displayed Asian America as irreducibly multiple and composed of conflicting imaginings, desires, and claims to the nation. Framing a discussion of postcolonialism through Yamanaka's novel and the debates surrounding it works to foreground the ways in which Asian American studies is necessarily implicated in and produced out of colonial histories and modes of knowledge production, as well as the pressing need to attend to the differences that structure the very category of Asian America.

Scholars working at the intersection of Asian American and postcolonial studies have pointed to an important distinction between *postcoloniality* and *postcolonialism,* where the former refers to the material set of social conditions and the latter to a mode of inquiry or critique. The grouping of colonialism and postcolonialism is itself a troubled one, because it assumes similarity or grounds for comparison between the two terms. However, postcolonial critique has specifically worked against the assumption that the *post* signifies a temporal or geographic distance from colonialism, or a state of being beyond domination. Rather, following author Qadri Ismail, postcolonial critique represents a politics that puts into question the logic of Eurocentrism. Approaching postcolonialism as a critique that poses particular challenges to Asian American studies, this entry suggests that postcolonial critique specifically foregrounds the politics of nation, empire/imperialism, and diaspora/migration within and for Asian America. At the same time, Asian American studies brings the theorizing of race and racial formations to the conversation, topics that are often overlooked in postcolonial studies.

NATION

A critique of nation and nationalism has been particularly central for Asian American studies in questioning the political objective of achieving national subjectivity or claiming the United States as home. Postcolonial scholarship has argued for the inherent complicity between nationalism and colonialism, thereby exposing the necessary paradox at the heart of anticolonial nationalism. As an epistemological concept, the nation-state is internally contradictory for the very reason that its promise of equality and contention of universality always relies upon a particular, or Other, against which to assert its claim to modernity. Moreover, the logic of inclusion that structures the identity of nation necessitates a constant expulsion of difference. Postcolonial and Asian American studies have often made parallel critiques of the nation: the former stressing its colonial structure and the latter, its implicit racism. Lisa Lowe's foundational work *Immigrant Acts* argues that the liberal promise of equality sutures together the contradictions of a capitalist order that necessarily relies upon the differentiation of its subjects. Lowe's critique of liberalism and multiculturalism suggests that the struggle for political recognition or claims to citizenship must be interrogated as the endpoint for Asian American studies. Recognizing the United States as a historical and contemporary imperial power, as Kandice Chuh has also suggested, confronts the limitations of placing the hope for justice within the hands of the nation-state. Indeed, the United States as a territorial and conceptual entity has always been constituted in and through colonial projects. The recent move to theorize the United States as a transnational formation attempts to foreground the ways in which America is formed out of global relations of power and has constantly reached beyond itself to secure its physical and imagined borders. Maintaining the nation as the uninterrogated ground for politics therefore risks reproducing the very structures of colonial domination being contested in the first instance. Following this logic, cultural nationalism must also be approached skeptically for its allegiance to colonial modes of knowing. Postcolonial feminists in particular have uncovered the gendered and sexualized norms operating within cultural nationalist assertions of identity and autonomy and have often had their arguments dismissed as inauthentic and traitorous by the self-appointed gatekeepers of Asian American culture. The pressing need to attend to the question of nation is eloquently captured in Kandice Chuh's call to "imagine otherwise" as expressed in the title of her 2003 book, that is, to risk imagining possibilities for justice that are not limited to the contours of the nation-state.

EMPIRE/IMPERIALISM

The modernization of the United States, as David Palumbo-Liu has noted, is deeply enmeshed and inseparable from the Pacific region. Expansion into East Asia and the Pacific enabled the importation of cheap labor, while broadening the United States' reach in the world economy. Within a neoliberal regime of economic restructuring, however, imperialism takes many forms that are often more subtle and diffuse than outright territorial colonialism. Economic sanctions, covert wars, border patrols, and corporate privatization of basic needs are all manifestations of modern empire-building. The violence of the military intervention in Southeast Asia, including Vietnam, remains a defining moment that spurred critiques of American imperialism and the military-industrial complex within Asian America. The intersection of Asian American and postcolonial studies specifically highlights the ways in which racial formations are produced through and articulated with imperial projects. Although the mechanisms for constructing difference shift and transform over time, the underlying epistemology of Othering remains similar. Recognizing these parallels allows connections to be made, for example, between **Japanese American internment** during **World War II** and immigrant detainment post 9/11. The conflicting needs of capital and nation that Lowe highlighted also link past exclusion acts with the immigration policies resulting from the Patriot Act.

The recent turn to the postcolonial within Asian American studies has been largely characterized by a renewed interest in the Philippines and Hawaii. Although these postcolonial locales figure very visibly within current scholarship, they often enter the conversation as exceptions to Asian America, that is, as the minority perspective acknowledged by the responsible majority. Attending to the legacy of colonialism is a project that is clearly far from complete, given that the categories of difference upholding Asian American studies as a distinct disciplinary field of study are themselves heirs of colonial epistemologies. The fraught relationship between the formations "Asian American" and "Arab American" highlights the ways in which Asian America is necessarily fractured by histories and geographies of colonial occupation. The continued struggle over the status of "Pacific Islander" as a subject-position and racial formation distinct from "Asian American" underscores the incommensurable differences brought about by the violence of modern empire-building.

Postcolonial critique has also been centrally concerned with theorizing the knowledge production that underpins colonial and imperial projects. Thinking critically about the politics of representation that constitutes Asia as a distinct entity separate from America and the Eurocentric discourses that have variously given rise to the **model minority** myth or stereotypes like the Asian butterfly have been important projects within Asian American studies. In her book *Compositional Subjects*, Laura Kang specifically traces the ways in which Asian American women are constituted as legible and coherent subjects by cultural texts, disciplinary knowledge, and the transnational economy. This body of scholarship has contributed a rich analysis of the colonial epistemes that continue to structure understandings and productions of difference.

DIASPORA AND MIGRATION

Asian American studies scholars such as Jigna Desai and David Eng approach diaspora as a mode of critique that interrogates notions of home, rootedness, and origins. This framework engages with the inequalities that structure transnational circuits of migration by attending to the dissonant and conflicted relationships between territoriality, identity, and belonging. A postcolonial approach to transnationality understands diaspora and migration as constituted out of colonialism and imperialism and views racial formations within the United States that produce Asian Americans as exterior to the nation as inseparable from the transnational racial processes of the nation-state. Diasporic critique has made significant interventions into narratives of globalization that emphasize time-space compression and the rise of the cosmopolitan subject. Stressing the ways in which capitalism relies upon and articulates with racial formations, this body of scholarship positions diaspora as complicit with post-Fordist globalization and attempts to theorize the new forms of state racism that emerge as a result of the shifting role of the nation-state within late capitalism. At the same time that borders have become increasingly porous to capital, the militarization of state lines restricts and prohibits the movement of certain bodies. Distinctions between voluntary and involuntary migration, forced relocation, and elite travel therefore underscore the irreducible difference between the subject positions of immigrant and refugee. In forwarding the specificities of mobility and movement as they are structured through capitalism, neocolonialism, and national discourses, Asian American critique has worked to displace the construction of the United States as homeland, while positioning processes of racialization within global geopolitics. **See also** Asian Diasporas; Asian Pacific Islanders; Hawaiian Literature; Multiculturalism and Asian America; Nationalism and Asian America; Orientalism and Asian America; Racism and Asian America.

Further Reading

Chuh, Kandice. *Imagine Otherwise: On Asian Americanist Critique*. Durham and London: Duke University Press, 2003.

Desai, Jigna. *Beyond Bollywood: The Cultural Politics of South Asian Diasporic Film*. New York and London: Routledge, 2004.

Eng, David. *Racial Castration: Managing Masculinity in Asian America*. Durham and London: Duke University Press, 2001.

Ismail, Qadri. *Abiding By Sri Lanka: On Peace, Place and Postcoloniality*. Minneapolis: University of Minnesota Press, 2005.

Kang, Laura. *Compositional Subjects: Enfiguring Asian/American Women*. Durham and London: Duke University Press, 2002.

Lowe, Lisa. *Immigrant Acts: On Asian American Cultural Politics*. Durham and London: Duke University Press, 1996.

Palumbo-Liu, David. *Asian/American: Historical Crossings of a Racial Frontier*. Stanford, CA: Stanford University Press, 1999.

Yamanaka, Lois-Ann. *Blu's Hanging*. New York: Farrar, Straus and Giroux, 1997.

DIANE DETOURNAY AND JIGNA DESAI

D

✦

✦ DESAI, KIRAN (1971–)

Indian American novelist and winner of Man Booker Prize, Kiran Desai has gained wide acclaim within a few years. The daughter of the celebrated writer Anita Desai, she was born on September 3, 1971, in New Delhi. Desai went along with her family to Great Britain at the age of 14. Afterward they migrated to the United States, and Desai finished her schooling in Massachusetts. She studied in Bennington College, Vermont University, and Columbia University. She took two years of leave while studying creative writing at Columbia to write her first novel, *Hullabaloo in the Guava Orchard*, which was published in 1988. Desai wrote the next novel, *The Inheritance of Loss*, which bagged the £50,000 Man Booker Prize for Fiction in October 2006. She was one of the six short-listed authors. Her mother Anita had been nominated thrice earlier, although she did not make it. Desai dedicated the novel to her mother. Desai also won the National Book Critics Circle Fiction Award for *The Inheritance of Loss*.

Hullabaloo in the Guava Orchard was set in the small town of Shahkot in India, and Desai was inspired to write the novel after reading a story about a holy person climbing a guava tree. Disillusioned with ordinary life, the protagonist of the novel, Sampath Chawla, had gone to lead a solitary life on a guava tree. He was privy to the mail of his town, while working in a post office earlier. The residents became convinced that he was a saint, because he was able to tell their inner thoughts. Sampath could do so because he had read their letters earlier. In the novel, there was description of monkeys who had descended into the orchard. There were also characters like the doting mother, preparing dishes for the son and a sister of Sampath, in love with an ice cream vendor. There were police officers and a man from the atheistic society bent upon exposing Sampath. The protagonist of the novel was a simpleton, naïve, and somewhat idiotic. In the end, he disappeared from the scene. Desai in her masterly way gives a vivid portrayal of characters lashed with humor. She also describes in detail the ordinary life of people and their beliefs in a superb way. The novel was praised by critics and by Salman Rushdie, who was impressed by it. It earned her the Betty Trask Award, given by the Society of Authors.

The Inheritance of Loss is about the life of a Cambridge-educated Indian, living a retired life at the foot of Mt. Kanchunjunga in the northeastern Himalayas. The backdrop is the Gurkha insurgency movement of mid-1980s India. Jemubhai Popatlal's life in the town of Kalimpong changes after the arrival of his granddaughter. Another character is the poverty-stricken cook Nandu, who bears with his master's peculiar request and laments the fate of the son after reading his letters. Jemubhai reminiscences about his preretired life. He had gone to Cambridge before **World War II**. He became an English gentleman after giving up his Indianness. But he struggled with two identities: Indian background and aspiration to become an English gentleman. He was in two worlds, and both rejected him. The other characters are refugee princesses from Afghanistan, the Anglophile sisters Lora and Noni, and Father Potty from Sweden. In a postcolonial world, the characters search for their identity amid a fast changing world. Desai addresses issues such as modernization, cultural identity, nationhood, and insurgency, while narrating the events. The 17-year-old granddaughter Sai Mistry is in love with Gyan, who is involved in the violent Gurkha liberation struggle. The cook, Nandu, has a son named Biju, who is leading the life of an illegal immigrant in the United States. The Anglophile Judge Patel becomes the target of the insurgency. Romance between Sai and Gyan is affected by violent struggles of the Gurkhas. The illegal alien Biju living in Manhattan soon returns to India. He has become homesick.

The Inheritance of Loss delves into the human mind in all its ramifications and highlights the national and global issues of the 1980s. Some of the issues persist until now. It seems as if Desai had anticipated the continuance of these problems. Although Gurkha insurgency has subsided, India is facing terrorist menaces from other quarters. The immigrant still feels cultural alienation. The condition of aliens staying illegally in the United States and other nations is miserable. In India itself, the Anglophiles continue to feel despair. Her style of writing is skilled, and she can describe any situation, event, or even state of mind with aplomb. She describes human behaviors vividly without moralizing. However, criticism against her has been rather harsh. She has been unjustly blamed for telling the story of the elite only. But this is far from the truth, as feelings of subalterns find an equal place. She rightly deserved the Man Booker Prize of 2006 for writing a stunning and brilliant piece of fiction. Even still, readers have found a major flaw in the novel and have complained about her lack of definitions of the Indian idioms. Moreover, her portrayal of the Nepalese diaspora and the people has angered many, and there were protests and demonstrations against her novel. The people did not take kindly to her description of Bhairav and Mt. Kanchenjunga.

An astute observer of human behavior, Desai writes with elegance, perception, clarity, and humor. She is quite at ease whether she is writing about the life of an aristocrat or of the common people. Desai is a worthy daughter of her mother. **See also** Asian Diasporas.

Further Reading

Clark, Alex. "The Inheritance of Loss." May 27, 2007. http://observer.guardian.co.uk/review/story/0,,2088900,00.html.

Desai, Kiran. *Hullabaloo in the Guava Orchard*. New York: Atlantic Monthly Press, 1998.

————. *Inheritance of Loss*. New York: Atlantic Monthly Press, 2006.

Mishra, Pankaj. "Wounded by the West." February 12, 2006. http://www.nytimes.com/2006/02/12/books/review/12mishra.html?ei=5070&en=4fc48d55ba24d33e&ex=1162094400&pagewanted=print.

Nelson, Emmanuel S., ed. *Asian American Novelists: A Bio-Bibliographical Critical Sourcebook*. Westport, CT: Greenwood Press, 2000.

Quinn, Judy. "Rushdie Causes Rush for First Novel." *Publishers Weekly* (April 14, 1998): 24–25.

PATIT PABAN MISHRA

✦ DIVAKARUNI, CHITRA BANERJEE (1956–)

Born in Calcutta, India, poet, novelist, essayist, children's writer, and social activist Chitra Banerjee Divakaruni is one of the most popularly known authors of Indian origin in the United States. She also has an international audience, as her work has been translated into several languages, including Dutch, German, and Japanese. In the last two decades, since writers such as Salman Rushdie and V.S. Naipaul have cemented the fact that a readership exists for Indian Anglophone writers, Divakaruni has been one of the most prolific to appear on the literary scene.

Divakaruni's father worked for an oil company, and her mother was an elementary schoolteacher in Calcutta. The Banerjees, a Hindu family, had four children, of which Chitra was the second-born and the only girl. She was schooled in a rigorous environment, attending the Loreto House, a convent school managed and taught by Irish nuns.

Early on, Divakaruni developed a love for the English language, which was a dominant lingua in postcolonial India. She enjoyed reading Rabindranath Tagore, the giant in Indian letters and winner of the 1913 Nobel Prize for Literature, as well as other international writers. As an undergraduate at Presidency College, part of the University of Calcutta, Divakaruni studied English and earned a bachelor's degree in 1976. At that point, only 19 years old, she decided to pursue a master's degree in the United States. She enrolled at Wright State University in Dayton, Ohio, where her eldest brother already lived. She graduated in 1978.

A year later, she married Murthi Divakaruni, an engineer, whom she met while completing her studies. Afterward, she attended the University of California at Berkeley and earned a PhD in English in 1984, completing her dissertation on "'For Danger Is in Words': Changing Attitudes to Language in the Plays of Christopher Marlowe." However, she had already begun to feel that her focus on Renaissance writers had little to do with her personal identity as a woman of color and an immigrant to the United States.

Banerjee's parents were hardly wealthy, so she had to help fund her own education. While working on her graduate degrees, she earned money doing various odd jobs. These included babysitting, washing equipment in a science lab, and working in an Indian boutique. Three years after graduating, she began teaching at Diablo Valley College, then took a position at Foothill College in Los Altos, California, in 1989. During this time, she realized that creative writing attracted her much more than academic writing. She joined a writers' group during the mid-1980s and found that poetry intrigued her. She had publishing success early; her first published poem, "At Muktinath," appeared in *Calyx* in 1986.

Her first book of poetry, *Dark Like the River*, was published a year later in 1987 by Writers Workshop, a Calcutta-based house. In these initial poems, she evokes themes that will later come to distinguish her writing, namely women's issues and feelings of exile. *The Reason for Nasturtiums*, her second poetry collection, appeared in 1990, published by the Berkeley Poets Workshop and Press. Calyx Press published her next collection, *Black Candle: Poems about Women from India, Pakistan, and Bangladesh*, in 1991, developing her interest in the lives and experiences of immigrant women. By this point, Divakaruni's reputation as a poet was well established, as was her interest in women's themes.

As a writer, she felt it important to explore other genres, namely fiction; she wanted to stretch her abilities and discover new avenues for expressing the themes that were a hallmark of her poetry. She enrolled in a fiction-writing course at Foothills College, where she was teaching, and applied herself to studying the craft. Her earliest drafts demonstrated her continuing interest in the experiences of women emigrating from South Asia.

Arranged Marriage, her debut short story collection, appeared in 1995, published by Anchor Books, and received critical acclaim. Most of the main characters are Indian women who find themselves newly arrived in the United States. Struggling to adapt to a new, often overwhelming American culture, they also face problems from their own community. Divakaruni writes vividly about the highlights and shortcomings of the Indian community, especially the way in which Indian women are sometimes oppressed or silenced by Indian men. She depicts these tensions as part of the difficulty of adapting to a new culture and new country. *Arranged Marriage* won the 1996 American Book Award and the PEN Oakland Award for Fiction for its examination of how a traditional institution—arranged marriage—fares when brought into a different environment.

Divakaruni was not without her critics, however. Some South Asian readers accused her of maligning the Indian immigrant community and giving credence to the stereotype that Indian women were oppressed and silenced by Indian men. Divakaruni responded by insisting that she wrote about the community she saw and witnessed and that she wanted her audience to care about her characters as humans rather than as representations of cultural or ethnic identity. Indeed, her work has remained consistently nonpolitical, focusing instead on personal and emotional relationships among people.

In 1997 she published her second work of fiction and first novel, *The Mistress of Spices*, also with Anchor Books. The novel demonstrates Divakaruni's interest in mystical storytelling and magic. The protagonist, Tilo, is an elderly woman who runs a spice shop in Oakland, California. However, she is actually one of a line of immortal mistresses of spices, trained in the arts of knowing which spices will help solve the problems of her customers, mostly first- and second-generation Indian immigrants. She evokes the powers of the spices to heal their pain, usually caused by the difficulty of leaving one world behind and seeking another. While American audiences loved the book, her critics again charged her with exoticizing Indian culture. However, others, such as Indian novelist Shashi **Tharoor**, praised the book for its unusual storyline, lush imagery, and magical realism; indeed, Divakaruni lists Gabriel Garcia Marquez, a pioneer of magical realism, as one of her literary influences. Her evocation of the experiences of Indian immigrant life also garnered her critical attention. *The Mistress of Spices* was named a Best Book of 1997 by the *Los Angeles Times*.

That same year, *Leaving Yuba City*, a fourth poetry collection was also published. It collected poems from her previous three collections as well as new works and helped establish her as a writer talented in multiple genres. *Leaving Yuba City* won the Allen Ginsberg Prize as well as a Pushcart Prize. It also garnered the author a Gerbode Foundation Award.

Sister of My Heart, her second novel, appeared in 1999 by Doubleday Books and traced the close relationship of cousins Sudha and Anju, born on the same day. (The novel is actually an extension of the story "The Ultrasound," which appeared in *Arranged Marriage* and featured the two cousins.) One is beautiful while the other is not, and the cousins are forced into arranged marriages that will test their personal strength and their sense of sisterhood. She returned to their story with *Vine of Desire*, her third novel, in 2002. Sudha, the cousin blessed with good looks but cursed in an abusive marriage, moves in with her cousin-sister Anju, though she struggles to resist the attentions of Anju's husband. Both books refrain from employing the magical realism that distinguished *The Mistress of Spices*, but they display Divakaruni's beautiful prose and talent for twisting plot lines.

The Unknown Errors of Our Lives, a second short story collection, was published in 2001 by Doubleday. Again Divakaruni explores the lives of Indian immigrants and their American-born children with grace and honesty. "Mrs. Dutta Writes a Letter," one of the stories in the collection, was selected for the *Best American Short Stories* anthology of that year. Divakaruni herself assembled two anthologies: *Multitude: Cross-cultural Readings for Writers* (McGraw-Hill, 1993) and *We, Too, Sing America* (McGraw-Hill, 1998), both of which feature writing by South Asian and other ethnic writers.

Most recently, Divakaruni published *The Queen of Dreams*, a compelling novel featuring Rakhi, a young woman who has always wished she shared her mother's talent as a dream interpreter. An artist living in Berkeley, California, Rakhi has a daughter but is separated from her husband; she runs a teashop with her friend, but a series of events, including her mother's death and the September 11, 2001, terrorist attacks, conspire to threaten her lifestyle and identity. The book's early reviews were filled with praise but reluctantly expressed dissatisfaction with the story's plotline; the main critique is that the storyline was overly dependent on coincidences and, as some critics charged, too many convenient events, such as the discovery of the journals of Rakhi's mother. Nevertheless, *The Queen of Dreams* continued Divakaruni's tradition of excellent storytelling.

In recent years, Divakaruni has also ventured into yet another literary genre: children's books. In 2002 she published *Neela, Victory Song*, a novel for middle school-aged readers and part of the Girls of Many Lands series by American Girl books. The story is set in India during the national struggle for independence from British colonialism. Set against the background of Mohandas Gandhi's civil disobedience movement, *Neela, Victory Song* follows its main character through a series of adventures and experiences. The action is fast paced, but the language exhibits Divakaruni's signature lushness for detail. She followed *Neela, Victory Song* with *The Conch Bearer*, by Roaring Book Press in 2003. Featuring a young boy as its protagonist, a departure for a writer whose female protagonists are one of her hallmarks, *The Conch Bearer* also uses Divakaruni's attraction for magical storylines and plot elements. Anand meets an elderly member of the Brotherhood of Healers, who convinces the 12-year-old to accompany him on a journey to the Himalayas to return the conch shell, which holds magical powers, to its original home. Like *Neela, Victory Song*, it offers young readers an exciting storyline, filled with plot twists and villains, while sustaining an engaging writing style.

An important component of Divakaruni's career has also been her social activism. Divakaruni considers writing to be an expression of a social consciousness, as exhibited in her underlying political message in *The Queen of Dreams* regarding the September 11, 2001, terrorist attacks on the United States (in the novel, a young Indian man is mistaken for an Arab and viciously attacked by a mob of angry American men). Much of her social work has been closely linked to her own ethnic roots, and she has striven to aid other immigrant Indian and South Asian women in making the difficult transition between home and the new world of the United States.

In 1991 Divakaruni founded MAITRI, a telephone helpline for battered and abused South Asian women. For years she had been working with battered women in other organizations, such as the Mid-Peninsula Support Network for Battered Women. However, she had noticed that few South Asian women sought help at these places, which made her wonder why. She realized that many were disconnected from mainstream American society and thus were unaware of the existence of organizations and networks that could help them, while a second reason was that they felt they were betraying their ethnic roots by seeking help from non-South Asians. MAITRI was established as a connection between the South Asian community and the organizations already in existence, and it aims to help abused women feel they are not being judged when they seek advice and counseling. The helpline receives about 15–20 calls a month, and counselors work with the women to reach a solution that is comfortable for them.

In 2005 Divakaruni supported the launch of a satellite radio program intended to reach rural Indian women. Equal Access, a San Francisco–based organization, uses such communication tools to educate and connect women who would have no other form of networking. The project, launched in the villages of the Uttaranchal Pradesh region, gives local women's groups radio and transmission equipment and trains them in production. They tape their own shows, focusing on various topics and issues, and send them to Delhi, where a station edits them and forwards the programs to a satellite station in Australia. The programs are then broadcast across the region and offer listeners information on various local issues, such as health, child marriage, and disaster management.

Divakaruni has won many other awards for her writing, including a Memorial Award from the Barbara Deming Foundation, a Bay Area Book Reviewers Award for Fiction, a Before Columbus Foundation Prize, and a California Arts Council Award. Her stories and essays have appeared in many mainstream publications, such as *Good Housekeeping, Atlantic Monthly*, and *Salon.com*. In addition, *The Mistress of Spices* has been adapted as a movie by director Gurinder Chadda. **See also**

Asian American Political Activism; Asian American Stereotypes; Colonialism and Postcolonialism.

Further Reading

Farmanfarmaian, Roxane. "Chitra Banerjee Divakaruni: Writing from a Different Place." *Publishers Weekly* (May 4, 2001): 46–47.

Milstead, Claudia. "Chitra Banerjee Divakaruni." In *Greenwood Encyclopedia of Multiethnic American Literature*, ed. Emmanuel S. Nelson. Vol. 2. Westport: CT: Greenwood Press, 2005. 591–594.

SUSAN MUADDI DARRAJ

E

✦

✦ EATON, EDITH MAUDE (SUI SIN FAR) (1865–1914)

Chinese North American journalist and short stories writer, Edith Maude Eaton published short stories depicting Chinese American life under the Chinese pen name of Sui Sin Far (differently spelled as Sui Seen Far or Sui Sin Fah, all meaning Water Lily). Her literary reputation mainly rests on a collection of short fiction titled *Mrs. Spring Fragrance* (1912), published two years before her death in 1914. She is now recognized as the first Asian American fictionist and the spiritual grandmother of Asian American literature, appreciated both for her ethnic authenticity and for her courage to speak for Chinese Americans at a time when Sinophobia ran rampant in North America. Born in Macclesfield, England, Eaton was the second child and the eldest daughter of a family of 14 children, one of whom, Winnifred **Eaton**, would become a successful writer of popular fiction, publishing most of her works under a purportedly Japanese pen name, Onoto Watanna. The father, Edward Eaton, was an Englishman and son of a silk merchant, and the mother, Grace A. Trefusis (Lotus Blossom), was a Chinese, adopted by English missionaries and educated in England. When Edith Eaton was about seven years old, the Eatons migrated to New York but eventually settled down in Montreal, Quebec. Due to family poverty, Eaton was withdrawn from school at the age of ten and started to support her parents and earn her own living.

Beginning in the 1880s, Eaton worked as a stenographer and a journalist while struggling to establish a literary reputation. She worked as a journalist for the *Montreal Star* and published her writings in the Montreal magazine *Dominion Illustrated*. Her first writings—eight pieces of short stories and essays ("A Trip in a Horse Car," "Misunderstood: The Story of a Young Man," "A Fatal Tug of War," "The Origin of a

Broken Nose," "Robin," "Abermarle's Secret," "Spring Impression: A Medley of Poetry and Prose," and "In Fairyland")—were published between 1888–1890 and bylined "Edith Eaton." Dealing with English or French Canadian subjects, these pieces have nothing to do with the Chinese American experience, the major subject of her journalistic writings and short fiction starting from the year 1896. In the same year, she visited the New York **Chinatown** and published under the pen name of Sui Seen Far a group of Chinatown short stories about violence arising from gambling ("The Gamblers"), the tragedy of misplaced identity ("Ku Yum"), the cost of cultural defiance ("The Story of Iso"), and star-crossed lovers ("A Love Story of the Orient" and "A Chinese Feud"). With the exception of "The Gamblers," a story of all-male Chinese characters, these stories depict women of Chinese descent and their tragic lives. "The Story of Iso," for instance, tells the story of a rebellious Chinese woman who defies cultural norms by refusing to marry the man chosen for her, disgraces herself by following foreigners across the sea, and dies in a strange land.

Eaton went to Kingston, Jamaica, in late 1896 to work briefly as a reporter for *Gall's Daily News Letter,* owned by a Canadian proprietor. In 1898 she went to the West Coast of the United States, living first in San Francisco and then in Seattle and earning a meager living as a stenographer and a teacher in a missionary school of Chinese immigrants. In the meantime, she published essays defending the Chinese immigrants and stories featuring Chinese men and women in America. A group of journalistic essays published in the *Los Angeles Express* in 1903 present various aspects of Chinatown life ("In Los Angeles' Chinatown," "Betrothals in Chinatown," "Chinatown needs a School," "Chinatown Boys and Girls," "Leung Ki Chu and His Wife," "Chinese in Business Here," and "Chinese Laundry Checking"). These pieces presented images markedly different from those portrayed with racial prejudice against the Chinese by providing fairly sympathetic and unbiased glimpses into the cultural, social, and economic activities of Chinese immigrants in the United States. The short stories explore individual lives of Chinese descent but at the same time tackle issues of broader social concerns. "Sweet Sin," a story that touches upon interracial marriages, is particularly significant in that, like Eaton who remained an unmarried Eurasian, the titular protagonist is a Eurasian daughter of a Chinese merchant and an American woman. Disliking the idea of marrying a Chinese man her father intends for her, Sweet Sin commits suicide on the eve of their departure for China. The name "Sweet Sin" plays on Eaton's own pen name, Sui Sin Far, both meaning water lily (the former mainly refers to the plant itself while the latter may mean both the plant and its flower). "Lin John" narrates a story similar to "Sweet Sin." Lin John saves to buy his sister out of prostitution and send her back to China to live an honest life, yet she frustrates his plan by stealing the money and refusing to be subservient to men. The story of "A Chinese Ishmael" deals with the tragic love affair between Leih Tseih and a slave girl (again with the name of Ku Yum), who drown themselves in the sea to escape the persecution by a Chinese villain named Loy Choy; the story also touches on such Chinatown issues as violence, gambling, passage fee, and the operations of the Chinese Six Companies. In these stories, Eaton departs from stereotypical representations of the Chinese immigrants and depicts her characters as ordinary human beings whose reactions are shaped by their historical circumstances.

In 1909 "Leaves from the Mental Portfolio of an Eurasian," Eaton's autobiographical essay, appeared in the *Independent*, a New York-based prestigious journal of the day. On the surface level, the essay consists of biographical incidents in her life—accused of being a storyteller and slapped by her mother at four, refused to be spoken to by a playmate for having a Chinese mother, scrutinized and judged to be an "interesting little creature" by an old Englishman, shocked by an awareness of the Chinese race in Hudson City, shouted at and bullied by white children for being of Chinese descent, psychologically burdened with "the cross of the Eurasian" in a Canadian school, troubled by identity, nationality, and life in a family of many Chinese Eurasian siblings, pleased with gratitude from the Chinese for writing for them in the papers, risen to the defense of the Chinese in an unnamed Midwest town when a Mr. K. slights the Chinese, misjudged to be a loose Chinese girl by an English sailor in the West Indies, and accepted by Chinese men and women on the West Coast. Despite its autobiographical nature, "Leaves" does not provide much matter-of-fact information about Eaton and her life; rather, they are just mental leaves selected from the psychological depth of a Eurasian woman who looks at both sides of her biological inheritance without preconceived bias. With the biographical incidents, Eaton exposes white prejudice against the Chinese; at the same time her unique Eurasian perspective allows her to perceive that she differs from both her parents and that her mother's race is as prejudiced as her father's. The same perspective also endows her with an appreciative attitude toward both sides, admiring the courage of Mr. K. for admitting his groundless prejudice against the Chinese and for apologizing to her. Her contacts with the Chinese lead her to believe that prejudice can be removed by association. Eaton is aware of the strategic routes of different Eurasian individuals and expresses her sympathy toward them. She pities the half-Chinese girls who pass for white or for Japanese and places the blame on those who compel them to use such strategies. As for herself, Eaton prizes individuality over nationality, claiming, "I give my right hand to the Occidentals and my left to the Orientals" (1995, 230). Yet what Eaton says in the narrative cannot be taken simply as factual; she, for instance, is referred to as "Miss Sui" by her nurse and addressed by Mr. K. as "Miss Far," when she should be known by her official name.

In 1910 Eaton relocated to Boston, where she remained until 1913. In May 1912 she published another autobiographical essay, "Sui Sin Far, the Half Chinese Writer,

Tells of Her Career," in the *Boston Globe*, summarizing her life and announcing the forthcoming publication of *Mrs. Spring Fragrance* and a second book to follow the next year. A.C. McClurg & Co. published the former under her pen name followed by "Edith Eaton" in parentheses, but the second book somehow never saw publication, even though it was mentioned several times in her correspondences that it had been completed and submitted to McClurg and was going through revisions.

Mrs. Spring Fragrance, a collection of 17 short stories and 20 children's stories, runs up to 347 large-print pages. Of the 37 pieces, about 11 were previously published and now incorporated into the book, in some cases, with slight revisions in the text (as in "Mrs. Spring Fragrance") or in the title (as in "The Story of One White Woman Who Married a Chinese" and "Children of Peace"). That most of the stories were published for the first time while a second book was in progress indicates that Eaton must have attained literary maturity, and the last few years of her life must have been the most productive period of her literary career. Like many of Winnifred Eaton's Japanese romances, the stories are printed on pages decorated with plum blossoms on the upper part and a bird perched on a twig of a tree branch. Apart from that, each odd page is imprinted on the lower right corner with three Chinese characters meaning "happiness, fortune, and longevity." The design must have been part of the marketing strategy to give the book a Chinese/Oriental flavor, though it is not clear whether it was the idea of Eaton or her publisher. The short stories are grouped under the subheading of "Mrs. Spring Fragrance," which is also the title of the first story, whereas the children's stories are given a group name, "Tales of Chinese Children," though not all of them deal with subjects specifically relevant to Chinese children. In "What about the Cat," the sixth children's story, for example, the princess hears different stories from her servants about what a cat is doing, when in fact it is all the while up in her sleeve. Except for the mention of the duck farm of Shinku, a name that sounds somewhat "Oriental," the different stories about the same cat and hiding the cat in one's sleeve suggest that the story is more Anglo American than Chinese.

The short stories are all love stories that explore manifold aspects of Chinese American experience, which contests stereotypical representations. The first two pieces present a slightly comic picture of Mrs. Spring Fragrance, the young Americanized wife of a Chinese merchant. In "Mrs. Spring Fragrance," she quotes lines of Tennyson and helps an 18-year-old Chinese girl neighbor named Laura (Mai Gwi Far) out of an undesired betrothal and into marriage to an Americanized youth, arousing her husband's suspicion of her as having lovers elsewhere. In "The Inferior Woman" she decides to follow the example of American women by writing an immortal book about Americans. In the process, she assists Will Carman in winning back Alice Winthrop, a working girl estranged from him by his mother, who contemptuously calls Alice the

Inferior Woman. The tragic story of "The Wisdom of the New" attends to the intense cultural conflicts experienced by Chinese Americans. In contrast to Wou Sankwei, who adapts successfully to American life, his wife Pau Lin clings to Chinese cultural traditions and murders their son to save him from American culture, which she calls the Wisdom of the New. The half-Chinese girl named Pan raised in Chinatown in "Its Wavering Image" feels hurt by Mark Carson, her white lover and a reporter who betrays her by selling his soul for a Chinatown story. "The Story of One White Woman Who Married a Chinese" and "Her Chinese Husband" substitute the white male and Chinese female pattern of interracial marriages with the marriage of a Chinese named Liu Kanghi and Minnie, a white woman who sees her Chinese husband in every way antithetical to the treacherous and threatening James Carsner, the white husband she has divorced.

"The Smuggling of Tie Co" and "Tian Shan's Kindred Spirit" are two unique stories, not only because they share the subject of smuggling across the U.S./Canadian border, thus related to exclusionary laws against the Chinese immigrants, but also because both focus on Chinese American women who resort to tricksterism in befriending the smugglers they love. In the first story, Tie Co, a Chinese Canadian laundry manager who disguises herself as a young man and offers to be smuggled into the United States to encourage the smuggling business of a professional smuggler named Jack Fabian, throws herself into the river to save Fabian from imprisonment when they are discovered by Customs officers. In the second story, Fin Fan, the daughter of a Canadian Chinese storekeeper, puts on her father's clothes and devises to have herself captured and deported to China when she hears of the coming deportation of Tian Shan, her smuggler lover. A story that directly confronts the inhumanity of immigration laws against the Chinese is "In the Land of the Free," which relates the sad experience of a Chinese couple with the immigration officers. Lae Choo, together with her two-year-old son, arrives in San Francisco from China to join her husband, Hom Hing, but, ironically, upon their arrival in the Land of the Free, their son is detained and taken away. When after 10 months of agonizing separation their son is returned to them, the boy bids the mother to "Go 'way."

Like the majority of Eaton's Chinese stories excluded from *Mrs. Spring Fragrance*, the ones included in the collection share a number of features. To various degrees, the stories seek to challenge stereotypical images of the Chinese and eradicate prejudices that have stigmatized them as exotic, inhuman, and inassimilable aliens. Mrs. Spring Fragrance, for example, quickly adjusts to her American environment and learns the language; after five years of residence in the United States, as her husband claims, "There are no more American words for her learning" (1995, 17). Her ambition to write a book counters the logic of racism by reversing the argument, for she wishes to explain the "mysterious, inscrutable, incomprehensible Americans" (33) to Chinese women. The stories are also characterized by a reconfiguration of the relationship between men and women. Characters such as Mrs. Spring Fragrance, Laura, Alice Winthrop, Pau Lin, Tie Co, and Fin Fan all pose as women of strong personality who refuse to be dictated to; in the case of Mrs. Spring Fragrance, it is she who gives the orders and her husband who obeys. The high visibility of women in these stories might be in disproportion to historical reality, yet it functions as a challenge to the notion of Chinese community as a bachelor society. Eaton's texts generally appear to be facile and direct in expression, yet underneath the surface there often lies a sense of irony that renders simple interpretations problematic. For instance, "The Inferior Woman" ends with Mrs. Spring Fragrance wishing for a daughter walking "in the groove of the Superior Woman" (41) which threatens to nullify all her efforts to exalt the Inferior Woman. Stylistically, Eaton's stories are sometimes tainted with a faint Chinese flavor in language style, as in her occasional use of flowers as names for her Chinese characters and in the substitution of *moon* for *month*, but she seldom goes to the extent of exoticizing things Chinese, and her Chinese characters rarely utter speeches unnecessarily distorted by their Chinese background. **See also** Racism and Asian America.

Further Reading

Ammons, Elizabeth. "Audacious Words: Sui Sin Far's *Mrs. Spring Fragrance*." *Conflicting Stories: American Women Writers at the Turn into the Twentieth Century*. New York: Oxford University Press, 1991. 105–120.

Ferens, Dominika. *Edith & Winnifred Eaton: Chinatown Missions and Japanese Romances*. Urbana and Chicago: University of Illinois Press, 2002.

Huang, Guiyou. "The Asian American Short Story—The Cases of Sui Sin Far, Yamamoto, and Penaranda." In *Asian American Short Story Writers: An A-To-Z Guide*, ed. Guiyou Huang. Westport, CT: Greenwood Press, 2003. xiii–xxxii.

Ling, Amy. "Creating One's Own Self: The Eaton Sisters." In *Reading the Literatures of Asian America*, eds. Shirley Geok-lin Lim and Amy Ling. Philadelphia: Temple University Press, 1992. 305–318.

————. "Pioneers and Paradigms: The Eaton Sisters." *Between Worlds: Women Writers of Chinese Ancestry*. New York: Pergamon, 1990. 21–55.

Solberg, S.E. "Sui Sin Far/Edith Eaton: First Chinese-American Fictionist." *MELUS* 8 (Spring 1981): 27–39.

Sui Sin Far. *Mrs. Spring Fragrance and Other Writings*, eds. Amy Ling and Annette White-Parks. Urbana and Chicago: University of Illinois Press, 1995. Rev. and rpt. of Sui Sin Far (Edith Eaton), *Mrs. Spring Fragrance*. Chicago: A.C. McClurg, 1912.

White-Parks, Annette. *Sui Sin Far/Edith Maude Eaton: A Literary Biography*. Urbana and Chicago: University of Illinois Press, 1995.

ZHIMING PAN

✦ EATON, WINNIFRED (ONOTO WATANNA) (1875–1954)

A Chinese North American journalist, novelist, short story writer, and scenarist, Winnifred Eaton was the first Chinese North American novelist mainly known for her Japanese American popular romances. Unlike her elder sister Edith Maude **Eaton**, Winnifred was a prolific writer who produced over 16 novels, numerous short stories, two autobiographies, a cookbook, and dozens of screenplays for Universal Studios and MGM. Her best known novel, *A Japanese Nightingale* (1901), was translated into several languages, adapted into a Broadway play and a silent film, and won the praise of William Dean Howells. Most of Eaton's novels are fairylike popular romances that are related to Japanese settings with Japanese or Japanese American characters and published under her invented Japanese pen name, Onoto Watanna, though they often reconfigure the conventional patterns of popular romance and contest or challenge cultural, social, and sexual discourses of her day, particular evolutionary interpretations of race.

That Eaton chose to deal with Japanese subject matters and adopted a Japanese persona for her literary career might have been the result of her family influence as well as the historical circumstances of her time. Born in Montreal, Canada, Eaton was the eighth of 14 children of Edward Eaton, son of an English silk merchant, and Grace A. Trefusis (Lotus Blossom), a Chinese adopted by English missionaries and educated in England. Mr. Eaton was an impoverished artist who had traveled to Japan and was infatuated with Japanese arts in the heyday of Japonisme. The slightly favorable conditions of the Japanese in America and the Japanese victory in the Sino-Japanese War of 1894–1895 might also have played a part in Eaton's decision to invent a Japanese family background and write for an American reading public thrilled with things Japanese.

Eaton claimed to have written a story at the age of 16 that won her the recommendation to work as a reporter for *Gall's Daily News Letter* owned by a Canadian in Kingston, Jamaica, in 1896. She went to the United States in the same year and worked for the *Cincinnati Commercial Tribune* in 1897–1898. "A Japanese Girl," her first Japanese story, was published in that paper, but another Japanese story, "A Japanese Love Story," came out in *Iroquois Magazine* in 1897, and was definitely bylined "Onoto Watanna." In 1898, she moved to Chicago where she did secretarial work in the meat-packing industry and continued to publish essays and stories about the Japanese.

Eaton's first novel, *Miss Numè of Japan: A Japanese-American Romance*, was published by Rand, McNally & Co. in 1899. Set in Japan, the novel tells the interracial love story as a result of partner-changing between a Japanese pair of lovers (Takashima and his sweetheart, Miss Numè) and an American pair (Arthur Sinclair and Cleo Ballard). On his voyage back to Japan after his Harvard education, Takashima falls victim to a coquettish American girl, Cleo Ballard, who, accompanied by her mother and her cousin Tom Ballard, is going to join her fiancé in Tokyo. Cleo desists from reciprocating Takashima's love, while Sinclair, the American diplomat prejudiced against Japanese women, meets Numè at a party and the two take a fancy in each other. In contrast to the love story of Sinclair and Numè, which consummates in happy marriage, that of Cleo and Takashima ends with the tragic suicides of Takashima, his father, and Numè's father when Cleo refuses to marry her Japanese lover. The novel resembles Japanese travel narratives by Pierre Loti (*Madame Chrysanthème* 1888) and John Luther Long (*Madame Butterfly* and *Miss Cherry-Blossom of Tokyo*, both published in 1895) in narrative pattern and language style, but Eaton's romance essentially refutes the American misconception of the Japanese. The deaths of the male Japanese characters disprove Tom Ballard's belief of the Japanese men as heartless, while Numè's love effectively challenges Sinclair's prejudice of the Japanese women as having no heart. In this sense, the insertion of the superficial "new woman" of Cleo into its plot and her incestuous marriage to her cousin as reported in the end of the novel might be regarded as a reversal of the American prejudice and as a punishment of her own heartlessness.

The Old Jinrikisha (1900), a novelette accounted by an old jinrikisha that assumes a feminine persona, reflects the vicissitudes of Japanese society, including the impact of the Meiji Restoration, Japanese contacts with the West, the evils of temporary marriages, and its effects upon the half-caste offspring. The story involves three generations of Japanese women with the same name of Natsu: the grandmother Natsu reduced to a geisha after her parents' deaths, induced by the dispossession of the samurai class from power; the mother Natsu's temporary marriage to an Englishman after the death of her Japanese husband; and the granddaughter Natsu's marriage to a liberal Japanese man. An important theme that the novelette tackles is interracial marriage. After being deserted by the English husband, the mother Natsu bleeds herself to death, leaving behind two daughters, Natsu by her Japanese husband and Koto by her English husband. Koto is patronized by Phil Evans, an American young man, who falls in love with her in the end.

In 1901 Eaton moved to New York, married Bertrand W. Babcock, and published *A Japanese Nightingale*. Lavishly decorated with color illustrations and printed on delicately predecorated pages featuring geishas playing samisen, jirinkisha runners, and Japanese landscapes, the novel depicts the romance of Jack Bigelow and Yuki, the former a rich American young man traveling in Japan and the latter a half-caste, the daughter of a Japanese woman and an Englishman whose death impoverished the family. Bigelow is charmed by Yuki's magic dance in the teahouse, resists her proposal of a temporary marriage to him but eventually marries her, despite warnings by Taro Burton, his half-caste Japanese classmate, against any temporary marriage before Bigelow's departure for Japan. However, instead of ending with the marriage, the novel

situates Bigelow and Yuki in the union early in its plot to put to test American mis-
conceptions about Japanese women. Soon after his marriage, Bigelow begins to be per-
turbed by Yuki's eccentric behaviors, usually misconceived as the immorality of
Japanese women. He is annoyed by the way she seizes every opportunity to extract
money from him by inventing fabulous and conflicting stories about her family and
her numerous siblings, the number of whom changes from moment to moment. Worse
yet, her unexplained habitual disappearances from his house further perplex him and
throw him into restlessness. Everything clears up when his classmate Taro Burton
returns from the United States and discovers that the woman that Bigelow has married is his sister, who has contracted the temporary marriage with Bigelow for money
to finance her brother's travel back. Yuki runs away and Taro dies of remorse, but
before Taro's death Bigelow promises to take care of Yuki. Eaton may have evoked the
story of Loti's *Madame Chrysanthème*, in which the temporary Japanese wife of a
French sailor is shown to be a woman devoid of morality and greedy for money. Unlike
Loti, whose French protagonist leaves the Japanese woman with a clear conscience
when he happens to see her counting money in his absence, Eaton, refusing to exempt
her American protagonist from moral accusation, reconfigures the plot so that what in
the beginning appears to be another story of temporary marriage turns into a bond of
eternity when Bigelow and Yuki reunite by the end of the novel.

After *A Japanese Nightingale*, Eaton produced in quick succession a series of Japanese
romances and a comic novel about an Irish maidservant. *The Wooing of Wistaria*
(1902), as the subtitle on its first page indicates, is "A Love Story of Japan," populated
only with Japanese characters. Set on the eve of Commodore Perry's Japanese cruises,
the novel revolves around the love story of Prince Keiki from the Mori family, loyal to
the emperor, and Wistaria who—brought up by the Catzu family, loyal to the
shogun—is ignorant of her low birth through her mother, a woman belonging to
the lowest social class of Eta. Prince Keiki, son of Lord of Mori, falls in love with
Wistaria and goes to the house of Lord of Catzu to court her in disguise. When her
family discovers Keiki's identity, Wistaria's father forces her to wrest military information from him by taking advantage of his love for her. Warned by Wistaria of his dangerous situation, Keiki escapes from the house but is captured by her father, who
intends to kill him to avenge his wife, who was murdered by the Mori samurais. To save
his life, Wistaria suggests her father punish Keiki by marrying her to him, thereby
reducing him to an Eta. Crushed by his marriage to the Eta girl, Keiki abandons
Wistaria and goes to fight for the emperor. Wistaria enters his service disguised as a
young man and eventually reunites with Keiki when class distinctions are abolished.
The novel crosses class barriers and gender lines through the use of boundary-crossing
and cross-dressing, strategies similarly used in such novels as *The Heart of Hyacinth*
and *The Daughters of Nijo*.

Both *The Heart of Hyacinth* (1903) and *The Daughters of Nijo* (1904) inquire into the relationship between culture and nature, a theme that becomes manifest in some of Eaton's later novels. Set in Sendai, *The Heart of Hyacinth* features two children named Koma and Hyacinth, the former the half-caste son of Madame Aoi and her English sailor husband, who dies at sea, and the latter, the daughter of an American couple entrusted to the care of Madame Aoi upon her birth by the wife, who has run away from her unfaithful husband. As he grows up, Koma goes to England, receives an English education, and acquires Western manners, while Hyacinth, unaware of her biological origin, accepts Japanese culture and religion and joins the Japanese children in ridiculing Christian missionaries. The interference of James Blount, the American missionary, brings the childless Mr. Lorrimer and his new wife to Sendai to claim his lost daughter. Unwilling to leave Japan, Hyacinth appeals to the parents of her Japanese fiancé for a hasty marriage but is rejected because of her white skin. In the end, Hyacinth's dilemma is finally sorted out when Koma reveals his love for her. The novel clearly argues for culture over nature, a concept embodied in the story of Hyacinth, who is biologically white but culturally Japanese. Cross-dressing in *The Daughters of Nijo* (1904) again looks into the issue of culture and nature. The novel slightly resembles Mark Twain's *The Prince and the Pauper* (1882) in storyline and in narrative structure, yet Eaton substitutes Twain's English story with a story of Japanese setting and female characters. Eaton's novel tells the story of two daughters of the Prince of Nijo, Sado-ko and Masago, who look identical in appearance. Sado-ko, the legal princess fostered by the Dowager Empress in seclusion, is a rebellious and sentimental girl. She dislikes the court life and feels ill fitted among the faddish ladies in the palace of Komatzu, her royal cousin to whom she is expected to marry. In contrast, Masago, the illegitimate daughter of Nijo, grows up in a rich merchant's family and admires the luxurious court life imparted to her by her mother. She is betrothed to Junzo, a well educated sculptor commissioned to work in Komatzu's palace, where he mistakes Sado-ko for Masago. Sado-ko recognizes Junzo as the boy she adored as a child in the castle of the Dowager Empress and falls in love with him. Out of jealousy, Sado-ko trades her position with Masago, puts on her clothes, and eventually marries Junzo, while Masago fits nicely into her new life in the court and marries Komatzu.

The Love of Azalea (1904), another Japanese American romance and similar to *A Japanese Nightingale* in tone and language style, centers on Richard Verley, an American missionary, and Azalea, a Japanese girl maltreated by her stepmother, Mrs. Yamada. To escape her unkind stepmother, Azalea claims to be Verley's convert, for she learns that he wins converts by bribing them. Meanwhile, Matsuda, the richest local merchant, determines to marry Azalea, partly out of revenge for having been insulted by Azalea's father. Her stepmother is anxious for the match, notwithstanding Azalea's aversion to Yamada. Azalea temporarily escapes from her trouble when Verley admits his love for her, but, soon after their marriage, Verley is called back to the United States, leaving behind Azalea, who gives birth to a baby in his absence. Verley is detained in America longer than expected, and Azalea suffers financially. She is reduced to begging when Matsuda, who has schemed to take the missionary's property into his control and intercepted Verley's letters to Azalea, drives her out of her house. Matsuda then takes Azalea into his house and prepares to marry her. Yet Verley returns on the day of their wedding and finds in the mission church Azalea, who has escaped with her baby from Matsuda. An important theme of the novel concerns issues related to Christian missions and their impact in Japan. Verley uses money in enlisting converts, while Azalea's misery in Verley's absence is partly induced by her conversion to Christianity and her forsaking Japanese religions as symbolized in her throwing away the family tablet on the day of her wedding.

Set in the time of the Russian-Japanese War, *A Japanese Blossom* (1906) reverses the conventional Caucasian male and Japanese female romance; it instead presents a fairylike picture of cross-cultural conflicts arising from the marriage of Kiyo Kurukawa, a Japanese widower and businessman, and his white American wife, Ellen Kurukawa, an American widow. Kurukawa takes his wife, their child, Ellen's American children, and their Irish maidservant back to Japan, where his Japanese children live with their maternal grandparents. Disgusted by the news of his father's marriage to a barbarian woman, Gozo, Kurukawa's eldest Japanese son, fakes an older age and goes to war to avoid the white stepmother. Stirred by the fervor of war, Kurukawa obtains the support of Ellen and joins the army. The novel ends when Kurukawa and Gozo return from the war, and the family gathers around to listen to a story that promises to be a fairy tale with its beginning "Once upon a time . . ." Despite the cultural conflicts, particularly those between the children, the novel sounds like a lighthearted fairy tale that probes into the possibility of harmonious existence of people of different races.

Lightheartedness also characterizes *The Diary of Delia: Being a Veracious Chronicle of the Kitchen with Some Side-Lights on the Parlour* (1907), but it departs from Eaton's Japanese theme and uses a humorous vernacular Irish dialect rather than the quaint Japanese Pidgin in representing Delia, an Irish maidservant, who records in her diary her experiences with the Wolleys, a middle-class New York family. Encouraged by her friend Minnie, Delia refuses to do the general housework for the Wolleys and decides to hire herself out as a cook only. She is invited back to the family to cook a week later by Claire, the Wolleys's daughter, who has failed to manage the housework herself that week. Claire assigns different housework to the unwilling family members who in time either hire others to do their jobs or enlist Delia's service.

After *The Diary of Delia*, Eaton returned to Japanese American romance in *Tama* (1910), a novel set in Fukui shortly after the Meiji Restoration. Through the depiction of an American professor of science, simply called *Tojin* (the foreigner) by the

Japanese, and his love for Tama, the blind daughter of a Japanese woman and an English sailor, living in the mountains after the murder of her parents, the novel inquires into problems caused by the introduction of Western science and culture. Tojin represents Western science, with which he imposes upon himself the mission to educate the superstitious Japanese, who regard Tama as a fox-woman. With the help of his Japanese students, he traps Tama and takes upon himself to protect her for belonging to his own race. The novel ends happily when Tama, restored to light, returns to Fukui and confesses her love for Tojin. On the surface, the romance of Tojin and Tama presents a dark picture tainted by a racist point of view, yet there is an obvious subversive stance encoded in its plot. Throughout the novel, Tojin the foreigner, befuddles science and culture with his conviction in scientism, which is encountered by his Japanese students, who acknowledge the usefulness of science in Japan's modernization but defy the cultural superiority of the West.

The Honorable Miss Moonlight (1912), another Eaton novel with an all-Japanese cast, is propelled not by love but by the force to pass on the family line. The novel tackles the problem of heredity by presenting the fate of three individuals who either transcend or fall victim of hereditary forces: Saito Gonji, who, as the only male member of his generation, shoulders the responsibility of passing on the family line; Miss Moonlight, a geisha whom Gonji loves and marries but who is forsaken for bearing him no child; Ohano, Gonji's distant relative and second wife, who is compelled to commit seppuku for being childless and for her unwillingness to take care of Miss Moonlight's child, born after she is turned out of the family. Gonji revolts against using him as a biological mechanism to carry on the family heredity, and after agonizing trials he is eventually reunited with Miss Moonlight, while Ohano's life ends tragically, not only because of her being childless but also because of the inability to free herself from the bindings of hereditary influence, which is reflected in her committing seppuku.

Published in *The Blue Book Magazine* in January 1915 and set in wartime Japan, *Miss Spring Morning* features the interracial marriage of an American man and a Japanese woman, Jamison Tyrrell and Spring-morning. A fanatic artist of Japonisme, Jamison witnesses the wedding of Yamada Omi and Spring-morning during his stay with a Japanese captain. The wedding is arranged on the very night he leaves for the war, so that Spring-morning should take care of Madame Yamada, mother of Omi. Upon Omi's departure, Madame Yamada takes Spring-morning to Yokohama, with the intention to force her into service in the Yoshiwara there. The destitute Spring-morning, however, attracts the attention of Edith Latimer, an American girl in missionary service, who arranges for her to work in the house of Mrs. Tyrrell, Jamison's mother, who has followed him to Japan, resolved to bring him back to the United States. Not knowing that Spring-morning is the very girl whose wedding he has witnessed, Jamison grows infatuated with her and, despite strong resistance from his mother, marries her. However, Jamison is kept in the dark that Spring-morning enters into the liaison with the intention to go back to Omi when he returns from the war. Upon his return from war, Omi comes to claim Spring-morning, but he gives up his claim upon the announcement of her pregnancy. Jamison is disillusioned when Spring-morning dies in childbirth and goes back to the United States with his mother. The novel, the least romantic in its gloomy representation, depends heavily upon coincidences, but it is important in presenting Jamison, who refutes the American notion of racial inferiority of the Japanese and of the **Yellow Peril**.

In 1915 Eaton anonymously published her autobiography *Me: A Book of Remembrance*, in which she traces a short period of her life between her departure for Kingston, Jamaica, in 1896 and her return to New York in 1901, in the name of Nora Ascough, a 17-year-old Canadian girl. The book opens with the narrator voyaging out to Jamaica, to be a reporter there, with only 10 dollars in her pocket. As the daughter of an English father and a mother from an unnamed far-distant land, she is filled with expectations of wealth, literary fame, and romance. In Kingston, a black Jamaican statesman forces kisses on her, an event that results in her decision to go to Richmond, Virginia, where she escapes from Dr. Manning, a lecherous surgeon she met in Kingston. With the financial support of Roger Avery Hamilton, whom she meets on the train to Richmond, she goes to Chicago where she works as a stenographer, writes stories, accepts the proposals of several men, all the while loving Hamilton, who visits her at intervals but refrains from seriously committing to her. She eventually discovers from the newspaper that Hamilton is a married man unfaithful to his wife. By the time the book ends and she departs for New York, she has achieved nothing of her expectations she held when she first voyaged out. The autobiography is far from a factual record of Eaton's life and much of it is fictional, inaccurate, and inauthentic, masking rather than revealing her life, particularly about her mother's Chinese identity. However, in some cases, it does faithfully tell the story of Eaton as the writer who produces romances under the pen name of Onoto Watanna.

Marion: The Story of an Artist's Model (1916), supposedly written "By Herself and the Author of 'Me'" as its title page states, is a biography of Eaton's sister, Sara Bosse. The book provides more information about the Eatons and their Canadian life under the mask of their fictional names: Winnifred as Nora, Sara as Marion, and Edith as Ada. The book, however, focuses on Marion, who learns painting and acting and struggles to be a woman artist. She is first discouraged by Reginald Bertie, her selfish English boyfriend, who disdains artists and seeks personal advancement. She then goes to Boston, where the artist she seeks help from discourages her artistic ambitions. She is later forced by starvation to pose nude for art students, runs away, and moves to New York, where she works in art studios and marries Paul Bonnat, an energetic and promising young painter.

In 1916 Eaton divorced her first husband, married Frank Reeve, and moved back to Canada with Frank and lived on her husband's Albertan ranch. However, she grew weary of her ranch life and wrote her last Japanese American novel, *Sunny-San*, in 1921, and it was published the next year both in Toronto (by McClelland and Stewart) and in New York (by George H. Doran Company). Its plot faintly echoes the 1900 short story of "A Father" in its crossing the international borders and the discovery of the American father, but, in critical purview and in tone, *Sunny-San* excels its predecessor. It tells the story of Sunny-San, the Eurasian daughter of Madame Many Smiles—herself a half-caste with a Russian father and a Japanese mother—and an American traveler named Stephen Holt Wainwright, who eventually becomes the Chicago Man of Steel and a U.S. senator. The romance begins with a party of American students (Jinx, Bobs, Monty, and Jerry) under the supervision of Professor Timothy Barrowes, enjoying themselves in a Japanese teahouse on a night when Sunny takes the place as the leading dancer after her mother's death. Upon discovering her maltreatment at the hand of Hirata (the teahouse owner), the students storm into the torture room and take Sunny away by force. They raise among themselves $10,000 and set up the Sunny Syndicate Limited for Sunny's education and future, depart for the United States, and soon forget their Japanese adventure. Sunny then follows them to the United States and moves into the studio of Jerry, who has become an artist, while Professor Barrowes busies himself in excavating dinosaur fossils in Canada. Like Nora in *Me*, three of her benefactors (Jinx, Bobs, and Monty) propose for her hand, and she accepts them all. Jerry's mother and the girl he is engaged to, however, drive Sunny away from his studio during his absence. Sunny then strikes the acquaintance of an Irish girl, who shares her meager subsistence with Sunny and accidentally discovers that Sunny's American father is Senator Wainwright, who being childless in his marriage with his American wife, happily reclaims his Japanese daughter. The romance ends with Sunny announcing her love for Jerry at her debutante ball.

After *Sunny-San*, Eaton forwent popular romance, relocated her literary field to Calgary ranches in Alberta, Canada, and reoriented her attention to themes related to but varying from those explored in her Japanese romances in her last two novels, *Cattle* (1924) and *His Royal Nibs* (1925), bylined respectively as Winifred Eaton and Winifred Eaton Reeve. In these novels, Eaton continues to engage current issues such as race, yet these issues go beyond the dichotomy between people of the Orient and the Occident. *Cattle* tells the story of various pioneers on the Canadian prairie. The domineering antihero of the romance is Bull Langdon, the proprietor of the Bar Q Ranch, whose success story as a cattle rancher primarily reflects the grab-and-keep logic of early frontier pioneers. He has started his cattle ranch by rustling unbranded Indian calves but finally becomes the owner of a large cattle ranch. When his neighboring ranch widower Dan Day dies, leaving 10 children behind, Bull takes the oldest girl named Nettie Day into his household to take care of his physically feeble wife, Mrs. Langdon, a former rural schoolteacher. Nettie is loved by Cyril Stanley, Bull's ranch hand, who helps Bull in breeding Prince Perfection, a specimen of thoroughbred cattle, and tries to build a home for Nettie in his spare time. Ever present in the story is Bull's illegitimate, half-breed son, Jake, half-witted and indecipherable in speech because of a knock on his head by Bull. He discovers Bull's rape of Nettie during Mrs. Langdon's absence but fails to make himself understood by Angella Loring, an English woman recluse on a neighboring ranch that has been given to her without her knowledge by Dr. McDermott in return for his education, which was financed by her father. Upon her return, Mrs. Langdon discovers the secret of Nettie's pregnancy and dies of shock. Meanwhile, Nettie runs away, is brought to Angella by Dr. McDermott, and gives birth to a baby. A sisterly sympathy gradually grows between Nettie and Angella, and, when Bull comes to claim his child, Angella frightens him away with a rifle. A plague breaks out in Alberta, and Nettie joins Dr. McDermott in medical service. Bull steals the baby and goes to claim Nettie, but he is gored to death by Prince Perfection, set free by the Chinese cook upon his flight from the plague. The baby dies of cold weather, but the romance ends with the happy union of Nettie with Cyril and that of Angella with Dr. McDermott.

Eaton's last novel, *His Royal Nibs*, again depicts the frontier life on an Albertan ranch through the love story between Hilda McPherson and Cheerio, the former the daughter of P.D. McPherson, who is the proprietor of O Bar O, an Albertan ranch managed by a foreman named Bully Bill, and the latter a young Englishman looking for a temporary job. Cheerio is hired, assigned to chores despised by cowboys, and looked down upon by almost everybody on the ranch, including Hilda, her brother Sandy, Bully, and Roughneck Holy Smoke, but he is content with his position, greets everybody with "Cheerio," by which he is known to the ranchers, sticks to taking a bath every morning, proves himself to be a first-rate rider, gradually wins the respect of the ranchers, devotes his spare time to searching for dinosaur fossils and finds a cave on a cliff in which he paints pictures of Indians and also of Hilda, for he begins to take a fancy in her. As a girl with desires for romance, Hilda's heart also throbs with constant curiosity for Cheerio, but at the same time she repulses and reviles everything associated with his presence, for his sleek dress, his habit of bath, his aristocratic English air, his fractured English speech, and his interest in dinosaur fossils stand for everything that her ranch life is not. Adding to these is her jealousy aroused by his gold locket, in which is a picture of a lovely woman whom Hilda mistakes for his fiancée. Her dislike for him reaches its zenith when he faints in a scene of cattle branding and in delirium reveals his cowardice to be a constitutional defect.

P.D. McPherson, who has been kept literally in the backdrop up to this point—the middle of the romance—comes to the fore with his obsession for winning the world championship of chess. P.D., as he is called in the romance, has built up a reputation as the chess champion of Western Canada and now determines to defeat the greatest chess player in the United States. Faced with being discharged from his job because of his cowardice, Cheerio proposes to P.D. that he stay on and play as his opponent at chess until he is defeated, which P.D. accepts. Cheerio turns out to be a better hand at chess and each time defeats P.D., who gradually sinks into gloom and neglects Bully's urge for him to give the order of the fall roundup. It is not until Cheerio detects the impending trouble for the cattle and secretly changes the position of chess pieces that P.D. finally gets the chance to win. This, together with his rescues of Hilda from Roughneck's lariat, eventually wins for him Hilda's affection. The defeat of P.D. in the meantime attracts the attention of the editor of the Calgary *Blizzard*, who sends Duncan Mallison to O Bar O to investigate the matter. He accidentally discovers Cheerio to be the lost son and heir of Lord Chelsmore. The novel thus ends happily with the reconciliation of Cheerio as duke of the O Bar O and Hilda as the darling duchess when Cheerio reveals his identity as Edward Eaton Charlesmore of Macclesfield and Coventry, an allusion to Eaton's father, Edward Eaton.

Eaton's short stories are not unlike her novels in subject matter. The largest group deals with Japanese subjects and Eurasian characters ("Two Converts," "Kirishima-San," "The Pot of Paint," "A Half Caste," "A Father," "An Unexpected Grandchild," and "A Daughter of Two Lands"), but others feature the Irish ("Delia Dissents: Her Diary Records the End of a Great Endeavor"), the Chinese ("Amoy, a Chinese Girl"), or Caucasians ("Eye That Saw Not"). Most of these stories attend to cross-cultural issues, though some have to do with issues of gender and artistic creation ("Margot" and "Eyes That Saw Not").

Further Reading

Birchall, Diana. *Onoto Watanna: The Story of Winnifred Eaton.* Urbana and Chicago: University of Illinois Press, 2001.

Cole, Jean Lee. *The Literary Voices of Winnifred Eaton: Redefining Ethnicity and Authenticity.* New Brunswick, NJ and London: Rutgers University Press, 2002.

Ferens, Dominika. *Edith & Winnifred Eaton: Chinatown Missions and Japanese Romances.* Urbana and Chicago: University of Illinois Press, 2002.

Lee, Rachel C. "Journalistic Representations of Asian Americans and Literary Responses, 1910–1920." In *An Interethnic Companion to Asian American Literature,* ed. King-Kok Cheung. New York: Cambridge University Press, 1997. 249–273.

Ling, Amy. "Creating One's Own Self: The Eaton Sisters." In *Reading the Literatures of Asian America,* eds. Shirley Lim and Amy Ling. Philadelphia: Temple University Press, 1992. 305–318.

———. "Pioneers and Paradigms: The Eaton Sisters." *Between Worlds: Women Writers of Chinese Ancestry.* New York: Pergamon, 1990. 21–55.

———. "Winnifred Eaton: Ethnic Chameleon and Popular Success." *MELUS* 11 (Fall 1984): 5–15.

Matsukawa, Yuko. "Cross-Dressing and Cross-Naming: Decoding Onoto Watanna." In *Trick-sterism in Turn-of-the-Century American Literature: A Multicultural Perspective*, eds. Elizabeth Ammons and Annette White-Parks. Hanover, NH: University Press of New England, 1994. 106–125.

Nguyen, Viet Thanh. "On the Origin of Asian American Literature: The Eaton Sisters and the Hybrid Body." *Race and Resistance: Literature and Politics in Asian America*. New York: Oxford University Press, 2002. 33–59.

ZHIMING PAN

F

✦

✦ FEMINISM AND ASIAN AMERICA

Feminism in Asian America is a collective response to racism, sexism, cultural nationalism, and a call for heterogeneity in various locations—feminist scholarship, organization, and activism. It aims to reconsider the gender and ethnicity paradigm around nexuses of race, ethnicity, gender, and class in Asian America. It emerges to challenge the Orientalism inflicted upon Asian women and the stereotypes American mainstreams hold of Asian American women. Contemporary Asian American feminism also attempts to extend its territory to other Asian subjects in a transnational context by including women across boundaries of race, class, and nationality.

Asian American feminism is profoundly attached to the **civil rights movement**, the second-wave feminist movement, and the Asian American movement in the 1960s and throughout the 1970s, when Asian American women interrogated the marginalization of women of color in these movements and asserted Asian American women's voices in the feminist and **Asian American studies** agendas. Simply put, the Asian American feminist movement arises from a conscious and strategic move to resist, interrogate, and analyze the ethnocentrism of white feminism, sexism, and cultural nationalism in the Asian American community.

In the 1970s Asian American women, together with African American or Hispanic women, became more aware of the barriers and struggles they faced as a group. On the one hand, they noticed that the white American feminist movement dismissed race as irrelevant to the feminist agenda. Asian American women were underrepresented in leadership roles, academia, and anthologies. These women also found Asian American women neglected in the early Asian American studies movement. As a result, there was an urgent need for Asian American women to counter racism and sexism at the same time.

In the earlier phase (1970s–1980s) of Asian American feminist conscious-raising and political and literary practice, Asian American feminists had to overcome many obstacles and make Asian American women's experiences relevant to both feminist and racial concerns.

Asian American feminist activists first introduced Asian American women's experiences into university classrooms. By virtue of limited written materials and resources available to examine Asian American women, universities such as the University of California at Berkeley and San Francisco State University made an effort to first introduce Asian women and then Asian American women's oral histories in their curriculum and offered courses on Asian American women to help raise Asian American feminist consciousness. The effort led to the first journal, *Asian Women*, being published in 1971. It included papers students wrote for the first class on Asian women at the University of California, Berkeley.

In the meantime, literature became a site of conflict, contestation, and resistance for Asian American women. Earlier feminist writers engaged themselves in auto/biographical and life writings to counter stereotypes, sexism, and racism. They primarily reflected immigrant women's efforts and struggles to construct their cultural identities. Chinese American women's writings played a leading role in creating new images of the self in self-representation or biographical writings and in forging matrilineal relations in their works.

Maxine Hong **Kingston's** award-winning memoir *The Woman Warrior* was published in 1976. It is seminal in that it incorporates inquiry of gendered identity in revisiting and revising history, memory, ethnicity, and culture from a feminist perspective. It unquestionably contributes to a feminist understanding of the gender politics in the Chinese American community and provides a useful theoretical frame to examine similar questions in other Asian American communities as well. Although the book received controversial reviews and critique from white feminists and Asian American male writers, it marks the beginning of Asian American feminist intervention to link literature to culture concerning gender and ethnicity. Most importantly, it indicates earlier feminist efforts to establish matrilineal relations to Asian American history, tradition, and home culture; to move away from male-dominant cultural nationalism; and to assert women's views of culture.

Ruth Lum McCunn's *Thousand Pieces of Gold: A Biographical Novel* (1981) was an acclaimed biography of a Chinese immigrant woman's journey from China to the United States, followed by her struggles for independence in the American West. Some Chinese American women writers, such as Amy **Tan**, also wrote about immigrant women's lives but used fictional forms. *The Joy Luck Club* (1989), focusing on four mothers, four daughters, and four families, portrays ways matrilineal relations are formed among Chinese American women—immigrant mothers and American-born daughters. It became a *New York Times* best seller. Nevertheless, like *The Woman Warrior*, the book was critiqued for its negative portrayal of Chinese men and was involved in the debate about feminist and cultural nationalist agendas.

Attention to matrilineal relations is also found in Japanese American women's writings. Mitsuye **Yamada** uses her poems and stories to reflect the role matrilineal relations play in Japanese American women's identity construction, while defying racism at various levels. Hisaye **Yamamoto's** *Seventeen Syllables and Other Stories* (1988) addresses issues concerning gender and ethnicity with focuses, among other things, on cultural conflicts and generation gaps between the **issei**—the first-generation Japanese Americans, and the **nisei**—American-born Japanese children.

Unlike Chinese or Japanese American women writers, Indian American women writers, such as Meena **Alexander** and Bharati **Mukherjee**, position their works in a postcolonial discourse or a diasporic world and write about the consequences of dislocation for immigrant women from India. Alexander's poetry and autobiographical writings reflect her search for home, whereas Mukherjee's *Jasmine* (1989) presents an Indian woman on a nonstop journey from India to the United States.

A number of Asian American feminist anthologies were also published in the 1970s and 1980s. Besides *Asian Women* (1971), a few more anthologies were published: *This Bridge Called My Back: Writings by Radical Women of Color* (1981), although addressing American women of color in general, also includes Asian American feminist scholarship. Two other anthologies—*The Forbidden Stitch: An Asian American Women's Anthology* (1989) and *Making Waves: An Anthology of Writing by and about Asian American Women* (1989)—are collective efforts to define Asian American feminism.

From the late 1980s until the early twenty-first century, although Asian American feminist studies and discussions of Asian American literature made further efforts to theorize gender in relation to ethnicity, they continued to recognize differences among Asian American women while finding common ground based on race considered. They deemed it more important to disrupt the homogeneity of Asian American women's experiences because they are not inherently monolithic or homogenous, especially given the diverse demographic features of the Asian American community. Therefore, demographic changes in the Asian American population and the influx of new immigrants from various Asian countries helped initiate a feminist paradigm shift to difference, diaspora, and heterogeneity, in addition to seeking connections between Asia and Asian America. In 1987 Esther Ngan-Ling Chow showed her concerns about a lack of feminist consciousness among Asian Americans and proposed to link the intersectionality of race, gender, class, and culture to Asian American women's experiences. Gayatri Chakravorty Spivak and Lisa Lowe are also among Asian American feminist scholars to orient to difference. Lowe's "Heterogeneity, Hybridity, Multiplicity:

Marking Asian American Differences" (1991) is a landmark essay for the feminist paradigm shift to difference. Echoing Spivak and Lowe, other Asian American feminists focus more on multiple nexuses of race, ethnicity, gender, sexuality, or class. Along the same line, Asian American feminist scholars started to consider the role that transnational feminism plays in Asian American women's experiences. They incorporated feminist activism and literary practices in forging connections, affiliations, or coalitions with border crossing and other categories of identities.

Beginning approximately in the mid-1990s, Asian American women writers wove transnational feminist concerns in their creative or life writings. A Vietnamese American woman writer, Lan **Cao**, published *Monkey Bridge* (1997), while a Japanese American woman writer, Kyoko **Mori**, produced *Polite Lies: On Being a Woman Caught Between Cultures* (1997). These works—fiction or prose—both reflect the authors' deliberate efforts to weave different cultures together and cross-examine gender politics or issues of cultural identities.

In the 1990s, Asian American feminist scholars and activists continued to publish anthologies such as *The State of Asian America: Activism and Resistance in the 1990s* (1994), *Making More Waves: New Writing by Asian American Women* (1997), *Dragon Ladies: Asian American Feminists Breathe Fire* (1997), *Dangerous Women: Gender and Korean Nationalism* (1998), and *Other Sisterhoods: Literary Theory and U.S. Women of Color* (1998). These anthologies, together with the body of literary works at the same period, continue Asian American feminist efforts to theorize feminism in Asian America. **See also** Asian American Stereotypes; Asian Diasporas; Orientalism and Asian America; Racism and Asian America; Sexism and Asian America.

Further Reading

Bow, Leslie. *Betrayal and Other Acts of Subversion: Feminism, Sexual Politics, Asian American Women's Literature*. Princeton: Princeton University Press, 2001.

Chow, Esther Ngan-Ling. "The Development of Feminist Consciousness among Asian American Women." *Gender and Society* 1.3 (1987): 284–299.

———. "The Feminism Movement: Where Are All the Asian American Women?" In *From Different Shores: Perspectives on Race and Ethnicity in America*, ed. Ronald Takaki. New York: Oxford University Press, 1994. 184–191.

Chu, Judy. "Asian American Women's Studies Courses: A Look Back at Our Beginnings." *Frontiers: A Journal of Women Studies* 8.3 (1986): 97–101.

Grice, Helena. "Asian American Feminism, Developments, Dialogues, Departures." *Hitting Critical Mass: A Journal of Asian American Cultural Criticism* 6.2 (2000): 1–20.

Lee, Rachel C. *The Americas of Asian American Literature: Gendered Fictions of Nation and Transnation*. Princeton: Princeton University Press, 1999.

Lim, Shirley Geok-lin. "Complications of Feminist and Ethnic Literary Theories in Asian American Literature." In *Challenging Boundaries: Gender and Periodization*, eds. Joyce W. Warren and Margaret Dickie. Athens: University of Georgia Press, 2000. 107–136.

————. "Feminist and Ethnic Literary Theories in Asian American Literature." *Feminist Studies* 19.3 (Autumn 1993): 570–595.

Ling, Amy. "Maxine Hong Kingston and the Dialogic Dilemma of Asian American Writers." In *Ideas of Home: Literature of Asian Migration,* ed. Geoffrey Kain. East Lansing: Michigan State University Press, 1997.

Lowe, Lisa. "Heterogeneity, Hybridity, Multiplicity: Marking Asian American Differences." *Diaspora* 1.1 (1991): 24–44.

Mazumbar, Sucheta. "A Woman-Centered Perspective on Asian American History." In *Making Waves: An Anthology of Writing by and about Asian American Women,* ed. Asian Women United of California. Boston: Beacon, 1989. 1–22.

Mohanty, Chandra Talpade. "Under Western Eyes: Feminist Scholarship and Colonial Discourses: Third World Women and the Politics of Feminism." In *Feminist Literary Theory: A Reader,* ed. Mary Eagleton. Oxford and Cambridge, MA: Blackwell, 1996.

Shah, Sonia, ed. *Dragon Ladies: Asian American Feminists Breathe Fire.* Boston: South End, 1997.

Wong, Sau-ling C. "Ethnicizing Gender: An Exploration of Sexuality as Sign in Chinese Immigrant Literature." In *Reading the Literatures of Asian America,* eds. Shirley Geok-lin Lim and Amy Ling. Philadelphia: Temple University Press, 1992. 111–129.

————. "Gender and Sexuality in Asian American Literature." *Signs* 25.1 (1999): 171–226.

DONG LI

✦ *FIFTH CHINESE DAUGHTER* (WONG)

Written by Jade Snow **Wong** (1922–2006) and published in 1945, this autobiographical novel "depicts the 'collision of worlds' between the traditions of the old world and the lure of American values and lifestyles. *Fifth Chinese Daughter* is one of the earlier works by Asian Americans where the dilemma of bridging two different cultures is addressed" (Ng 1995, 1673). Greatly appreciated by Maxine Hong **Kingston** as "the Mother of **Chinese American literature**" (Bloom 1997, 16), Jade Snow Wong depicts a perfect example of the qualities of traditional Chinese and American individuality and tries to deal with the two cultures harmoniously without damaging either one.

A CHINESE DAUGHTER AT HOME

Born in San Francisco in 1922, Jade Snow Wong lived in San Francisco's **Chinatown**, which was isolated from the white society, when she was a child. From her father, Wong learns Chinese calligraphy, ancient Chinese culture, and history because he thinks that all Chinese children in the United States should learn Chinese so that they could acquire the knowledge of Chinese culture and history. One evening he announces that Jade Snow would go to a Chinese evening school so that she could become acquainted with China's great rivers, T'ang poetry, and Chinese history. At home she helps her mother with housework, such as cooking and washing dishes, as a filial Chinese daughter should.

Young Jade Snow follows her father as he works to observe what he is doing, and she raises many questions because she is curious. To satisfy his young daughter's demand, her father begins to teach her Chinese history by asking her to recite after him such statements as "Wong Ti was the first king of China" (Wong 1995, 4). Jade Snow repeats such sentences repeatedly until they become rooted in her memory. By practicing like this, she learns Chinese language and history. These sentences are inscribed in her mind and have a far-reaching influence on her.

Her mother tells her that a girl should be polite and never rough enough for fist-fights. This kind of teaching has an unconsciously crucial influence on the young daughter living in a Chinese community. One day, a bigger girl hits Jade Snow with her fists. Jade Snow clenches her fists and has the impulse to strike back. But her mother's familiar reminder echoes in her ears: "Even if another should strike you, you must not strike him, for then your guilt would be as great as his" (Wong 1995, 14). What little Jade Snow can do is to control her fists and burst into tears for relief.

Filial piety is emphasized by her parents time and again. Family is most important to the Chinese, whereas filiality is the essence that keeps the family together. Her father quotes Confucius to teach her. "He who is filial toward elders and fraternal toward brothers and is fond of offending his superiors is rare indeed; he who is not fond of offending his superiors and is fond of making revolutions has never been known" (Wong 1995, 15). So offending superiors is considered *unfilial*.

As her father announces, the peace and stability of a nation depends upon proper relationships established in the home. Confucianism emphasizes the importance of family: if an emperor fails to handle the relationships among his family members, he cannot reign over the country peacefully and powerfully. That is to say, a harmonious family is the foundation of a peaceful country. When her father is hospitalized, Jade Snow's mother is worried that if something happens to him, the whole family will collapse. Thinking of the horrifying consequence, her mother bursts into tears in front of her. For the first time she not only understands the vulnerability of her mother but also feels a "novel closeness" (Wong 1995, 81) to her.

Nurtured in the Chinese culture, Jade Snow is proud of her origin, although racism visits her repeatedly. When she goes to English school where "Jade Snow would be forced to learn more English" (Wong 1995, 67), she finds herself the only Chinese student among the "foreign" classmates of her age. It is at the school that Jade Snow experiences racial discrimination. One day after school, for example, everyone has gone home except herself and a boy named Richard, who has been waiting for a chance like this to insult her. "With malicious intent in his eyes, he burst forth, 'Chinky,

Chinky, Chinaman'" (68). Astonished at the sudden challenge, she is sensible enough to keep silent, which provokes the racist boy. He picks up an eraser, throws it at her, and laughs. Faced with such provocation, Jade Snow resorts to Chinese civilization for consolation. "Everybody knew . . . that the Chinese people had a superior culture. Her ancestors had created a great art heritage and had made inventions important to world civilization—the compass, gunpowder, paper, and a host of other essentials" (68). Moreover, she looks down upon Richard, thinking that his "grades couldn't compare with her own, and his home training was obviously amiss" (68). It is encouraging that she is brave enough to compete with her classmates and to be proud of her Chinese heritage, instead of being confused and self-contemptuous. So far, Chinese identity has stayed rooted in her.

AN AMERICAN INDIVIDUAL OUTDOORS

Jade Snow's education begins to reward her. In grade four, she is surprised by the practices of her teacher, Miss Mullohand, who has wavy, blonde hair, fair skin, and blue eyes. One day in the schoolyard, Jade Snow is hit on the hand by a carelessly flung bat. The teacher holds her, feeling the sore hand and wiping away her tears. The teacher's consolation moves her to a strange feeling; she begins to be aware of the difference between the American lady and her mother, who never hugs her to comfort her.

Jade Snow picks up a sense of individuality little by little. When her graduation from high school approaches, she inquires about qualifications for a college education. Although she meets the academic requirements for the state university, the fees will be beyond her even if she has a part-time job. She consults her father, who surprises her greatly. According to her father, the sons must have priority over the daughters because they will perpetuate their ancestral heritage by permanently bearing the Wong family name and transmitting it through their bloodline. They will make pilgrimages to ancestral burial grounds and preserve them forever, while the daughters leave home at marriage to go to their husbands' families to carry on the heritage in their names. The dream "to be more than an average Chinese or American girl" (Wong 1995, 109) depends on the opportunity to go to college. Her father, however, withdraws financial support because he thinks that she has been "given an above-average Chinese education for an American-born Chinese girl" (109). Although frustrated by her father's decision, Jade Snow does not say anything, but her mind is undergoing a stormy protest. "I can't help being born a girl. Perhaps, even being a girl, I don't want to marry, just to raise sons! Perhaps I have a right to want more than sons! I am a person, besides being a female! Don't the Chinese admit that women also have feelings and minds" (110).

Later, with her own efforts, she attends San Francisco Junior College, where she takes one course, sociology, that "completely revolutionized her thinking shattering her

Wong-constructed conception of the order of things" (Wong 1995, 125). One day her instructor discusses the topic of the relationship between parents and children. The teacher argues that children are individuals and that their parents cannot demand their unquestioning obedience any more. The right thing for parents to do is to try to understand their children, who have their rights as well. The statement arouses Jade Snow's consciousness and consideration about herself as an individual. She has been docile to satisfy her parents' and brother's unquestioned demands. Her consciousness is saying, "I am an individual besides being a Chinese daughter. I have rights too" (125). For the first time she thinks that perhaps her parents are wrong in forgetting that their daughter will become a woman in new America, not in old China. Encouraged by the teacher's statement and realizing her own individuality, she calls a boy named Joe for a date. She gets dressed up, full of happy anticipation. But when she is ready, her father suddenly stops her by asking whether she has obtained permission from her parents to go out. Confronted with her father's demand, Jade Snow is brave enough to challenge his authority. All of a sudden, she bursts out her declaration of independence.

The debate between Jade Snow and her father becomes an argument between American culture and Chinese culture. The authoritarian father is symbolized by the saying that he has eaten more salt than she has eaten rice, whereas Jade Snow is represented by the belief that a girl is an individual. The former resorts to Confucianism for support, and the latter comes to this discussion from the perspective of an American, and of the teacher's ideas. The result is that Jade Snow is given the freedom to find some answers for herself. From then on, she comes and goes without being questioned. The family where she used to be nurtured turns out to be a site of her independence, a site for her to obtain a new identity. It is the first step for her to be recognized as an individual by her own family.

The fact that Jade Snow wins the debate does not mean that she has become a pure American at the cost of the Chinese identity as some Chinese Americans do. Her advantage is to stand between two cultures—she understands and accepts both of them without favoring either one. The Chinese culture has nurtured her, offering her a particular foundation for her future, such as the values of hard work and of the importance of a harmonious family. The American culture provides her with an opportunity to be an independent individual. The blend of the two cultures produces a special identity—to be both a Chinese woman and an American individual. In her declaration of independence, she tries to talk her parents into treating her as an individual with her own rights instead of as a child. But she keeps her Chinese identity—to be a filial daughter. When she finds her parents have conceded defeat, she understands that it is a hard blow to them and they have lost face. To soften the blow, she explains that to get along with others would help her deal with life more easily in her future. Moreover, she assures them, "You must have confidence that I shall remain true to the spirit of your teachings. I shall bring back to you the new knowledge of whatever I learn" (Wong 1995, 129–130).

After getting a measure of freedom, Jade Snow concludes that she should not discard her parents' teaching to accept the philosophy of foreigners as a substitute, because the foreign philosophy is also vulnerable to criticism. Her dialectic analysis of her situation indicates that she knows how to analyze a problem from the opposing side. This ability enables her to be wisely sensible to know who she is and where she is. She knows that she has grown up reading Confucius and learning to embroider and cook rice and that she cannot reject Chinese fatalism. Chinese culture is inscribed in her mind, like a poem carved onto a piece of stone or steel, so deep that it cannot be wiped away. But she is an American in a white society. It is impractical for her to be pure Chinese. So she has to find a middle way to accommodate two cultures.

Although the search is not easy, Jade Snow is determined to go on without turning back. Mills College offers her a full scholarship so that she can continue her study without worrying about tuition. The older she is, the more she learns about life and society. At 18 she re-reads a diary she wrote at the age of 16, when she proclaimed her declaration of independence, and sees many points of difference: she now is a very serious young woman. "That two years had made her a little wiser in the ways of the world, a little more realistic, less of a dreamer, and she hoped more of a personality" (Wong 1995, 132).

With a wider scope for life, Jade Snow improves her social status gradually. One day, she brings her instructor and classmates to visit her father's factory as a field trip. Her parents welcome them warmly. Although it is a smaller factory than the American one they visit next, Jade Snow does not show any contempt for her parents or reject her kinship with the factory. Following the project, she prepares a term paper for a year's course in the English novel. She has an opportunity to compare the English and Chinese approaches to novels and to link her past and present learning. Her English professor is pleased with her paper, "The Chinese Novel," and singles it out for reading at an English conference to be held at the college. By working hard and connecting with Chinese culture, she improves herself from "a mere spectator" to "a participant" (Wong 1995, 166).

A key to her success is to distinguish her social life from her family life. Jade Snow follows her father's advice—"Do not try to force foreign ideas into my home" (Wong 1995, 130). When she visits her parents during weekends, she is a Chinese daughter again by accompanying her mother to church as usual. "Jade Snow no longer attempted to bring the new Western learning into her Oriental family. When she entered the Wong household, she slipped into her pattern of withdrawal, and she performed her usual daughterly duties—shopping for Mama, doing household chores, writing business letters in English for Daddy—in the role of an obedient Chinese girl. But now she no longer felt stifled or dissatisfied, for she could return to another life in which she fitted as an individual" (169).

Jade Snow succeeds in being a dutiful Chinese daughter and an American individual simultaneously without confusion, although this kind of double identity is extremely difficult to maintain. The young man Narcissus in Roman mythology sees his image reflected in water and falls in love with it. The image is his other identity that he cannot handle properly and causes his death. So it is generally believed that double identities lead to confusion and possibly death of the subject. It is, however, a different case with Jade Snow. She not only grasps Chinese language and calligraphy but also understands Chinese civilization and history. She understands the differences between the two cultures and knows well how to deal with them. Her father visits the college art gallery with Jade Snow when he goes to Mills College for her graduation ceremony in 1942. Impressed by some pottery Jade Snow has created in an art class, he tells her that her grandfather is artistically talented and would have been very glad to see her work. It is obvious that her father is praising her indirectly. Jade Snow answers properly, "Is that so?" instead of "Thank you" (Wong 1995, 180). When she puts on her academic regalia in front of her mother, Mama says nothing with tears in her eyes. Everyone says congratulations to her at her moment of triumph except her parents. But Jade Snow understands their mute happiness—they are proud of her. Her father is proud because the college president, although busy at that ceremony, "gave face" to let him take some pictures of the president herself and Jade Snow. Her mother's tears are mingled with joy and excitement.

The success in claiming to be an individual daughter at home and a hardworking student in school is just the beginning of her career. Her graduation presents another serious question—can she be as competent in society as she has been in school? When she looks for a job, a white interviewer's advice stings her into speechlessness and numbness. "If you are smart, you will look for a job only among your Chinese firms. You cannot expect to get anywhere in American business houses. After all, I am sure you are conscious that racial prejudice on the Pacific Coast will be a great handicap to you" (Wong 1995, 188).

Racial discrimination does not thwart her ambition, though. Later she finds a job as a secretary for the Navy, but a morass of detail and monotonous copy typing irritates her. Her boss lets her find out how practical cold vaccines will be. Although her report is well organized with detailed data, she finds that her chance for promotion is slim because the American work world is a man's world. When she asks her boss for his ideas, she is told that a woman could not compete for equal pay in a man's world.

Her first attempt at a promising career failing, Jade Snow retreats to the Santa Cruz Mountains for a vacation—to introspect her identity in depth: although she is recognized by her parents as an individual, the white-dominated society has not accepted her as an equal. When reflecting, she suddenly finds a fresh path in front of her—she can write down her experience as a Chinese daughter and an American individual. But she is not sure whether she can make a living by writing because she has a vague impression that writers struggle for a living. The gene she inherits from her grandfather brings her through—she will sell her pottery for a living. Her autobiography, *Fifth Chinese Daughter*, was published in 1945, and she opened her own ceramics shop in Chinatown.

ADVANTAGE OF HER CHINESENESS

Jade Snow's success is based upon her Chinese identity to some extent. When she fails to advance in the white society, she resorts to the valuable and inexhaustible mine—Chinese culture. Her sound knowledge of Chinese language, history, and culture enables her to be a competent writer. Chinese American writers will need more chances to show themselves, their life, and their ancestral culture. Readers can discern the influence of Chinese culture in both her book and her life. When she was interviewed for *Contemporary Authors*, Jade Snow announced, "I give priority to women's responsibility for a good home life; hence, I put my husband and four children before my writing or ceramics" (Bloom 1997, 110).

Traditional Chinese ways of writing are embodied in the writing style of Jade Snow Wong's autobiography. Most white autobiographies are written in the first person to emphasize the emergence of the individual. *Fifth Chinese Daughter*, however, is told under the cloak of a third person. "I" is transformed into "she." As a result, the protagonist and the author merge into one. The reason that Jade Snow employs the third person is that she sticks to the personal modesty Chinese culture emphasizes. In "Author's Note to the Original Edition" and "Introduction to the 1989 Edition," Wong explains, "Although a 'first person singular' book, this story is written in the third person from Chinese habit. The submergence of the individual is literally practiced. In written Chinese, prose or poetry, the word 'I' rarely appears, but is understood. . . . Even written in English, an 'I' book by a Chinese would seem outrageously immodest to anyone raised in the spirit of Chinese propriety" (Wong 1995, xiii). Modesty is one of the Chinese virtues that requires respect for others. Jade Snow skillfully conflates it with her autobiography to illustrate the Chinese family teaching embodied in her.

In 1951, the State Department of the United States sent her on a four-month world tour as an example of the success of a Chinese American woman who, "born to poor Chinese immigrants, could gain a toehold among prejudiced America" (viii). The most valuable spirit found in this book is that Jade Snow Wong identifies herself with Chinese culture and adopts it as a guide for her family and social lives, just as she writes, "My Chinese heritage has been my strength and advantage" (xi). See **also** Chinese American Autobiography; Racism and Asian America.

Further Reading

Bhabha, Homi K. *The Location of Culture*. London: Routledge, 1994.

Bloom, Harold, ed. *Asian-American Women Writers*. Philadelphia: Chelsea House Publishers, 1997.

Kim, Elaine H. *Asian American Literature: An Introduction to the Writings and Their Social Context*. Philadelphia: Temple University Press, 1982.

Ng, Franklin, ed. *The Asian American Encyclopedia*. New York: Marshell Cavendish, 1995.

Wong, Jade Snow. *Fifth Chinese Daughter*, with a new introduction by the author. Seattle: University of Washington Press, 1995.

LONGHAI ZHANG

✦ FILIAL PIETY

Filial piety is the central part of a Confucian value system concerned with the need to produce beneficial behavior patterns from children who are expected to care for their parents. According to Confucius (551–487 BC), a variety of virtues is needed to maintain a strong society: filial piety, righteousness, love, loyalty, sincerity, justice, tranquility, moderation, and harmony. Filial piety stands as the most important. Even in today's Marxist/capitalist society of China, filial piety is still valued. *The Book of Filial Piety (Xiao Jing)* is the key text defining this Chinese virtue. In the text, through a series of conversations between Confucius and his pupil, Zeng Zi, the main points of the patriarchal pattern of obedience are examined in detail. The son is expected to be the highest model of filial piety, specifically the eldest son. Indeed, the original Chinese character or ideograph for filial piety, *xiao*, is composed of two characters: *lao* (old) and *zi* (son) (Ikels 2004, 3). It is the duty of the son, specifically the eldest son, to care for his parents. Therefore, this son is expected to sacrifice almost everything for his parents, for the true purpose of his life is to take care of his parents. Even after death, that son will pay his respect to the parents. The father-son relationship becomes the model for all relationships in society, which follows a prescribed hierarchy of power: husband-wife and older brother-younger brother. Other social relationships are also modeled on such relationships, such as emperor-minister and teacher-student. The model exists even in a friend-friend relationship if one friend is considerably older.

When Buddhism first tried to become part of Chinese culture, it was rejected. The old teachings of Theravada Buddhism were too austere for the public. After all, Lord Buddha left his parents to become enlightened. For Chinese, this act demonstrated the opposite virtue of filial piety: abandonment. For Buddhism to succeed in China, it had to emphasize stories about filial piety. A selfless aspect of Buddhism would in the end fit well with Chinese filial piety. In a Jataka story about Shan-tzu, the protagonist took care of his blind parents. With this story and others, Buddhism appeared Chinese. One day Shan-tzu went to get water, wearing deerskin as a disguise, so as not to upset the deer that watered there. Unfortunately, he was accidentally shot by the king. When the king found out what happened and that Shan-tzu's death would mean the death of his blind parents, the king promised to take care of them. When the parents learned that their son had died from a poisoned arrow, they grasped the dead body and cried. Miraculously, he was reborn, so he could take care of them. This story became famous and was repeated as a classic example of filial piety. Its connection to Buddhism was secondary.

A more important Buddhist story of filial piety would become part of Chinese lore and psyche. A religious holiday would be created based on the need to remember and respect the dead. Mu-lien, through hard study and discipline, had obtained the status of an arhat, an enlightened being with clairvoyant abilities. With such abilities, he saw his dead mother, who had been reborn as a hungry ghost. He tried to feed her, but it had no effect. Buddha suggested that special offerings be made. Mu-lien made the offerings and liberated his mother from the realm of the hungry ghosts. On the fifteenth day of the seventh month, the Festival of the Hungry Ghost is celebrated throughout China. Variations of this festival would occur in other Asian countries. In the eyes of Chinese, Buddhism and filial piety were now inseparable because a son could so love his mother that he could rescue her from hell. One could be Buddhist and Chinese. Buddhism would extend the possibilities of filial piety, as Kenneth Ch'en points out. Whereas Confucian virtue focused on the harmony of relationships here on Earth, Buddhism works for the liberation of all sentient beings in the afterlife, so they can be reborn and ultimately attain nirvana (1968, 97).

Another important pedagogical text for filial piety was popular among the common people of China: *The Twenty-four Paragons of Filial Piety*. Written in the Yuan Dynasty (1280–1368 CE) by scholar Guo Jujing from Fujian Province, this text, along with its drawings, was created primarily for children, who enjoyed the entertainment value of the tales while learning about the virtue of how parents should be the crucial focus of life. A dutiful son will do anything for his parents. He will fight demons, divorce a bad daughter-in-law, and even starve himself for his parents. Though these stories go to extremes, such is the nature of children's fables worldwide.

In one tale, Kuo Ju, an obedient son, decides to kill his only child, a son, so that there will be enough food to feed his mother. As he digs the grave so he can bury his son alive, he discovers gold. His son is kept alive. According to scholars Weimin Mo and Wenju Shen, the moral of the story is not that one should sacrifice one's son, but that one will be rewarded for such extreme sacrifice for one's parents (1999, 17). Such stories become powerful reminders of how children should respect their parents. In another story, a son even cuts part of his own body off to feed to his parent. The sacrifice is more than nutrition, for the act becomes the medicine or cure that is needed.

In *The Joy Luck Club* (1989), the Chinese American novelist Amy **Tan** mentions a similar story of a daughter making soup out of her flesh to feed her mother.

Filial piety originated in China and expanded to Korea, Japan, and other Asian countries that were influenced by the power of the middle country's cultural, political, and economic might. As Asian families immigrated to the United States, they brought such values of filial obligations with them. However, filial piety often conflicted with the values of Western society, which emphasized independence and individuality. Asian American literature is full of stories about how the "Americanized" children of "Asian" families had problems dealing with such conflicts as they tried to fit in while trying to maintain a show of respect toward their parents and elders; this is especially noticeable in another Chinese American writer, Jade Snow **Wong's** autobiography *Fifth Chinese Daughter*.

When Asians immigrated to the United States, they brought such stories of filial piety with them to tell their children. Other Chinese stories of filial piety became famous. The story of Hua Mulan comes from the *Ballad of Mulan* written in the sixth century. In a time of war, a daughter takes the place of her father, who is too old to fight. She goes off to war disguised, willing to sacrifice her life for the love of her father. Maxine Hong **Kingston** uses the story in her classic Asian American book *The Woman Warrior* (1976) to show what kind of dedication Asian American children are expected to give their parents. Such dedication can be overbearing for children, especially in a land where women's rights are proclaimed.

In Japan, one famous tale of filial piety is Momotaro, usually translated as peach boy. In some versions of the tale, a boy in a giant peach is sent from Heaven and is discovered by a woman who has no child. She raises him with her husband. When he becomes older, Momotaro leaves for the island of Onigashima to fight an *oni*, a demon. He returns as a dutiful hero who takes care of his parents. His whole life is about serving the needs of his parents. Momotaro is mentioned in the Japanese American writer John **Okada's** novel *No-No Boy* (1978), which examines the sacrifice that the oldest son must make during **World War II**. Ichiro and his family were sent to a **Japanese American internment** camp, where the boys were given a chance to show their patriotism to the United States by answering two simple loyalty questions, 27 and 28—Will you serve the United States in combat? Will you swear allegiance to this country? Ichiro was the oldest son, so out of duty to his mother, he said no-no. But he would pay a high price for his filial piety. He was despised by his Japanese American peers as a traitor.

Thus, as Asian "American" children grow up in a Western culture with its value system emphasizing independence and individuality, they are also brought up with the conflicting Asian values of being interdependent and obedient. This conflict returns repeatedly in Asian American literature.

Further Reading

Ch'en, Kenneth. "Filial Piety in Chinese Buddhism." *Harvard Journal of Asiatic Studies* 28 (1968): 81–97.

Ching, Hsiao. *The Book of Filial Duty.* Trans. Ivan Chen. Boston: Adamant Media Corporation, 2004.

Hashimoto, Akiko. "Culture, Power, and the Discourse of Filial Piety in Japan: The Disempowerment of Youth and Its Social Consequences." In *Filial Piety: Practice and Discourse in Contemporary East Asia,* ed. Charlotte Ikels. Stanford, CA: Stanford University Press, 2004. 182–197.

Ikels, Charlotte, ed. *Filial Piety: Practice and Discourse in Contemporary East Asia.* Stanford, CA: Stanford University Press, 2004.

Janelli, Roger L., and Dawnhee Yim. "The Transformation of Filial Piety in Contemporary South Korea." In *Filial Piety: Practice and Discourse in Contemporary East Asia,* ed. Charlotte Ikels. Stanford, CA: Stanford University Press, 2004. 128–152.

Mo, Weimin, and Wenju Shen. "The Twenty-Four Paragons of Filial Piety: Their Didactic Role and Impact on Children's Lives." *Children's Literature Association* 24.1 (1999): 15–23.

WAYNE STEIN

✦ FILIPINO AMERICAN ANTHOLOGY

Since **Filipino American literature** was first conceptualized as a distinct body of work in the Asian American anthology *Aiiieeeee!* (1974), at least a dozen Filipino American literary anthologies have been published in the United States or assembled by Filipino editors located in the United States. As part of the broader proliferation of Filipino American literature in recent years, these anthologies have facilitated the construction of Filipino American literature as an expressive field separate from the general category of Asian American literature. In the process, these texts have implicitly raised the question of what constitutes Filipino American literature, even if they have not always explicitly answered that question. When situated within a transnational history that extends as far back as the 1920s, contemporary Filipino American anthologies can be seen as part of a vibrant and complex literary tradition that is shaped, but not circumscribed, by its conditions of emergence—U.S. colonialism and imperialism in the Philippines and migration to the United States.

The period of the 1920s is often regarded as the golden age of Philippine literature in English, the moment when the first generation of Anglophone writers in Manila, under the general guidance and tutelage of the U.S. colonial regime, began to publish in great quantity. The first anthology of Filipino poetry in English, *Filipino Poetry (1909–1924),* was put together in Manila in 1924 by Rodolfo Dato. A few years later, educator and author Paz Marquez Benitez, whose own "Dead Stars" (1925) is considered the first modern Filipino short story in English, edited the earliest anthology of fiction called *Filipino Love Stories* (1927). Shortly thereafter, a young José Garcia **Villa** implicitly responded to Benitez's anthology by publishing *Philippine Short Stories: Best 25 Stories of 1928* (1929), borrowing his selection criteria from Edward J. O'Brien's *Best American Short Stories* series. According to Villa's brief preface, the anthology was meant to encourage Filipino writers in their artistic endeavors by giving them due recognition, to preserve the stories for posterity (especially since the usual mode of publication in this context was weekly or monthly Manila periodicals) and to cultivate an appreciative reading public. Although this was the only anthology to result from his editorial selections, Villa continued to survey and evaluate Philippine literature in English until 1941, even after he migrated to the United States in 1930. He renewed this practice, in a sense, after he stopped publishing his own poetry in the 1950s. While living in New York, Villa maintained his position as self-appointed arbiter of Filipino literary value from afar through the four editions of *A Doveglion Book of Philippine Poetry* (1962, 1965, 1975, 1993), all published in Manila.

Moving across the Pacific and into the **World War II** period, Filipino American writer Carlos **Bulosan** edited the first collection of Filipino poetry published in the United States, *Chorus for America: Six Philippine Poets* (1942). Whereas Villa's editorial criteria emphasized the aesthetic properties of literature and the metaphysical aspects of life, Bulosan foregrounded the political and revolutionary possibilities of literature. Published just weeks after the fall of Bataan, *Chorus for America* gathers a number of Filipino poets, including Villa, R. Zulueta da Costa (whose award-winning "Like the Molave" is excerpted), C.B. Rigor, R.T. Feria, and Bulosan himself (under his own name and under the pseudonym Cecilio Baroga). In his preface, Bulosan situates the anthology within a Philippine revolutionary tradition and offers the volume as engaged in the antifascist/popular front effort.

Villa's short story anthology and his "best of" essays, coupled with Bulosan's *Chorus for America*, constitute a kind of prehistory to contemporary Filipino American anthology-making. Such a history proper, when the self-conscious use of "Filipino American" (or "Pilipino American") takes root, begins with *Liwanag: Literary and Graphic Expressions by Filipinos in America*, published in San Francisco in 1975, one year after the appearance of *Aiiieeeee!* This multimedia anthology consists of poetry and fiction, as well as black-and-white photographs, drawings, and paintings. Collectively assembled and edited by several West Coast Filipino American artists, *Liwanag* (Tagalog for "light" or "illumination") reflects the ethos of its time. The introduction rejects the compulsion to assimilate into mainstream culture and seeks instead to construct a "whole" Filipino American identity. The most evident way that this process is thematized and achieved is through what might be considered generational transmission in reverse, a deliberate effort at maintaining or recovering what threatens to be lost in the first generation's migration to the United States. Thus, some of the works—such as the framing poem "Liwanag" or Joselyn Ignacio's poem "Memories of Dusty Bamboo Mats"—look to the "homeland" to retrieve (at times, "indigenous") Filipino cultural signifiers and practices. Similarly, other works—such as Prisco's poem "These are the forgotten Manong" and Serafin Syquia's poem "a sight for sour eyes"—aim to recover and connect with the history of the *manongs*, the first generation of mostly male Filipino immigrants who labored in the fields and in the canneries from the 1920s forward. The anthology contains work by a number of writers who would go on to publish books of their own (Virginia Cerenio, Jessica **Hagedorn**, Bayani Mariano, Oscar Peñaranda, Al Robles, and Cyn Zarco) as well as other important poets of the so-called Flips generation, such as Emily Cachapero, Lou and Serafin Syquia, and Sam Tagatac.

In its multimedia scope and ambition, *Liwanag* remains an important, if fleeting, attempt to engage in a cultural nationalist construction of Filipino American identity at a time when other social movements were absorbed in analogous strategies. Two anthologies—*Without Names* (1983) and *Liwanag: Volume 2* (1993)—follow in *Liwanag*'s wake. *Without Names* is a slim volume of poems written by many of the same writers in *Liwanag*; the latter resembles its predecessor in its multidisciplinarity and in its thematic concerns with laying claim to a Filipino American identity and culture. However, *Liwanag: Volume 2* also contains pieces, particularly by women artists, which insistently take up issues of gender and sexuality. Framed by Theo Gonzalves's preface, which highlights the rootedness of Filipino American culture within U.S. society, the volume is comprised of poetry, drama, fiction, and visual art by a new generation of artists, some of whom, such as Bino Almonte-Realuyo, Catalina Cariaga, Eugene Gloria, Vince Gotera, Rex Navarrete, Celine Salazar Parreñas, and Barbara Jane P. Reyes, have gone on to make names for themselves.

Since 1993, there has been a veritable explosion of Filipino American anthologies. Unlike the earlier anthologies, the contemporary ones seem to be concerned less with collecting and advancing a particular version or vision of Filipino American literature than with ensuring that writers of Filipino descent gain visibility in the U.S. literary marketplace. The result is an astonishing and sometimes bewildering array of Filipino American literary instantiations. Luis Francia's edited *Brown River, White Ocean: Philippine Literature in English* (1993) is the only recent anthology that provides a diachronic, historical survey of literature produced mainly, though not exclusively, in the Philippines. Divided generically into two sections—short stories and poetry—the book is arranged chronologically, with many of the early Philippine writers coinciding with those whom Villa had earlier included in his "honor roll" essays.

Most other anthologies, by contrast, aim to gather contemporaneous literature in an effort to document a segment of Filipino writing produced at a specific historical moment. These tend to be built around such categories as gender (*Babaylan: An*

Anthology of Filipina and Filipina American Writers, 2000; *Going Home to a Landscape: Writings by Filipinas*, 2003); genre (*Fiction by Filipinos in America*, 1993; *Contemporary Fiction by Filipinos in America*, 1997; *Returning a Borrowed Tongue: An Anthology of Filipino and Filipino American Poetry*, 1995); and theme (*Flippin': Filipinos on America*, 1996; *Growing Up Filipino: Stories for Young Adults*, 2003).

Despite these manifold orientations, what these recent anthologies have in common is that they are addressed to remedy some kind of lack, loss, or absence—what is generally regarded as Filipino invisibility within the U.S. cultural imaginary. For example, editor Cecilia Manguerra **Brainard** states that *Fiction by Filipinos in America* and its sequel *Contemporary Fiction by Filipinos in America* are intended to redress the perceived scarcity of Filipino American literature and the alleged voicelessness of Filipinos in the United States. Other editors understand Filipino invisibility to result not so much from the dearth or absence of an available literary archive but from the way colonial and/or U.S. education has ignored or subordinated Anglophone Filipino literature. In their respective introductions to *Brown River, White Ocean* and *Returning a Borrowed Tongue*, editors Luis Francia and Nick **Carbó** position their anthologies as responses to the lack of recognition this body of work has received, both in Philippine and in U.S. higher education. Given the colonial and imperial roots of these conditions (and the basic fact that Anglophone Filipino literature is a direct effect of U.S. colonial education), it is not surprising that these editors underscore the politics of language inherent in the use of English. The very title of *Returning a Borrowed Tongue* speaks to the complexities of linguistic imposition, reception, and appropriation. In her introduction to *Babaylan*, editor Eileen **Tabios** also focuses on language as a potentially contestatory tool.

Despite these avowed assertions of anti-imperial, self-representational, postcolonial stances, the actual works anthologized in the books undertake a wide range of thematic, political, and cultural initiatives. Nowhere is this heterogeneity more evident than in *Pinoy Poetics: A Collection of Autobiographical and Critical Essays on Filipino and Filipino-American Poetics* (2004). Documenting the extensive history of writing by Filipinos in the United States, editor Nick Carbó self-consciously situates the volume within the enduring tradition of Filipino anthology-making and seeks to challenge the condition of invisibility by inscribing a Filipino presence into world Anglophone literary history. However, the essays themselves—written by both Philippine- and U.S.-located poets—traverse a remarkably broad spectrum of aesthetic theories, from the overtly political (Mila D. Aguilar's "The Poetics of Clarita Roja," Marlon Unas Esguerra's "The Poetry of Rebolusyon," Barbara J. Pulmano Reyes's "The Building of 'Anthropologic,'" Tony Robles's "A Poetics of the Common Man(ong)") to the meditative and philosophical (Gemino H. Abad's "What Does One Look for in a Poem?" Eric Gamalinda's "Language, Light, and the Language of

Light"). Other poets theorize their poetics in relation to English (Ricardo M. de Ungria's "An English Apart," Kristin Naca's "The Cult of Language in Pinoy Poetry"), ethnic identity (Leslieann Hobayan's "Mo(ve)ments in Silence: Constructing 'Home' in the Gap Through Poetry and Letters," Patrick Pardo's "On Being a Filipino Poet," Oscar Peñaranda's "The Filipino American Sensibility in Literature," Jean Vengua's "Abilidad and Flux: Notes on a Filipino American Poetics"), and queer sexuality (Joseph O. Legaspi's "Boys in Skirts and Other Subjects That Matter," Joel B. Tan's "Brown Faggot Poet: Notes on Zip File Poetry, Cultural Nomadism, and the Politics of Publishing").

In general, then, contemporary Filipino American anthologies take up and enact a host of artistic and political projects. They anthologize the well established (Cecilia Manguerra Brainard, N.V.M. **Gonzalez**, Jessica Hagedorn, F. Sionil José, Bienvenido **Santos**, and Linda **Ty-Casper**) next to younger writers (Catalina Cariaga, Sarah Gambito, Paolo Javier, and Patrick Rosal), Philippine authors next to Filipino American authors, women writers next to male writers, colonial pasts next to postcolonial presents, poetry next to fiction, and experimental next to traditional forms, all the while staging the continuities and discontinuities that mark the history of Anglophone Filipino litera-ture. **See also** Colonialism and Postcolonialism; Filipino American Poetry, Filipino American Short Story.

Further Reading

Ancheta, Shirley, Jaime Jacinto, and Jeff Tagami, eds. *Without Names: A Collection of Poems*. San Francisco: Kearny Street Workshop Press, 1985.

Brainard, Cecelia Manguerra, ed. *Growing Up Filipino: Stories for Young Adults*. Santa Monica: PALH (Philippine American Literary House), 2003.

Bulosan, Carlos, ed. *Chorus for America: Six Philippine Poets*. Los Angeles: Wagon & Stars Publishers and Harvey Parker & Craftsman, 1942.

Carbó, Nick, ed. *Pinoy Poetics: A Collection of Autobiographical and Critical Essays on Filipino and Filipino-American Poetics*. San Francisco and St. Helena: Meritage Press, 2004.

———, ed. *Returning a Borrowed Tongue: An Anthology of Filipino and Filipino American Poetry*. Minneapolis: Coffeehouse Press, 1995.

Carbó, Nick, and Eileen Tabios, eds. *Babaylan: An Anthology of Filipina and Filipina American Writers*. San Francisco: Aunt Lute Books, 2000.

Francia, Luis H., ed. *Brown River, White Ocean: An Anthology of Twentieth-Century Philippine Literature in English*. New Brunswick: Rutgers University Press, 1993.

Francia, Luis H., and Eric Gamalinda, eds. *Flippin': Filipinos on America*. New York: Asian American Writers' Workshop, 1996.

Gonzalves, Theo, et al. eds. *Liwanag: Volume 2*. San Francisco: Liwanag Publications, 1993.

Igloria, Luisa A., ed. *Not Home, But Here: Writing from the Filipino Diaspora*. Manila: Anvil, 2003.

Liwanag Collective, eds. *Liwanag: Literary and Graphic Expressions by Filipinos in America*. San Francisco: Liwanag Publishing, 1975.

Ponce, Martin Joseph. "'The Labor of Un-Oneing': The Transnational Poetics of Anglophone Filipino Literature." PhD Diss., Rutgers University, 2005.

Shaw, Angel Velasco, and Luis H. Francia, eds. *Vestiges of War: The Philippine-American War and the Aftermath of an Imperial Dream 1899–1999*. New York: New York University Press, 2002.

Toribio, Helen C., ed. *Seven Card Stud with Seven Manangs Wild: An Anthology of Filipino-American Writings*. San Francisco: East Bay Filipino American National Historical Society, 2002.

Villa, José Garcia, ed. *A Doveglion Book of Philippine Poetry*. Manila: Katha Editions, 1962. Subsequent editions: *A Doveglion Book of Philippine Poetry in English: 1910 to 1962*. Manila: A.S. Florentino, 1965; *The New Doveglion Book of Philippine Poetry*. Manila: Caliraya Foundation on Consciousness and the Environment, 1975; *The New Doveglion Book of Philippine Poetry*. Manila: Anvil, 1993.

Villanueva, Marianne, and Virginia Cerenio, eds. *Going Home to a Landscape: Writings by Filipinas*. Corvallis, OR: Calyx Books, 2003.

MARTIN JOSEPH PONCE

✦ FILIPINO AMERICAN AUTOBIOGRAPHY

Autobiographical texts by Filipino Americans unveil the interconnection between historical writing, racial positioning, and literary experimentation. The earliest Filipino immigrants wrote autobiography to engage their personal experiences in the United States, most often in contrast to official or idealized versions of the country popular in the Philippines at the time. Filipinos, colonized by Americans from 1898–1946, generally believed in the notion of the American Dream, and many traveled there as workers or as *pensionados* (young men who received college scholarships to later return to the Philippines). The first three known Filipino American autobiographies—Carlos **Bulosan's** *America Is in the Heart: A Personal History* (1943), Manuel Buaken's *I Have Lived with the American People* (1948), and Benny F. Feria's *Filipino Son* (1954)—describe the experiences of those early immigrants. Bulosan's narrative, the founding Filipino American text and a classic of Asian American literature, centers on his experiences as a migrant worker in West Coast farms and Alaskan canneries and as a union organizer in the United States after his arrival in Seattle in 1930. Seduced by the idea of the American Dream to seek his fortune in the United States, Bulosan chronicles in detail the destruction of that fantasy as he encounters the economic hardships and racial oppression that many immigrants experienced. Having had only three years of schooling in the Philippines, Bulosan, afflicted with tuberculosis, which obliged him to spend years in a hospital, spent hours reading and writing, eventually becoming one of the most prolific Filipino American writers of poetry, essays, and novels. Extensive critical attention to *America Is in the*

Heart has focused on Bulosan's representation of the struggles of early Filipino immigrants, the representation of gender roles, race and class consciousness, notions of American democracy, and political commitment.

In opposition, Buaken's and Feria's texts are little known and have received no serious critical attention. Buaken's autobiography is written along the same lines as Bulosan's and describes the life of Filipino workers in California from the 1920s–1940s, ending with his 1942 enlistment into the 1st Filipino Infantry Regiment of the U.S. Army. But one notable exception makes this work a crucial complement to Bulosan's narrative: Buaken went to the United States as a scholarship student who was meant to study divinity at Princeton. He came from an upper-middle-class Protestant family, and his early life centered on education, music, and religion. His family sent him to the United States to prepare him to take over his father's church. But Buaken had other plans and remained in the West Coast. This led to an estrangement from his family and entrance into a life completely different from the one he was accustomed to, working as a dishwasher, a cook, and at stoop labor for menial pay. Buaken's autobiography also highlights the racism against Filipinos in California, including details of riots and institutionalized rejection of Filipinos. Finally, Buaken enters university part-time until he joins the Army.

Feria's *Filipino Son,* on the other hand, elides the negative perspectives on the United States and American racial attitudes patent in Bulosan's and Buaken's texts. Feria spent most of his time in the United States in Chicago, studying at DePaul University and the University of Chicago and participating actively in community events that included publishing the first Filipino American newspaper, the *Commonwealth Free Press.* The narrative ends with the account of the publication of his volume of poetry, *Never Tomorrow* (1947). Of doubtful literary value, *Filipino Son* nevertheless provides a description of the lives of Filipinos in the Midwest. Feria's chronicle is notable for his determined optimism regarding the treatment of Filipinos and other immigrants and his unquestioning acceptance toward the ideal of assimilation to the United States.

Remarkably, five decades passed before other autobiographies were produced, although this recent production is outstanding for its literary quality. Connecting thematically and chronologically with the early autobiographies, Peter Jamero's *Growing Up Brown: Memoirs of a Filipino American* (2006) is the story of the "bridge generation," the American-born children of the early immigrants. As a *campo* boy, whose family included the dozens of young Filipino American men working in farm labor camps, Jamero recounts his experience of the United States as a place where Filipinos occupied an ambivalent position. His autobiography, written during his retirement, covers over six decades of West Coast Filipino American life, giving readers a comprehensive perspective of the problems and opportunities the second generation of

Filipino Americans experienced. Other second-generation narratives include Pati Navalta Poblete's *The Oracles: My Filipino Grandparents in America* (2006), a heartfelt reminiscence of how her adolescence was transformed by the arrival of both her maternal and paternal grandparents to the United States, and Benny Agbayani's *Big League Survivor* (2000), the autobiography of a Major League Baseball player. Poblete focuses on the typical generational and cultural clash between grandparents and their grandchildren but also describes her growing appreciation of her family history and Filipino culture. Agbayani's autobiography, written in the tradition of other sports autobiographies, stresses his appreciation for Filipino American life in Hawaii, his struggle to enter the big leagues, and his success as a baseball player.

The experience of **biraciality** and biculturalism links Norman Reyes's *Child of Two Worlds: An Autobiography of a Filipino-American, or Vice Versa* (1995) and Patricia Justiniani MacReynolds's *Almost Americans: A Quest for Dignity* (1997), inviting readers to examine the ways in which Filipino Americans articulate hybrid positions. Reyes's autobiography of his childhood unveils perspectives on race in the Philippines, particularly during the American occupation, when his Filipino father returned from the United States with his American wife. The couple envisioned their children as a bridge between two worlds, and Reyes, reflecting the idea of the United States as the pathway to modernization, stresses the positive aspects of this position. From his privileged position in middle-class Filipino American life, Reyes consciously performs the role of a cultural guide who introduces the American public to the customs, traditions, and idiosyncrasies of the Philippines by describing the events that illustrate the similarities and differences between American and Filipino ways. MacReynolds's autobiography, set in Los Angeles, focuses on a multiethnic family—Filipino father, Norwegian mother, and American daughter—as they negotiate the racial and cultural demands of society. Most of the text centers on Patsy's childhood memories of trying to understand her parents and dealing with mainstream society's prejudice against interracial marriage. The eponymous notion of being "almost Americans" illustrates the ambivalence of persons who struggle to belong to a society that looks upon them with distrust.

Syndicated cartoonist Lynda **Barry's** *One Hundred Demons* (2002), an experimental graphic text structured in short, titled narrative pieces, is the coming-of-age story of a mixed-race Filipina artist. The independent sections are linked by the protagonist/narrator and by a series of motifs, notably the concept of the demon and the need to paint it to master it. Barry's "demons" are the objects, events, or concepts that remind her of the difficult emotional stages in her young life. She negotiates her ethnic position mostly through her Filipino family and their customs and, importantly, by intersecting issues of race, class, and her dreams of becoming a writer. Another singular text is Luis Francia's *Eye of the Fish: A Personal Archipelago* (2001), which weaves memories of this journalist's childhood and adolescence in the

Philippines with historical anecdotes, stories of his professional life in the United States, and commentaries on U.S.-Philippine cultural relations, in the context of several trips he takes as an adult back to his homeland. This sophisticated text explores the notions of hybrid Filipino identity and "home," the narration of history, and cross-cultural belonging.

These autobiographies reveal the predominant issues that have marked the history of Filipino American self-representation, such as changing attitudes toward Filipinos in American society and the possibilities of literary experimentation. By engaging narratives of the self, these Filipino American autobiographers focus our attention on the ways history nuances self-perception and how changing views on ethnic writing invite us to rethink the history that created particular communities. **See also** Assimilation/Americanization; Racism and Asian America.

Further Reading
Alquizola, Marilyn. "Subversion or Affirmation: The Text and Subtext of *America Is in the Heart*." In *Asian Americans: Comparative and Global Perspectives*, eds. Shirley Hune, Hyung-chan Kim, et al. Pullman: Washington State University Press, 1991. 199–209.
Davis, Rocío G. *Begin Here: Reading Asian North American Autobiographies of Childhood*. Honolulu: University of Hawaii Press, 2007.
De Jesús, Melinda Luisa. "Of Monsters and Mothers: Filipina American Identity and Maternal Legacies in Lynda J. Barry's *One Hundred Demons*." *Meridians* 5.1 (2004): 1–26.
Evangelista, Susan. "Carlos Bulosan." In *Dictionary of Literary Biography: Asian American Writers*, ed. Deborah Madsen. Vol. 312. Detroit, MI: Gale, 2005. 10–18.
Fuse, Montye P. "Benny P. Feria." In *Asian American Autobiographers: A Bio-Bibliographical Critical Sourcebook*, ed. Guiyou Huang. Westport, CT: Greenwood Press, 2001. 83–88.
Kim, Elaine H. *Asian American Literature: An Introduction to the Writings and Their Social Context*. Philadelphia: Temple University Press, 1982.
Lee, Rachel C. *The Americas of Asian American Literature: Gendered Fictions of Nation and Transnation*. Princeton: Princeton University Press, 1999.
San Juan, E., Jr. "Searching for the Heart of 'America' (Carlos Bulosan)." In *Teaching American Ethnic Literatures: Nineteen Essays*, eds. John R. Maitino and David R. Peck. Albuquerque: University of New Mexico Press, 1996. 259–272.

ROCÍO G. DAVIS

✦ FILIPINO AMERICAN LITERATURE

Filipino American literature is rooted in the experiences of the laborers who migrated from the Philippines to the United States in the early twentieth century, the U.S. **civil rights movement**, and the development of literature in the Philippines. Filipino American literature today is firmly tied to Philippine literature in English, which is itself a product of a long history of colonization and decolonization and which is understandable only in relation to the development of literatures in other languages in the Philippines.

Before Magellan's landfall (and subsequent death) on the eastern rim of the Pacific Ocean in 1521, the islands that would become known as the Philippines were part of a trading network that ringed the South China Sea and extended from Madagascar to Europe to Korea. During the Spanish colonial period, 1565–1899, precolonial indigenous cultural production suffered major attacks, but many forms were transformed and translated. Late in this period publishing in several indigenous languages and in Spanish flourished, and the circulation of texts was crucial for the growth of nationalist movements that would erupt in the Philippine Revolution of 1896. Writing in Spanish continued well into the next period, running from 1899 to 1946, the period of U.S, and, from 1942 to 1945, Japanese occupation. Filipinos began to produce writing in English in 1905, and by the end of the 1920s a tradition of writing in English was established and a body of writings in a number of genres—poetry, short stories, novels, essays, and plays—emerged that would later be called Philippine literature in English. Philippine literature in English began—and continues in the present—within a publishing context where only a small and generally privileged minority could read English, a context shared progressively less with the literature in another colonial language, Spanish, but progressively more with literatures in indigenous languages such as Tagalog (the basis of Filipino, the national language). About 150,000 Filipinos traveled to the United States during the first half of the twentieth century, most of whom were low-wage migrant workers such as Carlos **Bulosan**, whose autobiographical novel *America Is in the Heart* is likely the most widely read text within the canon of Filipino American literature. During this time Jose Garcia **Villa** would also travel to the United States, and, after briefly moving into the firmament of the U.S. avant-garde in poetry in the 1940s and early 1950s, he would largely be forgotten by people in the United States. However, Villa exerted a powerful influence on literature in the Philippines, and in particular poetry in English, from the 1930s until his death. In the late-1960s **Asian American political activism** provided a major impetus for the naming of a specifically Filipino American literature and movement, in which Filipino Americans were defined as U.S.-born, in contrast to people born in the Philippines who migrated to the United States. But with the massive influx of people who were Philippine-born after the immigration reforms of 1965 "Filipino America" has widened to include new immigrants. Since the People Power revolt of 1986 that ended the Marcos regime, Filipino American literature has developed increasingly close ties with Philippine literature in English, as a number of writers have traveled back and forth between the two countries and have worked, written about, and published in both.

LITERATURE IN THE PHILIPPINES DURING THE SPANISH PERIOD

Literature in Spanish in the Philippines was sharply limited because of the reluctance of colonial authorities to have the Christianized natives (*indios*) learn the language of power. However, with the relaxation in controls over trade early in the nineteenth century and the growth of the *principalia* class of elites made up of natives and mestizos (Chinese and Spanish), indios were sent to Europe to study. During this time indios were admitted to educational institutions administered by the religious orders in Manila. This group of young men, collectively known as *ilustrados*, would form the nucleus of Filipino nationalism, which became a revolutionary force when it inspired popular elements such as the Katipunan secret society, led by Andres Bonifacio, who was himself a Tagalog poet.

The outbreak of revolution in 1896 quickly led to the execution of José Rizal, arguably the father of Filipino nationalism. Rizal was a leader of the Propaganda Movement, which agitated in Barcelona and Madrid for reforms in the Philippines during the late 1880s and early 1890s. Rizal's writings have exerted a tremendous influence on the development of literature in the Philippines, and part of the reason for this influence was the adoption by the U.S. colonial regime of Rizal as the national hero of the Philippines.

LITERATURE OF THE U.S. COLONIAL PERIOD

According to the terms of the Treaty of Paris, which concluded the Spanish-American War of 1898, Spain ceded its claim to the Philippines to the United States. The Filipino revolutionary forces, which had already declared a constitutional republic and had won the whole of the archipelago from Spain with the exception of Manila, were not consulted in the negotiations, and in 1899 the Filipino-American War began. Even before the United States declared the war over in 1903, the processes were set in motion to transform Filipinos into colonial subjects through language and education. In 1900 English became the official language of instruction in public schools, and in 1901, 600 teachers arrived on the USS *Thomas* to begin in earnest the pacification-by-education project.

Some of the early contributions to Philippine literature in English owe their existence to two institutions. First, Filipinos named *pensionados* were selected to enter the colonial administration and were thus sent to U.S. colleges and universities. In 1905 the first poetry published by Filipinos in English was written by *pensionados* studying in California, and over the next few decades several thousand *pensionados* would study in the United States. Then, soon after the establishment of the University of the Philippines (UP) in 1908, a means for transmitting a canon of English-language literature, with its attendant dispositions and aesthetic norms, was set in place. Up to the present many of the most prominent figures in Philippine literature in English would be students and teachers at UP.

The spread of English created a limited audience and market, and through the early 1900s newspapers and magazines provided a vehicle for English-language writing. In 1921 the first novel in English appeared, followed in 1924 by the first poetry anthology. In 1925, Paz Marquez Benitez published what many critics have called the first "modern" short story by a Filipino writer in English, "Dead Stars," and in 1927 she edited the first anthology of Filipino short stories. By the late 1920s the Manila literary scene had consolidated to the point that revolts against established forms could occur, in particular with the founding of the UP Writers' Club in 1927.

However, the Manila literary scene was relatively isolated. Few people had the leisure to read or the money to buy reading materials; English instruction was of uneven quality and duration, and the majority of people in the archipelago seldom used the language in everyday life. The fact that English had not really established itself prompted the delegates to the 1934 constitutional convention that founded the Philippine Commonwealth to include a provision stating that one of the vernaculars would be the basis for a national language. By 1940, Tagalog received official support to be the basis for Filipino.

The Commonwealth Literary Contest of 1940, the largest literary contest up to that time in the Philippines, was indicative of the changing linguistic terrain of literature insofar as it included prizes for writing in Spanish, English, and Tagalog. However, the field of literature was also bifurcated by a movement toward asserting the autonomy of art and a countermovement toward more engagement between literature and society, a division sharply outlined in the debate between Villa, who had relocated to the United States in 1930, and Salvador Lopez. In the Philippines this debate was occurring at a moment when peasant movements were gaining strength, labor unrest in the United States was increasing as the Depression continued, and worldwide a broad united front was forming against fascism. Against this backdrop Villa acted as a major tastemaker with his annual selections of the "best" stories and poems from 1926 to 1941.

The aesthetics and social commitments Lopez outlined would find a measure of fulfillment in the work of Bulosan. Like Villa, Bulosan had also relocated to the United States in the early 1930s, but his trajectory was far different. Around 150,000 Filipinos, most of whom were men under 30 years old, had migrated to the United States from the Philippines during the early 1900s. Large numbers of Filipino "U.S. nationals" worked on the sugar plantations in Hawaii, the agricultural fields near the Pacific Coast, in the Alaskan canneries, and in low-wage service occupations across the United States. In 1934, however, the Tydings-McDuffie Act sharply curtailed the movement of Filipinos between the United States and the Philippines. Bulosan, who was born in a rural area near Manila that would be a center of the peasant guerrilla uprisings both during and after **World War II**, attempted to give artistic expression in his novels to both the struggles of Filipino laborers in the United States and to the peasant movements in the region where he was born.

POST-INDEPENDENCE PHILIPPINE LITERATURE IN ENGLISH

After the Philippines attained formal independence in 1946, the links between English-language literature in the Philippines and literature in the United States became tighter. Writers and literary scholars from the Philippines traveled to the United States to study and sometimes teach, and in many cases this travel was enabled by grants and fellowships. In the United States many of these writers participated in creative writing workshops, and the University of Iowa Workshop would play a particularly large role in shaping literature in the Philippines, because not only did several Filipinos participate in its writing program, but two of the most prominent among them, Edith and Edilberto Tiempo, returned to the Philippines and founded the Silliman University National Summer Writers Workshop, located in Dumaguete City in the Visayas in 1962. Most of the leading English-language writers in the Philippines today are alumni of the Silliman Workshop, as are several figures who have relocated to the United States.

On a world scale, the long 1960s were the high point of Third World decolonization movements. As colonial regimes fell, nationalist and Left movements in the Philippines gained confidence. In the Philippines Renato Constantino published in 1966 "The Miseducation of the Filipino," an essay that outlined the mechanisms, primarily through the imposition of the education system, by which the United States gained and maintained cultural hegemony. Massive protests against sending Filipino troops to Vietnam, and more generally against imperialism, feudal relations in the countryside, and bureaucratic capitalism in the urban centers, erupted in Manila and culminated in the First Quarter Storm of 1970 and the Diliman Commune of 1971.

DEFINING FILIPINO AMERICAN LITERATURE

In the United States, the 1968 **Third World Students' Strike** at San Francisco State became a defining event for what would soon emerge as Filipino American literature. The first anthology of **Filipino American poetry**, *Flips*, was published in 1971 by writers based in San Francisco, some of whom would define themselves in the introduction of *Aiiieeeee!* a few years later as specifically U.S.-born Filipinos, as opposed to Philippine-born Filipinos. The genealogy of this group would be rooted in the history of the *manongs*, the older generation of Filipinos whose lives were depicted by Bulosan and who would, after his death, play an integral part in the Delano Grape Strike of 1965 and the formation, in conjunction with Mexicans, of the United Farm Workers. These Filipino Americans were closely linked to the general Asian American movement in California, which would consolidate again in 1976 in defense of the

International Hotel, a building that provided low-income housing, primarily for Filipino and Chinese men, and housed offices for activist groups.

However, events in both the United States and the Philippines would work against the formation of a Filipino American identity in terms of only U.S.-born Filipinos. With the 1965 U.S. immigration reforms, the quotas that had tightly restricted immigration from the Philippines were lifted, and, through preferences for family reunification and for professionals, the numbers of Philippine-born U.S. citizens soon dramatically increased. The diaspora from the Philippines—both of contract workers to other parts of Asia and of middle-class professionals to the United States—further intensified when Ferdinand Marcos declared martial law in 1972. During the 1970s some U.S.-based groups concentrated political activity not only on local community issues but also on the struggle against martial law in the Philippines. Some writers in English, such as Bienvenido **Santos** and Ninotchka **Rosca**, went into political exile in the United States, and others, such as Mila Aguilar, Emmanuel Lacaba, F. Sionil Jose, and Bienvenido Lumbera, braved the political repression in the Philippines as the Marcos regime attempted to suppress communist and Muslim insurgencies.

Writers in exile and their continued engagement with the political situation in the Philippines played an important part in the creation of Filipino American literature. During the martial law years of the 1970s, institutional support in the United States developed to sustain, and in some ways create, **Asian American studies**, ethnic studies, Filipino American studies, and their attendant departments, classes, and publishing networks. At this time several writers from the Philippines taught at universities in the United States—Santos at Wichita State University, Epifanio San Juan Jr. at the University of Connecticut, and N.V.M. **Gonzalez** at California State University at Hayward.

During the Marcos regime there was a sharp decrease in the publication of literary texts, although some mainstream Manila publishers continued to release new works. To get around the censors, some publishing emanated from underground political organizations. However, after the assassination of Benigno Aquino in 1983, the middle classes participated in massive protests throughout the archipelago. These protests heralded both a revival in popular theater in the streets and a new assertiveness on the part of some publishers in printing works critical of the dictatorial regime. After an election clearly marked by fraud, the People Power revolt of 1986 finally forced Marcos to flee the country and thus ended the dictatorship.

Inequality and the impoverishment of the vast majority of the Filipino people was a major cause of the Marcos regime's collapse. However, after martial law ended the Philippine economy was still crippled by massive military outlays and payments to maintain the foreign debt accumulated under Marcos. In the succeeding years the Philippines has not shifted far from the economic course taken by the dictatorship, and the remittances of the Filipino diaspora have become increasingly important in sustaining the Philippine economy.

THE INTERSECTION OF FILIPINO AMERICAN LITERATURE AND PHILIPPINE LITERATURE IN ENGLISH

Despite the deepening economic crisis in the Philippines, Philippine literature in English has accomplished something of a renaissance since 1986. There has been a publication boom of works in English—New Day, Solidaridad, and Anvil Press have published a number of literary works, and UP, Ateneo de Manila University, and De La Salle University have collaborated in publishing literature in English. Creative writing workshops are conducted not only at these universities but also at other universities in Metro Manila and across the archipelago. A substantial number of writers' organizations have also formed that hold workshops and symposia in locations spread throughout the country. Literatures in languages such as Cebuano and Ilocano have been receiving increasing scholarly attention since the 1970s, and writing in English has established centers outside of the dominant Metro Manila-Silliman circuit in places such as Mindanao State University in Iligan and San Carlos University in Cebu City.

This revival of Philippine literature in English has had effects in the United States that are most strongly felt in both Asian American and Filipino American literature, and arguably the current boom of Philippine literature in English owes much to events in the United States. The struggles of the Asian American movement helped to open the canon of English-language literature in the United States to include some Asian American writers. The resulting academic and publishing support helped to create reading and writing publics for Filipino American literature that did not exist prior to the 1960s. New York, as the center of publishing in the United States, has become a particularly favored destination for writers arriving from the Philippines. Rosca and Jessica **Hagedorn** were both largely based in New York City when they made breakthroughs in getting their novels published by major presses in the late 1980s and early 1990s. Writers such as Luis Francia and Luis Cabalquinto participated in workshops with Villa in New York, and they were joined in the early 1990s by Eric Gamalinda. This group has been involved in publishing several important anthologies with the Asian American Writers' Workshop, and it has grown to include writers of Filipino descent who have grown up in the United States, such as Bino Realuyo. This group has also maintained particularly close ties with fellow writers in the Philippines, such as Gemino Abad, while building links with writers based in the San Francisco Bay Area, such as Eileen **Tabios**, and with institutions such as the University of Hawaii at Manoa.

An under-studied aspect of Filipino American literature is the writing and performance that is less consecrated by the academy and more community-based. Filipino student organizations at many universities have written and staged plays during Pilipino Cultural Nights, and several of these organizations have published collections of writings. Hip-hop and spoken word scenes rooted in community organizing have sprung up in Los Angeles, Seattle, San Francisco, Chicago, and New York. A substantial body of writing in Ilocano has been produced in Hawaii. In general, literary production by Filipinos and Filipino American communities beyond the centers in Manila, San Francisco, and New York needs more attention. **See also** Asian American Political Activism; Asian Diasporas; Filipino American Anthology; Filipino American Novel; Filipino American Poetry; Filipino American Short Story.

Further Reading

Abad, Gemino, ed. *Likhaan Anthology of Philippine Literature in English*. Manila: University of the Philippines Press, 1998.

Alegre, Edilberto, and Doreen Fernandez. *Writers and Their Milieu: An Oral History of the First and Second Generation Writers in English*. Manila: De La Salle University Press, 1993.

Francia, Luis, ed. *Brown River, White Ocean: An Anthology of Twentieth-Century Philippine Literature in English*. New Brunswick, NJ: Rutgers University Press, 1993.

Hidalgo, Cristina Pantoja, and Priscelina Patajo-Legasto. *Philippine Post-Colonial Studies: Essays on Language and Literature*. Manila: University of the Philippines Press, 1993.

Mojares, Resil. *Origins and Rise of the Filipino Novel: A Generic Study of the Novel until 1940*. Manila: University of the Philippines Press, 1983.

Valeros-Gruenberg, Estrellita. *The De La Salle University Reader: Writings from the Different Regions of the Philippines*. Manila: De La Salle University Press, 2000.

Zapanta-Manlapaz, Edna. *Filipino Women Writers in English, Their Story: 1905–2002*. Manila: Ateneo University Press, 2003.

SHERWIN MENDOZA

✦ FILIPINO AMERICAN NOVEL

Like much of Filipino literature in general, the Filipino American novel is heavily indebted to the work of the national hero of the Philippines, José Rizal. Rizal's two novels, *Noli Me Tangere* (1887) and *El Filibusterismo* (1891), were published in Europe, and both were realistic novels that depicted friar abuses and advocated for a Philippines in which Filipinos and Spaniards were equal to each other. Rizal was executed shortly after the Philippine Revolution broke out in 1896, and early in the U.S. colonial period he was chosen to be the hero of the not-yet-born nation. Rizal's legend would extend across the Pacific, and Carlos **Bulosan**, whose *America Is in the Heart* (1943) is likely the most widely read novel within the Filipino American canon, wrote in a letter in 1949 that he wanted to repeat what Rizal had done for

Philippine literature. The only possible rival for *America Is in the Heart* in terms of readership is Jessica **Hagedorn's** *Dogeaters* (1990). Set in Manila during the Marcos dictatorship of the 1970s and early 1980s, the novel's fragmented, cinematic narration ranges across a number of social strata, from shantytowns to the bastions of the elite. Between Bulosan and Hagedorn the major Filipino novelists in the United States were Bienvenido **Santos** and N.V.M. **Gonzalez**, both of whom were closely involved with the Filipino literary scene for writing in English, and their careers intertwined with writers based in Manila, such as Nick Joaquin and Francisco Sionil Jose. **Asian American political activism** and the rise of **Asian American studies** programs in the 1970s created an institutional space for Filipino American writers, but **Filipino American poetry** and the **Filipino American short story** took the lead as U.S.-born Filipinos wrote primarily in these forms. In the 1970s and early 1980s, many writers left the Philippines because of the political repression of the Marcos regime, and Linda **Ty-Casper** published novels in the 1980s that were critical of the dictatorship. Since the People Power revolt that deposed the dictator in 1986, a number of Philippine-born writers, such as Ninotchka **Rosca**, Bino Realuyo, and Noël Alumit, have published novels in the United States set in the martial law Philippines. The novels of Realuyo and Alumit are also coming-of-age stories, and Cecilia Manguerra **Brainard**, Sophia Romero, and R. Zamora Linmark have in recent years contributed to this subgenre.

THE NOVEL IN THE COLONIAL LANGUAGES OF THE PHILIPPINES

Rizal was born in 1861 in the Philippines, and he left for Spain in 1882 to study. While there he became a leading member of the Propaganda Movement, which consisted of men from the Philippines who agitated in Barcelona and Madrid for reforms in the Philippines. The propagandists were particularly critical of the Spanish friars who held much of the secular power in the Philippines, and Rizal's two novels—*Noli Me Tangere* (*Touch Me Not*) and *El Filibusterismo* (*The Subversive*)—both depicted friar abuses and advocated for reforms in the colonial administration in the Philippines. The novels were written in Spanish and published in Europe, but they were quickly banned in the Philippines, and, when he returned to the colony, Rizal was sent into exile on the southern island of Mindanao. When the revolution began in 1896, Rizal was executed, and as a martyr he became a rallying point for the revolution.

Bulosan, before publishing *America Is in the Heart* in 1944, published an essay in 1942 on the 1940 Commonwealth Literary Contest in which he cites a Filipino literary tradition with two branches, one in Tagalog running from Francisco Balagtas (1788–1862), who is best known for the metrical romance *Florante at Laura* (*Florante and Laura*), the other in Spanish running from Rizal. Bulosan would later think of himself as being in dialogue with Rizal, and he made plans to write a panoramic work covering 100 years of Philippine history. He died before this project was completed, but a portion, edited by E. San Juan Jr. and titled *The Cry and the Dedication*, was published posthumously in 1995.

In the years immediately after **World War II**, a number of Filipinos were in the United States as students, teachers, and writers. Edith and Edilberto Tiempo studied creative writing at the University of Iowa, and they have both written several novels in addition to founding and directing the Silliman University Workshop. Santos was doing graduate work in the United States during World War II, and after the war he published a number of novels in the 1960s. Gonzalez, who had made a name for himself as a journalist and novelist before he received a college degree, attended courses in a number of universities and colleges in the United States in the 1950s. His final novel, *The Bamboo Dancers* (1959), is set primarily in the United States and is reminiscent of Ernest Hemingway's *The Sun Also Rises*, but significant differences emerge because of the Filipino protagonist's position as a writer from a colony dealing with gender and sexuality in the metropole.

Joaquin and Jose were important figures in the literary scene that extended from Dumaguete City, where the Silliman University campus is located, to Manila to campuses and cities in the United States. Joaquin, whose career as a writer owed much to the praise of Jose Garcia **Villa**, wrote stories, drama, children's books, poems, history, but only one novel, *The Woman Who Had Two Navels* (1961). The novel tells the story of a group of Filipino expatriates in Hong Kong during the Chinese Civil War of 1946–1949, whose lives range over the Philippine revolution and the U.S. and Japanese occupations. The novel lovingly depicts Manila before the city's destruction during World War II, and Joaquin translates much from Spanish-language literature into an English-language novel. Jose is best known for his Rosales Saga, five novels—*The Pretenders* (1960), *My Brother, My Executioner* (1972), *Mass* (1976), *Tree* (1977), and *Po-on* (1984)—that span four generations in a family that migrates from the Ilocos in the north of the Philippines to a town in the province of Pangasinan, just north of Manila. The saga weaves the life of a single family into a history of revolts—against the Spanish colonizers, their U.S. successors, against the power of landlords, and finally against the neocolonial oligarchy.

THE NOVEL IN THE FILIPINO AMERICAN MOVEMENT

In the 1960s and 1970s, several events in both the Philippines and the United States would shape the later course of the Filipino American novel. As a result of the **civil rights movement**, ethnic studies and Asian American studies departments provided an institutional home for Filipino and Filipino American writers. In some early articulations of Filipino American identity, such as the one in the seminal anthology *Aiiieeeee!* a sharp line was drawn between Filipinos in the United States and U.S.-born Filipinos, with only the latter included within the category "Filipino American." However, this line was weakened as the number of immigrants from the Philippines increased dramatically after the 1965 immigration reforms and after the imposition of martial law by Philippine President Ferdinand Marcos in 1972.

Martial law had a profound effect on Filipino and Filipino American novelists. Santos's novel *The Praying Man* was set to be published by Jose's Solidaridad Press, but because of the novel's criticism of corruption the publication was delayed until 1982. Santos applied for U.S. citizenship, and during his exile due to martial law he taught at Wichita State University. Joaquin accepted the National Artist Award for Literature in 1976 on the condition that a fellow writer, Jose Lacaba, was released from prison. Ty-Casper, whose novel *The Peninsulars* (1964), was the first historical novel published by a Filipino, wrote a number of novels sharply critical of the Marcos regime's human rights abuses. One of these novels, *Awaiting Trespass* (1985), loosely draws inspiration from the *Pasyon*, a long poem recited during the Catholic Holy Week that tells the story of the crucifixion of Jesus.

Both Ty-Casper and Rosca have primarily been based in the United States since the Marcos regime fell in 1986, but the two writers are notable for publishing their novels both in the United States and in the Philippines, where imported books have been prohibitively expensive. As Oscar Campomanes has noted (1992, 72), Rosca's first novel, *State of War* (1988), is divided into three parts that correspond to three descriptions that Ty-Casper offers in the epigraph for *Awaiting Trespass*: a book of hours, a book of numbers, and a book of revelations. *State of War*, however, in its temporalities, baroque descriptive passages, and comic tone, more closely resembles Joaquin's novel as it tells the story of two women and a man who attend a festival that becomes a battlefield in the civil war between the Marcos regime and the revolutionary underground. Rosca's second novel, *Twice Blessed* (1992), is a roman à clef that satirizes Ferdinand and Imelda Marcos but also provides a map of the origins and workings of elite power in the Philippines.

As the Filipino American movement continued in the 1980s and 1990s, the work of some writers began to address issues and take on themes borrowed from that movement. A novel published in 1987 by Santos, *What the Hell for You Left Your Heart in San Francisco*, raises the question of Filipino American identity by tracing an editor's search for material for a magazine for Filipinos in the United States. The narrative moves through several segments of Filipino America, from old-timers in the United States, to the new middle class, to the U.S.-born youth, to the **Asian diaspora** of Filipino writers. Brainard's *When the Rainbow Goddess Wept* (1994), which was first published in the Philippines under the title *Song of Yvonne* (1991), tells the story of a middle-class family from Cebu that goes into hiding with the Japanese invasion during World War II. The novel takes a number of cultural motifs from the Filipino American identity movement in the United States: recipes are dramatized in the act of cooking; folk tales, myths, and epics become structuring devices; and contradictions surface about the role of imperial aggression—from Spain, the United States, and Japan—in shaping the Philippines and Filipino America.

Since 1995 several texts have appeared that highlight issues concerning gender and sexuality in the form of coming-of-age novels. R. Zamora Linmark's *Rolling the R's* (1995), in its use of **Hawaiian Pidgin**, dramatizes the resistance of young Filipinos, Native Hawaiians, and people of mixed race against the linguistic, national, gender, and sexual norms of a school system and wider state that consigns them to being second-class citizens. *Always Hiding* (1998), by Romero, takes its title from a translation of the Tagalog phrase *tago ng tago*, which, abbreviated to TNT, is a commonly used name for Filipinos in the United States who are in danger of being deported. The novel evokes a number of themes common in the Filipino diaspora, large portions of which extend not just to the United States but also to other parts of Asia: family separation, exploitation by employers and immigration lawyers, de-skilling and loss of status, and the desire for migrant workers and immigrants to escape or resolve problems in the Philippines by traveling overseas. In Realuyo's *The Umbrella Country* (1999) the narrator grows up in a struggling Manila neighborhood during martial law, and the patriarchal violence of the regime is reproduced within the boy's household. Noël Alumit's *Letters to Montgomery Clift* (2002) correlates the love for the dead movie star of a Filipino boy growing up in Los Angeles, with his love for his parents who were imprisoned by the Marcos regime. **See also** Asian Diasporas.

Further Reading

Campomanes, Oscar. "Filipinos in the United States and Their Literature of Exile." *Reading the Literatures of Asian America*, eds. Shirley Geok-lin Lim and Amy Ling. Philadelphia: Temple University Press,1992. 49–78.

Garcia, Neil. *The Likhaan Book of Philippine Criticism 1992–1997*. Manila: University of the Philippines Press, 2000.

Hau, Caroline. *Necessary Fictions: Philippine Literature and the Nation 1946–1980*. Manila: Ateneo University Press, 2000.

Isaac, Allen. *American Tropics: Articulating Filipino America*. Minneapolis: University of Minnesota Press, 2006.

Pison, Ruth. *Alternative Histories: Martial Law Novels as Counter-Memory*. Manila: University of the Philippines, 2005.

SHERWIN MENDOZA

✦ FILIPINO AMERICAN POETRY

Filipino American poetry is distinct from other Asian American poetries because of its Spanish and U.S. colonial history, which has resulted in poems negotiating multiple languages and an ambivalence toward the United States and the Philippines as real and imagined homelands. Filipino American poets in the 1970s, like other writers participating in broader **Asian American political activism**, constructed a history that traced a genealogy through the pre-Hispanic Philippines, the Philippine Revolution of 1896, and the struggles of the Filipinos who worked on farms, in Alaskan canneries, and in working-class service jobs, primarily bachelors who were collectively known as the *manongs*. The figure of the *manong* is often juxtaposed with recollections of an imagined homeland that questions the desirability and possibility of assimilation to the United States and the return to the Philippines. The poetry reflects the historical realities of **racism and Asian America** and the specific invisibility of a large Filipino American community in the ethnic imaginary of U.S. multiculturalism. Many innovations result from this Filipino American context in a poetic tradition that analyzes and exploits the inheritance of English as a colonial language through English mixed with Tagalog, other Philippine languages, and the language of the street. The poetic form is most often a short lyric, which is driven by a single speaking voice (usually the poet her- or himself) directly addressing the reader. More recently, some poets have experimented with forms that subsume the poet's authorial position as the speaking voice in a serial or long poem in which collaged material and other poetic voices compete with the traditional speaking voice of the lyric poem.

Filipinos wrote poetry in English as early as 1905, and a literary scene consisting of faculty and students at the University of the Philippines (UP), English-language periodicals and newspapers, and a small but significant readership consolidated itself by the mid-1920s in Manila, the political and economic capital of the colony. From the 1920s to the early 1940s, poetry by Filipinos oscillated between the poles of a cosmopolitan aestheticism and direct engagement with the social realities of the Philippines, such as class divisions, landlessness for peasants, and the impact of U.S. colonialism.

Jose Garcia **Villa**, arguably the most influential English-language poet in Filipino literary history, grew out of the early twentieth-century Manila literary context. Villa enrolled in UP in 1925, and he was a founding member of the UP Writers' Club in 1927. However, he would be suspended from the university in 1929 for publishing an allegedly obscene poem, "Man Songs," and shortly thereafter he immigrated to the United States. Villa's primary rival in UP's poetry scene was Angela Manalang, who was the literary editor for an important student publication but who also remained somewhat aloof from the UP Writers' Club. Her early poetry at UP superficially resembled symbolist and imagist poetry in Europe and the United States, but as she matured as a poet the impact of her more immediate environment became more pronounced in her work. Loss, unrequited love, and calls from a distant lover are dominant themes in her poems from 1925 to 1930.

Villa, as a single man, was able to travel to the United States in 1929; Manalang (who changed her name to Manalang-Gloria), on the other hand, married and moved back to her parents' town in the province of Albay. In the early 1930s, while Villa was giving up the short story form, Manalang-Gloria was repudiating the romantic aestheticism of her college days, and as the 1930s progressed she, in her own way, joined the more general movement away from the Art for Art's Sake position staked out by Villa and his supporters. In 1940, as the great struggle against fascism was reaching its climax, the Philippine Commonwealth government held the largest literary contest to date in the archipelago. One of the prizes was for poetry in English, and, in a statement made shortly after the contest, the chairman of the board of judges claimed that both aesthetics and social significance guided the board's assessments. Both Villa and Manalang-Gloria submitted collections of poems, but, whereas Villa received an honorable mention, Manalang-Gloria was completely snubbed by the judges, who did not recognize the feminist significance of her work.

In the decades following **World War II**, the New Criticism, which emphasized the formal qualities of literature rather than extrinsic determinants such as the intentions of writers and their historical contexts, played a major part in the development of English-language poetry in the Philippines, and its primary exponents were Edith and Edilberto Tiempo. The Tiempos enrolled in the creative writing program at the University of Iowa in the late 1940s, and they founded the Silliman National Writers Workshop in 1962. Edith Tiempo's *Tracks of Babylon and Other Poems*, which was published in the United States in 1966, is a collection of carefully crafted poems that shows a New Critical sensibility in its deployment of irony, images, and symbols. The tendency of the poems to make their settings ambiguous—neither straightforwardly U.S. nor Philippine—would contrast sharply both with the overtly political poetry inspired by the national democratic movements in the Philippines and with the specifically Filipino American poetry that would emerge in the late 1960s around San Francisco.

On the West Coast, Kearny Street Workshop and **Asian American studies** programs institutionally supported Filipino American poetry in the late 1960s to the present. In the Manilatown neighborhood on the edge of the financial district of San Francisco, over 2,000 people protested the closure of the I-Hotel, which housed several *manongs* and Chinese American men in affordable housing. This event galvanized the demand for Asian American studies at San Francisco State College and the University of California at Berkeley through the **Third World Students Strikes**. The strikes resulted in the establishment and growth of the institutional programs that helped to canonize Carlos **Bulosan** as the literary representative of the *manong* experience in poetry and prose, while affording the support of an engaged Filipino American community for new poets such as

Al Robles, Shirley Ancheta, Jaime Jacinto, Oscar Peñaranda, and Jessica **Hagedorn.**

From the 1970s to the present, the line between Filipino American poetry and Filipino poetry in English has been complicated by the movement of established poets from the Philippines to the United States. In particular, the Asian American Writers' Workshop, which was established in New York in 1991 and has since developed connections throughout the United States, has provided a space where Philippine-trained poets such as Luis Francia and Eric Gamalinda have been able to address Asian American and Filipino American audiences and thus participate in the formation of **Filipino American literature.**

The **Filipino American anthology** became crucial to the artistic growth of Filipino American poetry. Many of the poetry-specific anthologies represent the poetic rift between a lyric tradition and a postmodern aesthetic of constructed forms that make a speaking persona of the poem or the poet difficult to locate. Students at San Francisco State published *Flips: A Filipino-American Anthology* in 1971 and reclaimed the sobriquet of "Flips" for a generation of poets staking out their poetic space as Filipino Americans. Kearny Street Workshop later published *Without Names* in 1985, substantiating the lyric tradition, which was later picked up by younger poets in the 1990s in collections such as *Returning a Borrowed Tongue* and *Flippin': Filipinos on America.* The recent anthology *Babaylan* reclaims a women-centered poetics while consistently questioning the U.S.- and Philippine-based positions of women poets. Furthermore, the theorization of poetry and the related process of making meaning in general—poetics—has resulted in the *Pinoy Poetics*, which simultaneously engages and counters the turn to poetics in the U.S. experimental poetry community, which often neglects the Filipino American poetry contributions to U.S. poetry and reflects the continuation of the dynamic between figures like Villa and Bulosan inherited by twenty-first-century Filipino American poets.

Filipino American poetry is further complicated by poets' connection to creative writing MFA programs for education and employment as poets and literary critics. Filipinos such as the Tiempos were active in creative writing programs from the beginning of the Iowa Writers Workshop. Many Filipino American poets gain artistic employment as creative writing faculty, visiting writer positions, and the poetry reading circuit organized around the MFA programs centered in the United States. Poets such as Nick **Carbó**, Vince Gotera, Luis Francia, Eric Gamalinda, Eileen **Tabios**, Eugene Gloria, Barbara Jane Reyes, Marjorie Evasco, Catalina Cariaga, and R. Zamora Linmark comprise a new generation of poets who engage and expand the Filipino American tradition while building links with the Philippines. See also Assimilation/Americanization; Colonialism and Postcolonialism; Multiculturalism and Asian America; Racism and Asian America.

Further Reading

Ancheta, Shirley, Jaime Jacinto, and Jeff Tagami, eds. *Without Names: A Collection of Poems/Bay Area Pilipino American Writers.* San Francisco, CA: Kearny Street Workshop, 1985.

Carbó, Nick, ed. *Pinoy Poetics: A Collection of Autobiographical and Critical Essays on Filipino and Filipino-American Poetics.* San Francisco and St. Helena, CA: Mertiage Press, 2004.

Carbó, Nick, and Eileen Tabios, eds. *Babaylan: An Anthology of Filipina and Filipina American Writers.* San Francisco: Aunt Lute Books, 2000.

Francia, Luis H. and Eric Gamalinda, eds. *Flippin': Filipinos on America.* New York: Asian American Writers' Workshop, 1996.

J. GUEVARA AND SHERWIN MENDOZA

✦ FILIPINO AMERICAN SHORT STORY

Leopoldo Yabes, a major anthologist and critic of the Filipino short story, claimed in the early 1940s that the short story was the most developed of English-language literary forms in the Philippines. In the period from the 1920s up to **World War II**, while the Philippines was still a U.S. colony, short stories and poems in English could more readily find outlets for publication than novels, since many magazines in the colony published short fiction. One of the most noted short story writers during this early period, Paz Marquez Benitez, was also important as a teacher and supporter of English-language literature at the University of the Philippines. After World War II the short story as an artistic form would receive renewed attention as writers who had received training in the United States returned to teach creative writing in the newly independent country. In the late 1960s and early 1970s, short story writers of Filipino descent such as Oscar Peñaranda, Luis Syquia, and Sam Tagatac participated in more general **Asian American political activism**, and these writers would be influential in creating a Filipino American identity. The **Filipino American anthology** has become an important vehicle not only for short stories but also for defining **Filipino American literature** in general. Since the 1990s several anthologies have collected works set in both the Philippines and the United States, and contributors to these anthologies have been based in the Philippines, in the United States, or in both.

THE PHILIPPINE SHORT STORY IN ENGLISH

The two most celebrated stories from the U.S. colonial period are Benitez's "Dead Stars" and Manuel Arguilla's "How My Brother Leon Brought Home a Wife." "Dead Stars" was first published in 1925, and it tells the story of a couple whose long engagement is jeopardized when the fiancé meets the visiting daughter of his neighbor. However, whereas Benitez's story centers on middle-class characters with strong ties to the U.S. colonial administration, "How My Brother Leon Brought Home a Wife," the title story of the collection that won the first prize for short story in English in the Commonwealth Literary Contest of 1940, focuses instead on the impact of urbanization on a rural family. The story is told from the point of view of a boy in the countryside, and it dramatizes the events leading up to the encounter between his father and a brother who had gone to the city and married without his father's blessing.

In the two decades following World War II, the literary scene in English in the Philippines was dominated by New Criticism, which for the short story meant a close attention to the craft of forming narratives from the materials of words, images, and symbols. Edith and Edilberto Tiempo, who were both fiction writers, were the primary exponents of New Criticism, but perhaps the most admired writer in the Philippines at this time was Nick Joaquin. Joaquin's stories are consistently preoccupied with gender relationships and antagonisms, and the plots often turn on the travails of a Hispanized elite attempting to ward off both precolonial cultures and U.S. colonialism.

FILIPINO WRITERS IN THE UNITED STATES

Joaquin's career as a writer took off after he was noticed by Jose Garcia **Villa**, an important poet based primarily in New York who was nevertheless a major tastemaker in Manila from the 1930s until his death in 1997. Villa was best known as a poet, but, shortly after he moved to New York, he published his first—and last—collection of short stories in 1933. During this time Carlos **Bulosan** was working as a migrant laborer on the West Coast of the United States, and, in the first half of the 1940s, he began to publish stories that would be collected in *The Laughter of My Father* (1944). The collection, which drew from folk tales from around the world that were reworked to present a satirical image of the semifeudal order in the rural Philippines, was a best seller in the United States, and it was translated into several languages.

Bulosan is best known for his novel *America Is in the Heart*, which centered on the struggles of the *manongs*, young men who had migrated during the 1920s and 1930s to the United States and worked in agricultural fields, canneries, and in low-wage service jobs in the Pacific coastal states. After Bulosan's death in 1956, Bien-venido **Santos** would also write about the *manongs*, many of whom participated in the struggle to establish the United Farm Workers from 1965 to 1970, but who would be retired or nearing retirement as Santos wrote. Although Santos was not himself a manual laborer, his stories are notable for the sensitivity with which he depicts his characters' sense of loss and displacement as they attempt to make lives for themselves in the United States after World War II. On the other hand, Santos's friend N.V.M. **Gonzalez** wrote his stories of Filipinos in the Philippines. Like Bulosan, Gonzalez drew on memories of rural provinces in the Philippines for much of his material. He is best known for his accounts of people on the island of Mindoro, from swidden farmers to sailors to the middle class of clerks and teachers.

When Ferdinand Marcos declared martial law in 1972, both Santos and Gonzalez were abroad, and they would spend much of the period of the Marcos dictatorship teaching in the United States. Ninotchka **Rosca**, on the other hand, was among the writers and journalists detained as part of the general clampdown on critics of the regime. After her release Rosca fled to the United States, and her *Monsoon Collection* (1983), which was first published in Australia, alternates between stories set in the Philippines and scenes of imprisonment and torture under the Marcos regime. The stories are highly sensitive to gender and power, and these topics would inform Rosca's work as a member of the Gabriela Network, an organization that aims to build solidarity between women in the United States and the Philippines.

THE FILIPINO AMERICAN SHORT STORY AND FILIPINO AMERICAN IDENTITY

Santos, Gonzalez, and Rosca were beneficiaries of both Asian American political activism and the subsequent rise of **Asian American studies**, which provided publication opportunities, institutional recognition, and audiences that would not have been available to earlier writers. An important center for specifically Filipino American activism and literature was the San Francisco Bay Area, which was the base for the group of writers who produced the *Flips* anthology of poetry in 1971. Three writers from this scene—Peñaranda, Syquia, and Tagatac—would contribute to the watershed *Aiiieeeee!* anthology of 1974. Tagatac's contribution, "The New Anak," is a story that reads like film reels spliced together and projected, with images ranging from the International Hotel to mountains in the Philippines to a montage of U.S. military ventures in Asia. The contributors to *Aiiieeeee!* and several of the *Flips* writers would also contribute to *Liwanag* (1975), a publication that, like Tagatac's story, attempted to combine literary and visual art within a single text.

Peñaranda, Syquia, and Tagatac's preface to *Aiiieeeee!* like the preface on Japanese and **Chinese American literature**, insisted on a difference between writers from Asia and those born in the United States—the former would be Chinese, Japanese, or Filipino whereas the latter would be Chinese American, Japanese American, or Filipino American. However, by the 1990s the line between Filipino American and Filipino literature was difficult to find. Both Peñaranda and Tagatac contributed stories to a collection, *Fiction by Filipinos in America*, that was published in Metro Manila in 1993. "The Visitor," Peñaranda's story, was first published as "Musings" in *Liwanag* and depicts a laborer in Alaska whose Native American lover had married and had a child in his absence. Tagatac's story, "Small Talk at Union Square," tells of an encounter between a young middle-class Filipino American and a Filipino old-timer who, ironically, seems to have more in common with the Navajo man who got him a job in construction in San Francisco.

Cecilia Manguerra **Brainard**, the editor of *Fiction by Filipinos in America*, has been an important figure in linking Filipino and Filipino American literature. While *Fiction by Filipinos in America* brought a wide variety of stories, in particular about the *manongs*, to the Philippines, a collection that she edited and published in 2003, *Growing Up Filipino*, brought stories by writers based in the Philippines to the United States. In general, the **Filipino American anthology** has been an important medium for bridging the gap between Filipino American literature and Philippine literature in English, and currently writers, audiences, and the institutional and publishing infrastructure for these literatures are becoming more transnational and more tightly linked. **See also** Asian American Political Activism; Colonialism and Postcolonialism.

Further Reading

Abad, Gemino, ed. *Likhaan Anthology of Philippine Literature in English*. Manila: University of the Philippines Press, 1998.

Gamalinda, Eric, and Alfred Yuson, eds. *Century of Dreams*. Honolulu: University of Hawaii Press, 1997.

Villanueva, Marianne, and Virginia Cerenio, eds. *Going Home to a Landscape: Writing by Filipinas*. St. Paul, MN: Calyx, 2003.

Yabes, Leopoldo, ed. *Philippine Short Stories 1925–1940*. Manila: University of the Philippines Press, 1997.

———, ed. *Philippine Short Stories 1941–1955*. Manila: University of the Philippines Press, 1981.

SHERWIN MENDOZA

✦ FU MANCHU

Fu Manchu is a stereotype of Chinese created in 1913 by Sax Rohmer (1883–1959), a British writer. It is consistent with **Yellow Peril**, denoting a masculine threat of military and sexual conquest. This image's negative influence was far-reaching and pushed forward the anti-Chinese movement in the United States at the beginning of the twentieth century.

The creation of the stereotype is coincidental. One night in an alley in London's **Chinatown**, Rohmer happened to see a mysterious Chinese man and thought that he was kingpin of a dope-smuggling coven. This experience inspired Rohmer's two short stories and 13 novels from 1913 to 1959 about "the diabolic, torture-loving, gloriously mad Fu Manchu" (Mank 1994, 61), including *The Insidious Dr. Fu Manchu, The*

Mystery of Dr. Fu Manchu, The Mysterious Dr. Fu Manchu, The Mask of Fu Manchu, and *Emperor Fu Manchu*.

The reason that this stereotype is so influential is that it echoes the then Yellow Peril and the anti-Chinese movement. Chinese began to immigrate on a large scale to the United States at the news of the gold rush. Although they proved efficient and hardworking and played a major role in California's statehood celebration in 1850, by the 1880s they were so strongly hated that the U.S. government passed laws to keep them out of the country. They became "strangers in America" and were considered a "population born in China, reared in China, expecting to return to China, living while here in a little China of its own, and without the slightest attachment to the country—utter heathens, treacherous, sensual, cowardly and cruel" (Takaki 1989, 109). The slogan—"The Chinese must go"—reflects the white worker's anxiety and hatred. After contributing to their adopted country, the Chinese laborers "had no more right to be in California than 'flocks of blackbirds have in a wheat field'" (50–51). The *New York Times* warned the whites of the heathenish dangers: "If there were to be a flood-tide of Chinese population—a population befouled with all the social vices, with no knowledge or appreciation of free institution or constitutional liberty, with heathenish souls and heathenish propensities . . . we should be prepared to bid farewell to republicanism" (100–101).

Yellow Peril, as the Chinese were called by the whites in the late nineteenth century, indicated the whites' anxiety. The white workers attributed their unemployment and low salary to the Chinese laborers' competition. They complained, for example, if there had not been Chinese labor forces for the **transcontinental railroad**, the companies would have been compelled to hire white workers with a high and satisfactory pay. When economic depression came, the Chinese laborers were set in the foreground as a target. According to Gary Y. Okihiro, the Yellow Peril perhaps originated from Charles H. Pearson, an English historian, who said in his *National Life and Character* (1893) that the whites' desire for tropical products and colonizing these areas brought technology and medicines that strengthened the nonwhites and introduced them to white science and industry. As a result, the nonwhites might become powerful enough to be the rivals of the whites (Okihiro 1994, 130–131).

The first time Fu Manchu shows up in Rohmer's first novel, *The Insidious Dr. Fu Manchu* (1913), he drew the attention of the mainstream readers: "Imagine a person, tall, lean and feline, high-shouldered, with a brow like Shakespeare and a face like Satan, a close-shaven skull, and long, magnetic eyes of true cat-green. Invest him with all the cruel cunning of an entire Eastern race, accumulated in one giant intellect. . . . Imagine that awful being, and you have a mental picture of Dr. Fu Manchu, the yellow peril incarnate in one man" (Mank 1994, 61).

The Eastern intellect not only speaks fluent English but also is physically and intelligently strong. Furthermore, he knows very well how to combine the

Eastern/Chinese knowledge with the Western to control and rule the whites. His favorite statement indicates the source of his strength. "I'm a doctor of philosophy from Edinborough. I'm a doctor of Law from Christ's College. I'm a doctor of medicine from Harvard. My friends, out of courtesy, call me Doctor" (Mank 1994, 68). Such a deeply learned man poses a big threat because he vows the destruction of the whites. He competes incessantly with his stiff-upper-lip adversaries Sir Dennis Nayland Smith of Scotland Yard and Dr. Petrie, the narrator of the tales. It is a battle of wits, supernatural forces, and science. Fu Manchu is the first Asian leader in Anglo American literature, and he is an imminent presence in the Chinatown of Britain and America. This spooky crook and bad guy is always associated with murder and the darkness of night. The mainstream helps teach him something about technology. In return, Fu Manchu poses a peril because he is masculine, although his masculinity is tempered by femininity. He challenges and then threatens Western supremacy. He sometimes tortures the whites madly in incredible ways, and sometimes tries to extricate information he needs, even at the cost of his own daughter's virtue. But no matter how cruel and smart he is, victory goes to Sir Dennis Smith at the end of every story. That is to say, Fu symbolizes the cruel, dark, and evil, whereas Sir Nayland is the angel of justice. Worth mentioning is the fact that Fu Manchu dies at the end of two stories, and his creator had to bring him back to life to continue his series.

The wide spread of the stereotypical image of Fu Manchu results from the involvement of movie companies such as MGM and Paramount. MGM decided to make the tale into movies, and in 1932 Metro borrowed Boris Karloff, Frankenstein's monster, from Universal City to act as the Eastern monster in *The Mask of Fu Manchu*. It goes that Fu Manchu tries to find out the location of Genghis Khan's tomb to claim the tyrant's golden mask and scimitar so that he can declare himself Genghis Khan come to life again and lead millions of men to sweep the world, while Sir Lionel and Sir Nayland spearhead archaeologists to thwart the mad man's ambition.

The tales of Fu Manchu are really Orientalistic and exotic—the East is cruel, evil, ambitious, and sexy, in sharp contrast to the West's cooperation, bravery, and strength. Fu wants to be another Genghis Khan to lead Asians to sweep the world, to "Conquer and breed! Kill the white man, and take his women" (Mank 1994, 80). This image was projected in the advertisement for the premiere of *The Mask of Fu Manchu* in New York City in 1932. "Mad, Oriental tortures! Crazed, heartless desires! This oriental monster almost wrecked civilization with his love-drug" (82). Such an image, of course, ignites the whites' horror and hatred and provokes antagonism between the West and the East. But the success of this movie makes it one of the two horror films by MGM in 1932. Other movie companies follow suit, and the "kids would wet their beds after seeing it" movies did not slow down until World War II, when the Chinese government mounted a strong protest. **See also** Asian American Stereotypes.

Further Reading

Mank, Gregory William. *Hollywood Cauldron: Thirteen Horror Films from the Genre's Golden Age.* Jefferson: McFarland & Company, Inc., Publishers, 1994.

Okihiro, Gary Y. *Margins and Mainstreams: Asians in American History and Culture.* Seattle: University of Washington Press, 1994.

Takaki, Ronald. *Strangers from a Different Shore: A History of Asian Americans.* New York: Penguin Books, 1989.

LONGHAI ZHANG

G

✦

✦ GANESAN, INDIRA (1960–)

Indira Ganesan is an Indian American novelist, essayist, short story writer, reviewer, editor, interpreter of Indian culture, feminist, and professor of English. Ganesan teaches writing and literature courses at Southampton College of Long Island University, New York, and Lesley University and serves as the fiction editor of *Many Mountains Moving: A Literary Journal of Diverse Contemporary Voices*.

Born on November 5, 1960, in Srirangam in Tamil Nadu, India, Ganesan came to the United States with her parents at the age of five. The Ganesan family settled in Rockland County, New York. After high school, Ganesan attended Vassar College, graduating with a major in English in 1982, and then she graduated with an MFA in 1984 from the University of Iowa. She has written two novels, *The Journey* (1990) and *Inheritance* (1998). She is working on a third novel titled *Finding Her Way Home*. Her other writings have appeared in *Newsday, Antaeus, Glamour, Seventeen,* the *Mississippi Review,* the *Women's Review of Books,* and the anthology *Half and Half: Writing on Growing Up Biracial & Bicultural*. Ganesan excels in her appeal to the reader' senses, as she describes the sights, sounds, smells, and tastes of India, pleasant and unpleasant, giving a flavor of real India. In *The Journey* she describes Indian customs, such as the thirteenth-day feast to celebrate "the soul's passage from life to life" (27) and pilgrimage to the Trivandur's Temple of 500 steps (37), and in *Inheritance* the Hindu tradition of showing a girl to a prospective match and his family and worship at the temple (46–54, 128–29). The protagonists in both her novels are young women who desire fulfilling lives. Like Stephen Dedalus of James Joyce's *A Portrait of the Artist as a Young Man,* Renu and Sonil, the respective protagonists of *The Journey* and *Inheritance*, come to realize that they must create their own individualities.

In *The Journey*, 19-year-old Renu Krishnan returns from the United States with her mother and younger sister Manx to Pi, an imaginary island in the Bay of Bengal that serves as the setting for both of Ganesan's novels, to grieve for her "twin" cousin Rajesh, who died in an Indian train accident. Being a creature of two cultures, Renu, who was born in Pi but raised in Long Island, fears that her own death is imminent: "The women of her mother's village say that if one twin dies by water, the other will die by fire" (3). She often dreams of three giantesses who threaten her with dire consequences if she renounces her "inherited weights." She fears that if she returns to the American way of life, she will face the fury of the gods.

The novel brings out the prejudices of westerners against Indians and of Indians against westerners, as well as the irrational partiality of each for the other's culture. When Renu's uncle Adda Krishnamurthi seeks the permission of Alvirez, the father of the European Alphonsa, Alvirez refuses: "No citizen would rest knowing a brown man sweeps a white woman into his arms at night" (65). And when Adda brings his European wife to his parents' home in India, she receives a cold reception. The look that Adda's mother gave her made Alphonsa lose her voice, and "for the rest of her life [she] would speak to no one save her husband and his best friend, Amir" (66). Ultimately, Alphonsa is driven to enter a convent, where she kills herself. On the other hand, Freddie Flat, an American hippie, loves all things Indian: "[H]e adopted Eastern ways, gave up meat for a while, exchanged his mother's blue-eyed Madonna for a goddess sitting on an open, perfumed lotus" (93–94). And, Manx, Renu's 15-year-old sister, treasures all things American, resulting in an affair with Freddie, who is twice her age.

Ganesan repudiates the Indian system of arranged marriages as the main cause of failed marriages. The narrator observes that "most of the women [in Renu's family] tended to marry with their eyes shut," and "disappointments were not uncommon" (46) even though matchmakers tried to match horoscopes.

The novel also criticizes a society that does not sanction widows' remarriage but cannot tolerate an unattached woman. Renu journeys to the interior of Pi to a place called Trippi, where she meets Marya the seer, who offers the possibility of self-creation. Marya confides in Renu why she became Marya the seer. She explains that she could have died of neglect after she left her husband because of his infidelity. Although people have differing opinions of her choice, she "chose [her] light" (127). She asks Renu why she is "stuck with the memory of the dead, this necrophilia." When Renu answers that "Rajesh is my twin," she exclaims, "But he doesn't exist as he was, only as you have created him." The seer advises Renu that "each one of us can be our own light. You can even be the Light of the World" (126). The novel ends triumphantly, as Renu gets ready to return to the States "away from her superstitions and fears, away from her self-wrought sickness," "stepping away from her inherited weights" (173–74).

In Ganesan's second novel *The Inheritance,* the 15-year-old Sonil comes from mainland India to stay with her grandmother on Pi to recover from chronic bronchitis. Sonil, who has been brought up by her aunts in India, is eager to learn about her aloof mother Lakshmi, who lives on Pi, and her father, who departed India before she was born and who she later discovers is white. A *bildungsroman*, the novel describes Sonil's experiences of love, rejection, and loss and her eventual self-realization and liberation.

The strength of *Inheritance* lies in its strong female characters that include Sonil's mother, her aunts, who run their joint household without their husbands who work abroad, her beloved grandmother, and Sonil herself. The only man in the house is her opium addict great uncle, a "wraith-like man" (41) whose goings and comings are imperceptible. Sonil does not seem to mind the absence of a male presence: "We were a family of women . . . I didn't think we needed men. My aunts largely managed without them and prospered. In fact, I think, without men we were stronger" (43).

When Sonil's cousin Jani leaves their grandmother's house to enter a convent, Sonil finds companionship in Richard, a 30-year-old American who is seeking spiritual enlightenment in India. They begin an intense affair, described in sensuous language. Kissing and being kissed by Richard gives her a dizzy sensation and makes her feel as if she were "transported in another world" (91). Sonil says of Richard: "He was everything that no one in my family was; it was everything I wanted to be" (146). When Richard abruptly ends the relationship, Sonil begins to understand and to forgive her mother's neglect of her. Having once compared her mother to "the bird which abandoned her young in other birds' nests" (117), Sonil now realizes that her mother had perhaps herself been abandoned by Sonil's American father. When her mother's second lover, Ashoka Ram, visits on the death of Sonil's grandmother, her mother reveals her past to Sonil. She refuses to marry Ashoka.

Sonil's cousin Jani also refuses to marry the man her family has chosen for her. Jani escapes the marriage by entering a convent. When Sonil visits her at the convent, she learns why Jani will not marry C.P. Iyengar: "Loving Asha, she couldn't love C.P." (156). Sonil herself feels the urge "to kiss Jani, pull her toward me, make her leave the convent. Who needed boys anyway?" (156–157). The novel ends with Sonil realizing the true meaning of her inheritances: "My family is ingrained in my actions. . . . Yet there are parts of me that are nothing like them. . . . I do not have to be like my mother. . . . Yet a shard of her exists in everything I do" (192). She is now set on a course to determine her own identity.

Further Reading

Curtis, Sarah. Rev. of *Inheritance*. *The Times Literary Supplement* 18 July 1997: 22.

Dery, Mark. Rev. of *The Journey*. *New York Times Book Review* 9 Sep. 1990: 26.

Ganesan, Indira. *The Inheritance*. New York: Alfred A. Knopf, 1998.

————. *The Journey*. New York: Alfred A. Knopf, 1990.

Hower, Edward. "Spice Island"—Rev. of *Inheritance*. *The New York Times Book Review* 29 Mar. 1998: 16.

HARISH CHANDER

✦ GAWANDE, ATUL (1965–)

Atul Gawande is an Indian American surgeon, science writer, and professor at Harvard Medical School and Harvard School of Public Health. Born in Brooklyn, New York, to immigrant parents, Gawande was raised in rural Athens, Ohio. The son of a urologist father and pediatrician mother, he attended Stanford University where he received a BSA in 1987. He then completed a master's degree at Oxford University as a Rhodes Scholar (1989) before earning an MD (1995) and an MPH (1999), both from Harvard University. A physician actively engaged in both research and writing, Gawande has been recognized for his ability to combine an interdisciplinary perspective with the more accessible voice of a popular science writer. His appeal is comparable to that of Stephen Jay Gould or Oliver Sacks. His capacities as a teacher and critical observer are inextricable from the responsibilities and privileges of his role as a public intellectual and innovator in the field of medical science.

Written in the autobiographical mode, Gawande's earliest publication appeared in the online magazine *Slate,* where he chronicled five adrenalin-soaked days as a surgery resident. This foray into writing led to a more sustained study of his experiences as a physician-in-training. He reached a wider readership in 2002 when he published *Complications: A Surgeon's Notes on an Imperfect Science*. It was a National Book Award finalist for nonfiction and a *New York Times* Notable Book. Translated into 17 languages and published in more than 100 countries, *Complications* received other honors as well: it was named an American Library Association Notable Book, a *Boston Globe* Best Book, a *Discover* magazine Best Science Book, and a finalist for the L.L. Winship/ PEN New England Award.

The text, a collection of essays, is divided under three section headings: fallibility, mystery, and uncertainty. Through detailed analyses of actual cases (among them, morbid obesity, chronic pain, and necrotizing fasciitis, or flesh-eating disease), Gawande explains how all three concepts are interpretive lenses through which the American medical system and the practice of doctoring may be viewed. He highlights the prevalence of error in medical care as a function of collective as well as individual failings; he also illustrates the ways in which diagnoses often fall short of the desired results because certain medical phenomena are just outside of the range of typical understanding. Gawande's approach does not so much undermine or apologize for the medical profession's weaknesses as claim a space for change, flux, and, ultimately, informed evaluation and improvement. Overall, his writing is characterized by an anecdotal, self-referential style interlaced with qualitative and quantitative observations about his professional milieu. By using a subjective "I," he positions himself explicitly in an active knowledge-making community but also recognizes his limitations as a scholar-practitioner. His target audiences are not only physicians or affiliates in the health-care field but also readers interested in the moral, legal, ethical, and philosophical dilemmas that ensnare the medical profession.

Gawande's work acknowledges that because patient care is essentially a series of diverse interactions within structured institutions, it is profoundly risky and unpredictable. He thus situates his writing in the interrogatory space between authority and expertise on the one hand and uncertainty and experimentation on the other. As suggested by the honesty of his book's title, Gawande values a physician's ability to analyze and improve the status quo. His concern has translated into practical improvements in surgery protocol, especially in conjunction with the Center for Surgery and Public Health at Brigham and Women's Hospital where he has served as assistant director since 2004. He has been involved with devising a bar code system to prevent surgeons from inadvertently leaving instruments or other operating room paraphernalia in patients, as well as a 10-point scale that gauges the likelihood of postsurgical complications. Evaluating and improving surgical performance, implementing better safety measures, and alleviating errors are among his top concerns as an academic.

Whether he discusses the high costs of medical malpractice, the efficacy of publicly rating physician care, or the frustrations experienced by medical trainees and patients alike, the breadth of topics that Gawande tackles reveals a comprehensive investment in the human drama of illness and recovery. Since 1998, he has served as a staff writer of the *New Yorker* and contributed to the *New England Journal of Medicine*'s "Notes of a Surgeon" column. His work has appeared in *The Best American Essays 2002* and *The Best American Science Writing 2002*. He has composed or collaborated on articles for such peer-reviewed journals as *American Journal of Surgery, Annals of Internal Medicine, Surgery, Health Affairs,* and the *New England Journal of Medicine*.

Since 2003, Gawande has multitasked as an assistant professor of surgery at his alma mater, Harvard Medical School, and as a general and endocrine surgeon at Brigham and Women's Hospital in Boston. In 2004, he joined the faculty of Harvard School of Public Health as an assistant professor in the Department of Health Policy and Management. Recognition for his writing and research initiatives has been steady;

the American Association for the Advancement of Science awarded his 2004 *New Yorker* article "The Bell Curve" its annual Science Journalism Award. In it, Gawande examines relative levels of care offered to patients suffering from cystic fibrosis, a genetic disease that compromises lung function and eventually proves fatal. Intermingling personal narrative, institutional analysis, and case study-type examples, he writes from the point of view of an investigative journalist. He examines the multiple dimensions of the patient-caregiver relationship and determines the ways in which qualifiers like "poor," "average," and "best" in terms of treatment (and when applied to doctors) rely on a number of factors beyond technical expertise or reputation. In 2006 Gawande received a "genius grant" from the John D. and Catherine T. MacArthur Foundation as part of the organization's annual Fellows Program. The $500,000 award acknowledges the demonstrated merits, intellectual potential, and innovative thinking of a number of American leaders in various disciplines. Improving global health-care remains among Gawande's ongoing research goals.

Further Reading

Gawande, Atul. "Harvard Medical School Commencement Address, 2005." Speech presented at the Harvard Medical School and Harvard School of Dental Medicine Commencement, Cambridge, MA, June 2005.

Exum, Kaitlen, J. "Atul Gawande, Surgeon and Medical Writer." *Current Biography* 66.3 (2005): 37–40.

Feinstein, Karen Wolk. "An Error by Any Other Name." *Health Affairs* 21.6 (2002): 264–265.

McLellan, Faith. "Lunch with the *Lancet:* Atul Gawande." *The Lancet* 361.9352 (11 Jan. 2003): 188.

"Under the Microscope': Interview with Atul Gawande." *The Atlantic Monthly* June 2002. *The Atlantic Monthly* Web site. http://www.theatlantic.com/doc/prem/200205u/int2002-05-01.

NANCY KANG

◆ GAY MALE LITERATURE

Gay male Asian American literature may be defined as literature produced by Asian American authors that represents male homosexuality, homoeroticism, and/or other modes of nonnormative sexuality and desire. (For information on lesbian or queer female Asian American literature, see **Lesbian Literature**.) Since the majority of texts that contain identifiably gay or queer male characters have been published since the 1980s and since the scholarly field of queer **Asian American studies** has emerged even more recently, each of the terms in *gay Asian American literature* is open to debate. Here, *gay* designates male characters or speakers who either self-identify with that label or whose predominant mode of sexual attraction is directed toward other males.

Asian American includes both U.S. and Canadian writers of Asian descent (regardless of where the literary work itself is set), whereas *literature* mainly refers to novels, short stories, personal essays, plays, and poems. These delimitations leave aside "gay" literature written by Asian authors in locations other than North America and works originally published in Asian languages and translated into English. Nonetheless, even within these boundaries, there has been an extraordinary proliferation of gay Asian American literature during the past 20 years or so whose thematic concerns and literary styles are as diverse and variegated as the larger field of Asian American literature itself.

This body of work acquires much of its significance when read within the context of the history of Asian immigration and racialization in North America. Many scholars have noted how the legal, economic, and cultural means by which peoples from Asia were ascribed "racial" characteristics from the nineteenth into the twentieth centuries simultaneously attributed gendered and sexualized traits onto the immigrants and their descendants. Although these processes of ascription were by no means uniform (being differentiated, for example, according to specific Asian ethnicities), they generally resulted in stereotypes that continue to persist into the present. With regard to the gender and sexuality of males of Asian descent, those stereotypes have typically revolved around images of effeminacy and emasculation, passivity or asceticism. Scholars such as Richard Fung, David Eng, and Nguyen Tan Hoang, among others, have analyzed the ways in which these stereotypes are referenced and reinforced in various forms of cultural expression, especially film and literature.

The most infamous response to this coalescing of the feminized or asexual Asian male was voiced in the introductions to the Asian American literary anthology *Aiiieeeee!* (1974). In the preface and in the essay "An Introduction to Chinese- and Japanese-American Literature," the editors criticized racist portrayals of male Asians as effeminate and homosexual and consequently called for a remaking of Asian American manhood, particularly through the reinvigoration of language. Although feminist critics have challenged the masculinism intrinsic to this cultural nationalist position, it is only recently that queer Asian American studies scholarship has begun to acknowledge how these conditions have placed gay Asian American literature in an acutely fraught position. In addition to the homophobia and racism that permeates North American culture, gay Asian American literature must also contend with masculinist and homophobic impulses within Asian American communities and families, as well as with racialized vectors of desire and disgust within largely white gay social arenas. It is within the context of these broad historical and cultural forces that the politics of gay Asian American literature acquires its most resonant critical edge.

This complex history, coupled with the perceived lack of images of Asian men as attractive and desirable in mainstream popular culture, has rendered the politics of representation—and its corollary, the politics of interracial (predominantly Asian-white) desire—important and pervasive themes. Andy Quan's title story in his fiction collection *Calendar Boy* (2001), for example, satirizes the protagonist's attempts to recreate the Asian male image according to the same standards of physical beauty that permeate Western culture, even as it recognizes the motivation to do so. Another story in *Calendar Boy,* "What I Really Hate," humorously plays up the rice queen/potato queen dynamic (white men who pursue Asian men/Asian men who pursue white men) operating at gay clubs. Its devastating irony notwithstanding, Quan's story reveals the complicated positioning of Asian men within these highly wrought spaces of desire by showing how the Chinese Canadian narrator is both repelled by and craves the rice queen's regard, while simultaneously distancing himself from what he deems the naive and embarrassing behavior of gay Chinese immigrants.

Perhaps the most notorious treatment of this queer interracial dynamic resides in David Henry **Hwang's** Tony Award-winning *M. Butterfly* (1988), a play set during the **Vietnam War** era in which the French diplomat Rene Gallimard engages in a 20-year-long affair with the Chinese communist spy Song Liling, presumably under the delusion that Song is a woman. Troping on Western Orientalist fantasies of the East and redeploying the myth of the submissive self-sacrificing Japanese woman's abiding love for the arrogant American soldier Pinkerton in Puccini's opera *Madama Butterfly* (1904), Hwang reverses the gender roles at the end of the play, with Song revealing himself as a man and Gallimard donning the kimono before committing ritual suicide. In doing so, *M. Butterfly* deconstructs the gendered, sexualized, and racialized means by which the East and the West are culturally and politically represented.

As *M. Butterfly* demonstrates, interracial power relations are especially politically charged in texts set in imperial or neocolonial contexts. Jessica **Hagedorn's** acclaimed *Dogeaters* (1990), for instance, features as one of its first-person narrators the queer hustler/DJ Joey Sands, whose pedigree as the son of a Filipina prostitute and an African American GI references one of the "byproducts" of decades of U.S. military presence in the Philippines. The sexualization of neocolonialism is further illustrated in Joey's backstory relationship with the American GI Neil Sekada, as well as in his hookup with the German art film director Rainer. In the course of their week-long liaison, Rainer asks his "informant" about the legendary shower boys who lather themselves with soap on stage for the pleasure of the mostly Western tourists and GIs, showing again the exploitation of racialized bodies and the commodification of colonial desire. Monique **Truong's** exquisite *The Book of Salt* (2004) also underscores the hierarchies of power that inhere in interracial, colonial relationships. Drifting back and forth between the narrator Binh's past in Vietnam and his present during the interwar period in Paris as Gertrude Stein and Alice B. Toklas's live-in cook, the novel describes how Binh is first ejected from Saigon when his clandestine affair with the

French Chef Bleriot is exposed and then is abandoned by the racially mixed American expatriate Lattimore, who uses Binh to pilfer Stein's notebooks. As if patriotically responding to this sexualized layering of French and U.S. imperial interventions in Vietnam, at the end of the novel Truong has Binh seek out Nguyen Ai Quoc, his fellow countryman with whom he spent one night in Paris two years prior, and who would later be known in the annals of history as Ho Chi Minh.

The conflicted father-son relationship in *The Book of Salt*—Binh's father condemns his son's homosexuality even from beyond the grave—is also central to Bino Realuyo's *The Umbrella Country* (1999). Set in Manila during the martial law period of Marcos's rule, the novel delineates the emergent gay sexualities of Gringo, the reticent 11-year-old narrator, and his older brother Pipo, whose proclivities for transgender activities (he is the three-time winner of the neighborhood children's "Miss Unibers" contest) earn him his father's wrath in the form of physical beatings. Despite Daddy Groovie's imperious lectures on how to be a "man" and his drunken violence, the two boys manage to express their understated desires—Pipo through a painful encounter with the *bakla* Boy Manicure and through sexual explorations with a circle of neighborhood boys, and Gringo through his affectionate friendship with the newspaper seller Boy Spit. Like *The Umbrella Country*, R. Zamora Linmark's *Rolling the R's* (1995) takes up issues of transgender play and father-son struggle, mixing humor and cutting irony in its nonlinear, multigeneric portrayals of the fifth graders of Kalihi, Hawaii. In contrast to Edgar Ramirez's unapologetic gender-bending homosexuality, for example, the less gay-assertive Vicente de los Reyes is severely reprimanded by his father when he plucks up the courage to sing Donna Summer's "Enough Is Enough" on the youth's makeshift stage. *Funny Boy* (1994) by Shyam **Selvadurai** provides another example of these intertwined themes of gender nonconformity, emergent homoeroticism, and displacement. Similar to *The Umbrella Country*'s merging of the personal and sexual with the public and political, *Funny Boy* charts Arjie's cross-gender identifications and sexual awakening against the backdrop of the 1970s Sri Lankan conflict between Sinhalese and Tamils, closing with the family's forced exile to Canada.

Whereas patriarchal authority in these texts frequently asserts itself over and against the son's nascent homosexuality, intergenerational relationships between nonfamilial males assume an array of meanings. In addition to the texts above, several personal essays gathered in Justin Chin's *Burden of Ashes* (2001)—such as "The Beginning of My Worthlessness," "The Swedish Psychologist," and "The French Ambassador," set during the author's youth in Singapore—display cross-age and cross-race sexual encounters. Whereas Chin largely represents his younger self as an actively desiring subject, Alexander Chee explores the difficult terrain of child sexual abuse and its aftermath in his novel *Edinburgh* (2001). In highly allusive and introspective prose, *Edinburgh* traces how the Korean American protagonist Fee deals, on the one hand, with the love and loss of his childhood friend Peter, and on the other, with the molestation of himself and 11 other choirboys by the director Big Eric. Although the novel is cognizant of the politics of interracial desire, its primary focus lies in disentangling gay male love between adults from pederastic exploitation.

These coming-of-age portraits of sexually emergent gay youth constitute part of the larger field of "coming out" narratives. Noël Alumit's *Letters to Montgomery Clift* (2001) embeds these elements within the trajectory of the immigrant narrative. The novel tracks the experiences of the Filipino narrator Bong, who is dispatched to California following the capture and torture of his parents during the Marcos regime, finds comfort in composing letters to and seeing visions of the dead closeted movie star Montgomery Clift, learns of his father's brutal torture and execution, slowly recovers from his practice of self-mutilation, forms a relationship with the Japanese American screenwriter Logan, and finally reunites with his mother in the Philippines. Joel Barraquiel Tan's poignant and hilarious essay "San Prancisco" (anthologized in *Growing Up Filipino,* 2003) also pays respect to the mother-son relationship, starkly contrasting his mother's no-nonsense compassion with his estranged father's denunciation of his son's homosexuality.

To the extent that homosexuality in diasporic Asian cultures is interpreted at times as a Western affliction, it is interesting to note that some texts represent the process of returning to the protagonist's Asian "homeland" as an integral part of becoming a gay or queer Asian American subject. In various ways, Norman Wong's title story in *Cultural Revolution* (1994), Lawrence Chua's novel *Gold by the Inch* (1998), several stories in Russell **Leong's** *Phoenix Eyes* (2000), and Han Ong's novel *The Disinherited* (2004) engage with this theme, demonstrating that relations of power and desire are not only structured by racial difference but also by class, age, and national affiliation.

Although the majority of gay Asian American literature has taken prose forms, there have been a number of poetry books and dramatic productions that explore such issues as homoeroticism, race, body image, stranger sex, religion, and AIDS. Formally ranging from the highly mannered and restrained to the unruly and open-ended, these texts include Russell Leong's *The Country of Dreams and Dust* (1993); Timothy Liu's *Vox Angelica* (1992), *Burnt Offerings* (1995), *Say Goodnight* (1998), *Hard Evidence* (2001), *Of Thee I Sing* (2004), and *For Dust Thou Art* (2005); Justin Chin's *Bite Hard* (1997) and *Harmless Medicine* (2001); Andy Quan's *Slant* (2001); Joel B. Tan's *Monster* (2002); and R. Zamora Linmark's *Prime Time Apparitions* (2005). Noted playwright Chay Yew's dramatic trilogy *Whitelands*—which includes *Porcelain* (1992), *A Language of Their Own* (1994), and *Half-Lives* (1996)—similarly addresses themes of interracial desire and violence, immigration and AIDS, and father-son relationships. Justin Chin has also published a collection of performance pieces titled *Attack of the Man-Eating Lotus Blossoms* (2005).

In addition to several collections of Asian American lesbian literature, there also exist a number of anthologies that include gay-themed texts and erotica, such as *On a Bed of Rice: An Asian American Erotic Feast* (1995), *Rice: Explorations into Gay Asian Culture and Politics* (1998), *Queer PAPI Porn* (1998), *Take Out: Queer Writing from Asian Pacific America* (2001), and *Best Gay Asian Erotica* (2004). **See also** Asian American Stereotypes; Orientalism and Asian America; Queer Identity and Politics; Racism and Asian America; Sexism and Asian America.

Further Reading

Eng, David L. *Racial Castration: Managing Masculinity in Asian America.* Durham, NC: Duke University Press, 2001.

Eng, David L., and Alice Y. Hom, eds. *Q & A: Queer in Asian America.* Philadelphia: Temple University Press, 1998.

Eng, David L., Judith Halberstam, and José Esteban Muñoz, eds. *What's Queer about Queer Studies Now?* Spec. issue of *Social Text* 23.3–4 (2005): 1–308.

Fung, Richard. "Looking for My Penis: The Eroticized Asian in Gay Video Porn." In *Asian American Sexualities,* ed. Russell Leong. New York: Routledge, 1996. 181–198.

Gopinath, Gayatri. *Impossible Desires: Queer Diasporas and South Asian Public Cultures.* Durham, NC: Duke University Press, 2005.

Manalansan, Martin F., IV. *Global Divas: Filipino Gay Men in the Diaspora.* Durham, NC: Duke University Press, 2003.

Nguyen Tan Hoang. "The Resurrection of Brandon Lee: The Making of a Gay Asian American Porn Star." In *Porn Studies,* ed. Linda Williams. Durham, NC: Duke University Press, 2004. 223–270.

Parikh, Crystal. "'The Most Outrageous Masquerade': Queering Asian-American Masculinity." *Modern Fiction Studies* 48 (2002): 858–898.

Takagi, Dana Y. "Maiden Voyage: Excursion into Sexuality and Identity Politics in Asian America." In *Asian American Sexualities,* ed. Russell Leong. New York: Routledge, 1996. 21–35.

Wat, Eric. *The Making of a Gay Asian Community: An Oral History of Pre-AIDS Los Angeles.* Lanham, MD: Rowman and Littlefield, 2002.

Wong, Sau-ling, and Jeffrey J. Santa Ana. "Gender and Sexuality in Asian American Literature: Review Essay." *Signs: Journal of Women in Culture and Society* 25 (1999): 171–226.

MARTIN JOSEPH PONCE

✦ GILL, MYRNA LAKSHMI (1943–)

Born to an East Indian father and a Spanish Filipina mother, Lakshmi Gill was raised in Manila, Philippines, a product of two cultures. A poet, novelist, short story writer, editor, and English instructor, Gill has published many volumes of poetry that include *Rape of the Spirit* (1961), *During Rain, I Plant Chrysanthemums* (1966), *Mind-walls*

(1970), *First Clearing, An Immigrant's Tour of Life* (1972), *Novena to St. Jude Thaddeus* (1979), *Land of the Morning* (1980), and *Gathered Seasons* (1983). Indubitably personal in character, Gill's poems bring forth her experiences as a woman, daughter, sister, wife, parent, and teacher, as well as her eclectic religious views, her deep love for her philosophical father, and her metaphorical homelessness as an immigrant. She collected some of her best poems in *Returning the Empties: Selected Poems, 1960s–1990s* (1998). She has contributed poems and short stories to multicultural and world literature anthologies, in addition to editing an anthology of poems written by Asians in Canada and Asian Canadians for the spring 1981 issue of the *Asianadian* magazine. *The Third Infinitive* (1998), which recounts the protagonist's search for identity, is Gill's only published novel to date and echoes her own life experiences. She married William Godfrey, with whom she has three children, Marc, Evelyne, and Karam Keir. Gill has held English teaching positions at Notre Dame University, Nelson, British Columbia; Mount Allison University; University of Victoria, Victoria; and the University of British Columbia, Vancouver. She presently lives in Vancouver, British Columbia, and is working on a second novel.

Growing up in two cultures, Asian and North American, Lakshmi Gill aspires to "achieve a synthesis of the two cultures" (Murphy 1970, 418). Gill's poetry and fiction are thus autobiographical in their subject matter and themes. In the poem titled "In This Country," included in *Returning the Empties,* the poet sees herself as "the playground clown standing astride the seesaw of seasons, in a balancing act" (21). A few of her poems in this collection, such as "April 4," "Storyteller," and "Puja for Papa," are memorials for her father. "Puja for Papa," for example, reflects her deep love for her father, as she hears his voice assuring her in a dream that one day she will come home to India and "you will flow back into your beginnings" (167). In "I Tell You, Mr. Biswas," the poet responds to the title character in V.S. Naipaul's *A House for Mr. Biswas* (1961), who struggles his whole life to build his own home and thereby gain independence; in Gill's poem, the speaker declares that "my homelessness is my freedom," disavowing any effort to cultivate roots in a particular place (90). A number of her poems, such as "My Son Dreams in Sackville," "A Winter Scene," "Marc, Gatherer," "Returning the Empties," and "Mixed Conditionals," celebrate her children. In "Mixed Conditionals," written on her fiftieth birthday, the poet counts her life's blessings, considering even her failures as blessings in disguise (20). "The Night Watch" brings out the narrator's responsibilities as a mother. "On the Third Year after Her Death" is a poem written in remembrance of her sister who died of breast cancer. Poems like "The Poeteacher" and "Legacy" explore the hard lot of a teacher. The first poem describes the harsh reality faced by the speaker, who must raise three children on the meager salary she receives as a half-time teacher after her husband leaves her. "Legacy" shows the immigrant teacher's hurt when an Asian student complains to her department head: "Why is she teaching English?" (19). The speaker of "In Search for New Diction" ponders the ways humankind has visualized its relation to gods: "What need for perfection/Who will burn the old words?" (26) Leslie Sanders has aptly remarked in the *Toronto Review* that Gill's poems reveal "the lifelong reflections of a woman who sees, thinks, and feels deeply, turning her estrangement and pain into understanding and insight" (1999, 105). And in her short story "Carian Wine," which tells of a girl trying to get her drunken father to bed, Gill seems to be reminiscing her experience with her own father.

The Third Infinitive relates the story of a half-Indian, half-Filipina girl named Jazz who grows up in the Philippines. The novel describes her convent school education and her struggles in her search for a national and religious identity. Jazz is clearly based on the author's own experience growing up in Manila in the 1950s and recalls Stephen Dedalus of James Joyce's *A Portrait of the Artist as a Young Man*. Joyce's protagonist rejects his family, religion, and country, professing that "I will not serve that in which I no longer believe" (247). Like Joyce's Stephen, Gill's Jazz rejects Filipino culture and nationalism, as well as blind faith in religion, seeking instead the freedom to choose her own path. Jazz's sisters, on the other hand, embrace nationalism, Filipino culture, and religious faith. Jazz is puzzled at Mary's behavior that she was so silent and compliant when Jesus suffered: "What a life! To have borne a child into the world, just to see it suffer. And be unable to do anything about it" (61). Jazz dares to question the catechism, demanding to know from the Jesuit priest why the world needs to be saved again if Christ has already saved it (59). Out of the three infinitives of the catechism—"To know Him, to love Him, and to serve Him" (64)—Jazz chooses the third infinitive of service to God, which is really the service of fellow humans to create "a new day" for humankind (140). Unlike Stephen Dedalus, Jazz's determination of her life plan comes not from an epiphany but rather from logical reasoning and her father's influence.

The Third Infinitive deplores the role of women in the patriarchal society of the Philippines. Although Jazz's father and mother seek to develop their daughters' talents fully, Philippine society denies women equal opportunities. Jazz's father shudders at the thought of his daughters being treated as "chattel," and therefore decides to send them abroad (136). Ironically, however, her father is less liberal when it comes to his wife, having "stopped her education" and not permitting her "to strike out on her own, to release her creativity" (95). He can never accept her doing any business on her own. Once when he goes away from the country for almost a year, she runs a successful restaurant; however, when he returns, he closes it. What he expects from her is "to be at his side during business dealings, host the endless cocktail parties, look very attractive" (95).

Further Reading

Galdon, Joseph A. Rev. of *The Third Infinitive*. *World Literature Today* 69.1 (Winter 1985): 232.

Gill, Lakshmi. *Returning the Empties: Selected Poems, 1960s–1990s*. Toronto: TSAR, 1998.

——. *The Third Infinitive*. Toronto: TSAR Publications, 1993.

Joyce, James. *A Portrait of the Artist as a Young Man*. 1916. New York: Penguin Books, 1977.

Murphy, Rosalie, ed. *Contemporary Poets*. London: St. James Press, 1970. 416–419.

Sanders, Leslie. "Plenitude"—A Review of *Returning the Empties*. *The Toronto Review* 17.3 (Summer 1999): 103–105.

Taylor, Wanda. "Postimperial Identities"—A Review of *The Third Infinitive*. *Canadian Literature* 149 (Summer 1996): 184–185.

HARISH CHANDER

✦ GISH, LILLIAN. *See* Jen, Gish

✦ GOLD MOUNTAIN

Coming to America, immigrants have carried with them their own notions about the meaning of the New World. Whereas the Puritans came to build "a city upon a hill," the Chinese ventured across the Pacific Ocean to find the Gold Mountain. Invented by the early Chinese immigrants who came to California shortly after the discovery of gold, the notion "Gold Mountain" has been used in reference not only to California but also to the city of San Francisco, which for a long time was the most important port of entry and home to the nation's largest Chinese community. The term was used in reference to the United States later on, when the Chinese population began to disperse to other parts of the nation beyond California. Rather than being a precise geographical term, the term reveals Chinese immigrants' economic motivation and their perception of the New World, a motivation and perception that have been shared by millions of immigrants from other parts of the world.

From the beginning of Chinese emigration to the 1960s, an overwhelming majority of Chinese immigrants in the New World came from the Pearl River Delta region in Guangdong Province in South China. That region was one of the first areas in China to be connected to global markets in modern history. And for a long time during the Qing Dynasty, the provincial capital, Canton (present-day Guangzhou), existed as the sole port for China's international trade. People in the Delta region were the first in China to learn about the United States and the gold in California.

It is not surprising, therefore, that early California-bound immigrants from this region were motivated by economic considerations. To further understand the extent of their economic motivations, it is necessary to consider the longstanding gulf in income between China and the United States, which was expansive in the late nineteenth century.

In the 1860s, for example, a Chinese working for the Central Pacific Railroad Company in the West would receive a monthly wage of about $31. Others working in different occupations and locations got paid less, including those who would agree to work in agriculture in the South for $22 a month. According to contemporary estimates, rural workers in the immigrants' native land at the time earned $8 to $10 a year, which means that the average immigrant worker's earning was 26 to 46 times higher than the wage of his fellow villager back in China. Therefore, sending a family member, who was invariably a young male, to America was often a family strategy in taking advantage of opportunities in the increasing global economy at the time. The young immigrant bore grave responsibilities and, as is evident in so many cases, regularly sent money to the loved ones back home. The money that the immigrants made and saved would also improve their class status, turning lower-middle-class people into landlords and property owners.

The standard of living in the United States was also considerably better than that in China, especially in the villages in rural south China. There was much more and better food, especially meat, in America than in the homeland communities. Chinese immigrant laundry workers in pre–**World War II** Chicago, for example, could have chicken every Saturday. Back home in the villages, by comparison, few could afford to have it once a month. They could also have soda several times a day, which was a luxurious item that was out of the reach of ordinary people in the villages.

The image of the United States as a land of economic opportunities has remained strong among the Chinese. This is because the economic gap continued to widen between China and the United States until recent years, when China's unprecedented growth began to shift the longstanding economic relationship between the two countries. A large number of the post-1970s Chinese immigrants are intellectuals, who have arrived in the United States since the 1980s as graduate students. Though they came for the declared purpose of pursuing knowledge and doing research, the unstated economic benefits for coming to the United States are obvious. By becoming a graduate student at an American university, a fresh Chinese college graduate could make at least five to six times more than an established university professor did in China in the late 1990s, who earned a monthly salary of less than $150.

But the image of Gold Mountain does not represent an entirely and simplistically romantic picture. From the very beginning, the Chinese have been aware of the uncertainties and hazards that were intimately associated with the lives of "Golden Mountaineers." The pursuit of their dream meant long—often decades-long—absences from their family. And the dream remained unrealized in many cases, as some struggled with poverty and others simply vanished. Therefore, folksongs in the emigrant communities as early as the late nineteenth and early twentieth centuries contained not only praises for the Gold Mountaineers but also stern warnings for young girls not to marry them.

More importantly, for the Chinese, the Gold Mountain was also a place full of racialized discrimination, which started to surface soon after the arrival of the Chinese forty-niners. Discriminatory activities came primarily in two forms: legislation and violence. Such legislation existed at the local, state, and federal levels, undercutting the economic interest of the Chinese, attacking their cultural traditions, and even threatening to erase their presence in the United States. As examples of legislation at the state level, early in the 1850s, California levied a foreign miners' tax, primarily targeting the Chinese. The state legislature of California also tried to ban immigration from China, but its measure was declared unconstitutional because immigration was in the jurisdiction of the federal government. Government's anti-Chinese policies also existed at the local level. San Francisco, in particular, passed numerous anti-Chinese ordinances. One of the most notorious is the Queue Ordinance, which stipulated that Chinese inmates must have their hair (queue) cut right after their arrival at the county jail. Because the queue had acquired much symbolic significance for the Chinese, the 1867 ordinance was a blatant attack on the cultural identity of the Chinese. The United States Congress started to pass anti-Chinese legislation with the Page Act of 1875, which intended to restrict the arrival of Chinese women. In 1882 Congress passed the infamous **Chinese Exclusion Act**, banning Chinese labor immigration for 10 years and reiterating the principle that no Chinese could become naturalized citizens. The principle had been established by the 1790 Naturalization Act, which stipulated that only free white men could become naturalized citizens. The ban on Chinese immigration became permanent in 1904. The Exclusion Act is just an indication of institutionalized anti-Chinese racism in the legal system, which affected every aspect of Chinese American life.

Chinese in nineteen-century America also encountered violence. Besides assaults that Chinese suffered individually, numerous physical attacks occurred on Chinese communities throughout the American West, destroying property, killing innocent individuals, and driving away the rest. One of the most violent is the 1885 massacre, in which mobs killed 51 Chinese laborers who worked in the largest coal mines along the Union Pacific Railroad in Rock Springs, Wyoming. Although the brutal massacre shocked the entire nation, no culprits were brought to justice, and the surviving Chinese moved out. The lack of justice in cases like this is attributable in part to the anti-Chinese sentiments that had wide popular support throughout the country.

It must be noted that the Chinese did fight such institutionalized racism. In the court of law, for example, they fought numerous battles to protect their rights and fundamental constitutional principles. They won a few battles, but it was extremely difficult for the politically powerless and numerically small community to win the war for social justice by itself. Social injustice prompted some Chinese to question the validity of the United States as a Gold Mountain, which became the subject of debates among Chinese Americans in the prewar years. Some argued that the Gold Mountain for them now existed in China.

Since then, especially since the **civil rights movement** of the 1960s, the Gold Mountain has changed significantly. Institutionalized racism has decisively diminished. In 1943, the United States government abolished all the Chinese exclusion acts, giving Chinese immigrants the right to become naturalized citizens and allowing 105 Chinese to enter the country each year, which was based on the racist quota system established by the 1924 immigration act. The 1965 Immigration Reform Act abolished the quota system, opening the door for Asian immigration. As a result, Chinese emigration from Hong Kong, Taiwan, and ethnic Chinese communities in places such as Southeast Asia and Korea increased dramatically. The post-Mao reform that started in the late 1970s triggered a new wave of emigrants from mainland China. Post-1965 immigration has transformed and dramatically regenerated Chinese America. Anti-Chinese racism had significantly curbed the growth of the Chinese American population, which was only slightly over 102,000 in 1930, more than eight decades after the arrival of the Chinese forty-niners. Slowly, it went up to about 150,000 in 1950. In 2000 it exceeded 2.8 million—a twelvefold growth since 1960.

Chinese America is also far more diverse than ever before. Unlike in the early years when Chinese immigrants came predominantly from the Pearl River Delta, today Chinese immigrants arrive from different parts of China and from different Chinese communities throughout the world. Moreover, for a long time before 1970, the Chinese were concentrated heavily in two service occupations, namely the laundry business and the restaurant industry. Today, the Chinese population is far more diversely distributed in many industries. One of the new industries in which the Chinese have achieved a high profile is in high tech. It is their remarkable achievement in education that has enabled an increasing number of Chinese Americans (both U.S.-born and immigrants) to take advantage of opportunities in such newly emerged and high-paying industries. In much of the twentieth century, even white ethnic Americans had to wait at least one generation before they could join the ranks of the middle class. Now a significant number of Chinese newcomers can achieve their Gold Mountain dream just a few years after arriving in the United States. Although many Chinese Americans live in poverty and the struggle for social justice is far from over, there is a widespread belief among the Chinese that the Gold Mountain remains golden. **See also** Racism and Asian America.

Further Reading

Chen, Yong. *Chinese San Francisco 1850–1943: A Transpacific Community*. Stanford, CA: Stanford University Press, 2000.

Hsu, Madeilne Y. *Dreaming of Gold, Dreaming of Hope: Transnationalism and Migration Between the United States and South China, 1882–1943*. Stanford, CA: Stanford University Press, 2000.

Tong, Benson. *The Chinese Americans.* Boulder: University Press of Colorado, 2003.

Yung, Judy, Gordon H. Chang, and Him Mark Lai, eds. *Chinese American Voices: From the Gold Rush to the Present.* Berkeley: University of California Press, 2006.

YONG CHEN

✦ GONZALEZ, N.V.M. (1915–1999)

Nestor Vicente Madali Gonzalez, fictionist, poet, and essayist, born on September 8, 1915, is universally acknowledged to be among the first-ranking writers of the Philippines, though his works also enjoy international acceptance, with translations into German, Russian, Chinese, and Bahasa Indonesian. Among the many honors bestowed on him are such impressive recognitions as three Rockefeller grants (1949–1950, 1952, and 1964), first prizes in the *Philippines Free Press* short story contest (1964) and the Palanca short story contest (1971), a Union of Writers of the Philippines Award (1989), a Cultural Center of the Philippines Award (1990), and the Philippine Centennial Award for Literature (1998). Gonzalez's principal occupation was professor, although he failed the University of the Philippines' entrance examination and never earned a college degree. In 1949 he became the first nondegree holder to teach courses at the University of the Philippines, from whose faculty he retired in 1967. He was visiting professor at the University of California, Santa Barbara, from 1966 to 1968 and thereafter was tenured at California State University, Hayward, retiring in 1982. In 1987 he received an honorary doctorate from the University of the Philippines. In 1998–1999 he was the Regents Professor at UCLA. He did no significant scholarly studies, however. Instead, he wrote a substantial number of essays that contextualize Philippine literature and address problems faced by writers. The most salient essays have been reprinted in his collections *The Father and the Maid: Essays on Filipino Life and Letters* (1990); *Kalutang: A Filipino in the World* (1995); and *The Novel of Justice: Selected Essays, 1968–1994* (1996).

Gonzalez's 65-year literary career began with prestigious publications. At age 16 his poem "Guitarist" was published in *Philippine Magazine,* the most revered periodical in the prewar Philippines. In January 1934, four of his poems were published under the variant surname "Gonzales" (which he used in the 1930s) in *Poetry* magazine in the United States. Despite his poetic precocity, Gonzalez turned to prose fiction, beginning with a short story in the September 1933 issue of *Philippine Magazine.* However, he never ceased to write poetry.

The linchpins of Gonzalez's reputation are his short stories, which he assembled into seven volumes: *Seven Hills Away* (1947), *Children of the Ash-Covered Loam* (1954), *Look, Stranger, on This Island Now* (1963), *Selected Stories* (1964), *Mindoro and Beyond*

(1979; emended edition 1989), *The Bread of Salt and Other Stories* (1993), and *A Grammar of Dreams and Other Stories* (1997). As in his uncollected short stories, Gonzalez's prose style is simple, direct, and empirical, reminding more than one critic of Ernest Hemingway. The plots, however, are so static that they recede into vignette, even tableau. Some readers attribute this to the faithful representation of slow-moving peasant life, the nonlinear plots conveying the rhythmic patterns of life of the Mindoro *kaingineros* (slash-and-burn farmers) in particular. Others consider the stories plotless, even pointless, because, as an anthologist remarked in 1958, "Nothing much happens in them" (Roseburg 1958, 150). The cause of this torpor, according to the anthologist, is the style: "At times it leaps and then all of a sudden slows down and becomes sluggish and lumbers along like a debris-loaded stream" (Roseburg 1958, 151–152). The possibility that the languor merely boils down to the imitative fallacy, however, is countered by the careful construction of the stories.

Critics have detected Joycean and Jamesean strains in the schema, and the architectonics are often symbolic, as they are in "Dry Heaven." More than an ironic juxtaposition of the pointless quest for fish by two sport fishermen and the pointed quest for souls by Father Eugenio, the overarching motif involves the futility of much human questing. Like the individual stories, the collections are architected. A case in point is *Mindoro and Beyond*, consisting of 21 stories drawn from three previous volumes. Each of the six sections into which the stories are grouped increases the degree of sophistication, subtlety of tone, and juxtaposition of components. The reprinting of stories from volume to volume might even replicate the effect of the circular plots, creating recurrent but fixed points of reference in individual stories and collections.

Perhaps because Gonzalez's artistic vision is cosmic, his stories sometimes seem inscrutable or ambiguous. In the appropriately titled "In the Twilight," for example, readers are left to determine whose account to accept—Major Godo's or Dan's. This tiptoe situation reminds us that truth is not always transparent. The Gonzalez worldview, seemingly involving timeless, immutable physical objects accurately perceived by our senses, accommodates the contrary view that our perceptions of reality may be tenuous, even unreliable. That Gonzalez should not be thought of as merely a bucolic local colorist is evident not only from his worldview but also from the social criticism embedded in his stories. He does not inject the venom of Ninotchka **Rosca** nor does he historically contextualize as Linda **Ty-Casper** does, but he nonetheless lacerates unjust social practices and arrangements, often by reportage, depicting apparently personal afflictions such as loneliness or suffering. Readers connect the individual predicament with the social malady (e.g., "Pare Lucio" is not solely the story of one man's encounter with the judiciary; it exposes arbitrary "justice" in general at the *municipio* level). In *Seven Hills Away* the transition from the specific situation of the individual to the more widespread human condition is facilitated by the absence of the first-person singular point of view. Another aspect of Gonzalez's fiction that has generally received accolades is his renderings in English of peasant dialect. That he was well qualified to translate from Tagalog to English was established by 1943, when he placed third in the *Liwayway* Tagalog short story contest. But the degree to which he succeeded in rendering local and regional expressions has drawn praise even from harshly critical commentators such as the foremost Filipino formalist critic, Edilberto Tiempo, who considers Gonzalez largely an artistic failure.

Two of Gonzalez's three novels have garnered major literary prizes, *The Winds of April* (1940), an Honorable Mention in the first Commonwealth Literary Contests, and *The Bamboo Dancers* (1959), both the Jose Rizal Pro-Patria Award and a Republic Cultural Heritage Award. *A Season of Grace* (1956), however, the best of the three, won no such prizes, and even it has elicited a good deal of negative critical reaction. *The Winds of April,* an autobiographical first-person narrative, has a *bildungsroman* quality about it and is picaresque in its episodic construction. It has virtually no plot, instead consisting of lengthy descriptive passages (sometimes finely rendered) and accounts of events such as the narrator's visit to the city and his lumber-selling trip to Capiz. The characters do not grow, even when they are fetchingly presented, as in the case of the narrator's father and the Japanese medicine salesman. Gonzalez did achieve an objective narrative stance and did attempt social criticism through the narrator's contacts with different settings and people of varied social strata. As a whole, however, *The Winds of April* is a series of fragments; the one unifying element—the narrator's controlling consciousness—is insufficient to impart full coherence to the text.

A Season of Grace exhibits the maturation of Gonzalez's work in the succeeding 16 years. The local color is still present, but it does not preclude a narrative flow, which *A Season of Grace* has, albeit a sluggish one. *A Season of Grace* also has a five-part overall design: three middle sections sandwiched between two shorter ones, which constitute a prologue and an epilogue respectively. The scenes that recur, with variations, at the beginning and end reinforce this structure. For instance, a coerced "gift" of mats to a corrupt *municipio* official is exacted at both the beginning and the end. Throughout the novel the cyclical nature of the lives of the *kaingineros* is depicted. Just 12 major incidents happen in the approximate one-year time setting of the novel, and these involve recurrent problems unanchored in any definite time frame. Furthermore, events from the past are recalled and combined with the events of the time setting, thus adding to the aura of timelessness that the novel exudes. The lives of the main characters, Doro and Sabel, revolve around the crop cycle: clearing the land, planting, trying to defend the growing grain from predators such as rats, and harvesting. Meanwhile, the parallel human life cycle of birth, growth, aging, and death links humans to external nature, leading readers to realize that the fictional world is not so much temporally defined as spatially explicit. Palpably specific are the ash-covered loam and the mangrove swamps; elusively ephemeral are the time markers.

Adding substance to the novel is the transparent social criticism, far better integrated into the artistry of the work than it was in *The Winds of April*. An enduring element of the cyclical life patterns of the *kaingineros* is the human predators, in the novel embodied in the rapacious Epe Ruda and his wife Tiaga. They are the only available suppliers of such staples as clothes and kerosene. Credit is extended on the *duplihan* (double-borrowing) system—the debtor must return twice the amount borrowed. This arrangement ensures that the already impoverished farmers only sink more hopelessly into even further debt with each passing year. Though such exploitive practices are presented objectively and without didacticism in both *The Winds of April* and *A Season of Grace,* in the former we encounter them as spectators; in the latter we experience them because they are interwoven into the texture of the tale. For instance, the fact that Sabel and Doro have, at the end, two children (Eloy and Porton) and Sabel is again pregnant, whereas Tiaga has just suffered a miscarriage and so is still childless, is a powerfully ironic commentary on the riches, accumulated through greed, of the Rudas of the world, and the impoverishment, due to honest, hard work, of the Doros and Sabels.

There is consensus that *The Bamboo Dancers* is a retrogression from Gonzalez's standard. For the first time, Gonzalez leaves rural Mindoro, which he knew intimately from experience, and attempts an international novel, set in the United States, Canada, Japan, and Taiwan. The gravitation of Gonzalez's plots toward the disunified is, predictably, exacerbated by such a wide scope of settings, leading one critic to conclude that the story is "a mere travelogue" (Daroy 1966, 31) and another to opine that "as a work of art, the novel is a failure" (Demetillo 1987, 69).

The protagonist, Ernie Rama, is a sculptor, but his creativity has been stultified. His brother Pepe suggests that he try driftwood art, a sardonic reflection on his rudderless meanderings around the world. He is ambivalent in many ways, including his sexual orientation, which of course symbolically reinforces his lack of artistic fecundity. The book's title prepares us for his unsettled status, referring as it does to the *tinikling* (bird dance), a traditional Filipino art in which dancers must deftly leap to prevent the ankles from being clipped by bamboo poles, alternately opening and closing. The two poles symbolize Asian and Western orientations respectively, the two cultural influences that produce Ernie's ambivalence (a trait of his character that Gonzalez himself called attention to) and intellectual paralysis. Gonzalez has also emphasized that Ernie is no hero. In fact, his name is ironic, a pale reflection of the truly intrepid Ernest Hemingway (Ernie to his associates), whose manly exploits in male proving grounds (e.g., bullring, battlefield, big game hunt) put into the shade Rama's excursions, for instance to the carp pond of a hotel. "Rama" in Hinduism is a deified hero, an incarnation of Vishnu, precisely what Ernie is not. Ernie's American counterpart is Herb Lane, ambivalent and innocuous in the United States but a juggernaut of destruction in Taipei, where he gets drunk, attacks his girlfriend, and runs over a Chinese girl with his jeep. His name, too, is an ironic misfit. An herb is often used for medicinal purposes, but Herb Lane is not the path to healing the alienation and self-divisions of humans in the modern world. The havoc wrought by Lane may only be a microcosm of the cataclysm that humans can bring on themselves, as the Hiroshima locale may ominously remind the reader. Although Ernie's near drowning may betoken a rebirth, there is no certainty that this is the case. Ernie's self-imposed isolation from others, especially older people (who embody traditional cultural values), may ultimately lead to self-annihilation.

Further Reading

Bayuga, Rosy May. "Gonzalez Sabel: A Brown Madonna." *Philippine Studies* 45 (1997): 124–134.

Cabanos-Lava, Josefa. "Rhythms in Fiction." *The Literary Apprentice* 19 (1955): 59–70.

Casper, Leonard. "N.V.M. Gonzalez." In *New Writing from the Philippines: A Critique and Anthology.* Syracuse, NY: Syracuse University Press, 1966. 42–55.

Daroy, Petronilo Bn. "The Colonial Question." *The U.P. Research Digest* July 1966: 28–33.

Demetillo, Ricaredo. "Reflections on N.V.M. Gonzalez as a Fiction Writer." In Demetillo, *Major and Minor Keys.* Quezon City: New Day, 1987. 66–72.

Gonzalez, N.V.M. "Notes on a Method and a Culture." *General Education Journal* 4 (1962): 87–94.

Grow, L.M. "Modern Philippine Poetry in the Formative Years." *Ariel* 15.3 (1984): 81–98; rpt. in Grow, *World Enough and Time: Epistemologies and Cosmologies in Modern Philippine Poetry.* Quezon City: Giraffe Books, 2000. 20–39.

Guzman, Richard P. "'As in Myth, the Signs Were All Over': The Fiction of N.V.M. Gonzalez." *Virginia Quarterly Review* 60 (1984): 102–118.

Roseburg, Arturo G. "N. V. M. Gonzalez." In *Pathways to Philippine Literature in English*, ed. Arturo B. Roseburg. Quezon City: Phoenix Press, 1958. 148–152.

Tiempo, Edilberto K. *Literary Criticism in the Philippines and Other Essays.* Manila: De La Salle University Press, 1995. 281–319.

L. M. GROW

✦ GOTANDA, PHILIP KAN (1951–)

A **sansei** (third-generation) Japanese American playwright, producer, director, and actor, Gotanda is primarily known as a playwright and has received a Guggenheim Foundation scholarship, three National Endowment for the Arts Artist Grants, three Rockefeller Playwriting Awards, the 1989 Will Glickman Playwriting Award, a PEW

Theater Community Group National Theatre Artist Award, a Gerbode and McKnight Foundation Fellowship, the Theatre Communication Group/National Endowment for the Arts Directing Fellowship, and Lila Wallace-Reader's Digest Writer's Award.

Born on December 17, 1951, in Stockton, California, Philip Kan Gotanda was exposed to the arts while growing up, and he wrote songs about being **Asian American** and played in bands from junior high school through college. He eventually befriended David Henry **Hwang**, a Chinese American playwright who is also a musician, because of their mutual interests in music. They played in a rock band, Bamboo, with R.A. **Shiomi**. Gotanda attended the University of California at Santa Cruz in 1969, intending to study psychology to eventually become a psychiatrist. In 1970 he went to Japan and studied pottery with artist Hiroshi Seto, and he received a BA in Asian studies from the University of California at Santa Barabara in 1973. His experiences in the pottery field later informed his plays, *Ballad of Yachiho* (1996) and *Yohen* (1997). He studied law at Hastings School of Law in San Francisco to satisfy his parents, who expected him to become a lawyer, completing his law degree in 1978. Following in the footsteps of Frank **Chin**, a pioneer in creating the Asian American theater community during the post-World War II era, Gotanda is an influential dramatist of the 1980s and 1990s, part of the so-called second-wave Asian American theater community, along with David Henry Hwang, Momoko **Iko**, and Wakako **Yamauchi**. He nurtured the next wave of Asian American writers, such as Cherylene Lee, Jeannie **Barroga**, Han Ong, Canyon Sam, and Charlie Chin.

As Gotanda was always interested in music, his first play, titled *The Avocado Kid, or Zen and the Art of Guacamole*, was a musical inspired by "Momotaro," a famous Japanese folktale. Catching the attention of Mako, artistic director of the East West Players, the first professional Asian American theatre company in the United States, founded in 1965, this musical was staged in Los Angeles by the East West Players in 1979. Then it was staged in San Francisco by the Asian American Theatre Company, founded in 1973, the third professional Asian American theatre company. At this time, Gotanda was a clerk at North Beach-**Chinatown** Legal Aid in San Francisco, but eventually he gave up his career in the legal field. He never took the bar exam. His second musical about a third-generation Japanese American rockstar titled *Bullet Headed Birds* was staged by the Asian American Theatre Company in 1981 and the Pan Asian Repertory Theater in New York in November 1981.

Despite the fact that Gotanda was born after the internment of Japanese Americans during **World War II**, many of his plays are drawn from the internment experiences of his parents' generation. His father, Wilfred Itsuta Gotanda, was from Kauai, Hawaii, and, upon completing his medical degree at the University of Arkansas, he opened his medical practice in Stockton, California. Gotanda's mother, Catherine Matsumoto, was a schoolteacher from Stockton. At the outbreak of World War II, Gotanda's parents were separately sent to an internment camp in Rohwer, Arkansas, and Wilfred Gotanda married Catherine Matsumoto and settled in Stockton after they returned from the internment camp. Gotanda was the youngest of their three sons. Although Gotanda's parents did not talk about their internment camp experiences very often, theirs as well as their generation's experiences in the internment camps and their lasting effects became a central theme in many of Gotanda's plays, such as *A Song for a Nisei Fisherman* (directed by David Henry Hwang, produced by the Asian American Theatre Company in San Francisco in 1980), *The Wash* (produced in San Francisco by Eureka Theatre Company in 1987), *Fish Head Soup* (produced in Berkeley, CA, by Berkeley Repertory Theatre in 1991), and *Sister Matsumoto* (produced in Seattle by Seattle Repertory Theater in 1997). Unlike his contemporary playwrights such as Lane **Nishikawa**, whose internment camp plays are set in the camps, Gotanda's internment camp plays are set after the war and explore the lasting psychological effects of racism and camp experiences on Japanese Americans, including internalized racism and self-hatred.

A Song for a Nisei Fisherman, a play drawn from Gotanda's father's experience, is considered the opening part of a Japanese American family trilogy that includes *The Wash* and *Fish Head Soup. A Song for a Nisei Fisherman* is about Itsuta "Ichan" Matsumoto, a **nisei** (second-generation Japanese American) son from a family involved in the fishery business, who wants to be a doctor. Though the play is not chronologically arranged, it shows Itsuta's life through a series of scenes, from his impoverished Hawaiian childhood and experience in an internment camp to fatherhood and retirement. While depicting the protagonist's struggles in racist American society and pressures from his Japanese American family, Gotanda explores the theme of emotional isolation and the generational gaps.

Gotanda's next play, *The Dream of Kitamura,* is a punk-rock fantasy play drawn from stories collected from Gotanda's family, friends, and his dreams, and it was produced in San Francisco in 1984, whereas the aforementioned surrealistic play titled *Bullet Headed Birds* was produced at the Pan Asian Repertory Theatre in New York in 1981. However, what gained Gotanda's entrance into mainstream American theatre was the production of *A Song for a Nisei Fisherman* and *The Wash* at the Mark Taper Forum in Los Angeles in 1991. Whereas *A Song for a Nisei Fisherman* is based on nisei men's experiences, including Gotanda's father's, *The Wash* is drawn from the story of a nisei wife who left her neglectful husband to begin a new life as an independent woman, even though such self-asserting behavior was unheard of in her generation. This play's dramatic action occurs 40 years after the internment camp, and its main female character, Masi Matsumoto, replaces her husband's dirty laundry with clean clothes every week. Exploring the husband-wife relationship on the one hand, Gotanda exposes racism within the Japanese American community on the other. For example, the husband Nobu opposes interracial marriage and does not recognize his daughter Judy's marriage to an African American man. Consequently, he refuses to meet his only grandson, Timothy. The play was originally workshopped at the Mark Taper Forum's New Theater for the Now Festival in 1985 and then premiered at San Francisco's Eureka Theater in 1987. It was made into a motion picture in 1988, with the screenplay by Gotanda and directed by Michael Toshiyuki Uno.

Unlike the first two plays in the Japanese American family trilogy that focus on second-generation Japanese Americans, *Fish Head Soup* is about a sansei (third-generation Japanese American) son named Matt Iwasaki, who stages his death by drowning to erase his Asian American identity. Consequently, Matt's father is devastated by his son's death and becomes emotionally unavailable to his family; Matt's mother begins an affair with a Caucasian man whose obsession is Oriental femininity; Matt's brother suffers from the shock and guilt of his experiences in the **Vietnam War**. The self-centered Matt returns home in San Joaquin Valley to mortgage the family house to help finance his film about his dysfunctional family, and he reveals the secret of the supposed drowning to his family. While facing typical problems with the racist film industry, the son also faces opposition from his mother for filming only Japanese Americans because she believes that no one is interested in Japanese Americans, who—she unconsciously believes as her son does—are second-class citizens. Thus, the play demonstrates internalized racial prejudice that was passed on generationally after the **Japanese American internment**.

Sisters Matsumoto, a Chekhovian realistic drama, deals with the camp experience's immediate psychological impact, as the play is set in late 1945 Stockton, California, when three sisters of a wealthy family, Grace, Chiz, and Rose, are released from the Rohwer camp, with their parents dead and the prewar family fortune gone. Grace, the oldest sister, is rational and traditional, while the middle sister, Chiz, is an assimilationist who wants to be integrated into mainstream America. The youngest sister, Rose, for whom the older sisters are trying to arrange a marriage, is nostalgic. Their differences cause different views toward love, family, and identity. Although the victimization of Japanese Americans during World War II is a prominent theme in Gotanda's plays, he also exposes faults within the Japanese American community, as he does in *The Wash*. As Gotanda displays in *A Song for a Nisei Fisherman*, when Itsuta expresses his racist bias toward his son's relationship with a Chinese American woman, and in *The Wash*, in which the father refuses to acknowledge the existence of his only grandson, a product of interracial marriage, in *Sisters Matsumoto*, with the war and camp experience in the backdrop of the play, Gotanda reveals classist bias within the community while examining Japanese Americans' struggles in a racist culture and the economic aftermath of war. Although the play feels autobiographical and is, in fact, drawn from Gotanda's mother's life and grounded in historical events, it is fictitious and explores Japanese American women's reintegration into American society. The play premiered at the Seattle Repertory Theater with Gotanda's friend and artistic collaborator Sharon Ott as a director and in three-way collaboration with the San Jose Repertory Theatre and the Asian American Theatre Company in 1999, and later it was coproduced with Boston's Huntington Theatre Company in 2000. The play received mixed reviews.

Some of Gotanda's plays problematize the Asian American stereotypes and discrimination perpetuated in the media, an issue many of his contemporary Asian American dramatists, such as Edward **Sakamoto** and Lane Nishikawa, addressed. Gotanda was inspired by various veteran Asian American actors and created the main character Vincent Cheng. *Yankee Dawg You Die* contrasts Vincent, an experienced Asian American actor, to Bradley Yamashita, a young novice actor, and creates intergenerational conflicts between Vincent, who sells out to the typecasting practices, and Bradley, who despises Vincent's willingness to accept demeaning Asian roles. In the end, their roles are reversed when Vincent lands on a respectable role in a Japanese American production whereas Bradley cannot refuse a stereotypical yet lucrative role. This dramatic satire of two generations of Japanese American actors in a racist movie industry was drawn from Gotanda's first experiences working with Asian American dramatic artists and was one of the first Asian American plays to depict a dignified homosexual Asian American character (Vincent). It was produced by the Berkeley Repertory Theater in 1988.

In the 1990s, Gotanda turned his attention to the film industry, producing *The Kiss* (1992), *Drinking Tea* (1996), and *Life Tastes Good* (1999). *The Kiss,* a 13-minute, black-and-white movie Gotanda wrote, directed, produced, and starred in, recounts the story of an introvert named Wilfred Funai, who accidentally finds his previously unknown potential as a hero when his gay colleague chokes during a meal. Gotanda presented this film to various film festivals, including the Sundance Film Festival, and received San Francisco's Golden Gate Award in 1994. *Drinking Tea* (1996) is another film that Gotanda wrote, directed, and produced. It is 30 minutes long and is about the process and effect of dying on an old, second-generation Japanese American couple. This film was also presented at the Sundance Film Festival. Gotanda wrote and directed a feature-length, color movie titled *Life Tastes Good* with Dale Minami as a coproducer. This film was also presented at the Sundance Film Festival and other film festivals, including the San Francisco Asian Film Festival.

While working on films, Gotanda wrote *Ballad of Yachiyo,* a play based on his paternal aunt, Yachiyo Gotanda, who was born and raised in the small town of Mana on the island of Kauai and committed suicide by taking ant poison at the young age of 17. Gotanda's father hardly talked about his oldest sister, but she was mentioned accidentally during dinner, and Gotanda worked on this play for 10 years until he finally started writing its draft when his wife Diane was in the hospital. He has seen two pictures of his aunt—one taken around the time of her death and the other at her funeral. To write this play, Gotanda interviewed his relatives and conducted research at the Oral History Center at the University of Hawaii. Set in Kauai, Hawaii, in 1919, the play is about the coming of age of the female title character Yachiyo, who is sent to a pottery artist, Hiro Takamura, and his wife to become a live-in servant while acquiring the social polish necessary for a Japanese bride through tea ceremony and flower arrangement lessons. It chronicles the changing relationships among Yachiyo, the artist, and his wife, until Yachiyo becomes pregnant and commits suicide.

Although Gotanda's indebtedness to Asian American theatre companies is well-known, his plays have also been produced or coproduced by non-Asian theatres since the 1990s. *Fish Head Soup* premiered at Berkeley Repertory Theatre and was directed by Oskar Eustis, who also directed *Day Standing on its Head* at the Manhattan Theatre Club in 1994. Berkeley Repertory Theatre and Costa Mesa's South Coast Repertory co-commissioned *Ballad of Yachiyo*, a play about a love triangle that went tragically wrong. It premiered in Berkeley in 1995 and was produced in Costa Mesa in the following year. Likewise, the Asian American Theater Company, San Jose Repertory Theater, and Seattle Repertory Theatre collaborated on *Sisters Matsumoto*.

Critics praise Gotanda for his abilities to create a wide range of plays that have distinct styles, themes, and techniques, such as realism, surrealism, and musical. To keep the inspiration and the process of making plays fresh, Gotanda restructures the way he creates every five to seven years. Despite the fact that many of his plays, such as *Fish Head Soup and Other Plays* and *No More Cherry Blossoms: Sisters Matsumoto and Other Plays* are published by the University of Washington Press, his plays have not received wide scholarly attention yet. Perhaps *Yankee Dawg You Die* is the only play that has attracted scholarly interest. Some of the critical studies on *Yankee Dawg You Die* include James Moy's *Marginal Sights: Staging the Chinese in America* (1993), Robert Vorlicky's *Act Like a Man: Challenging Masculinities in American Drama* (1995), and Josephine Lee's *Performing Asian America* (1997). In the interviews by David Henry Hwang and by Robert Ito, Gotanda expresses his concerns regarding the financial troubles Asian American theatres such as the Asian American Theatre Company, the East West Players, and the Pan Asian are facing in recent years.

Gotanda's other plays include *American Tattoo* and *Jan Ken Po*. *American Tattoo* is a play based on Japanese American internment camp experiences, and it was read on stage in Berkeley, California, by the Berkeley Repertory Theatre in 1982. Gotanda wrote *Jan Ken Po* in collaboration with David Henry Hawang and R.A. Shiomi, and it was produced in San Francisco by the Asian American Theatre Company in 1986. *Day Standing on Its Head* is a Kafkaesque play featuring a middle-age Japanese American law professor named Harry Kitamura. It was produced in New York by the Manhattan

Theatre Club in 1993 and received mixed reviews. This play was anthologized in *Asian American Drama: 9 Plays from the Multiethnic Landscape* and in *But Still, Like Air, I'll Rise,* both published in 1997. In collaboration with Dan Kuramoto, Danny Yamamoto, and Taiji Miyagawa, Gotanda wrote and privately published *in domination of the night*. It is a spoken-word performance with a combination of jazz and poetry in which Gotanda plays the role of Ozu, and his coauthor Kuramoto plays Mr. Moto. It was produced in San Francisco by the Asian American Theatre Company in 1994. *Beans* from *Pieces of the Quilt* was produced in San Francisco by Magic Theatre in 1996. *Yohen,* a play that deals with a troublesome interracial marriage between an African American, James, and his Japanese war bride, named Sumi, was produced by Berkeley Repertory Theater in San Francisco in 1997 with Timothy Douglas as a director. It was later produced in Los Angeles by the East West Players in collaboration with the African American Robey Theatre Company in 1999. *[F]loating weeds* was produced in San Francisco by Campo Santo and Intersection Theater in 2001, and it was during this time that Gotanda was inspired to write a play about the cycle of male violence, *A Fist of Roses*. *The Wind Cries Mary* is a one-act play inspired by *Hedda Gabler* by Henrik Ibsen and was produced by the San Jose Repertory Theatre in 2002. This play portrays a Japanese American version of Ibsen's nineteenth-century heroine and a nisei daughter of an entrepreneur named Eiko, who is based on Gotanda's cousin. The play is included in *No More Cherry Blossoms,* along with *Sisters Matsumoto, Ballad of Yachiyo,* and *Under the Rainbow,* a play of two one-acts. *Under the Rainbow* was informally read at Locus Arts in San Francisco in 2002 and includes a one-act play titled *natalie wood is dead* and *white manifesto and other perfumed tales of self-entitlement.* The former one-act play depicts an unhealthy relationship between a mother who pursues Hollywood perfection and her daughter who is not willing to live up to her mother's expectations; the latter work looks at white males' obsession with Oriental women. *A Fist of Roses* premiered in 2004 and is an all-male-cast play that deals with male violence in relationships. This play also involves the audience, as they are asked to answer questions on a card and turn it in before the play starts. Later in the play, the actors read the cards filled out by the audience that briefly describe the audience's involvement in violence. *After the War* is set in postwar Japantown in San Francisco, and *Manzanar: An American Story* is an orchestral work about the Japanese American internment during World War II with spoken text written by Gotanda. He collaborated with Kent Nagano, maestro of the Berkeley Symphony and Berlin Philharmonic, and composers Jean-Pascal Beintus, David Benoit, and Naomi Sekiya.

As a director, Gotanda worked on *Uncle Tadao* by R.A. Shiomi, and *The House of Sleeping Beauties* by David Henry Hwang. An associate artist at the Seattle Repertory Theatre, Gotanda lives in San Francisco with his actress-producer wife Diane Takei. They have no children. He is also a cofounder of the Asian American Musicians

Organization. He collaborates with diverse types of American theatres, as well as international theatres, to expose his works to a wide range of audiences. In interviews, Gotanda expressed that as a playwright working off camaraderie among multiethnic groups and dealing with the issues of what it means to be Asian American, he was concerned that there was a lack of unity among the multiethnic communities in the early 1990s. What has worried him in recent years is the financial difficulties facing Asian American theatre communities. **See also** Asian American Stereotypes; Racism and Asian America.

Further Reading

Gotanda, Philip Kan. "Fist of Roses: An Excerpt and Commentary." *Amerasia Journal* 31.3 (2005): 133–139.

Gotanda, Philip Kan. March 2007. Philip Kan Gotanda Web site. http://www.philipkangotanda.com.

Hwang, David Henry. "Philip Kan Gotanda." *Bomb* 62 (Winter 1998): 20–26.

Ito, Robert B. Interview. "Philip Kan Gotanda." In *Words Matter: Conversations with Asian American Writers,* ed. King-Kok Cheung. Honolulu, HI: University of Hawaii Press, 2000. 173–185.

Kaplan, Randy Barbara. "Philip Kan Gotanda (1951–)." In *Asian American Playwrights: A Bio-Bibliographical Critical Sourcebook,* ed. Miles Xian Liu. Westport, CT: Greenwood Press, 2002. 69–88.

Lee, Josephine. *Performing Asian America: Race and Ethnicity on the Contemporary Stage.* Philadelphia: Temple University Press, 1997.

Maczyńska, Magdalena. "Philip Kan Gotanda." *Dictionary of Literary Bibography, Vol. 266: Twentieth-Century American Dramatists,* Fourth Series. Farmington Hills, MI: Thomson Gale, 2002. 116–127.

Moy, James. *Marginal Sights: Staging the Chinese in America.* Iowa City: University of Iowa Press, 1993.

Vorlicky, Robert. *Act like a Man: Challenging Masculinities in American Drama.* Ann Arbor: University of Michigan Press, 1995.

KYOKO AMANO

✦ GOTO, HIROMI (1966–)

Born in Chiba-Ken, Japan, Hiromi Goto immigrated to British Columbia, Canada, in 1969. Eight years later, Goto's family moved to the small town of Nanton, Alberta, where her father began to cultivate mushrooms on a farm. Much of Goto's literature is influenced by her childhood experiences of social and political racism and the effects of bigotry—especially on children. In 1989, Goto graduated with a Bachelor of Arts degree from the University of Calgary—although some sources claim it was the University of Alberta—,where she participated in the university's reputable Creative Writing Department, under notable authors such as Nicole Markotic,

Aritha Van Herk, and Fred **Wah**. Goto currently resides in British Columbia, where, from 2003 to 2004, she was the writer in residence at the Emily Carr Institute of Art and Design in Vancouver.

Chorus of Mushrooms (1994) is Goto's first novel, and the winner of the regional Commonwealth Writers' Prize for Best First Book. The novel features Marasaki (Muriel) as its protagonist, as she experiences many forms of the intergenerational conflicts that are common to many Asian North American novels (in Canada, for instance, Judy Fong **Bates's** *Midnight at the Dragon Café* and Wayson **Choy's** *The Jade Peony*). Murasaki searches for her missing grandmother, Naoe (a partial narrator of the story), while the text interweaves magic realism and mythology into the original plot; the reader must interpret the actual events that have occurred from the folktales that seep in. The novel addresses the significance of the subconscious, especially in terms of dreams and memory, fantasy and storytelling. *Chorus of Mushrooms* is a significant text as it moves away from the tradition of Japanese Canadian memoir and historical fiction that re-creates **World War II** or directly discusses the aftermath of **Japanese American internment** (Joy **Kogawa**, another Japanese Canadian author, famously wrote *Obasan* in 1981 at the beginning of Japanese Canadians' fight for redress). Instead, it likens itself with the Asian American literary genres that address intergenerational domestic struggles and minority isolation in small-town Canada. The distance that is suggested between Naoe and her daughter, who is fully assimilated and refuses to speak Japanese, is painful but eased by Marasaki's curiosity in the Japanese language. *Chorus of Mushrooms* has been awarded the co-winner of the Canada-Japan Book Award in 1995 and the Grant MacEwan College Book Award, 2000–2001.

Goto's second full-length novel is intended for adolescents but continues to address ideas of racism, isolation, and fantasy. *The Water of Possibility* (2001) is a text through which Goto can access a younger generation with the aim of teaching them about the ideas of migration and ethnic unbalance for a more youthful audience. Sayuri, the 12-year-old hero of *The Water of Possibility*, moves with her family to a small town in Alberta, where she and her brother, Keiji, discover a secret world through their cellar door. In this magical place, Japanese mythology becomes reality, as animals talk and folktales come alive. In a highly allegorical manner, Keiji is captured by Patriarch, a dominating fox, from whom Sayuri must rescue her little brother. After overcoming various fantastical obstacles, Sayuri is able to save Keiji and eliminate the overbearing power of Patriarch. Again, Goto's interest in magical realism is employed as a bridge between the Eastern and Western worlds, feminism and patriarchal oppression—the contemporary twenty-first century and the myths and legends of previous generations. Like in the medieval romances in the Western literary canon, Goto uses allegorical characters and supernatural figures as metaphors for contemporary social ills: racism, alienation by the dominant group, and the necessity of fighting against racist discourses.

Also published in 2001 is Goto's speculative fiction novel *The Kappa Child*—winner of the James Tiptree Jr. Award, an honor bestowed on novels that address gender within the science fiction and fantasy genres. Again set in the Canadian prairies, *The Kappa Child* combines Japanese folklore with the Western intertext of *Little House on the Prairie*—a source that Goto admits to being personally fond of while she was a child. The novel features four Japanese Canadian sisters as they suffer under their father's tyranny in different ways. The protagonist struggles with the patriarchy of her abusive father and dysfunctional family (she initially distances herself and cannot relate to her sisters) but is able to gain subjectivity through her immaculate conception pregnancy of a Kappa Child. Goto's typical marriage of Japanese mythology and Canadian realism is interjected with visual/popular culture and science fiction (it is revealed that the protagonist's mother is a former alien abductee). With this text, Goto joins other Asian Canadian novelists, such as Larissa **Lai** (*When Fox Is a Thousand* [1995], *Salt Fish Girl* [2002]), who address Asianess, gender, and sexuality through a mergence of the speculative genre with ethnic studies.

In her collection of short stories, *Hopeful Monsters* (2004), Goto elaborates on her previous work by inserting atypical characters into realist situations. The works undermine the Victorian (and beyond) notion that femaleness is monstrous, by examining gender and corporeality ironically, subversively, and, most importantly, empathetically. Again, Goto counters racist ideologies by recalling experiences from her childhood as an Asian Canadian in a predominantly white, prairie community. Monsters appear in various forms throughout the collection, ranging from the villains featured in childhood nightmares (bogeymen in the closet, creatures under the bed), archetypal figures like the mummy or a city-crushing lizard, to contemporary, psychological monsters, such as sociopaths and pedophiles. Yet Goto's monsters are not "Others," but members of twentieth-century society, as they argue with their mothers, nurture their children, and use the washroom—to highlight the arbitrariness of marginalization and alienation. "Camp Americana" features a Japanese grandfather of Asian Canadian children. The assimilated grandchildren disgust him with their disrespectful and abhorred behaviour; he, in turn, frightens them with his severity and rage. Maternity is another theme addressed in *Hopeful Monsters*, as one mother is devastated by the guilt of running over her child, and another woman is ostracized for refusing to breastfeed. Women, at numerous times throughout the text, consider themselves to be monstrous when their bodies change or refuse to regain their prepregnancy shapes. Again, intergenerational conflict appears in *Hopeful Monsters*, as second- and third-generation Japanese Canadians are deemed monstrous by their elders for excessive assimilation. In "Drift," a Japanese Canadian mother is repulsed by her daughter's overt sexuality, and, more specifically, her lesbianism; whereas other stories address issues of interracial marriage and racial hybridity. *Hopeful Monsters* forces the reader to adopt the perspective at times of the dominant ideology and at other times, of the marginalized Other, to highlight both the inherent monstrosity in us all and the constructedness of self-other binaries.

In addition to her published books, Goto's short fiction has appeared in various publications, including George Bowering's edited collection *And Other Stories* (2001), Smaro Kamboureli's anthology *Making a Difference, Canadian Multicultural Literature* (1996), and in journals such as *Blue Buffalo* (Summer 1992), *Grain* (Fall 1992), and *Ms.* (Fall 1996). Goto is also an accomplished poet whose work has appeared in anthologies like Taien Ng-Chan's *Ribsauce* (2001) and journals such as *Prairie Fire* (Winter 1997) and *Contemporary Verse 2* (Winter 1994). Furthermore, Goto contributes to the literary world with her critical theory, in which she examines ideas of alienation, marginalization, corporeality, and migration. Some of her essays include "Alien Texts, Alien Seductions: The Context of Colour Full Writing" that appeared in Christl Verduyn's collection, *Literary Pluralities* (1998), and "Translating the Self: Moving Between Cultures," which was featured in *WestCoastLine* (Fall 1996). **See also** Assimilation/Americanization; Feminism and Asian America; Japanese American Internment; Racism and Asian America.

Further Reading

Beauregard, Guy. "Hiromi Goto's *Chorus of Mushrooms* and the Politics of Writing Diaspora." *West Coast Line, A Journal of Contemporary Writing and Criticism* 29/3 (1995): 47–62.

Colavincenzo, Mar. "'Fables of the Reconstruction of the Fables': Multiculturalism, Postmodernism, and the Possibilities of Myth in Hiromi Goto's *Chorus of Mushrooms*." In *Towards a Transcultural Future: Literature and Society in a 'Post'-Colonial World*, eds. Geoffry Davis, Peter H. Marsden, et al. New York: Rodopi, 2005. 223–230.

Condé, Mary. "Japanese Generations in Hiromi Goto's Novel *Chorus of Mushrooms*." *Études Canadiennes* 51 (December 2001): 131–143.

Daris Beautell, Eva. "Hiromi Goto's *Chorus of Mushrooms*: Cultural Differences, Visibility and the Canadian Tradition." *Revista Alicantina de Estudios Ingleses* 16 (November 2003): 35–53.

Libin, Mark. "Lost in Translation: Hiromi Goto's *Chorus of Mushrooms*." *Canadian Literature* 163 (Winter 1999): 121–140.

———. "'Some of My Best Friends . . .': Befriending the Racialized Fiction of Hiromi Goto." *Essays on Canadian Writing* 73 (Spring 2001): 93–121.

Miki, Roy. "Asiancy: Making Space for Asian Canadian Writing." In *Privileging Positions: The Sites of Asian American Studies*, eds. Gary Y. Okihiro, et al. Pullman: Washington State University Press, 1995. 135–151.

Pivato, Joseph. "Commentary: *Chorus of Mushrooms*." *Comparative Canadian Literature: Study Guide*. Athabasca, AB: Athabasca University, 1996 and 2001.

Sasano, Mari. "Words Like Buckshot: Taking Aim at Notions of Nation in Hiromi Goto's *Chorus of Mushrooms*." *Open Letter, De:Scribing Alberta*, Part 2 (1998). http://www.athabascau.ca/cll/writers/goto/msasano.pdf.

JENNY HEI JUN WILLS

◆ GRAPHIC NOVEL

Asian American graphic novels, a longer form of the comic book, usually about 100 pages, are now coming of age and winning awards. Oriental villains, such as **Fu Manchu**, have been a part of the comic book narratives since the beginning. Now such stereotyped figures are less prominent as Asian American comics emerge. The sequential art form of the graphic novel evolved from its original discourse forms of the daily and Sunday cartoon strips, the political cartoons, and the comic book formats. Art Spiegelman created a graphic memoir about the Holocaust, *Maus: A Survivor's Tale*, which won a special Pulitzer Award in 1992. Its sequel, *Maus II*, won the Eisner and Harvey Awards, special cartoon and graphics awards. With such recognition, other publishers started to release their own graphic novels. Then followed Asian American graphic novels, such as *One Hundred Demons* (2002), *Same Difference* (2004), *American Born Chinese* (2006), and Adrian Tomine's *Shortcomings* (2007). However, there are some important precursors to these important novels: the works of Henry Kiyama and Stan Sakai.

Perhaps the first graphic representation of sequential art of the Asian American experience is *Four Immigrants Manga: A Japanese Experience in San Francisco* (1904–1924) by Henry Kiyama. He was born in Neu in Tottori Prefecture, Japan, in 1885. Kiyama studied at the San Francisco Art Institute and the New York Art Students League. His interests were in perfecting classical Western art, yet the irony is that he will probably gain more importance in Asian American literature for being its first cartoonist. Frederick L. Schodt, a researcher and translator who discovered the manga in 1999, claims *Four Immigrants* may very well be the first comic book or graphic novel ever printed. *Famous Funnies: A Carnival of Comics* with its 36 pages published in 1933, is often considered the first comic book. However, *Four Immigrants* with its 52 episodes at 104 pages was published in San Francisco in 1931.

Four Immigrants was originally published in a dual language format in which the participants speak in their own languages—the Japanese immigrants speaking Japanese and the American natives speaking English, though the translated version by Schodt uses only English. The book examines in graphic detail the story of four Japanese emigrants, who renamed themselves with the English names of Henry (the artist), Frank (the businessman), Charlie (the politician), and Fred (the farmer). These historically important episodes cover such events as landing at **Angel Island**, trying to find jobs in San Francisco, seeing President Taft, surviving the great earthquake, witnessing the trials and tribulations of picture brides, participating in the patriotism of World War I, gambling in **Chinatown**, and, finally, leaving for home.

In episode 45 about World War I, an **issei** (first-generation) Japanese decided to fight to prove he was patriotic, though in the end he was still denied citizenship. Another important theme is how the Japanese experience compares to the lives of

Chinese immigrants. Whereas the Chinese tried to maintain their culture, the Japanese immigrants dressed in Western attire and tried to assimilate, yet they were often confused as Chinese or another Asian. In episode 26, San Francisco authorities tried to segregate the Japanese school students by putting them with the Chinese students, keeping both away from the Caucasian children. However, Japan protested and Theodore Roosevelt pressured the school system to have the policy changed, and Japanese children were again allowed to attend regular schools with the Caucasian children. The Chinese children remained segregated.

The last episode, 52, ends with a mention of the Immigration Act of 1924 (see **National Origins Act**), which would prevent Asians from immigrating to America, though not restricting Europeans. Kiyama himself did not leave in 1924, and he probably would have remained in America until his death. However, while visiting his homeland in 1937, **World War II** broke out. Not being able to return, he remained in Japan until his death in 1951.

Another important influential cartoonist is Stan Sakai, whose character Usagi Yojimbo remains an important figure in Asian American graphic novels. Sakai has received over 20 Eisner Award nominations and has won three times. This character, Usagi Yojimbo, first appeared along with Peter Laird's Teenage Mutant Ninja Turtles in 1984 in the comic *Albedo*, volume 1, number 2. Sakai has since published over 20 graphic novels using the same character, including a space version: Space Usagi. Usagi, a rabbit, is based on the seventeenth-century samurai Miyamoto Musashi (Japan's greatest samurai) and the character in the famous film by Akira Kurosawa: *Yojimbo* (bodyguard). These graphic novels, though about Japanese samurai lore, were written from a Western or an Asian American point of view. These novels were part of the invasion or appropriation of Asian pop culture with its anime, manga, and games that would become part of American pop culture. Usagi would even make cameos in the television animated series *Teenage Mutant Ninja Turtles*. Other cartoonists such as Frank Miller would also explore the samurai tradition in *Ronin* (1983–1984), situated in a futuristic dystopia. *Samurai Jack* (2001–) and *Afro Samurai* (2007) also use the Japanese samurai mythos in a Western context.

The Filipino American perspective is one of the backgrounds for the graphic novel *One Hundred Demons* by Lynda **Barry**, which delves into her life while growing up in a multicultural neighborhood in Seattle. Barry is multiracial with a Filipina mother and Caucasian father. The book is part autobiographical, with some of the chapters focusing on the relationship between herself and her mother. Furthermore, the tension between her mother and her Filipina grandmother is explored.

An important Korean American graphic novel is Derek Kirk Kim's *Same Difference and Other Stories* (2003), which won three awards: Eisner, Harvey, and Ignatz Awards. Kim was born in 1974 in Kumi, Korea. He moved to America at the age of eight and lived in Korea for two years when he became an adult. The book, though fictional in nature, has autobiographical elements, especially the parts about growing up as a Korean American. Kim completed the book with monies from a Xeric Foundation Grant established by Peter Laird, a cocreator of the Teenage Mutant Ninja Turtles. "Same Difference" is the longest story or novella at 86 pages with an additional 12 much shorter stories. In the novella, Simon Moore and Nancy, two Korean American friends, share many experiences in Oakland and the Pacifica. He ponders upon what could have been as he tries to salvage his lost youth. One day in Oakland while eating in a restaurant with Nancy, he sees Irene waiting for a bus and tells the story about the high school dance. Irene wanted to go to the dance with Simon, not as a date, but just as friends. Simon made up a story that he could not go. This lie caused him much pain because he liked Irene, but he did not want others to think that Irene was the only person he was capable of getting on a date, which was probably true, but in retrospect it should not have mattered that Irene was blind, while Simon was a Korean American geek. It was all the same difference.

In another overlapping story, Nancy had been receiving letters from Ben Leland, who was writing to a Sara Richardson. Sara must have lived in Nancy's place before. Nancy was curious and opened a letter. It was a love letter, and Nancy wrote back as Sara. When Nancy wanted to know what Ben looked like, Nancy and Simon traveled to Pacifica, Ben Leland's home address. Pacifica is also Simon's hometown, where he went to high school. Surprisingly, they discover that Ben is Asian. In the end, Simon bumps into Irene and discovers that she is doing well and getting married. He bumps into a married couple, Jane and Eddie, whom he knew in high school. They seem happy and have a child with another one on the way. According to Simon, everyone's life seems to have improved and seems to be better than his own. The story ends with Nancy leaving an apology note for Ben on his doorstep. This apology becomes the perfect coda to the story, for it shows a maturation in Nancy for her chaotic actions. Perhaps it also points to a way out for Simon, who is stuck in his neurotic stasis.

American Born Chinese (2006) by Gene Yang emerged as another important graphic novel. It won an Eisner Award for Best Graphic Album (2007). *American Born Chinese* is in color and continues to win critical awards and favorable reviews. Three simultaneous story lines are told: one about the legendary and rambunctious Monkey King from Chinese lore; one about Jin Wang, a middle school student just trying to fit in; and another about Danny, a white student who is embarrassed by his Chinese cousin Chin-Kee, a living and breathing stereotype. In the end, all three plots collide literally, and things are not what they seem.

Adrian Tomine, a Japanese American cartoonist, released the graphic novel *Shortcomings* (2007). Previously, Tomine won the Harvey Award for Best New Artist. He is a forth-generation Japanese American whose stories are not usually about Asian

American topics. This artistic power is in his ability to write realistic female characters and write about the complexities of male/female relationships. *Shortcomings* is about the adventures of Ben Tanaka, who deals with his Asian cultures trying to survive in the American landscape. It also covers those complexities about gender relationships that he is known for in his other writings.

Asian Americans have been a part of the comic book establishment for years. Artists and writers such as Korean American Jim Lee helped to invigorate and influence the industry. Lee personally revitalized Marvel Comic's X-men series. However, what is different now is that Asian American comic artists such as Adrian Tomine are seeing that the Asian American experience itself is a worthy topic in its own right.

Further Reading
Barry, Lynda. *One Hundred Demons*. Seattle: Sasquatch Books, 2002.
Kim, Derek Kirk. *Same Difference and Other Stories*. Marietta: Top Shelf, 2003.
———. Web site. http://www.lowbright.com.
Kiyama, Henry. *Four Immigrants Manga: A Japanese Experience in San Francisco (1904–1924)*. Trans. Frederik L. Schodt. Berkeley, CA: Stone Bridge Press, 1999.
McCloud, Scott. *Making Comings: Storytelling Secrets of Comics, Manga and Graphic Novels*. New York: Harper, 2006.
Sakai, Stan. *The Ronin: Usagi Yojimbo*. Vol. 1. Seattle: Fantagraphic Books, 1997.
Tomine, Adrian. *Shortcomings*. Montreal: Drawn and Quarterly, 2007.
Yang, Gene. *American Born Chinese*. New York: First Second, 2006.

WAYNE STEIN